The Times

HOUSE OF COMMONS

1910

With FULL RESULTS *of the* POLLING *and* BIOGRAPHIES *of* MEMBERS *and* SUCCESSFUL CANDIDATES *and a* COMPLETE ANALYSIS AND STATISTICAL TABLES

Introduction by John Antcliffe

London:
Smithfield Consultants, 10 Aldersgate Street, EC1
www.smithfieldgroup.com

The Times Guide
to the
House of Commons
1910

First published in Great Britain 1910 by *The Times*

This edition published 2010 by
Methuen
8 Artillery Row
London
SW1P 1RZ

10 9 8 7 6 5 4 3 2 1

The Times Guide to the House of Commons 1910
Copyright © *The Times* 1910
Introduction copyright © John Antcliffe 2010

This book is copyright under the Berne Convention.
No reproduction without permission.
All rights reserved.

A CIP catalogue record for this book is available from the British Library

ISBN 978 184 275 034 6

Printed and bound in Great Britain by CPI William Clowes Beccles NR34 7TL

This book is sold subject to the condition that it shall not, by way of trade or otherwise be lent, resold, hired out or otherwise circulated in any form of binding or cover other than that in which it is published and without a similar condition, including this condition, being imposed on the subsequent purchaser.

Contents

Introduction
by John Antcliffe, Chief Executive,
Smithfield Consultants
page vii

The Times Guide to the House of Commons 1910

Introduction

The General Election of January 1910 was a turning point in one of the most bitter and prolonged political battles of the twentieth century: the fight for supremacy between the Liberal Government of Herbert Henry Asquith and the Unionist dominated House of Lords. The longest election in British history, after polling spread over 26 days and a record turnout, the Unionists secured 300,000 more votes than the Liberals but failed to carry the House of Commons.

The struggle began in April 1909 with the announcement of the "People's Budget" by the Chancellor of the Exchequer, David Lloyd George, continued through two general elections and a Constitutional Conference and finally ended in August 1911 when the House of Lords reluctantly passed the Parliament Bill by a majority of 17.

The battle lines were drawn in the 1909 parliamentary session during which there were no less than 895 divisions in the House of Commons, of which 554 were on the Budget, and culminated in a general election fought on the issue of "the Peers against the People".

The Political Backdrop

The Liberal Government entered 1909 facing a number of challenges. First, although elected in 1906 with an unprecedented majority, it had achieved disappointingly little as ten major bills passed by the House of Commons were either amended out of recognition or thrown out by the House of Lords.

Secondly, the Government was losing support among the electorate: during 1908 the Unionists had won a series of by-elections including Ashburton, Newcastle-on-Tyne, Peckham, Pudsey, Ross-on-Wye and Shoreditch as well as North-West Manchester where Winston Churchill had unsuccessfully sought re-election upon being appointed President of the Board of Trade.

Introduction

Thirdly, the new Chancellor of the Exchequer, Lloyd George, who had succeeded Asquith as Chancellor in 1908, needed to raise significantly more revenue in the coming financial year. This was required to meet the costs of the new old age pensions and naval rearmament in the face of growing German naval power, the First Lord of the Admiralty, Reginald McKenna, arguing that a minimum of six new Dreadnoughts should be built as soon as possible.

Increased expenditure on the Navy was unpopular with many in the Liberal Party and its Labour and Irish Nationalist allies. Lloyd George proposed, therefore, to raise the necessary revenue through a radical combination of measures likely to anger the opposition but to win him support in his own party. His proposals were regarded as controversial even among his own Cabinet colleagues and were discussed and examined at no less than 14 Cabinet meetings between mid-March and the end of April.

The People's Budget

On 29 April 1909 Lloyd George finally unveiled his "People's Budget" in the House of Commons in a speech lasting four and a half hours. The sums involved now seem remarkably small: the Government wished to raise £164 million against the £151 million revenue received the previous financial year, and the £148 million which it was calculated existing taxes would raise in the financial year just starting.

This left Lloyd George with a prospective deficit of £16 million and he proposed to raise £13.5 million in new or increased taxation, and to make up the balance from the Sinking Fund. The new taxes were to include a super-tax of 6d in the £ on the amount by which incomes of £5,000 or more exceeded £3,000; a 20 per cent tax on the "unearned increment" of land values to be paid either when the land was sold or when it passed at death; an annual duty of a halfpenny in the £ on the capital value of undeveloped land; motor vehicle taxes according to horsepower; a 3d per gallon tax on petrol; and a liquor licence tax of roughly half the annual proceeds from the sale of drink.

In addition, income tax was to go up from 1s to 1s 2d in the £ on unearned incomes, and on earned incomes of over £3,000 a year, while estate and stamp duties were to be substantially raised, as were the duties on tobacco and spirits which would increase the price of whisky by a halfpenny per glass.

The Government's proposals prompted a wave of criticism both inside and outside Parliament. The Leader of the Opposition, Arthur Balfour, denounced the Budget as "based on no principle, and injurious to the productive capacity of the country" whilst the former Liberal Prime Minister, Lord Rosebery, criticised it as being "inquisitorial, tyrannical and Socialistic."

In the City 21 leading financiers sent a letter to the Prime Minister on 15 May, noting that "..... while prepared to bear their full share of increased taxation, which they recognised as necessary, [they] expressed alarm at the increasing disproportion of the burden placed on a small class."

On 23 June 1909 Lord Rothschild chaired a protest meeting "representative of all interests in the City, and independent of political associations" at the Cannon Street Hotel. Over 1,000 people attended and approved a resolution that "the main proposals in the Budget weaken the security in all private property, discourage enterprise and thrift, and would prove seriously injurious to the commerce and industries of the country." Other protest meetings took place around the country, mainly under the auspices of the Budget Protest League led by Walter Long, Unionist MP for Dublin County South.

Opposition to the Budget was equally strong in the House of Commons where the Unionists fought the Finance Bill clause by clause. There was almost no summer recess, and for nearly five weeks the House sat regularly through the night prompting a Tory complaint that during the all-night sitting on 17-18 August, Winston Churchill (MP for Dundee since 1908) had been present "in his pyjamas".

The battle continued into the Autumn and after 70 Parliamentary days and 554 divisions, the Budget was finally sent to the Lords on 20 November.

For most of the Summer and early Autumn, it was widely assumed that even though the Unionists would vigorously oppose the Finance Bill in the House of Commons, they would not challenge a constitutional convention over 250 years old and reject a Finance Bill in the House of Lords – "That way revolution lies" predicted Asquith.

Balfour and the Unionist Leader in the House of Lords, Lord Lansdowne, were initially reluctant to see the Lords veto the Budget and instead preferred amendment to rejection. The political temperature was, however, raised by a series of speeches by Government Ministers, particularly Lloyd George who at a meeting in Limehouse on 30 July argued in colourful and provocative language that the proposed land taxes were justified by the extortionate profiteering of many landowners, particularly the Dukes. This personalised attack angered many Peers, prompted a letter of rebuke from King Edward VII and convinced leading Unionists that it was their duty to challenge the Government by rejecting the Budget in the House of Lords and so prompt a general election.

Thus, on 30 November, after five parliamentary days devoted to a second-reading debate, the House of Lords took a political gamble, defied precedent and rejected the Budget, voting for a resolution by 350 to 75 that stated that "This House is not justified in giving its consent to this Bill until it has been submitted to the judgement of the country". Only one Unionist peer voted against the resolution.

Asquith, who had been Prime Minister since 1908 following the resignation of Sir Henry Campbell-Bannerman, responded to the challenge on 2 December, when he moved in the House of Commons that "the action of the House of Lords in refusing to pass into law the financial provision made by this House for the

Introduction

service of the year is a breach of the Constitution and a usurpation of the rights of the Commons". In the course of his speech he announced an immediate dissolution – "at the earliest possible moment we shall ask the constituencies of the country to declare that the organ and voice of the free people of this country is to be found in the elected representatives of the nation". The resolution, supported by both the Irish Nationalists and the Labour Party, was carried by 349 votes to 134 and Prorogation took place the next day.

The dates of the election were not immediately known, but on 23 December it was announced that the writs would be issued on 10 January, and that polling would begin on 15 January and end on 9 February – it was not until the 1918 General Election that all voting took place on the same day, except in the university seats.

The Electorate

Electoral arrangements in 1910 were largely based on the Representation of the People Act 1867 as modified by the 1872 Ballot Act and the 1885 Redistribution of Seats Act. These arrangements differ from those in force today in a number of areas.

First, the franchise was still restricted with only 7.7 million voters (28 per cent of all adults) on the electoral roll. Even after the three extensions of the franchise during the nineteenth century that began with the 1832 Reform Act, just 58 per cent of male adults were entitled to vote and despite the efforts of the Suffragettes, all women were still excluded from voting. It was not until the 1918 Representation of the People Act that women over the age of 30 were enfranchised, women aged between 21 and 30 having to wait a further decade.

Secondly, about half a million electors had plural voting rights in several constituencies. This applied to owners of land, occupiers of business premises and to university graduates who returned an additional nine MPs, including the formidable Sir Edward Carson who sat as a Unionist Member for Dublin University.

Thirdly, the 1910 Parliament still included a full contingent of Irish MPs, the House of Commons falling in size by 95 Members in 1922 following the creation of the Irish Free State.

Finally, constituencies varied enormously in size. When boundaries were last redrawn in 1885, the principle that constituencies should be approximately equal in size was specifically rejected. Population movements since then had compounded these anomalies, particularly in the fast growing suburbs around London and other major cities. As a result, whilst Wandsworth had 38,523 registered voters in 1910, Whitechapel had a mere 3,986.

Introduction

The Parties

At the dissolution of Parliament, the Liberal-led Government comprised 502 MPs made up of 373 Liberals, 46 Labour Members and 83 Irish Nationalists who together enjoyed a "Ministerial" majority of 334 over the Unionists.

In 1910 the Unionists comprised both Conservative and Liberal Unionists. The latter had split from the Liberal Party in 1886 and mainly appealed to the growing industrial middle class at a time when the Tory party was seen as predominantly representing landed interests. For election purposes the Unionists were effectively one party in Ireland in 1910 but in the mainland the Liberal Unionists were to remain an independent party until May 1912 when they formally merged with the Conservatives.

The dominance of the two main parties was constrained by two other parties: the Irish Nationalists, led by John Redmond, MP for Waterford, which dominated Irish politics, and the Labour Party, still a new political force in 1910.

Following the formation of the Labour Representation Committee in 1900, an informal pact had been agreed with the Liberal Party in 1903 and in the general election three years later, Labour had fielded 51 candidates of whom 30 were elected. This number was supplemented by gains at by-elections including North East Derbyshire, Jarrow, Sheffield Attercliffe and Mid-Derbyshire. The party had, however, suffered a serious setback in 1909 when following a legal challenge brought by a Liberal trade unionist, W.V. Osborne, the House of Lords had ruled that trade union contributions to political parties were illegal. As a result, many local Labour parties collapsed leaving Labour candidates in the general election desperately short of money.

The Campaign

Campaigning began as soon as the dissolution was announced with the merits of the Budget attracting as much early attention as the behaviour of the Peers. Other issues including the size of the Navy, Home Rule for Ireland and, inevitably, Tariff Reform v. Free Trade soon emerged.

Electioneering in 1910 was very different to today with most campaigning led at a regional, not national level. Travelling long distances was usually undertaken by rail as travel by road was unreliable and slow: in 1910 there were only 155,000 licensed motor vehicles including buses, trolley buses and tractors.

Telephones were also relatively new, the General Post Office only providing services to 122,000 subscribers in 1910, including Southern Ireland, and in these pre-wireless days, there was limited national media. Despite rising circulations and the establishment of regional printing plants to which copy was transmitted by private wire, most London-based newspapers had limited influence outside the South East. Instead, such papers as the Manchester Guardian, Yorkshire Post,

Introduction

Birmingham Daily Post, Glasgow Herald and Scotsman continued to be of major regional importance.

The Prime Minister formally opened his campaign at the Royal Albert Hall on 10 December. Addressing an audience of some 10,000 described by The Times as "boiling over with enthusiasm", Asquith said that there were three major issues at stake: "the absolute control of the Commons over finance; the maintenance of Free Trade; and the effective limitation and curtailment of the legislative powers of the House of Lords."

On the same day the Unionist leader, Arthur Balfour, issued his election address to his constituents in the City of London stating that the attack on the House of Lords, was the culmination of a long-drawn conspiracy to secure a single-chamber legislature. These "conspirators" wished the Commons to be independent not only of the Peers, but of the people. Struck down with pulmonary catarrh, Balfour was, however, prevented from active campaigning until the New Year.

Another prominent Unionist, Joe Chamberlain, now 73, also played a limited part in the campaign. Standing for re-election in West Birmingham, he was unable to leave his Kensington house, incapacitated by a stroke since 1906, instead writing letters in support of many candidates.

The most effective speakers on the Tory side were Joe Chamberlain's son Austen, Shadow Chancellor of the Exchequer; Andrew Bonar Law who, standing again in Dulwich, was still in mourning following the sudden death of his wife at the end of October; and F.E. Smith who was seeking re-election in Liverpool Walton. After addressing large audiences around the country, F.E. Smith spent the last few days before polling in Walton where his meetings were regularly broken up by hired heavies until he mustered twelve men from the Salvidge Brewery who, dressed in frock-coats, henceforth maintained order.

The stars of the Liberal campaign were Winston Churchill and Lloyd George. Assured of re-election in Dundee, Churchill spoke at meetings across Scotland including addressing a meeting on New Year's Day 1910 in the Prime Minister's East Fife constituency. He also spoke at many meetings around England, particularly in Lancashire where he was still thought to have a strong following, and published a 150 page pamphlet entitled "The People's Rights." As the campaign wore on, the emphasis in his speeches changed from the need to reform the House of Lords to free trade and tariff reform.

Meanwhile Lloyd George, the People's Champion, maintained an even more punishing schedule. He opened his campaign in his own constituency of Caernarvon Boroughs addressing an audience of over 7,000 in the Pavilion at Caernarvon in English and Welsh. He then returned to London in time to be on the platform for Asquith's Albert Hall speech, and during the following week addressed meetings around London. On 21 December he spoke three times in Cardiff and once in Swansea, before going on to other towns in South Wales and then to Criccieth for Christmas.

Introduction

On New Year's Eve he again spoke in London and appeared at a rally in Reading the next day. Between 4 and 7 January he addressed more meetings in London, and spent the next weekend in Plymouth and Falmouth. Following visits to Stockport and York, he made a polling day trip to Grimsby, where he was met by a rowdy crowd and forced to make a hasty escape, and then returned to Wales, where he spoke at Newtown, Montgomeryshire, on 18 January. Results were already coming in and his own was declared on the 22 January. He then continued electioneering in later-polling constituencies, ending his campaign in the West Midlands.

The Suffragette Threat

Security was very tight at many public meetings as since 1905, a series of prominent politicians had been subject to violent physical attacks by militant Suffragettes.

Shortly before the campaign began, Winston Churchill had been attacked as he left a train at Bristol Temple Meads station by a woman who tried to strike him in the face with a riding whip. When he seized her wrists in self defence, she attempted to push him off the platform into the path of the departing train and was only stopped by the swift intervention of Churchill's wife, Clementine.

A few days later Lloyd George was locked in a car outside the Queen's Hall in London by, and with, a Suffragette and on 8 December in Bolton, a young woman was arrested for hurling a heavy piece of iron wrapped in a political leaflet at a car carrying Churchill. She refused to pay a 40 shilling fine and was instead sent to prison for seven days.

When Asquith launched his campaign on 10 December at the Albert Hall, women were excluded from the audience. Shortly before the meeting began, a woman was extricated from the organ and another, disguised as a telegraph boy, had to be prevented from entering the auditorium during the Prime Minister's speech.

Finally, on 1 January 1909 two Suffragettes sought to disrupt Lloyd George's meeting in a tramcar garage in Reading where over 7,000 people had gathered to hear him speak. The only women granted access to the garage were those on the platform and when Lloyd George rose to address the audience, two women appeared shouting from under the platform before being ejected by the stewards. Following this interruption, the Suffragettes called off their attempts to break up meetings for the rest of the election campaign.

The Nation's Verdict

Polling began on 15 January and a close result was widely forecast with the Irish Nationalists expected to hold the balance of power. 75 MPs were returned unopposed, including 55 of the 82 Irish Nationalists elected.

London and Lancashire were regarded as the key areas in which sweeping

Introduction

Unionist gains would be needed if the Liberal-led majority was to be destroyed. The first results were encouraging for the Unionists with three gains in London and three in Lancashire. By the end of the first week of polling, however, with almost three quarters of the results declared, the Unionists had a net gain of 75 seats, and it was clear that whilst neither of the two main parties could secure a clear majority, the Liberal Party, with its allies, would be in a position to continue in office.

By the end of the month all the returns, except for the Scottish Universities and Orkney and Shetland, were complete. The Unionists had achieved a net gain (over their 1906 position) of 116 seats, with 273 MPs including 31 Liberal Unionists. This was only two less than the 275 seats won by the Liberals who saw their 1906 majority vanish.

82 Irish Nationalists were returned, including 11 "Independent" Nationalists led by William O'Brien who successfully ran for election in two constituencies, Cork City and North East Cork.

Despite a gain from the Unionists at Wigan, the Labour Party had a poor campaign and lost a net 11 seats, falling back to 40. This reflected the Party's weak financial position and the difficulty of attracting electoral support in the face of a more radical Liberal Party.

The Government and its allies therefore had a "Ministerial" majority of 124 which, although far short of its nominal majority of 357 in 1906, was still the second biggest majority enjoyed by any Liberal Government since 1832.

The Unionists made particular progress in England gaining 112 seats and winning 239 seats against the Government's 226. The gains were generally heavier in the south than in the north, and occurred more in county constituencies and in small boroughs than, with the exception of London, in big towns. Thus whilst Unionist gains included twelve seats in London and constituencies such as Bath, Cambridge, Chester, Exeter, Rochester, and Warwick, in Lancashire and Yorkshire the Government only suffered a net loss of six seats. The Unionists did, though, win the majority of seats in Liverpool, Sheffield Nottingham and Wolverhampton and again carried all seven seats in Birmingham.

By contrast, Unionist gains outside England were limited. In Scotland the Liberals actually gained one net seat, in Wales the Unionists made only two gains (Radnorshire, where their candidate won by 14 votes, and Denby District) and in Ireland the Unionists gained three seats: North Antrim and South Tyrone from the Liberals and Mid-Tyrone from the Nationalists.

Successful Candidates

Unlike the 1906 General Election, when the Liberal landslide carried with it many prominent Unionists including Balfour, there were few high profile casualties in January 1910, the Chief Government Whip, J.A. Pease, losing in Saffron Walden and the Paymaster General, R.H. Causton, losing in Southwark West. However,

Introduction

the broader social composition of the 1906 House of Commons continued, the 40 Labour Members elected balancing the many aristocratic MPs who were either the sons or grandsons of Peers.

This social division is well illustrated in Derbyshire where William Harvey, a former miner who began work in the pits as a boy, was returned as the Labour Member for Derbyshire North-East whilst the Eton and Oxford educated Earl of Kerry, the eldest son of the Lord Lansdowne, was elected as the Unionist MP for Derbyshire West.

Other working class, largely self-taught Members included Alfred Grill, Labour MP for Bolton, who began work at the age of seven selling newspapers, John Wilson, the Liberal MP for Mid-Durham, who began work at Stanhope Quarries "at an early age" before becoming a miner at the age of 13, and the Labour MP for Rhondda, William Abraham, who began work in the mines at the age of 10. MPs were not paid until 1912 and most Labour MPs relied on the Labour Party for financial support.

By contrast, the new Unionist MPs elected included the eldest son of Lord Burnham, Harry Lawson (Eton and Balliol College, Oxford) who regained Mile End; the son of the Earl of Bessborough, Viscount Duncannon (Harrow and Trinity College, Cambridge) who gained Cheltenham; Lord Henry Cavendish-Bentinck, half brother of the Duke of Portland, who gained Nottingham South; and Viscount Lewisham, eldest son of the Earl of Dartmouth, who gained West Bromwich.

The 75 MPs returned unopposed included the leader of the Irish Nationalists, John Redmond, who was re-elected in Waterford, and the six MPs representing Cambridge, Dublin and Oxford Universities. Other candidates re-elected included Stanley Baldwin in Bewdley, Ramsay MacDonald in Leicester, Philip Snowden in Blackburn and Keir Hardie in Merthyr Tydvil.

The 1910 Parliament

The new Parliament met in February 1910 and the reintroduced Finance Bill passed its third reading in the House of Commons on 27 April by 324 to 231 votes. The bill passed to the House of Lords the next day where the second-reading debate lasted less than three hours. There was no division and the remaining stages passed without debate allowing Royal Assent to be secured on 29 April, exactly one year after Lloyd George's original budget speech.

The Government's determination to restrict the powers of the House of Lords remained but following the unexpected death of King Edward VII the following week, a brief "Truce of God" was declared by the main political parties.

A Constitutional Conference comprising 4 Liberals led by Asquith and 4 Unionists led by Balfour then convened with the aim of agreeing how to limit the ability of House of Lords to veto legislation and so avoid a serious political crisis, particularly at the start of a new reign. The first meeting took place in the Prime Minister's room in the House of Commons on 17 June but after 21 meetings, the

Introduction

Conference collapsed in deadlock on 11 November 1910. Following a request from Asquith, the new King, George V, dissolved Parliament on 28 November and a further general election took place the next month.

John Antcliffe
December 2009

The Times Guide
to the
House of Commons
1910

The Times

HOUSE OF COMMONS

1910

With Brief Biographies of Members and Full Details of the Polls: also an ANALYSIS OF THE RESULTS AND COMPARISONS WITH PREVIOUS ELECTIONS, A Survey of Changes in Counties and Boroughs, Statistical Tables, &c.

LONDON:
PRINTED AND PUBLISHED BY JOHN PARKINSON BLAND AT THE TIMES OFFICE
PRINTING HOUSE-SQUARE, E.C.

1910.

CONTENTS.

	PAGE
INDEX TO CANDIDATES	1
RESULT OF THE GENERAL ELECTION	8
PARTY GAINS AND LOSSES	10
COMPOSITION OF THE HOUSE OF COMMONS	10
AN ANALYSIS OF THE VOTING	11
THE CONSTITUENCIES: A COMPARATIVE RECORD IN 1900, 1906, AND 1910	16
POLLS AND BIOGRAPHIES:—	
ENGLAND——LONDON	21
,, —BOROUGHS	30
,, —COUNTIES	54
WALES ——BOROUGHS	88
,, —COUNTIES	90
SCOTLAND —BURGHS	93
,, —COUNTIES	98
IRELAND —BOROUGHS	104
,, —COUNTIES	106
UNIVERSITIES	114
INDEX TO CONSTITUENCIES	116
THE NEW PARLIAMENT	121

The first pollings took place on January 15; and the last (Orkney and Shetland) on February 8 and 9.

B—2

ALLIANCE
ASSURANCE COMPANY, Ltd.,

Head Office: **BARTHOLOMEW LANE, LONDON, E.C.**

Established 1824.

Accumulated Funds exceed, £17,000,000.

Directors.
The Right Hon. LORD ROTHSCHILD, G.C.V.O., Chairman.

IAN H. AMORY, Esq.	JOHN CATOR, Esq., M.P.	Hon. HENRY BERKELEY PORTMAN.
CHARLES EDWARD BARNETT, Esq.	His Grace The DUKE OF DEVONSHIRE.	Hon. N. CHARLES ROTHSCHILD.
F. CAVENDISH BENTINCK, Esq.	Col. the Hon. EVERARD C. DIGBY.	Sir MARCUS SAMUEL, Bart.
A. V. DUNLOP BEST, Esq.	Captain GERALD M. A. ELLIS.	H. MELVILL SIMONS, Esq.
FRANCIS AUGUSTUS BEVAN, Esq.	JOHN HAMPTON HALE, Esq.	HUGH COLIN SMITH, Esq.
PERCIVAL BOSANQUET, Esq.	C. SHIRREFF HILTON, Esq.	Right Hon. LORD STALBRIDGE.
HON. KENELM P. BOUVERIE.	W. DOURO HOARE, Esq.	HENRY ALEXANDER TROTTER, Esq.
THOMAS HENRY BURROUGHES, Esq.	ALFRED H. HUTH, Esq.	The RIGHT HON. THE EARL OF VERULAM.
FRANCIS WILLIAM BUXTON, Esq.	FRANCIS ALFRED LUCAS, Esq.	SIR CHARLES RIVERS WILSON, G.C.M.G., C.B.

THE OPERATIONS OF THE COMPANY EMBRACE ALL BRANCHES OF INSURANCE.

DEATH DUTIES.—Special forms of Policies have been prepared by the Company providing for the payment of Death Duties, thus avoiding the necessity of disturbing investments at a time when it may be difficult to realise without loss.

INCOME TAX.—Under the provisions of the Act, Income Tax is not payable on that portion of the Assured's income which is devoted to the payment of premiums on an assurance on his life. Having regard to the amount of the Tax, this abatement (which is limited to one-sixth of the Assured's income) is an important advantage to Life Policyholders.

Full particulars of all classes of Insurance, together with Proposal Forms and Statement of Accounts, may be had on application to any of the Company's Offices or Agents.

ROBERT LEWIS, General Manager.

INDEX TO CANDIDATES.

In the following list of candidates those who were unsuccessful are distinguished by italics. Members of the last Parliament are indicated by asterisks.

A	PAGE
*Abraham, Rt. Hon. W.	92
*Abraham, W.	107
*Acland, F. D.	85
*Acland-Hood, Rt. Hon. Sir A. F.	78
Acworth, W. M.	86
Adam, Maj. W. A.	30
Adamson, R.	100
Addinsell, W. A.	51
Addison, C.	28
Adkins, W. R.	69
*Agar-Robartes, Hon. T.	57
Aggs, W. Hanbury	42
Agnew, G. W.	49
*Ainsworth, J. S.	98
Akers-Douglas, Rt. Hon. A.	67
*Alden, P.	73
*Allen, A. A.	36
*Allen, C. P.	64
Allen, J. H.	30
Amery, L. S.	53
Anderson, A.	98
Anderson, W. C.	56
*Anson, Sir W.	114
*Anstruther-Gray, Major W.	97
Arbuthnot, G. A.	35
Archer-Shee, Maj. M.	23
*Arkwright, J. S.	39
Armitage, R.	40
Armstrong, Sir G.	90
Ashley, W. W.	67
Ashton, T. G.	54
Ashworth, P.	33
Aske, Dr. R. W.	39
*Asquith, Rt. Hon. H. H.	100
Assinder, G. F.	68
Astor, Waldorf	47
*Atherley-Jones, L., K.C.	62
Atkins, R. Wallace	55
Attenborough, W. A.	31
*Aubrey-Fletcher, Rt. Hon. Sir H.	81

B	
Bagley, E. A.	41
Bagot, Lieut.-Col. J. F.	83
Bailey, A. J.	49
Baird, J. L.	82
Baker, H.	68

	PAGE
Baker, H. A.	65
*Baker, J. A.	23
Baker, Sir R.	61
*Balcarres, Lord	68
*Baldwin, S.	83
*Balfour, Rt. Hon. A. J.	21
Balfour, Major Kenneth	50
*Balfour, R.	101
*Banbury, Sir F.	21
Bannington, A. C.	35
Barclay, Sir T.	32
*Baring, Capt. G. V.	53
*Baring, Godfrey	65
*Barker, Sir J.	46
Barlow, C. Montague	48
*Barlow, Sir J. E.	78
*Barlow, P.	31
*Barnard, E. B.	65
Barnes, F. G.	45
*Barnes, G. N.	95
Barnston, H.	56
*Barran, R. H.	41
*Barran, Sir J.	96
*Barrie, H. T.	111
*Barry, E.	107
Barry, M.	107
*Barry, Redmond, K.C.	113
Bartlett, E. Ashmead	87
Barton, A. W.	46
Bates, Col. C. L.	75
Bathurst, Col. the Hon. A. B.	64
Bathurst, Charles	83
Batten, T. H.	34
Battersby, T. S. F., K.C.	109
Baumann, A. A.	96
Baxter, Sir W.	106
*Beach, Hon. M. Hicks	64
*Beale, W. P., K.C.	98
*Beauchamp, E.	79
Beauchamp, F. B.	78
Beck, A. E.	36
*Beck, Cecil	83
*Beckett, the Hon. Gervase	85
Beddoes, Lt.-Col. H.	66
Belilios, R. E.	26
Bell, Sir H. L.	21
Bell, J., Junr.	96
Bell, Mackenzie	27
*Bellairs, C.	49
*Belloc, H.	48

	PAGE
Benn, A. Shirley	21
Benn, I. H.	23
*Benn, Sir J. W.	37
*Benn, W. Wedgwood	29
*Bennett, E. N.	76
Bennett, T. W.	110
Bentham, G. J.	71
Beresford, Lord C.	47
Bernacchi, L. G.	70
Bernard, F. T. H.	57
*Berridge, T. H.	52
Bethell, Commander	84
*Bethell, Sir J. H.	63
*Bethell, T. R.	63
Bigland, A.	31
*Bignold, Sir A.	97
Birchall, J. D.	41
Bird, A. F.	53
*Birrell, Rt. Hon. A.	34
*Black, A. W.	54
Black, W. G.	94
Blackburn, R. F. L., K.C.	100
Blaiklock, G.	24
Blease, W. L.	68
Bliss, J.	68
Blyth, B. H.	100
*Boland, J. P.	110
Borwick, G.	60
Borwick, G. O.	28
*Bottomley, H.	24
*Boulton, A. C. F.	66
Bowen, Oscar	82
*Bowerman, C. W.	23
*Bowles, G. Stewart	32
Bowles, T. G.	40
Boyle, D.	111
Boyle, W. L.	74
Boyton, J.	26
*Brace, W.	92
Brackenbury, Capt. H. L.	72
Bradley, A. M.	37
Brady, P. J.	105
Brampton, A.	31
Brampton, C. H.	82
*Bramsdon, Sir T. A.	47
*Branch, J.	73
Brassey, H. L. C.	75
Brassey, Capt. R. B.	76
Brett, Hon. O.	66
*Bridgeman, W. C.	77
*Brigg, Sir J.	86

Name	Page
Brigg, J. J.	85
Bright, Allan	51
Brock, H.	99
*Brocklehurst, Col. W. B.	57
*Brodie, H. C.	80
Bromley-Davenport, Col. W.	57
Brooke, Sir A. De Capell-	75
*Brooke, Stopford W.	28
Brookes, Warwick	26
Brooks, J. L.	83
*Brotherton, E. A.	52
Brown, J.	98
Browne, J. H. Balfour	33
Brownlie, J. T.	101
*Brunner, J. F. L.	57
Brunskill, G. F.	113
*Bryce, J. A.	93
*Buckmaster, S. O., K.C.	35
*Bull, Sir W. J.	24
Bulley, A. K.	68
*Burdett-Coutts, W. L. A. B.	30
Burgess, J.	97
Burgoyne, A.	25
Burke, J. M.	107
Burn, Col. C. R.	98
*Burns, Rt. Hon. J.	21
Burrows, H.	28
*Burt, Rt. Hon. T.	44
Burt, W.	84
Burton, B. H.	40
Bury, Viscount	56
Butcher, J. G., K.C.	54
*Butcher, S. H.	115
Butler, A. E.	32
Buxton, C. R.	60
Buxton, C. S.	80
Buxton, Noel	74
*Buxton, Rt. Hon. S.	29
*Byles, W. P.	48
Byrne, H. M.	69

C

Name	Page
Cadogan, Hon. E.	40
Cairns, A.	67
Calley, Col. T. C. P.	83
Cameron of Lochiel	103
Cameron, A. G.	42
Cameron, J.	73
*Cameron, R.	62
Campbell, Capt. D.	97
Campbell, J. G. D.	76
*Campbell, Rt. Hon. J. H. M., K.C.	115
Campbell, R.	90
Campion, W. R.	84
*Carlile, E. H.	66
Carmichael, E. G. M.	73
Carpenter, Capt. A. Boyd	85
Carpenter, J. Boyd	104
Carpenter, W. B. Boyd	48
*Carr-Gomm, H.	28
*Carson, Rt. Hon. Sir E. H., K.C.	115
Cassel, Felix, K.C.	24
*Castlereagh, Viscount	43
Cator, J.	66
*Causton, R. K.	28
Cautley, H. S.	81
*Cave, G., K.C.	80
Cavendish-Bentinck, Lord H.	46
*Cawley, Sir F.	69
Cawley, H. T.	69
Cayzer, Sir C.	44
*Cecil, E.	30
Cecil, Lord Hugh	114
*Cecil, Lord R.	32
Chaloner, Col. R. G. W.	42
*Chamberlain, Rt. Hon. Austen	84
*Chamberlain, Rt. Hon. J.	32
Chamberlain, N.	57
Chamberlayne, A. R.	96
Chambers, J., K.C.	104
Chancellor, H. G.	28
*Channing, Sir F. A.	75
*Chaplin, Rt. Hon. H.	81
Chapman, S.	97
Chapple, A.	103
Charlesworth, J. S.	86
Chatterton, H.	34
Chaytor, Sir W. C.	61
*Churchill, E. G. Spencer	52
*Churchill, Rt. Hon. Winston S.	94
Churchman, A. C.	40
*Clancy, J. J.	108
Clark-Hutchinson, G. A.	98
Clarke, W. H.	41
Clay, Capt. H. Spender	67
*Cleland, J. W.	95
Clifford, A. W.	64
*Clive, Capt. P. A.	65
Clonmell, Earl of	82
*Clough, W.	88
Clow, W. M.	106
*Clyde, J. A., K.C.	94
*Clynes, J. R.	43
*Coates, Major E. F.	26
Coates, Dr. G.	79
Coats, S. A.	23
Cochrane, A. H. J.	75
*Cochrane, Hon. T.	98
Cochran-Patrick, N. K.	97
Coit, Dr. S.	52
Colefax, H. A.	44
*Collings, Rt. Hon. J.	31
Collins, G. P.	96
*Collins, S.	25
*Collins, Sir W.	27
Compton, Lord A. F.	72
*Compton-Rickett, Sir J.	86
*Condon, T. J.	113
Conner, H. D., K.C.	105
Constable, A. H. B., K.C.	95
Constable, N. B.	99
Conybeare, C. A. V.	72
Cooper, Capt. Bryan	109
Cooper, R. A.	52
*Corbett, A. Cameron	96
*Corbett, C. H.	81
*Corbett, T. L.	103
*Cornwall, Sir E. A.	22
*Cory, Sir C. J.	58
Costello, L. W. J.	28
*Cotton, Sir H.	45
Cotton, H. E.	22
Cotton, W. F.	109
*Courthope, G. L.	82
*Cowan, W. H.	98
Cox, H. B.	94
*Cox, Harold	48
Coysh, F.	79
Crabb-Watt, J.	98
*Craig, C. C.	106
*Craig, H. J.	52
*Craig, Capt. J.	108
Craig, Norman C., K.C.	67
*Craik, Sir H.	115
Cranston, Sir R.	97
Crawshay-Williams, E.	41
*Crean, E.	107
Cremlyn, W. J.	91
Crichton-Stuart, Lord N.	88
Cripps, Sir C. A., K.C.	55
Croft, H. Page	36
*Crooks, W.	30
*Crosfield, A. H.	52
*Cross, A.	95
Crossley, Rt. Hon. Sir S.	25
*Crossley, Sir W. J.	56
*Cullinan, J.	113
Cuninghame, J. C.	103
*Curran, P.	62
Cusack, J.	105
Cuthbertson, T.	62

D

Name	Page
*Dalrymple, Viscount	103
Dalziel, D.	25
*Dalziel, Sir J. H.	96
Davies, A. C. Fox	89
*Davies, D.	92
*Davies, Ellis W.	91
*Davies, T.	72
*Davies, Sir W. H.	34
Dawes, J. A.	26
Dawson, J.	32
*de Eresby, Lord Willoughby	72
de Forest, Baron	70
*Delany, W.	112
Denman, Hon. R. D.	35
Dent, B.	37
Derry, J.	49
Devereux, Hon. R. C.	90
*Devlin, J.	104
*Dewar, A., K.C.	94
*Dewar, Sir J. A.	100
Dickinson, R. E.	27
*Dickinson, W. H.	27
*Dilke, Rt. Hon. Sir C. W.	64
*Dillon, J.	111
Disraeli, Coningsby	76
Dixon, C. H.	35
*Donelan, Capt. A. J. C.	107
Doris, W.	111
Dorman, C.	44
*Doughty, Sir G.	38
Doyle, N. Grattan	38
Dransfield, J. H.	87
Du Cros, Alfred	28
*Du Cros, Arthur	39
*Duffy, W. J.	109
Duke, H. E., K.C.	37
Dummett, R. E.	73
*Dumphreys, J.	28
*Duncan, C.	31
Duncan, J. B.	93

INDEX TO CANDIDATES.

	PAGE
*Duncan, J. H.	87
*Duncan, R.	101
Duncannon, Viscount	35
*Dunn, A. E.	57
Dunn, Sir W. H.	28
*Dunne, Major E. L.	52
Durand, Rt. Hon. Sir H. M.	47
Durning-Lawrence, Sir E.	58

E

	PAGE
Eastham, Dr. T.	56
*Edwards, A. C.	89
*Edwards, E.	39
*Edwards, Sir F.	93
Edwards, W. S.	61
Egan, B.	111
*Elibank, Master of	99
Elliott, G., K.C.	54
*Ellis, Rt. Hon. J. E.	76
Ellis, R. G.	86
Elphinstone, Hon. M. W.	99
Elverston, H.	38
Emery, J. N.	77
*Emmott, Rt. Hon. A.	46
*Esmonde, Sir T.	114
*Essex, R. W.	64
Esslemont, G. B.	93
Evans, L. Worthington	36
*Evans, Sir S. T., K.C.	92
Evatt, Surgeon-Gen.	34
Eyres-Monsell, B.	84

F

	PAGE
Faber, D.	25
*Faber, G. D.	21
*Faber, Capt. W. V.	64
*Falconer, J.	100
Falle, B. G.	47
Fallon, W.	107
*Farrell, J. P.	111
Farrer, R.	66
*Fell, A.	38
*Fenwick, C.	76
*Ferens, T. R.	39
*Fetherstonhaugh, G., K.C.	109
*Ffrench, P.	114
*Field, W.	105
*Fiennes, Hon. Eustace	76
Filmer, Sir R.	41
Finlay, Rt. Hon. Sir R. B., K.C.	115
Fisher, W. Hayes	23
Fitch, Cecil	74
FitzGerald, Sir E.	104
Fitzroy, E. A.	75
Flannery, Sir F.	63
*Flavin, M. J.	109
Fleming, V.	76
*Fletcher, J. S.	24
Flower, Sir E.	33
Foot, I.	61
Forbes, Capt. the Hon. D.	26
Ford, P. J.	94
Forestier-Walker, L.	73
Forsdike, P. F.	77
*Forster, H. W.	67
Foster, H. S.	79
Foster, J. K.	36
*Foster, P. S.	82
*Foster, Rt. Hon. Sir W.	59

	PAGE
Fox, C.	64
Foxcroft, C. T.	78
Fox-Pitt, St. G. L.	66
France, G.	86
Francis, F.	59
Fraser, Sir E.	40
Fraser, J. Foster	41
Fraser, Capt. Sir K.	71
Fremantle, Hon. T. F.	55
*Fuller, J. M. F.	83
*Fullerton, H.	58
*Furness, Sir C.	39

G

	PAGE
Gageby, R.	104
Galbraith, J. F. W.	38
*Gardner, E.	55
Garfit, T. Cheney	56
Gaskell, F. H.	92
Gastrell, Maj. H.	25
Gee, W.	30
Gelder, Sir W. A.	71
Gibbs, Lt.-Col. G. A.	34
*Gibson, Sir J.	94
Giles, C. T., K.C.	50
*Gilhooly, J.	108
*Gill, A. H.	33
Gilmour, Capt. J.	103
*Ginnell, L.	114
Glanville, H. J.	23
Glass, J.	94
*Glover, J.	48
Glyn, R. G. C.	100
*Goddard, Sir D.	40
Goldman, C. S.	46
Goldney, F. B.	35
Goldsmid, S. H.	22
Goldsmith, F.	80
*Gooch, G. P.	31
*Gooch, H. C.	22
Gordon, J.	40
*Gordon, J., K.C.	111
Gorst, Rt. Hon. Sir J.	48
*Goulding, E. A.	54
Graham, J. E., K.C.	96
Graham, Marquis of	79
Grant, J. A.	58
Gray, E.	29
*Grayson, A. Victor	85
Greenall, T.	70
Greene, Raymond	24
Greenlees, L.	29
*Greenwood, G. C.	47
*Greenwood, Hamar	54
Greig, Colonel	103
Grenfell, C. A.	57
*Gretton, J.	77
*Grey, Rt. Hon. Sir E.	75
Gribble, J.	45
*Griffith, J. Ellis	90
Griffith-Boscawen, Major	37
Griffiths, J. N.	52
Grimwood, J.	30
Gritten, W. G. H.	39
Grogan, Capt. E. S.	45
Groser, A. W.	85
Grylls, H. B.	57
Guest, Capt. the Hon. F.	61
Guiney, P.	107
*Guinness, Hon. R.	28

	PAGE
*Guinness, Hon. W.	35
*Gulland, J. W.	93
*Gwynn, S. L.	105
Gwynne, R. S.	84

H

	PAGE
Hackett, J.	113
*Haddock, G. B.	68
*Haldane, Rt. Hon. R. B., K.C.	100
Hall, Douglas B.	65
Hall, E. Marshall, K.C.	42
*Hall, F.	87
Hall, W. Clarke	40
Hambro, Angus V.	61
Hamersley, A. St. G., K.C.	76
Hamilton, Lord C.	25
*Hamilton, Marquis of	105
*Hancock, J. G.	59
*Harcourt, Rt. Hon. Lewis	68
*Harcourt, R. V.	97
*Hardie, J. Keir	89
*Hardy, G. A.	80
*Hardy, L.	66
Hare, Sir T. L.	74
Hargreaves, G. de la P.	87
*Harmood-Banner, J. S.	42
*Harmsworth, Cecil	84
*Harmsworth, R. Leicester	99
Harrington, Col. Sir J.	56
*Harrington, T.	105
*Harris, F. Leverton	29
Harris, H. P.	27
Harris, P.	73
Harrison, T.	108
Harrison-Broadley, Col. H. B.	84
Hart, Heber	53
*Hart-Davies, T.	24
Hartley, E. L.	35
Hartley, E. R.	33
*Harvey, A. G.	48
*Harvey, T. E.	41
*Harvey, W. E.	59
Harwood, G.	33
*Haslam, J.	58
*Haslam, L.	44
Havelock-Allan, Sir H.	61
*Haviland-Burke, E.	110
Haworth, A. A.	44
*Hay, Hon. Claude	28
Hayden, J. P.	112
Hayward, E.	62
*Hazel, Dr. A. E. W.	52
*Hazleton, R.	109 & 111
*Healy, M.	104
Healy, T. M., K.C.	111
Heath, Col. A. H.	79
Heathcoat-Amory, I.	60
Heaton, J. Henniker	35
Hedderwick, T. C. H., K.C.	55
*Hedges, A. P.	67
*Helme, N. W.	68
*Helmsley, Viscount	85
*Hemmerde, E. G., K.C.	91
Hemphill, Captain F.	23
Hemsley, T. W.	102
*Henderson, A.	61
Henderson, Maj. H. G.	55
Henderson, J. M.	98

Name	PAGE
Henderson, Capt. R. R.	71
Henlé, F. H.	27
*Henry, C. S.	77
*Herbert, Col. Sir I.	73
Herbert, Hon. Aubrey	78
*Herbert, T. Arnold	55
Herdman, E. C.	113
*Hermon-Hodge, Sir R.	23
Hewins, Prof. W. A. S.	87
Hickman, Col. T.	53
Hicks, Harold	77
*Higham, J. S.	88
*Hill, Sir C. L.	50
Hillier, Dr. A.	66
*Hills, J. W.	37
Hill-Wood, S.	59
Hilton, J.	46
Hinchliffe, W. A. S.	88
Hindle, F. G.	68
Hinmers, E.	59
Hirst, F. W.	80
Hoare, Sir S.	45
Hoare, S. J. G.	22
Hobart, Lieut.-Col.	30
*Hobart, Sir R.	65
*Hobhouse, Rt. Hon. C.	34
Hocking, Silas K.	36
*Hodge, J.	69
Hodgkinson, S.	67
Hoffgaard, E.	22
*Hogan, M.	113
Hohler, G. F., K.C.	35
Holland, A. L.	81
*Holland, Sir W.	87
*Holt, R. D.	75
Holzapfel, A. G.	80
*Hooper, A. G.	37
Hope, H.	99
*Hope, J. D.	100
*Hope, J. F.	49
Horne, Rev. C. Silvester	40
Horne, F.	85
Horne, R. S.	103
Horne, W. E.	80
Horner, A. L., K.C.	113
*Horniman, E. J.	22
House, Ald. W.	61
*Houston, R. P.	43
Howard, F. G.	24
*Howard, Hon. Geoffrey	58
Howard, Col. H. R. L.	91
Howell, H. E.	43
Howick, Viscount	33
*Hudson, W.	44
Hughes, A. E.	91
Hughes, F.	31
Hughes, S. L.	51
Hulbert, M. B.	72
Hume-Williams, W. E., K.C.	76
*Hunt, R.	77
Hunter, Sir C.	31
Hunter, W., K.C.	101
Hutchinson, St. J.	82
*Hyde, C. G.	52
Hyndman, H. M.	35

I

Name	PAGE
*Illingworth, P.	87
Irving, D.	48
Inskip, T. W. H.	75
*Isaacs, Rufus, K.C.	48

J

Name	PAGE
Jackson, Capt. C. Ward	44
Jackson, G.	78
Jackson, Sir J.	37
Jackson, Lt.-Col. J. A.	53
*Jackson, R. S.	23
Jardine, E.	78
*Jardine, Sir J.	103
Jardine, W.	85
Jebb, R.	26
Jellicoe, E. G.	43
*Jenkins, J. H.	35
Jenkins, S. R.	38
Jessel, A. H., K.C.	68
Jessel, Capt. H. M.	27
Jodrell, N. P.	74
*Johnson, J.	38
Johnson, J. S.	63
*Johnson, W.	82
*Jones, Sir D. Brynmor	90
Jones, E.	89
Jones, E. P.	57
Jones, Haydn	92
*Jones, Leif	82
*Jones, W.	91
Jones, W. S. Glyn	29
Jones-Morris, R.	92
*Jordan, J.	109
Joseph, F. L.	43
*Jowett, F. W.	33
*Joyce, M.	105
*Joynson-Hicks, W.	44

K

Name	PAGE
*Keating, M.	110
Kebty-Fletcher, J. R.	68
Keeves, J. H. T.	24
Keightley, Dr. S. R.	111
Keith, H. S.	95
Kellaway, F.	75
Kelly, E.	108
Kelly, F.	88
Kemp, Sir G.	44
Kennedy, T.	93
*Kennedy, V. P.	107
Kerr, J. G.	109
Kerrison, Col. E. R.	74
Kerr-Smiley, P.	106
*Kerry, Earl of	59
Kessack, J. O'C.	95
*Keswick, W.	80
Kettle, T. M.	113
*Kilbride, D.	110
Kimber, Sir H.	29
*King, A. J.	56
King, H. D.	74
*King, Sir H. S.	39
King, J.	78
King, W.	78
King-Farlow, S.	49
Kinloch-Cooke, Sir C.	37
Kipling, J. G.	21
Kirkley, J.	62
Kirkwood, J. E. Morrison	63
Knight, Capt. E. A.	40
Knight, M. E.	112
Knight, S. Holford	55
Knott, J.	51
Knott, J. L.	62
Kyd, D. H.	51

L

Name	PAGE
*Laidlaw, Sir R.	103
*Lamb, E.	65
*Lamb, E. H.	48
*Lambert, G.	60
Lambert, R. C.	47
*Lambton, Hon. F. W.	62
*Lamont, N.	99
*Lane-Fox, G. R.	85
Lang, P. K.	95
Lang, R. T.	67
Lansbury, G.	28
Lapworth, C.	49
*Lardner, J. C.	112
Laverty, C.	112
*Law, A. Bonar	22
*Law, H. A.	108
Lawrence, Sir A.	26
Lawson, Hon. H. L. W.	29
Lawson, Sir Wilfrid	58
*Layland-Barratt, Sir F.	60
Lea, J.	42
Leach, C.	85
*Lee, A. H.	65
*Lehmann, R. C.	71
Lely, Sir F.	67
Leon, A. L.	23
Leslie, Shane	105
Lester, W. R.	74
*Lever, A. Levy	63
*Lever, W. H.	70
Levita, Major C. B.	58
*Levy, Sir M.	71
*Lewis, J. H.	91
Lewis, J. W.	85
Lewisham, Viscount	52
Lias, W. J.	43
Lincoln, J. T.	36
Lister, R. A.	64
Lithgow, S.	37
Lloyd, G. A.	79
*Lloyd George, Rt. Hon. D.	89
Lloyd, Harold	92
Lloyd, J. S.	94
Locker-Lampson, G.	49
Locker-Lampson, O.	66
*Lockwood, Rt. Hon. Col. A. R. M.	63
Long, R. C. C.	83
*Long, Rt. Hon. W.	28
*Lonsdale, J. B.	106
Lopes, Sir H. Buller	60
Lord, W. G.	70
*Lough, Rt. Hon. T.	25
Low, Sir F., K.C.	45
Low, W.	97
*Lowe, Sir F. W.	32
Lowther, Hon. Claude	58
*Lowther, Rt. Hon. J. W.	58
Lucas, Col. F. A.	25
Luke, W. B.	60
*Lundon, T.	110
Lunn, Dr. H. S.	33
*Lupton, A.	72
*Luttrell, H. C. F.	60

INDEX TO CANDIDATES.

	PAGE
*Lyell, C. H.	94
Lygon, Hon. H.	46
*Lynch, A.	107
*Lynch, H. F. B.	87
*Lyttelton, Rt. Hon. A	27
Lyttelton, Hon. J. C.	84

M

	PAGE
*McArthur, C.	42
McCallum, J.	97
*McCalmont, Col. J. M.	106
*Macassey, L.	108
*MacCaw, W. J.	108
McCurdy, C. A.	45
*Macdonald, J. A. M.	95
*MacDonald, J. R.	41
MacIlwaine, Capt.	25
McIntyre, T. W.	98
*McKean, J.	112
McKenna, P.	114
*McKenna, Rt. Hon. R.	73
Mackinder, H. J.	95
McLachlan, J.	44
*McLaren, Rt. Hon. Sir C.	71
McLaren, F.	72
*McLaren, H. D.	79
*Maclean, D.	31
Maclean, N.	103
Macleod, Sir R.	100
Macmaster, D., K.C.	80
*McMicking, Major	101
McMicking, T.	96
*Macnamara, Dr.	22
*MacNeill, J. G. Swift	108
McNeill, R.	93
Maconochie, A. W.	101
Macpherson, J. A.	103
*Macpherson, J. T.	48
*MacVeagh, J.	108
*Maddison, F.	35
Maddocks, H.	82
Magee, P. J.	104
*Magnus, Sir P.	115
Main, A. P.	96
Malcolm, Ian	48
Mallaby-Deeley, H. C.	73
*Mallet, C. E.	47
*Manfield, H.	75
Manningham-Buller, Capt.	69
*Markham, A. B.	76
*Marks, G. C.	57
Marsden-Smedley, J. B.	59
Marshall, Sir H.	71
Martin, Hon. J., K.C.	27
Mason, D. M.	96
*Mason, J. F.	53
Mason, W. J. P.	23
*Massie, J.	83
*Masterman, C. F. G.	29
Mathias, R.	36
Mattinson, W., K.C.	33
Maxwell, Sir J. Stirling	95
*Meagher, M.	110
*Meehan, F. E.	110
*Meehan, P. A.	112
*Menzies, Sir W.	102
Methuen, A. M. S.	80
Meynell, F.	31
*Meysey-Thompson, E. C.	78
*Micklem, N., K.C.	66

	PAGE
*Middlebrook, W.	41
*Middlemore, J. T.	32
*Mildmay, F. B.	61
Millar, J. D.	97
Mills, Hon. C. T.	73
{ Mitchell, J. D.	102
Mitchell, W. Foot	66
*Mitchell-Thomson, W.	101
Molloy, M.	106
Molson, J. E.	22
*Molteno, P. A.	99
Monckton-Arundell, Hon. G. V. A.	49
*Mond, A.	90
*Money, L. G. Chiozza	26
*Montagu, Hon. E. S.	55
Montefiore, R. M. Sebag	39
Moon, Dr. R. O.	26
*Mooney, J. J.	105
*Moore, W., K.C.	106
*Morgan, G. Hay	58
Morgan, J.	54
Morgan, J. H.	32
*Morgan, J. Lloyd, K.C.	91
Morgan, L.	92
Morgan, W. Pritchard	89
*Morpeth, Viscount	32
Morison, H.	81
*Morrell, P.	76
Morrison, Captain J. A.	45
Morrison, T. B., K.C.	102
Morrison-Bell, Maj. A. C.	60
*Morrison-Bell, Capt. E. F.	60
Morrison-Bell, Capt. E. W.	55
Morrow, F. St. John	59
Mortimer, R.	50
*Morton, A. C.	103
Moulsdale, W. E.	77
Mount, W. A.	55
Moy, A., junr.	42
*Muldoon, J.	114
Munro, R.	97
*Munro-Ferguson, R. C.	97
Murison, Prof.	95
*Murnaghan, G.	113
*Murphy, J.	109
Murphy, Dr. W.	104
*Murray, Capt. the Hon. A. C.	100
Murray, Hon. A. D.	102
Murray, W.	99
Muspratt, M.	42
*Myer, H.	25

N

	PAGE
*Nannetti, J. P.	104
*Napier, T. B.	67
Neal, A.	50
Needham, C. T.	44
*Neilson, J.	56
Neville, R. J.	53
Newbolt, F. G.	80
*Newdigate-Newdegate, F.A.	82
Newman, J. R. Pretyman	73
*Newnes, F.	76
Newton, H. K.	63
*Nicholls, G.	75
*Nicholson, C. N.	86
Nicholson, Col. J. S.	61
Nicholson, W.	41

	PAGE
*Nicholson, W. G.	65
Nickalls, M.	34
*Nield, H.	72
*Nolan, J.	111
*Norman, Sir H.	53
Norris, F.	84
*Norton, Capt. C.	26
Nugent, G.	79
*Nugent, Sir W.	114
*Nussey, Sir W.	47
*Nuttall, H.	69

O

	PAGE
*O'Brien, Patrick	105
{ O'Brien, W.	104
{ O'Brien, W.	107
O'Connor, Major G. B.	104
*O'Connor, James	114
*O'Connor, John	110
*O'Connor, T. P.	42
*O'Doherty, P.	108
*O'Donnell, J.	111
*O'Donnell, T.	110
*O'Dowd, J.	112
*Oddy, J. J.	87
Ogden, F.	87
*O'Grady, J.	41
*O'Kelly, Conor	111
*O'Kelly, J.	112
O'Leary, D.	108
*O'Malley, W.	109
O'Neill, Hon. A.	106
*O'Neill, Dr. C.	106
Orde-Powlett, Hon. W. G. A.	85
Orlebar, R. R. B.	45
Ormsby-Gore, Hon. W.	89
*O'Shaughnessy, P. J.	110
*O'Shee, J. J.	113
O'Sullivan, E.	109
Outhwaite, R. L.	81

P

	PAGE
Page, A.	36
Paget, A. H.	35
Paget, T. G. F.	75
Pakenham, Lt.-Col. H. A.	27
Palmer, G.	62
*Parker, Sir G.	38
*Parker, J.	38
*Parkes, E.	31
Parkin, G. H.	72
*Partington, O.	59
Paul, E.	36
*Pearce, R.	79
*Pearce, W.	28
Pearson, R. B.	100
Pearson, W. H. M.	79
*Pease, H. Pike	36
*Pease, Rt. Hon. J. A.	63
Peel, Mervyn	91
Peel, Capt. R. F.	80
*Peel, Hon. W.	51
Percy, C.	76
Perkins, W. F.	65
Permewan, Dr.	70
Perowne, Col.	60
Peto, B. E.	83
*Philipps, Lt.-Col. Ivor	50
*Philipps, Sir O. C.	90

	PAGE
*Phillips, J.	111
Phillips, V.	43
Pickering, J. J.	101
*Pickersgill, E. H.	22
Pickles, W.	86
Pierpoint, R.	62
*Pirie, D. V.	93
Platt, Major E.	38
Plummer, Sir W. R.	44
Pocock, S. J.	73
*Pointer, J.	49
Pole-Carew, Lt.-Gen. Sir R.	57
*Pollard, Sir G. H.	68
Pollock, E. M., K.C.	52
Pollock, Sir F.	115
*Ponsonby, A.	97
Potter, C. H.	69
Powell, E.	77
*Power, P. J.	113
Pownall, Assheton	28
Preston, W. R.	27
*Pretyman, E. G.	62
*Price, C. E.	94
*Price, Sir R. J.	74
*Priestley, A.	38
Priestley, C. F. L.	91
*Priestley, Sir W. E.	33
Primrose, Hon. Neil	56
Pringle, W. M. R.	101
Proby, Col. D. J.	63
Prothero, R. E.	54
Pryce-Jones, Col. E.	89
Purcell, A. A.	49
Purvis, Sir R.	47

Q

Quelch, H.	45
Quilter, W. E. C.	80

R

*Radford, G. H.	24
Radford, G. W.	59
Raffan, P. W.	70
Raine, G. E.	51
*Rainy, A. R.	96
Ralston, Gavin W.	100
Ramsden, G. T.	86
*Randles, Sir J. S.	58
Rankin, Sir J.	65
Rankin, J. S.	51
*Raphael, H. H.	59
*Ratcliff, R. F.	78
*Rawlinson, J. F. P., K.C.	115
Rawson, Col. R. H.	81
*Rea, Russell	38
*Rea, W. Russell	49
*Reddy, M.	110
*Redmond, J.	105
*Redmond, W.	107
*Rees, J. D.	89
Reiss, R.	81
*Remnant, J. F.	23
*Rendall, A.	64
*Renton, Major A. L.	48
Renton, J. H.	64
*Renwick, G.	44
Rhys, D.	91
Rice, J. H.	105
Rice, Hon. W. F.	34

	PAGE
*Richards, T.	73
*Richards, T. F.	53
*Richardson, A.	46
Richardson, A.	22
Ricketts, G. W.	53
Ridgeway, Sir J. West	115
Ridley, Hon. Jasper	44
Ridley, S. F.	48
Rittner, G. H.	39
Robb, E. Elvy	43
*Roberts, C.	41
Roberts, Capt. F.	90
*Roberts, G.	45
*Roberts, Sir J. H.	91
Roberts, R. O.	90
*Roberts, S.	49
*Robertson, Sir G.	33
*Robertson, J. M.	75
Robertson, W.	93
*Robinson, S.	90
Robson, Sir H.	25
*Robson, Sir W., K.C.	50
*Roch, W. F.	93
*Roche, A.	104
*Roche, J.	109
*Roe, Sir T.	36
*Rogers, F. N.	83
Rolleston, Sir J.	65
Rollit, Sir A.	80
*Ronaldshay, Earl of	73
*Rose, Sir C. D.	56
Rose, F. H.	56
Rose-Innes, P., K.C.	69
Rosenheim, F.	26
Rothschild, Lionel	55
Roundell, R. F.	88
*Rowlands, J.	66
Rowntree, A.	54
Royce, W. S.	72
Royds, E.	72
*Runciman, Rt. Hon. W.	37
*Russell, Rt. Hon. T. W.	113
Russell-Taylor, E.	68
*Rutherford, J.	68
*Rutherford, Dr. V. H.	72
*Rutherford, W. W.	43
Ryan, E. A.	113

S

St. Maur, H.	37
Saise, Dr. T. J.	34
*Salter, A. C., K.C.	64
Samson, E. M.	93
Samuel, A. M.	69
*Samuel, Rt. Hon. H.	85
Samuel, Sir H.	26
Samuel, J.	51
Samuel, S.	41
*Samuel, Stuart	29
Sanders, R. A.	77
Sanders, W. S.	47
Sanderson, L., K.C.	82
Sandy, J.	65
Sandys, G. J.	78
*Sandys, Col. T. M.	70
*Sassoon, Sir E.	40
Saunderson, A. D.	113
*Scanlan, T.	112
*Scarisbrick, Sir T. L.	61
*Schwann, Sir C.	43

	PAGE
*Scott, A. H.	30
Scott, D. A.	94
Scott, Lord Henry	103
Scott, Leslie, K.C.	42
*Scott, Sir S.	26
Scott-Brown, R.	93
*Scott Dickson, Rt. Hon. C., K.C.	95
Scrymgeour, E.	94
*Seaverns, J. H.	25
*Seddon, J. A.	70
*Seely, Col.	42
Seely, C. H.	41
Seton-Karr, Sir H.	98
Sexton, J.	43
*Shackleton, D. J.	68
Shafto, A. D.	62
Sharp, A.	53
*Shaw, Sir C. E.	50
Shaw, Col. J. R.	47
Sheehan, D. D.	107
*Sheehy, D.	112
*Sheffield, Sir B.	71
Sheppard, F.	34
Sherburn, Sir J.	40
*Sherwell, A. J.	39
Shortt, E.	44
*Silcock, T. B.	78
Simmons, P. C.	29
Simner, P.	92
*Simon, J. A., K.C.	63
Simpson, Sir A.	115
*Sloan, T. H.	104
Small, R.	101
Smillie, R.	101
Smith, F. C.	70
*Smith, F. E., K.C.	43
Smith, G.	98
Smith, Harold	39
Smith, H.	86
Smith, H. B. Lees	45
Smith, Rt. Hon. J. Parker	96
Smith, Riley	54
Smith, T.	68
Smith, W. C., K.C.	102
Smith-Carington, N. W.	71
Smyth, Capt. G. H. S.	38
*Smyth, T. F.	110
Snell, H.	39
Snowden, H. G.	45
*Snowden, P.	32
Soames, A. W.	74
*Soares, E. J.	60
Spear, J. W.	60
*Spicer, Sir A.	24
Sprot, Col. A.	100
Stack, T. N.	109
*Stanier, B.	77
*Stanley, Hon. A.	70
*Stanley, Albert	79
*Stanley, Hon. A. L.	56
Stanley, Capt. G. F.	48
Stapley, Sir R.	23
*Starkey, J. R.	76
*Staveley-Hill, H.	79
*Steadman, W. C.	23
Steel, S. Strang	102
Steel-Maitland, A. D.	32
Stephenson, J. J.	32
Stewart, G.	57

INDEX TO CANDIDATES.

Name	PAGE
Stewart, Sir M. J. McT.	101
*Stewart-Smith, D., K.C.	83
Stobart, H. G.	61
Storey, S.	51
Stott, P. S.	46
*Strachey, Sir E.	78
Strain, L. H.	99
*Straus, B. S.	29
Strauss, A.	25
*Strauss, E. A.	55
Streatfeild, Maj. H.	62
Stroyan, J.	51
Stuart, G. H.	68
*Stuart, Rt. Hon. J.	51
Sturdy, E. V.	73
Sullivan, J.	101
*Summerbell, T.	51
Summers, J. W.	89
*Sutherland, J. E.	94
Sutton, J. E.	43
Swift, R., K.C.	48
Sykes, A. J.	56
Sykes, Major Mark	84
Symmons, I. A.	63

T

Name	PAGE
*Talbot, Lord E.	81
*Taylor, J. W.	62
*Taylor, T. C.	69
*Tennant, Sir E.	49
*Tennant, H. J.	98
Terrell, G.	83
Terrell, H., K.C.	38
*Thomas, Sir A.	92
*Thomas, A., K.C.	91
*Thomas, D. A.	88
Thomas, J. H.	36
Thomas, Lewis, K.C.	39
Thompson, F. W.	36
*Thompson, J. W. H.	78
Thompson, R.	104
Thompson, S.	91
Thompson, W. W.	87
*Thorne, G. R.	53
*Thorne, W.	30
Thynne, Lord A.	31
Tilby, H. A.	89
Tillett, Ben	90
Timmis, S.	86
Tiverton, Viscount	88
Tobin, Alfred A., K.C.	48
*Tomkinson, Rt. Hon. J.	56
Touche, G. A.	24
Toulmin, G.	35
*Trevelyan, C. P.	86
Tryon, Capt. G. C.	34
Tullibardine, Marquis of	102
Tweedy-Smith, R.	39
Twist, H.	53

U

Name	PAGE
*Ure, Rt. Hon. A., K.C.	102

V

Name	PAGE
*Valentia, Viscount	46
Valentine, J.	113
Vaudrey, Sir W. H.	43
*Vaughan-Davies, M. L.	90
Venables-Llewellyn, C. T.	93
*Verney, F. W.	55
Verney, H. C.	83
Verrall, G. H.	56
Vickers, D.	49
Vincent, H. C.	89
*Vivian, H.	31

W

Name	PAGE
*Wadsworth, J.	86
*Walker, H. de R.	71
*Walker, Col. W. H.	70
Walker, W.	97
Wallis, J. E.	64
Wallis, R. B.	76
Walls, P.	44
*Walrond, Hon. W. L. C.	60
*Walsh, S.	70
Walsh, V. Hussey	35
*Walters, J. T.	49
*Walton, J.	85
Wandless, W. H.	53
Ward, A. S.	66
Ward, Hon. Cyril A.	64
*Ward, D.	50
*Ward, J.	51
*Warde, Col. C. E.	67
*Wardle, G. J.	51
*Waring, Capt. W.	98
*Warner, T. C.	79
Warren, W.	29
*Wason, Rt. Hon. E.	99
*Wason, J. C.	102
*Waterlow, D. S.	24
*Watt, H. A.	95
Webb, H.	65
*Wedgwood, J. C.	45
Weigall, J. W. W.	67
*Weir, J. Galloway	103
Wertheimer, C.	24
Whale, G.	46
Wheler, G. C. H.	67
White, E.	69
White, H.	69
*White, J. D.	99
White, Maj. Dalrymple	70
*White, Sir G.	74
*White, Sir L.	84
*White, P.	112
Whitehead, J. P.	58
*Whitehead, R.	63
Whitehouse, J. H.	101
Whiteley, H.	30
*Whitley, J. H.	38

Name	PAGE
*Whittaker, Rt. Hon. Sir T. P.	88
Whitworth, C. W.	86
Whitworth, J. H.	50
Whyte, A. F.	97
*Wiles, T.	25
*Wilkie, A.	94
Williams, A.	47
Williams, Basil	81
Williams, C.	57
Williams, G. H.	92
*Williams, J.	92
Williams, J. R.	88
Williams, P.	44
*Williams, Col. R.	61
Williams, R. Vaughan	50
*Williams, W. Llewellyn	88
*Williamson, Sir A.	100
Williamson, G. H.	63
Willoughby, Maj. the Hon. C.	72
*Willoughby de Eresby, Lord	72
*Wills, A. W.	61
*Wilson, Hon. Guy	40
*Wilson, H. J.	86
Wilson, J. R.	101
*Wilson, John	62
*Wilson, J. W.	84
Wilson, Capt. Leslie	29
*Wilson, P. W.	27
*Wilson, Maj. Stanley	84
Wilson, T. F.	101
*Wilson, W. T.	69
*Winfrey, R.	74
Wing, T.	38
*Winterton, Earl	81
Wodehouse, Hon. P.	64
*Wolff, G. W.	104
Wolmer, Viscount	70
Wood, Capt. C. P. B.	77
Wood, Hon. E.	87
Wood, J.	103
Wood, J.	51
*Wood, T. McKinnon	96
Woodcock, W. D.	35
Woods, M. H.	34
*Wortley, Rt. Hon. C. B. Stuart	50
Wright, Col. J. R.	90
*Wyndham, Rt. Hon. G.	37
Wynn, A. W. W.	92

Y

Name	PAGE
Yate, Col. C.	71
Yerburgh, R.	35
Young, Hilto	84
*Young, S.	106
Young, W.	102
*Younger, G.	93
Younger, W.	102
*Yoxall, Sir J. H.	46

1—2

THE RESULT OF THE GENERAL ELECTION.

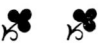

THE General Election of 1910 arose from the refusal of the House of Lords to pass the Finance Bill of the preceding year until it had been submitted to the judgment of the country. The Finance Bill embodied the Budget of Mr. Lloyd George, Chancellor of the Exchequer, and though it had been considerably amended in the course of prolonged debates in the House of Commons, it was found to contain when it reached the House of Lords many novel proposals of an important nature. When Lord Crewe, the leader of the House, had formally moved the second reading of the Bill, Lord Lansdowne, the leader of the Opposition in the House of Lords, moved as an amendment :—

> That this House is not justified in giving its consent to this Bill until it has been submitted to the judgment of the country.

After a debate which lasted from November 22 until November 30 the amendment was carried, 350 Peers voting for it and 75 against—majority 275.

The next day Mr. Asquith, the Prime Minister, went down to the House of Commons and informed a crowded and excited assemblage of members that "after consulting the authentic record of the proceedings of the other House" he had found that the Finance Bill passed by the House of Commons had been refused a second reading by the House of Lords. He gave notice of a resolution, which he moved at the succeeding sitting of the House. It was as follows :—

> That the action of the House of Lords in refusing to pass into law the financial provision made by this House for the service of the year is a breach of the Constitution and a usurpation of the rights of the Commons.

This resolution was debated briefly, Mr. Asquith announcing that the King would be advised to dissolve Parliament at the earliest possible moment; and it was then carried by 349 votes to 134—majority 215.

Parliament was prorogued on December 3, and it was dissolved on January 10. But politicians did not wait for the Dissolution to begin the campaign in the country. The leaders on both sides addressed meetings night after night until the close of the pollings. A feature of the election was the large number of speeches made by Peers, who went before the electors to explain why the House of Lords had declined to pass the Budget and also in order to defend the record of that House as a Second Chamber. Discussion was by no means confined to the Budget. There was much said about Tariff Reform and Free Trade, the Navy, Home Rule for Ireland, the position of the House of Lords in the Constitution, and many other familiar questions. The broad controversy between the two main parties in the State was conducted with extraordinary keenness, and there were disturbances in various parts of the country. When the pollings had finished it was found that in nearly every constituency an unprecedentedly high percentage of the electorate had voted.

The Ministerialists left the late House with

a nominal majority of 334, the parties standing thus:—

Liberals			373 ⎫	
Labour members			46 ⎬	.. 502
Nationalists			83 ⎭	
Unionists				168
Majority				334

The Unionists had to win 168 seats to secure a majority in the new House, and it was very soon obvious that for their gains they would have to look almost exclusively to England. In the first days of the election the Unionist gains came slowly, and the defeat of Mr. Pike Pease, the Liberal Unionist Whip, at Darlington, and of Sir George Doughty, a prominent Unionist speaker, at Grimsby, were disquieting omens of the state of opinion in the North. At the same time, however, Sir Henry Norman, the organizer of the Budget League, which had done a great deal to help the Liberals, was beaten in Wolverhampton; and his defeat proved to be an accurate indication of a revival of Unionism in the Midlands. Though the Unionists had not done quite so well as they had hoped to do in the boroughs, it was found when the borough pollings had closed that they had made a net gain of 40 borough seats. But it was when the county pollings began that Unionist gains were accelerated and succeeded one another at a rate which astonished Liberals and Unionists alike. At one time it seemed likely that the Unionists would be the largest single party in the House of Commons; then a tie between the two chief parties appeared to be probable; and, finally, the advantage of the lead was secured by the Liberals through the gain of a seat in the North of Scotland.

After the election the balance of parties in Scotland remained unchanged, and in the North of England, too, Unionists and Liberals remained pretty much as they had been at the Dissolution. In Cheshire, Nottinghamshire, Lincolnshire, Suffolk, Staffordshire, Oxfordshire, Berkshire, Herts, Essex, Middlesex, Kent, Sussex, Surrey, Hants, Dorset, Wilts, Gloucestershire, and Somerset the Unionists made considerable gains, 23 English counties besides London giving them a clear majority of the representation, counting boroughs and divisions together. They have all the seats for Kent, Surrey, Sussex, Herts, and Westmorland; all but one in Middlesex, Wilts, and Warwickshire; and all but two in Northamptonshire and Essex. South of Derbyshire and Cheshire the country is overwhelmingly Unionist in sentiment; north of that line, while the Unionists have improved upon their former position, there is a preponderance of Liberals. The antitheses north and south, town and country, have been used to suggest the cleavage between the Liberalism and the Unionism of England as disclosed by the General Election of 1910. Both, however, are only true with important exceptions.

The net result of the General Election is that the Unionists have gained 105 seats, and the parties now stand:—

Liberals			275 ⎫	
Labour members			40 ⎪	
Nationalists			71 ⎬	397
Independent Nationalists			11 ⎭	
Unionists				273
Ministerial majority				124

In practice the Ministerial majority will probably be found to be much smaller than the figure here given, as the Independent Nationalists are hostile to much of the policy of Mr. John Redmond, and consequently still more hostile to portions of the Liberal programme. It is by no means certain that even Mr. Redmond's followers will all support the Government in important divisions. The list of members of the last Parliament who were defeated at the poll includes the names of the following well-known politicians, most of whom are pretty certain to sit in the House of Commons again:—Colonel Seely, Under-Secretary for the Colonies; Mr. J. A. Pease, Parliamentary Secretary to the Treasury and Chief Government Whip; Mr. F. D. Acland, Financial Secretary to the War Office; Mr. R. K. Causton, Paymaster-General; Mr. T. W. Russell, Vice-President of the Irish Board of Agriculture; Sir Henry Norman, Assistant Postmaster-General; Mr. H. Pike Pease, Liberal Unionist Whip; Sir George Doughty, Lord Robert Cecil, Mr. Harold Cox, Mr. F. W. Lambton, Mr. Russell Rea, Mr. S. O. Buckmaster, K.C., Mr. Joynson-Hicks, Sir Henry Cotton, and Mr. Chiozza Money.

PARTY GAINS and LOSSES.

The following table shows the respective gains:—

MINISTERIALISTS.

Ayrshire, N.	1
Bermondsey	1
Blackburn	1
Darlington	1
Devon (Ashburton) ..	1
Durham, S.E. ..	1
Grimsby	1
Haggerston	1
Hoxton	1
King's Lynn	1
Lanark (Govan) ..	1
Lanark (North-West)	1
Lancashire (Darwen)..	1
Lincolnshire (Gainsborough)	1
Lincolnshire (Brigg)..	1
Manchester, N.W. ..	1
Newcastle-on-Tyne ..	1
St. Andrews	1
Stockton-on-Tees ..	1
Wick Burghs	1
Wigan	1
Yorkshire (Pudsey) ..	1
	22

OPPOSITION.

Antrim, N.	1
Bath	2
Bedford	1
Berkshire (Abingdon)	1
Berkshire (Newbury)	1
Boston	1
Bow and Bromley ..	1
Brighton	2
Brixton	1
Bucks (Wycombe) ..	1
Burnley	1
Buteshire	1
Cambridge	1
Cambridge (Newmarket)	1
Chatham	1
Chelsea	1
Cheltenham	1
Cheshire (Eddisbury)	1
Cheshire (Knutsford)	1
Cheshire (Wirral) ..	1
Chester	1
Christchurch	1
Colchester	1
Coventry	1
Cumberland (Egremont)	1
Denbigh Boroughs ..	1
Devonport	2
Dorset, N.	1
Dorset, S.	1
Essex (Harwich) ..	1
Essex (Maldon) ..	1
Essex (Saffron Walden)	1
Essex, S.E.	1
Exeter..	1
Finsbury, C.	1
Fulham	1
Glasgow (Camlachie)..	1
Gloucester	1
Gloucester (Cirencester)	1
Greenwich	1
Hackney, N.	1
Hants (Isle of Wight)	1
Hereford (Leominster)	1
Herts (Hitchin) ..	1
Herts (Watford) ..	1
Hants (New Forest) ..	1
Hunts (Huntingdon)..	1
Hunts (Ramsey) ..	1
Kensington, N. ..	1
Kent (Dartford) ..	1
Kent (Tunbridge) ..	1
Kent (Faversham) ..	1
Kidderminster ..	1
Kirkcudbright ..	1
Lambeth, N.	1
Lancashire (Southport)	1
Lincolnshire (Louth)..	1
Lincolnshire (Sleaford)	1
Liverpool (Abercromby)	1
Liverpool (East Toxteth)	1
Manchester, S.W. ..	1
Middlesex (Brentford)	1
Middlesex (Enfield) ..	1
Middlesex (Harrow) ..	1
Mile-end	1
Norfolk (Mid).. ..	1
Northants, N... ..	1
Northants, S... ..	1
Nottingham, E. ..	1
Nottingham, S. ..	1
Nottinghamshire (Bassetlaw)	1
Oxfordshire (Banbury)	1
Oxfordshire (Henley)	1
Oxfordshire (Woodstock)	1
Paddington, N. ..	1
Penryn and Falmouth	1
Perthshire, W. ..	1
Portsmouth	2
Preston	2
Radnorshire	1
Renfrewshire, E. ..	1
Rochester	1
St. Pancras, S. ..	1
Salisbury	1
Somerset (Bridgwater)	1
Somerset, E.	1
Somerset (Wells) ..	1
Southwark, W. ..	1
Staffordshire (Leek) ..	1
Staffordshire, W. ..	1
Stalybridge	1
Suffolk (Lowestoft) ..	1
Suffolk (Sudbury) ..	1
Suffolk (Stowmarket)	1
Suffolk (Woodbridge)	1
Sunderland	2
Surrey (Chertsey) ..	1
Surrey (Guildford) ..	1
Surrey (Reigate) ..	1
Sussex (East Grinstead)	1
Sussex (Eastbourne)..	1
Tyrone, S.	1
Tyrone (Mid)	1
Walsall	1
Warwick and Leamington	1
Warwickshire (Rugby)	1
Wednesbury	1
West Bromwich ..	1
Westmorland (Appleby)	1
Westmorland (Kendal)	1
Whitehaven	1
Wiltshire (Cricklade)	1
Wiltshire (Chippenham)	1
Wiltshire (Devizes) ..	1
Wiltshire (Wilton) ..	1
Wolverhampton, S. ..	1
Wolverhampton, W.	1
Woolwich	1
Worcester (Droitwich)	1
Yorkshire (Richmond)	1
Yorkshire (Ripon) ..	1
	127

COMPOSITION OF THE HOUSE OF COMMONS.

	Total seats	Ministerialists.				U.
		L.	Lab.	N.	Ind. N.	
ENGLAND— 465 seats:						
London ..	62	26	2	—	—	34
Boroughs ..	164	69	17	1	—	77
Counties ..	234	96	15	—	—	123
Universities ..	5	—	—	—	—	5
WALES— 30 seats:						
Boroughs ..	11	9	1	—	—	1
Counties ..	19	15	3	—	—	1
SCOTLAND— 72 seats:						
Burghs ..	31	25	2	—	—	4
Counties ..	39	34	—	—	—	5
Universities ..	2	—	—	—	—	2
IRELAND— 103 seats:						
Boroughs ..	16	—	—	11	1	4
Counties ..	85	1	—	59	10	15
Universities ..	2	—	—	—	—	2
	670	275	40	71	11	273
			397			273
			670				

AN ANALYSIS OF THE VOTING.

The following tables, A, B, and C, show the total votes cast for Ministerial and Opposition candidates in all the contested elections in the borough and county constituencies in England, Wales, and Scotland, with the exception of that in Orkney and Shetland, together with the Party representation which has resulted from the voting. For the purposes of the calculation, Ministerial has been taken to include Labour and Socialist candidates, the Nationalist member for the Scotland Division of Liverpool, Commander Bethell, who opposed Mr. Stanley Wilson (U.) in the Holderness Division of Yorkshire as an Independent Free-trader, and the " Prohibitionist " candidate at Dundee. On the other hand, the votes polled by Mr. S. Storey, who stood as an Independent Tariff Reformer at Sunderland, Mr. C. H. Seely, the Unionist Free-trade candidate at Lincoln in opposition to the official Unionist, and the Woman Suffrage candidate in the Rossendale Division of Lancashire have been reckoned in the Opposition aggregate.

In two-member constituencies, where there were four candidates, the figures taken are one-half the total of the votes cast respectively for the Ministerial and the Opposition candidates, but where one candidate opposed two candidates either of the same or of allied political complexion the total votes cast for both his opponents have been divided by two. In Table D, owing to the difficulty of determining the extent of cross-voting in two-member constituencies, the total votes actually cast are reckoned, without division. Commander Bethell is, for this purpose, accounted a Liberal, and the Woman Suffrage and " Prohibitionist " votes are ignored.

No account is taken in these tables of the contests in the London and Scottish Universities, in which the total Unionist vote was 12,709, the Liberal vote 4,521, and the Unionist Free-trade vote 4,411 ; or of those in Ireland, where the political conditions do not lend themselves to a comparison similar to that which has been made in England, Wales, and Scotland. Perhaps the most interesting feature of the elections in Ireland has been the birth of a new party—that of the Independent Nationalists, who have secured eleven seats (including Mr. W. O'Brien's double return), and whose total poll, including that of the unsuccessful candidates, amounted to 45,550 votes, as compared with 78,154 votes given to the followers of Mr. John Redmond in contested constituencies throughout Ireland.

TABLE A. ENGLAND.

	Members. M.	Members. O.	Boroughs. M.	Boroughs. O.	Counties. M.	Counties. O.	Total. M.	Total. O.
London	28	34	282,108	321,168	—	—	282,108	321,168
Bedfordshire	2	1	2,750	2,919	14,577	13,100	17,327	16,019
Berkshire	1	4	6,434	6,895	12,594	20,042	19,028	26,937
Buckinghamshire	1	2	—	—	16,763	20,671	16,763	20,671
Cambridgeshire	2	2	4,081	4,667	15,151	14,566	19,232	19,233
Cheshire	8	5	22,239	20,949	54,844	49,786	77,083	70,735
Cornwall	6	1	1,412	1,593	30,419	22,220	31,831	23,813
Cumberland	2	3	5,724	4,003	14,000	13,109	19,724	17,112
Derbyshire	8	1	10,266	7,995	54,234	42,057	64,500	50,052
Devonshire	7	6	18,045	17,977	39,461	41,663	57,506	59,640
Dorset	1	3	—	—	18,039	20,446	18,039	20,446
Durham	12	2	48,127	38,932	67,681	36,515	115,808	75,447
Essex	2	7	2,926	3,717	72,752	78,079	75,678	81,796
Gloucestershire	6	5	34,859	29,758	28,130	25,633	62,989	55,391
Hampshire	2	10	27,875	31,309	28,447	43,959	56,322	75,268
Herefordshire	—	3	1,533	2,320	8,669	9,895	10,202	12,215
Hertfordshire	—	4	—	—	20,834	28,013	20,834	28,013

ENGLAND (Continued).

	Members M.	O.	Boroughs M.	O.	Counties M.	O.	Total M.	O.
Huntingdonshire	—	2	—	—	5,014	5,816	5,014	5,816
Kent	—	15	18,473	26,263	43,996	69,357	62,469	95,620
Lancashire	39	18	184,779	151,494	186,357	160,396	371,136	311,890
Leicestershire	6	—	14,490	8,370	30,849	25,620	45,339	33,990
Lincolnshire	6	5	16,737	16,493	35,130	36,648	51,867	53,141
Middlesex	1	6	—	—	66,330	86,894	66,330	86,894
Monmouthshire	4	—	6,496	5,391	31,629	14,290	38,125	19,681
Norfolk	8	2	17,086	14,327	29,662	25,758	46,748	40,085
Northamptonsh.	5	2	10,356	7,392	23,622	22,890	33,978	30,282
Northumberland	8	—	28,871	21,000	34,518	20,201	63,389	41,201
Nottinghamshire	3	4	20,732	18,963	32,472	22,608	53,204	41,571
Oxfordshire	—	4	3,707	4,918	11,940	14,578	15,647	19,496
Rutland	—	1	—	—	1,531	2,235	1,531	2,235
Shropshire	1	4	1,994	2,596	16,741	19,826	18,735	22,422
Somerset	3	7	5,302	5,831	34,658	37,636	39,960	43,467
Staffordshire	7	9	57,989	52,532	39,280	43,323	97,269	95,855
Suffolk	3	4	6,039	5,667	25,135	27,601	31,174	33,268
Surrey	—	6	—	—	35,783	63,557	35,783	63,557
Sussex	—	9	11,322	16,230	25,103	43,549	36,425	59,779
Warwickshire	1	12	27,162	61,186	21,777	29,902	48,939	91,088
Westmorland	—	2	—	—	5,594	6,613	5,594	6,613
Wiltshire	1	5	1,485	1,803	23,789	25,572	25,274	27,375
Worcestershire	2	6	13,730	15,066	26,568	37,709	40,298	52,775
Yorkshire	39	13	170,523	118,605	194,461	130,130	364,984	248,735
Total	225	229	1,085,652	1,048,329	1,478,534	1,452,463	2,564,186	2,500,792

TABLE B. WALES.

	M.	O.	M.	O.	M.	O.	M.	O.
Anglesey	1	—	—	—	5,888	2,436	5,888	2,436
Brecknockshire	1	—	—	—	6,335	3,865	6,335	3,865
Cardiganshire	1	—	—	—	6,348	2,943	6,348	2,943
Carmarthenshire	3	—	4,197	1,965	13,303	4,510	17,500	6,475
Carnarvonshire	3	—	3,183	2,105	12,341	4,329	15,524	6,434
Denbighshire	2	1	2,430	2,438	12,719	6,150	15,149	8,588
Flintshire	2	—	2,150	1,723	6,610	4,454	8,760	6,177
Glamorganshire	10	—	45,630	23,198	61,256	22,523	106,886	45,721
Merionethshire	1	—	—	—	6,065	1,873	6,065	1,873
Montgomeryshire	2	—	1,539	1,526	4,369	2,697	5,908	4,223
Pembrokeshire	2	—	3,582	2,877	6,135	3,291	9,717	6,168
Radnorshire	—	1	—	—	2,208	2,222	2,208	2,222
Total	28	2	62,711	35,832	143,577	61,293	206,288	97,125

TABLE C. SCOTLAND.

	M.	O.	M.	O.	M.	O.	M.	O.
Aberdeenshire	4	—	12,390	6,747	12,501	7,156	24,891	13,903
Argyllshire	1	—	—	—	4,443	3,617	4,443	3,617
Ayrshire	3	1	12,531	9,348	16,823	12,744	29,354	22,092
Banffshire	1	—	—	—	4,066	2,053	4,066	2,053
Berwickshire	1	—	—	—	2,992	2,060	2,992	2,060
Buteshire	—	1	—	—	1,372	1,531	1,372	1,531
Caithness-shire	2	—	1,537	1,262	2,643	590	4,180	1,852
Clackmannan & Kinross	1	—	—	—	3,971	2,703	3,971	2,703
Dumbartonshire	1	—	—	—	8,640	7,607	8,640	7,607

AN ANALYSIS OF THE VOTING.

SCOTLAND (CONTINUED).

	Members. M.	O.	Burghs. M.	O.	Counties. M.	O.	Total. M.	O.
Dumfriesshire ..	2	—	2,303	1,730	4,666	4,091	6,969	5,821
Edinburghshire	5	1	35,063	23,377	9,062	5,427	44,125	28,804
Elgin & Nairn ..	2	—	3,031	1,201	2,917	1,734	5,948	2,935
Fife ..	4	—	6,542	3,128	16,137	5,177	22,679	8,305
Forfarshire ..	4	—	16,806	6,037	6,789	4,284	23,595	10,321
Haddingtonshire	1	—	—	—	3,771	3,026	3,771	3,026
Inverness-shire	2	—	2,440	1,650	4,599	2,774	7,039	4,424
Kincardineshire	1	—	—	—	3,926	1,891	3,926	1,891
Kirkcudbrightsh.	—	1	—	—	2,620	2,661	2,620	2,661
Lanarkshire ..	11	2	43,309	31,692	56,601	38,305	99,910	69,997
Linlithgowshire	1	—	—	—	6,451	3,536	6,451	3,536
Peebles & Selkirk	1	—	—	—	1,941	1,735	1,941	1,735
Perthshire ..	2	1	2,841	2,103	7,450	6,567	10,291	8,670
Renfrewshire ..	3	1	11,045	6,523	15,251	15,276	26,296	21,799
Ross & Cromarty	1	—	—	—	4,430	1,418	4,430	1,418
Roxburghshire..	2	—	3,261	2,268	2,943	2,626	6,204	4,894
Stirlingshire ..	3	—	10,995	6,794	10,122	6,417	21,117	13,211
Sutherland ..	1	—	—	—	1,607	951	1,607	951
Wigtownshire ..	—	1	—	—	2,142	2,777	2,142	2,777
Total ..	60	9	164,094	103,860	220,876	150,734	384,970	254,594

TABLE D   SUMMARY.

	Lib.	Lab.	Soc.	Nat.	U.
England	2,319,168	419,089	17,406	2,943	2,682,332
Wales	174,100	47,201	1,451	—	97,125
Scotland	353,686	39,740	1,344	—	259,040
Total	2,846,954	506,030	20,201	2,943	3,038,497
		3,376,128			3,038,497

ANOTHER ANALYSIS.

During the progress of the General Election a statistical Correspondent supplied to *The Times*, at intervals, analyses of the voting, brought up to date, showing the aggregate vote polled by each party, the percentage of recorded votes to the electorate, &c. The same correspondent has now prepared an analysis, on the same basis, of the complete results, and it is given below. As the method of calculation adopted is different, the figures do not quite agree with those in the detailed tables above :—

Any attempt to gauge the opinion of the electorate by an analysis of the voting at a General Election is complicated by two disturbing elements—first, the uncontested elections ; secondly, the two-member constituencies.

With regard to the first, which cannot be altogether left out of account, it has, in the following figures, been thought fair to assume that of the registered electorate in any uncontested constituency 10 per cent. would have abstained from voting, 60 per cent. would have been in sympathy with the candidate returned unopposed, and 30 per cent. would have voted for an opposition candidate had there been one. If there is any objection to be urged against this estimate it is not material for the net result in England, Wales, and Scotland is merely to add a balance of some 11,600 votes to the Unionist Party as the measure of nine uncontested Unionist seats and one uncontested Liberal seat.

As to constituencies returning two members, it is obviously impossible to include the number of total votes recorded, seeing that each voter has two votes. It has been thought fair to take in each case the average of the votes polled for two candidates of the same party, but where a Liberal and Labour candidate have stood together each has been credited with half the votes recorded for him.

LONDON.

The County of London is, from an electoral point of view, merely a large town, which, like Manchester, Liverpool, and others, is subdivided into electoral districts.

It consists of 60 constituencies returning each one member, and one constituency (the City of London) returning two. In all 62 members, with a registered electorate of 726,959.

	Votes.
34 Unionist members were returned by	320,463
26 Liberal ,, ,,	249,194
2 Labour ,, ,,	30,046
62 Total effective votes ..	599,703
Wasted votes on Labour candidates ..	2,167
,, ,, on a Socialist candidate	701
,, ,, on an Independent Tariff Reformer	702
Total of votes polled ..	603,273

or nearly 83% of the electorate.

ENGLISH BOROUGHS.

The other Boroughs, exclusive of those which go to form London, consist of 124 constituencies each returning one member and 20 constituencies returning two members each—total, 164 members, with a registered electorate of 1,739,146.

	Votes.
77 Unionist members were returned by	734,316
69 Liberal ,, ,,	648,749
17 Labour ,, ,,	124,256
1 Nationalist ,, ,,	2,943
164 Total effective votes ..	1,510,264
Wasted votes on Liberal candidates..	13,914
,, ,, Labour ,,	27,720
,, ,, Socialist ,,	11,847
,, ,, Unionist ,,	3,479
Total of votes polled ..	1,567,224

or over 90% of the electorate.

Taking then, together, all the Boroughs of England, including London, we get this singular result of the effective voting:—

	Votes.
95 Liberal members were returned by	897,943
19 Labour ,, ,,	154,302
1 Nationalist member was returned by	2,943
115	1,055,188
111 Unionist members were returned by	1,054,779
4 Liberal majority by	409

votes electoral majority.

But there is a further interesting result to be obtained by a closer study of the figures. The Liberal electoral majority of 409 in all English urban centres, though it has gained an excess of four seats for the party, is not a very imposing one, and it has been deemed necessary to offer as an explanation the statement that the larger and more important centres have been overborne by Cathedral cities and small towns. This statement is not only inaccurate, but, so far at least as England is concerned, is the exact reverse of the fact.

There are in England 32 towns or cities which have been deemed of sufficient importance to have more than one member each. They are accordingly represented by 153 members, while 73 towns are still left with one member apiece.

Now in these 32 more important centres
71 Unionists have been returned by 753,640 votes; and
82 Liberals, Labour, and Nationalists have been returned by 745,607 votes.

In the 73 less important centres
40 Unionists have been returned by 301,139 votes; and
33 Liberal and Labour have been returned by 309,581 votes.

THE ENGLISH COUNTIES.

The English counties consist of 234 constituencies each returning a single member. The registered electorate is 3,377,941.

	Votes.
123 Unionist members were returned by	1,469,044
96 Liberal ,, ,,	1,323,077
15 Labour ,, ,,	139,506
234 Total effective votes ..	2,931,627
Wasted votes on Labour candidates	27,452
,, ,, Socialist ,,	3,149
,, ,, Woman Suffrage ,,	639
Total of votes polled ..	2,962,867

or nearly 88% of the electorate.

THE UNIVERSITIES.

The English Universities return five members

AN ANALYSIS OF THE VOTING.

for a registered electorate of 20,110. Four of these members were returned by uncontested elections, but, adopting the system explained above, the voting would be:—

	Votes.
5 Unionist members returned by	11,649
0 Liberal ,, ,,	6,141
	17,790

Taking the whole of England we get the following result:—

	Members.	Returned by	Votes.
Unionists	239		2,535,472
Liberals	191	2,227,161	
Labour	34	293,808	
Nationalist	1	2,943	
	226		2,523,912
	13		11,560

Unionist electoral majority.

WALES.

The 29 constituencies of Wales, returning 30 members, have a registered electorate of 357,566.

	Votes.
2 Unionist members were returned by	97,125
24 Liberal ,, ,,	162,737
4 Labour ,, ,,	40,280
30 Total effective votes	300,142
Wasted votes on Labour candidates	3,629
,, ,, Socialist ,,	1,451
Total votes polled	305,222

or more than 85% of the electorate.

SCOTLAND.

The 71 constituencies of Scotland, returning 72 members, have a registered electorate of 785,208, but deducting that of the Orkneys and Shetland, which cannot be included in this summary, the number is 778,093.

	Votes.
11 Unionist members were returned by	254,678
58 Liberal ,, ,,	351,603
2 Labour ,, ,,	9,869
71 Total effective votes	616,150
Wasted votes on Labour candidates	27,552
,, ,, Socialist ,,	1,344
,, ,, Prohibitionist ,,	1,512
Total votes polled	646,558

or over 83% of the electorate.

IRELAND.

The 101 constituencies of Ireland, returning 103 members, have a registered electorate of 688,787, but as

	Electors.
10 Unionists were returned unopposed by	79,695
and 55 Nationalists were returned unopposed by	345,629
only 38 seats were contested by an electorate of	263,463
	688,787

In these contested elections—

		Votes.
16 Nationalists	were returned by	74,663
11 Unionists	,, ,, ,,	74,754
10 Ind. Nationalists	,, ,, ,,	37,171
1 Liberal	was ,, ,,	24,290
38	Total effective votes	210,878
	Wasted votes	5,613
		216,491

or over 82%.

SUMMARY.

Members.
669 were returned by electorate of 7,688,602
75 were returned unopposed do. 493,712

594 returned by electorate of 7,194,890

For these the total votes cast, including votes wasted, were:—

	Votes		Members
Unionist	2,929,927	returning	254
Liberal	2,754,439	,,	273
Labour	432,477	,,	40
Nationalist	77,606	,,	17
Ind. Nationalist	42,784	,,	10
Socialist	18,492	,,	0
Woman Suffrage & Prohibitionist	2,151	,,	0
	6,257,876		594

The 75 uncontested elections returned—

Unionists	19
Liberal	1
Nationalists	55
and the Orkney seat	1
brings the total to	670

THE CONSTITUENCIES.
A COMPARATIVE RECORD.

The following table shows at a glance the variations in the political representation of the constituencies in 1900, 1906, and 1910.—

LONDON.

	1900.	1906.	1910.
City of London (2)	U.U.	U.U.	U.U.
Battersea	L.	L.	L.
Bethnal Green, N.E.	U.	L.	L.
„ S.W.	U.	L.	L.
Camberwell, Dulwich	U.	U.	U.
„ N.	L.	L.	L.
„ Peckham	U.	L.	U.
Chelsea	U.	L.	U.
Clapham	U.	U.	U.
Croydon	U.	U.	U.
Deptford	U.	La.	La.
Finsbury, Central	U.	L.	U.
„ E.	U.	L.	L.
„ Holborn	U.	U.	U.
Fulham	U.	L.	U.
Greenwich	U.	L.	U.
Hackney, Central	U.	L.	L.
„ N.	U.	L.	U.
„ S.	U.	L.	L.
Hammersmith	U.	U.	U.
Hampstead	U.	U.	U.
Islington, E.	U.	L.	L.
„ N.	U.	L.	L.
„ S.	U.	L.	L.
„ W.	L.	L.	L.
Kensington, N.	U.	L.	U.
„ S.	U.	U.	U.
Lambeth, Brixton	U.	L.	U.
„ Kennington	U.	L.	L.
„ N.	U.	L.	U.
„ Norwood	U.	U.	U.
Lewisham	U.	U.	U.
Marylebone, E.	U.	U.	U.
„ W.	U.	U.	U.
Newington, W.	L.	L.	L.
„ Walworth	U.	L.	L.
Paddington, N.	U.	L.	U.
„ S.	U.	U.	U.
St. George's, Hanover-square	U.	U.	U.
St. Pancras, E.	U.	L.	L.
„ N.	U.	L.	L.
„ S.	U.	L.	U.
„ W.	U.	L.	L.
Shoreditch, Haggerston	L.	L.	L.
„ Hoxton	U.	L.	L.
Southwark, Bermondsey	U.	L.	L.
„ Rotherhithe	U.	L.	L.
„ W.	L.	L.	U.
Strand	U.	U.	U.
Tower Hamlets, Bow and Bromley	U.	L.	U.
„ Limehouse	U.	L.	L.
„ Mile End	U.	L.	U.
„ Poplar	L.	L.	L.
„ St. George's	U.	L.	L.
„ Stepney	U.	U.	U.
„ Whitechapel	L.	L.	L.
Wandsworth	U.	U.	U.
West Ham, N.	U.	L.	L.
„ S.	U.	La.	La.

	1900.	1906.	1910.
Westminster	U.	U.	U.
Woolwich	U.	La.	U.

ENGLAND : BOROUGHS.

	1900.	1906.	1910.
Ashton-under-Lyne	U.	L.	L.
Aston Manor	U.	U.	U.
Barrow-in-Furness	U.	La.	La.
Bath (2)	U.U.	L.L.	U.U.
Bedford	U.	L.	U.
Birkenhead	U.	L.	L.
Birmingham, Bordesley	U.	U.	U.
„ Central	U.	U.	U.
„ E.	U.	U.	U.
„ Edgbaston	U.	U.	U.
„ N.	U.	U.	U.
„ S.	U.	U.	U.
„ W.	U.	U.	U.
Blackburn (2)	U.U.	U.La.	L.La.
Bolton (2)	U.L.	L.La.	L.La.
Boston	U.	L.	L.
Bradford, Central	U.	L.	L.
„ E.	U.	L.	L.
„ W.	U.	La.	La.
Brighton (2)	U.U.	L.L.	U.U.
Bristol, E.	L.	L.	L.
„ N.	U.	L.	L.
„ S.	U.	L.	L.
„ W.	U.	U.	U.
Burnley	U.	L.	L.
Bury	U.	L.	L.
Bury St. Edmunds	U.	U.	U.
Cambridge	U.	L.	U.
Canterbury	U.	U.	U.
Carlisle	L.	L.	L.
Chatham	U.	La.	U.
Cheltenham	U.	L.	U.
Chester	U.	L.	U.
Christchurch	U.	L.	U.
Colchester	L.	L.	U.
Coventry	U.	L.	U.
Darlington	U.	U.	L.
Derby (2)	L.La.	La.L.	L.La.
Devonport (2)	L.L.	L.L.	U.U.
Dewsbury	L.	L.	L.
Dover	U.	U.	U.
Dudley	U.	L.	L.
Durham	U.	U.	U.
Exeter	U.	L.	U.
Gateshead	L.	La.	L.
Gloucester	U.	L.	U.
Grantham	L.	L.	U.
Gravesend	U.	U.	U.
Great Grimsby	U.	U.	U.
Great Yarmouth	U.	U.	U.
Halifax (2)	U.L.	L.La.	L.La.
Hanley	U.	La.	La.
Hartlepool	L.	L.	L.
Hastings	L.	U.	U.
Hereford	U.	U.	U.
Huddersfield	L.	L.	L.
Hull, Central	U.	U.	U.

CONSTITUENCIES.—RECORD.

	1900.	1906.	1910.
Hull, E.	U.	L.	L.
,, W.	L.	L.	L.
Hythe	U.	U.	U.
Ipswich (2)	L.U.	L.L.	L.L.
Kidderminster	U.	L.	U.
King's Lynn	U.	L.	L.
Leeds, Central	U.	L.	L.
,, E.	U.	La.	La.
,, N.	U.	L.	L.
,, S.	L.	L.	L.
,, W.	L.	L.	L.
Leicester (2)	L.U.	L.La.	L.La.
Lincoln	U.	L.	L.
Liverpool, Abercromby	U.	L.	U.
,, East Toxteth	U.	U.	U.
,, Everton	U.	U.	U.
,, Exchange	U.	L.	U.
,, Kirkdale	U.	U.	U.
,, Scotland	N.	N.	N.
,, Walton	U.	U.	U.
,, West Derby	U.	U.	U.
,, West Toxteth	U.	U.	U.
Maidstone	L.	U.	U.
Manchester, E.	U.	L.	La.
,, N.	L.	L.	L.
,, N.E.	U.	La.	La.
,, N.W.	U.	L.	L.
,, S.	U.	L.	L.
,, S.W.	U.	La.	U.
Middlesbrough	U.	L.	L.
Monmouth District	U.	L.	L.
Morpeth	L.	L.	L.
Newcastle-on-Tyne (2)	U.U.	La.L.	L.La.
Newcastle-under-Lyme	U.	L.	L.
Northampton (2)	L.L.	L.L.	L.L.
Norwich (2)	U.U.	La.L.	L.La.
Nottingham, E.	U.	L.	U.
,, S.	U.	L.	U.
,, W.	L.	L.	L.
Oldham (2)	L.U.	L.L.	L.L.
Oxford	U.	U.	U.
Penryn and Falmouth	L.	L.	L.
Peterborough	U.	L.	L.
Plymouth (2)	U.U.	L.L.	L.L.
Pontefract	L.	L.	L.
Portsmouth (2)	U.U.	L.L.	U.U.
Preston (2)	U.U.	La.L.	U.U.
Reading	L.	L.	L.
Rochdale	U.	L.	L.
Rochester	U.	L.	U.
St. Helen's	U.	La.	La.
Salford, N.	U.	L.	L.
,, S.	U.	L.	L.
,, W.	U.	L.	L.
Salisbury	U.	L.	U.
Scarborough	L.	L.	L.
Sheffield, Attercliffe	L.	L.	La.
,, Brightside	U.	L.	L.
,, Central	U.	U.	U.
,, Ecclesall	U.	U.	U.
,, Hallam	U.	U.	U.
Shrewsbury	U.	U.	U.
Southampton (2)	U.U.	L.L.	L.L.
South Shields	L.	L.	L.
Stafford	L.	L.	L.
Stalybridge	U.	L.	L.
Stockport (2)	L.U.	La.L.	La.L.
Stockton	U.	U.	L.
Stoke-on-Trent	U.	L.	L.

	1900.	1906.	1910.
Sunderland (2)	U.U.	L.La.	U.U.
Taunton	U.	U.	U.
Tynemouth	U.	L.	L.
Wakefield	U.	U.	U.
Walsall	L.	L.	U.
Warrington	U.	L.	L.
Warwick and Leamington	U.	L.	U.
Wednesbury	U.	L.	U.
West Bromwich	U.	L.	U.
Whitehaven	U.	L.	U.
Wigan	U.	U.	La.
Winchester	U.	U.	U.
Windsor	U.	U.	U.
Wolverhampton, E.	L.	L.	L.
,, S.	L.	L.	L.
,, W.	U.	La.	U.
Worcester	U.	U.	U.
York (2)	U.U.	L.U.	L.U.

ENGLAND : COUNTIES.

	1900.	1906.	1910.
Bedfordshire, Biggleswade	U.	L.	L.
,, Luton	L.	L.	L.
Berkshire, Abingdon	U.	L.	U.
,, Newbury	U.	L.	U.
,, Wokingham	U.	U.	U.
Bucks, Aylesbury	U.	U.	U.
,, Buckingham	U.	L.	U.
,, Wycombe	U.	L.	U.
Cambridge, Chesterton	U.	L.	L.
,, Newmarket	U.	L.	L.
,, Wisbech	L.	L.	L.
Cheshire, Altrincham	U.	L.	L.
,, Crewe	L.	L.	L.
,, Eddisbury	U.	L.	U.
,, Hyde	U.	L.	L.
,, Knutsford	U.	L.	U.
,, Macclesfield	U.	L.	L.
,, Northwich	L.	L.	L.
,, Wirral	U.	L.	L.
Cornwall, Bodmin	U.	L.	L.
,, Camborne	L.	L.	L.
,, Launceston	L.	L.	L.
,, St. Austell	L.	L.	L.
,, St. Ives	U.	L.	L.
,, Truro	U.	L.	L.
Cumberland, Cockermouth	U.	L.	U.
,, Egremont	U.	L.	U.
,, Eskdale	U.	L.	L.
,, Penrith	U.	U.	U.
Derbyshire, Chesterfield	L.	La.	La.
,, High Peak	L.	L.	L.
,, Ilkeston	L.	L.	L.
,, Mid	L.	L.	La.
,, N.E.	L.	L.	La.
,, S.	U.	L.	L.
,, W.	U.	U.	U.
Devonshire, Ashburton	L.	L.	L.
,, Barnstaple	L.	L.	L.
,, Honiton	U.	U.	U.
,, South Molton	L.	L.	L.
,, Tavistock	U.	L.	L.
,, Tiverton	U.	U.	U.
,, Torquay	L.	L.	L.
,, Totnes	U.	U.	U.
Dorset, E.	L.	L.	L.
,, N.	U.	L.	U.
,, S.	U.	L.	U.
,, W.	U.	U.	U.
Durham, Barnard Castle	L.	La.	La.

	1900.	1906.	1910.		1900.	1906.	1910.
Durham, Bishop Auckland	L.	L.	L.	Leicestershire, Melton	U.	L.	L.
,, Chester-le-Street	L.	La.	La.	Lincolnshire, Brigg	L.	L.	L.
,, Houghton-le-Spring	L.	L.	L.	,, Gainsborough	U.	L.	L.
,, Jarrow	L.	L.	L.	,, Horncastle	U.	U.	U.
,, Mid	L.	L.	L.	,, Louth	L.	L.	U.
,, N.W.	L.	L.	L.	,, Sleaford	U.	L.	U.
,, S.E.	U.	U.	L.	,, Spalding	L.	L.	L.
Essex, Chelmsford	U.	U.	U.	,, Stamford	U.	U.	U.
,, Epping	U.	U.	U.	Middlesex, Brentford	U.	L.	U.
,, Harwich	U.	L.	U.	,, Ealing	U.	U.	U.
,, Maldon	U.	L.	U.	,, Enfield	U.	L.	U.
,, Romford	U.	L.	L.	,, Harrow	U.	L.	U.
,, Saffron Walden	L.	L.	U.	,, Hornsey	U.	U.	U.
,, S.E.	U.	L.	U.	,, Tottenham	U.	L.	L.
,, Walthamstow	U.	L.	L.	,, Uxbridge	U.	U.	U.
Gloucester, Cirencester	U.	L.	U.	Monmouthshire, N.	L.	L.	L.
,, Forest of Dean	L.	L.	L.	,, S.	U.	L.	L.
,, Stroud	L.	L.	L.	,, W.	L.	La.	La.
,, Tewkesbury	U.	U.	U.	Norfolk, E.	L.	L.	L.
,, Thornbury	U.	L.	L.	,, Mid	L.	L.	U.
Hampshire, Andover	U.	U.	U.	,, N.	L.	L.	L.
,, Basingstoke	U.	U.	U.	,, N.W.	L.	L.	L.
,, Fareham	U.	U.	U.	,, S.	L.	L.	L.
,, Isle of Wight	U.	L.	U.	,, S.W.	U.	L.	L.
,, New Forest	U.	L.	U.	Northamptonshire, E.	L.	L.	L.
,, Petersfield	U.	U.	U.	,, Mid	L.	L.	L.
Herefordshire, Leominster	U.	L.	U.	,, N.	U.	L.	U.
,, Ross	U.	L.	U.	,, S.	U.	L.	U.
Hertfordshire, Hertford	U.	U.	U.	Northumberland, Berwick	L.	L.	L.
,, Hitchin	U.	L.	U.	,, Hexham	L.	L.	L.
,, St. Albans	U.	U.	U.	,, Tyneside	U.	L.	L.
,, Watford	U.	L.	U.	,, Wansbeck	L.	L.	L.
Hunts, Huntingdon	U.	L.	U.	Nottinghamshire, Bassetlaw	U.	L.	U.
,, Ramsey	U.	L.	U.	,, Mansfield	L.	L.	L.
Kent. Ashford	U.	U.	U.	,, Newark	U.	U.	U.
,, Dartford	U.	L.	U.	,, Rushcliffe	L.	L.	L.
,, Faversham	U.	L.	U.	Oxfordshire, Banbury	U.	L.	U.
,, Isle of Thanet	U.	U.	U.	,, Henley	U.	L.	U.
,, Medway	U.	U.	U.	,, Woodstock	U.	L.	U.
,, St. Augustine's	U.	U.	U.	Rutland	U.	U.	U.
,, Sevenoaks	U.	U.	U.	Shropshire, Ludlow	U.	U.	U.
,, Tunbridge	U.	L.	U.	,, Newport	U.	U.	U.
Lancashire, Accrington	L.	L.	L.	,, Oswestry	U.	U.	U.
,, Blackpool	U.	U.	U.	,, Wellington	U.	L.	U.
,, Bootle	U.	U.	U.	Somerset, Bridgwater	U.	L.	U.
,, Chorley	U.	U.	U.	,, E.	U.	L.	U.
,, Clitheroe	L.	La.	La.	,, Frome	L.	L.	L.
,, Darwen	U.	U.	L.	,, N.	U.	L.	L.
,, Eccles	U.	L.	U.	,, S.	L.	L.	L.
,, Gorton	U.	La.	La.	,, Wellington	U.	U.	U.
,, Heywood	U.	L.	L.	,, Wells	U.	L.	U.
,, Ince	U.	La.	La.	Staffordshire, Burton	U.	U.	U.
,, Lancaster	L.	L.	L.	,, Handsworth	U.	U.	U.
,, Leigh	L.	L.	L.	,, Kingswinford	U.	U.	U.
,, Middleton	U.	L.	L.	,, Leek	U.	L.	U.
,, Newton	U.	La.	La.	,, Lichfield	L.	L.	L.
,, N. Lonsdale	U.	U.	U.	,, N.W.	U.	L.	La.
,, Ormskirk	U.	U.	U.	,, W.	U.	L.	U.
,, Prestwich	L.	L.	L.	Suffolk, Eye	L.	L.	L.
,, Radcliffe - cum - Farnworth	L.	L.	L.	,, Lowestoft	U.	L.	U.
,, Rossendale	L.	L.	L.	,, Stowmarket	U.	L.	U.
,, Southport	U.	L.	U.	,, Sudbury	L.	L.	L.
,, Stretford	U.	L.	L.	,, Woodbridge	U.	L.	U.
,, Westhoughton	U.	La.	La.	Surrey, Chertsey	U.	L.	U.
,, Widnes	U.	U.	U.	,, Epsom	U.	U.	U.
Leicestershire, Bosworth	L.	L.	L.	,, Guildford	U.	L.	U.
,, Harborough	L.	L.	L.	,, Kingston	U.	U.	U.
,, Loughborough	L.	L.	L.	,, Reigate	U.	L.	U.
				,, Wimbledon	U.	U.	U.

CONSTITUENCIES—RECORD.

	1900.	1906.	1910.
Sussex, Chichester	U.	U.	U.
,, Eastbourne	U.	L.	U.
,, East Grinstead	U.	L.	U.
,, Horsham	U.	U.	U.
,, Lewes	U.	U.	U.
,, Rye	U.	U.	U.
Warwickshire, Nuneaton	U.	La.	La.
,, Rugby	L.	L.	U.
,, Stratford-on-Avon	U.	L.	U.
,, Tamworth	U.	U.	U.
Westmorland, Appleby	L.	L.	L.
,, Kendal	U.	L.	U.
Wiltshire, Chippenham	U.	L.	U.
,, Cricklade	U.	L.	U.
,, Devizes	U.	L.	U.
,, Westbury	L.	L.	L.
,, Wilton	U.	L.	U.
Worcestershire, Bewdley	U.	U.	U.
,, Droitwich	U.	U.	U.
,, E.	U.	U.	U.
,, Evesham	U.	U.	U.
,, N.	U.	L.	L.
Yorkshire, Barkston Ash	U.	U.	U.
,, Barnsley	L.	L.	L.
,, Buckrose	L.	L.	L.
,, Cleveland	L.	L.	L.
,, Colne Valley	L.	L.	L.
,, Doncaster	U.	L.	L.
,, Elland	L.	L.	L.
,, Hallamshire	L.	La.	La.
,, Holderness	U.	U.	U.
,, Holmfirth	L.	L.	L.
,, Howdenshire	U.	U.	U.
,, Keighley	L.	L.	L.
,, Morley	L.	L.	L.
,, Normanton	L.	La.	La.
,, Osgoldcross	L.	L.	L.
,, Otley	L.	L.	L.
,, Pudsey	L.	L.	L.
,, Richmond	U.	L.	U.
,, Ripon	U.	L.	U.
,, Rotherham	L.	L.	L.
,, Shipley	U.	L.	L.
,, Skipton	L.	L.	L.
,, Sowerby	L.	L.	L.
,, Spen Valley	L.	L.	L.
,, Thirsk and Malton	U.	U.	U.
,, Whitby	U.	U.	U.

WALES: BOROUGHS.

	1900.	1906.	1910.
Cardiff District	L.	L.	L.
Carmarthen District	L.	L.	L.
Carnarvon District	L.	L.	L.
Denbigh District	U.	L.	U.
Flint District	L.	L.	L.
Merthyr Tydvil (2)	L.La.	L.La.	L.La.
Montgomery District	U.	L.	L.
Pembroke and Haverfordwest	U.	L.	L.
Swansea District	L.	L.	L.
,, Town		L.	L.

WALES: COUNTIES.

	1900.	1906.	1910.
Anglesey	L.	L.	L.
Brecknockshire	L.	L.	L.
Cardiganshire	L.	L.	L.

	1900.	1903.	1910.
Carmarthenshire, E.	L.	L.	L.
,, W.	L.	L.	L.
Carnarvonshire, Arfon	L.	L.	L.
,, Eifion	L.	L.	L.
Denbighshire, E.	L.	L.	L.
,, W.	L.	L.	L.
Flintshire	L.	L.	L.
Glamorganshire, E.	L.	L.	L.
,, Gower	L.	La.	L.
,, Mid	L.	L.	L.
,, Rhondda	L.	L.	L.
,, S.	U.	La.	La.
Merionethshire	L.	L.	L.
Montgomeryshire	L.	L.	L.
Pembrokeshire	L.	L.	L.
Radnorshire	L.	L.	U.

SCOTLAND: BURGHS.

	1900.	1903.	1910.
Aberdeen, N.	L.	L.	L.
,, S.	L.	L.	L.
Ayr Burghs	U.	U.	U.
Dumfries Burghs	L.	L.	L.
Dundee (2)	L.L.	L.La.	L.La.
Edinburgh, Central	L.	L.	L.
,, E.	L.	L.	L.
,, S.	U.	L.	L.
,, W.	U.	U.	U.
Elgin Burghs	L.	L.	L.
Falkirk Burghs	U.	L.	L.
Glasgow, Blackfriars	U.	La.	La.
,, Bridgeton	U.	L.	L.
,, Camlachie	U.	U.	U.
,, Central	U.	L.	U.
,, College	U.	L.	L.
,, St. Rollox	U.	L.	L.
,, Tradeston	U.	U.	L.
Greenock	U.	L.	L.
Hawick Burghs	L.	L.	L.
Inverness Burghs	L.	L.	L.
Kilmarnock Burghs	U.	L.	L.
Kirkcaldy Burghs	L.	L.	L.
Leith Burghs	L.	L.	L.
Montrose Burghs	L.	L.	L.
Paisley	L.	L.	L.
Perth	L.	L.	L.
St. Andrews Burghs	U.	U.	L.
Stirling Burghs	L.	L.	L.
Wick Burghs	U.	U.	L.

SCOTLAND: COUNTIES.

	1900.	1903.	1910.
Aberdeenshire, E.	U.	L.	L.
,, W.	L.	L.	L.
Argyllshire	U.	L.	L.
Ayrshire, N.	U.	U.	U.
,, S.	U.	L.	L.
Banffshire	L.	L.	L.
Berwickshire	L.	L.	L.
Buteshire	U.	L.	U.
Caithness-shire	L.	L.	L.
Clackmannan and Kinross	L.	L.	L.
Dumbartonshire	U.	L.	L.
Dumfriesshire	U.	L.	L.
Edinburghshire	L.	L.	L.
Elgin and Nairn	U.	L.	L.
Fife, E.	L.	L.	L.
,, W.	L.	L.	L.

THE TIMES HOUSE OF COMMONS

	1900.	1906.	1910.
Forfarshire	L.	L.	L.
Haddingtonshire	L.	L.	L.
Inverness-shire	L.	L.	L.
Kincardineshire	L.	L.	L.
Kirkcudbrightshire	U.	L.	U.
Lanarkshire, Govan	L.	U.	L.
„ Mid	L.	L.	L.
„ N.E.	L.	L.	L.
„ N.W.	L.	U.	L.
„ Partick	U.	L.	L.
„ S.	U.	L.	L.
Linlithgowshire	L.	L.	L.
Orkney and Shetland	U.	L.	L.
Peebles and Selkirk	U.	L.	L.
Perthshire, E.	L.	L.	L.
„ W.	U.	L.	U.
Renfrewshire, E.	U.	L.	U.
„ W.	U.	L.	L.
Ross and Cromarty	L.	L.	L.
Roxburghshire	U.	L.	L.
Stirlingshire	U.	L.	L.
Sutherland	U.	L.	L.
Wigtownshire	U.	U.	U.

IRELAND: BOROUGHS.

	1900.	1906.	1910.
Belfast, E.	U.	U.	U.
„ N.	U.	U.	U.
„ S.	U.	U.	U.
„ W.	U.	N.	N.
Cork (2)	N.N.	N.N.	I.N.N.
Dublin, College Green	N.	N.	N.
„ Harbour	N.	N.	N.
„ St. Patrick's	N.	N.	N.
„ St. Stephen's	N.	N.	N.
Galway	U.	N.	N.
Kilkenny	N.	N.	N.
Limerick	N.	N.	N.
Londonderry	U.	U.	U.
Newry	N.	N.	N.
Waterford	N.	N.	N.

IRELAND: COUNTIES.

	1900.	1906.	1910.
Antrim, E.	U.	U.	U.
„ Mid	U.	U.	U.
„ N.	U.	U.	U.
„ S.	U.	U.	U.
Armagh, Mid	U.	U.	U.
„ N.	U.	U.	U.
„ S.	N.	N.	N.
Carlow	N.	N.	N.
Cavan, E.	N.	N.	N.
„ W.	N.	N.	N.
Clare, E.	N.	N.	N.
„ W.	N.	N.	N.
Cork, E.	N.	N.	N.
„ Mid	N.	N.	I.N.
„ N.	N.	N.	I.N.
„ N.E.	N.	N.	I.N.
„ S.	N.	N.	N.
„ S.E.	N.	N.	I.N.
„ W.	N.	N.	I.N.
Donegal, E.	N.	N.	N.
„ N.	N.	N.	N.
„ S.	N.	N.	N.
„ W.	N.	N.	N.
Down, E.	U.	U.	U.

	1900.	1906.	1910.
Down, N.	U.	U.	U.
„ S.	N.	N.	N.
„ W.	U.	U.	U.
Dublin, N.	N.	N.	N.
„ S.	N.	U.	U.
Fermanagh, N.	U.	U.	U.
„ S.	N.	N.	N.
Galway, Connemara	N.	N.	N.
„ E.	N.	N.	N.
„ N.	N.	N.	N.
„ S.	N.	N.	N.
Kerry, E.	N.	N.	I.N.
„ N.	N.	N.	N.
„ S.	N.	N.	N.
„ W.	N.	N.	N.
Kildare, N.	N.	N.	N.
„ S.	N.	N.	N.
Kilkenny, N.	N.	N.	N.
„ S.	N.	N.	N.
King's County, Birr	N.	N.	N.
„ Tullamore	N.	N.	N.
Leitrim, N.	N.	N.	N.
„ S.	N.	N.	N.
Limerick, E.	N.	N.	N.
„ W.	N.	N.	N.
Londonderry N.	U.	U.	U.
„ S.	U.	U.	U.
Longford, N.	N.	N.	N.
„ S.	N.	N.	N.
Louth, N.	N.	N.	I.N.
„ S.	N.	N.	N.
Mayo, E.	N.	N.	N.
„ N.	N.	N.	N.
„ S.	N.	N.	I.N.
„ W.	N.	N.	N.
Meath, N.	N.	N.	N.
„ S.	N.	N.	N.
Monaghan, N.	N.	N.	N.
„ S.	N.	N.	I.N.
Queen's County, Leix	N.	N.	N.
„ Ossory	N.	N.	N.
Roscommon, N.	N.	N.	N.
„ S.	N.	N.	N.
Sligo, N.	N.	N.	N.
„ S.	N.	N.	N.
Tipperary, E.	N.	N.	N.
„ Mid	N.	N.	N.
„ N.	N.	N.	N.
„ S.	N.	N.	N.
Tyrone, E.	N.	N.	N.
„ Mid	N.	N.	U.
„ N.	N.	L.	L.
„ S.	U.	L.	U.
Waterford, E.	N.	N.	N.
„ W.	N.	N.	N.
Westmeath, N.	N.	N.	I.N.
„ S.	N.	N.	N.
Wexford, N.	N.	N.	N.
„ S.	N.	N.	N.
Wicklow, E.	N.	N.	N.
„ W.	N.	N.	N.

UNIVERSITIES.

	1900.	1906.	1910.
Oxford (2)	U.U.	U.U.	U.U.
Cambridge (2)	U.U.	U.U.	U.U.
London	U.	U.	U.
Edinburgh and St. Andrews	U.	U.	U.
Glasgow and Aberdeen	U.	U.	U.
Dublin (2)	U.U.	U.U.	U.U.

HOUSE OF COMMONS, 1910.

The figures within parentheses show the number of registered electors in the constituency. The figures 2, 3, &c., after the name of a borough or county indicate the number of members it returns. Members of the last Parliament who have stood again as candidates for the same constituencies are distinguished by asterisks, and those who have stood for other constituencies by daggers. The figures in smaller type, after the result, give the numbers polled in 1906 and 1900, and also the majority by which each of the three previous General Elections was won:—

LONDON.

CITY OF LONDON (2) (30,010).—No change.

*Balfour, Rt. Hon. A. J. (U.)	17,907
*Banbury, Sir F. G. (U.)	17,302
Bell, Sir Hugh (L.)	4,623
Unionist majority	12,679

By-election, 1906.—U., 15,474; L., 4,134—U. maj., 11,340.
By-election, 1906.—U. unop.
1906.—U., 16,019; U., 15,619; L., 5,313; L., 5,064—U. maj. over L., 10,706.

Mr. ARTHUR JAMES BALFOUR, the leader of the Unionist Party in the House of Commons, has played a large and important part in the public and political life of the United Kingdom since he became member for Hertford in 1874. From 1878 to 1880 he acted as Private Secretary to the late Marquis of Salisbury when Foreign Secretary, and was attached to the special Salisbury-Beaconsfield Mission to Berlin. He has been President of the Local Government Board, Secretary for Scotland, Chief Secretary for Ireland in the stormy years between 1887 and 1891, First Lord of the Treasury and leader of the House of Commons in 1891-2, and from 1895 to 1905, becoming Prime Minister in 1902. In 1904 he was President of the British Association.

SIR FREDERICK BANBURY, who was born in 1850, has represented the City of London since 1906. He is a director of the Great Northern Railway and of the London and Provincial Bank, and for many years he was a partner in the firm of Frederick Banbury and Sons, stockbrokers. He is a J.P. for Hunts and Wilts, was created a baronet in 1902, and sat in the House of Commons for Peckham from 1892 to 1906, when he was defeated.

BATTERSEA AND CLAPHAM (2).

BATTERSEA (18,927).—No change.

*Burns, Rt. Hon. J. (L.)	8,540
Benn, A. Shirley (U.)	7,985
Liberal majority	555

1906.—L., 7,387; U., 5,787—L. maj., 1,600.
1900.—L., 5,860; U., 5,606—L. maj., 254.
1895, L. maj., 253; 1892, L. maj., 1,559; 1886, L. maj., 186.

Mr. JOHN BURNS is the first working-man in this country to attain Cabinet rank. Born in London in 1858, he worked first in a candle factory, and afterwards as an engineer; was concerned in the Trafalgar-square riots of 1886-7, and sent to prison for three months; took a leading part in the London dockers' strike in 1889; was a prominent member of the London County Council for several years. First returned as member for Battersea in 1892; was appointed President of the Local Government Board in 1906, and as such has disappointed his former Socialist and Labour friends by his moderation.

CLAPHAM (22,611).—No change.

*Faber, G. D. (U.)	10,743
Kipling, J. G. (L.)	8,762
Unionist majority	1,981

1906.—U., 7,912; L., 7,816—U. maj., 96.
1900.—U., 7,504; L., 3,084—U. maj., 4,420.
1895, U. maj., 2,021; 1892, U. maj., 644; 1886, U. maj., 469.

Mr. GEORGE DENISON FABER, who sat as one of the members for York from 1900 to the dissolution, s brother of Lord Faber and of Captain Faber, who represented the Andover Division of Hampshire in the late Parliament ; born in 1852, and educated at Marlborough College and University College, Oxford, and called to the Bar in 1879 ; for several years Registrar of the Privy Council, now a partner in the banking firm of Beckett and Co., Leeds ; an active critic of the late Government's Licensing Bill and the licensing clauses of the Budget.

BETHNAL-GREEN (2).

North-East (7,554).—No change.

*Cornwall, Sir E. A. (L.)	3,842
Molson, Dr. J. E. (U.)	2,435
Liberal majority	1,407

1906.—L., 4,127 ; U., 2,130—L. maj., 2,003.
1900.—U., 2,988 ; L., 2,609—U. maj., 379.
1895.—U. maj., 160 ; 1892, L. maj. over U., 597 ; 1886, L. maj., 372.

Sir Edwin A. Cornwall, born in 1863, was first elected for this division in 1906, when he won the seat for the Liberals. He has been a prominent member of the London County Council for many years, and was knighted during his year of office as Chairman in 1905. He is also a member of the Port of London Authority.

South-West (7,103).—No change.

*Pickersgill, E. H. (L.)	3,328
Hoffgaard, E. (U.)	2,350
Liberal majority	978

1906.—L., 3,542 ; U., 2,064—L. maj., 1,478.
1900.—L., 2,862 ; L., 2,514—U. maj., 348.
1895.—L. maj., 279 ; 1892, L. maj., 1,035 ; 1886, L. maj., 549.

Mr. Edward Hare Pickersgill, son of Mr. T. Pickersgill, architect, York ; born 1850, educated York Grammar School, King's College, London, and London University ; served for some time in Civil Service (Post Office) ; called to the Bar, 1884 ; sat for S.W. Bethnal-green, 1885-1900, and was again elected in 1906.

CAMBERWELL (3).

Dulwich (16,478).—No change.

*Law, A. Bonar (U.)	8,472
Cotton, H. E. (L.)	6,054
Unionist majority	2,418

By-election, 1906.—U., 6,709 ; L., 5,430—U. maj., 1,279.
1906.—U., 6,639 ; L., 6,282—U. maj., 357.
1900.—U. unop.
1895, U. maj., 3,082 ; 1892, U. maj., 2,180 ; 1886, U. unop.

Mr. Andrew Bonar Law was born at New Brunswick, Canada, where his father was a Presbyterian minister. He was educated in Canada and at Gilbertfield School, Hamilton, and Glasgow High School. He entered business as an iron merchant and was chairman of the Scottish Iron Trade Association. Elected for the Blackfriars Division of Glasgow in 1900, he became Parliamentary Secretary to the Board of Trade two years later. He was defeated for Glasgow in 1906, but after a few months' interval was elected for the Dulwich Division.

North (11,918).—No change.

*Macnamara, Dr. (L.)	5,593
Goldsmid, S. H. (U.)	4,511
Liberal majority	1,082

1906.—L., 6,314 ; U., 3,497—L. maj., 2,817.
1900.—L., 4,820 ; U., 3,485—L. maj., 1,335.
1895, U. maj over L., 693 ; 1892, L. maj., 845 ; 1886, U. maj. over L., 365.

Dr. Thomas James Macnamara, born at Montreal, 1861, the son of Sergeant Thomas Macnamara, of the old 47th Regiment, now the Loyal North Lancashire ; educated at an Exeter Board school, and served as school teacher from 1876 to 1892 ; editor of the *Schoolmaster* from 1892 till 1907 ; a member of the London School Board from 1894 to 1903 ; first entered Parliament for North Camberwell at General Election of 1900 ; appointed Parliamentary Secretary of the Local Government Board in January, 1907, and Parliamentary Secretary to the Admiralty in April, 1908.

Peckham (12,341).—No change.

*Gooch, H. C. (U.)	5,330
Richardson, A. (L.)	5,247
Unionist majority	83

By-election, 1908.—U., 6,970 ; L., 4,476—U. maj., 2,494.
1906.—L., 5,903 ; U., 3,564—L. maj., 2,339.
1900.—U., 4,453 ; L., 3,061—U. maj., 1,392.
1895, U. maj., 1,023 ; 1892, U. maj. over L., 183 ; 1886, U. maj., 751.

Mr. Henry Cubitt Gooch was born in 1871, educated at Eton and Trinity College, Cambridge, and was called to the Bar in 1894. He represented Peckham on the London School Board in 1897 and again in 1900, and served on the London County Council as vice-chairman of the Education Committee. In 1908 he won a notable Parliamentary victory at Peckham shortly after the introduction of the Licensing Bill. He is a member of the Royal Statistical, Geographical, and Philharmonic Societies, a Governor of Belgrave Hospital, Kennington, and a member of the Committee for the Removal of King's College Hospital to South London.

CHELSEA (11,257).—Unionist Gain.

Hoare, S. J. G. (U.)	5,610
*Horniman, E. J. (L.)	4,048
Unionist majority	1,562

1906.—L., 4,660 ; U., 4,031—L. maj., 629.
1900.—U., 4,637 ; L., 3,306—U. maj., 1,331.
1895.—U. maj., 1,920 ; 1892, U. maj., 566 ; 1886, U. maj., 176.

Mr. Samuel John Gurney Hoare is the eldest son of Sir Samuel Hoare, who was for 20 years member for Norwich. Born in 1880, he was educated at Harrow and at New College, Oxford. He served as assistant private secretary to Mr. Lyttelton when Secretary for the Colonies, and as Assistant Secretary of the Royal

Commission on Ecclesiastical Discipline. He unsuccessfully contested Ipswich in 1906.

CROYDON (27,350).—No change.

*Hermon-Hodge, Sir R., Bt. (U.)	12,223
Leon, A. L. (L.)	11,327
Unionist majority ..	896

By-election, 1909.—U., 11,989; L., 8,041; Lab., 886—U. maj. over L., 3,948.
1906.—U., 8,211; L., 7,573; Lab., 4,007—U. maj. over L., 638.
1900.—U. unop.
1895, U. maj., 2,229; 1892, U. maj., 1,694; 1886, U. unop.

SIR R. HERMON-HODGE was a well-known athlete both at Clifton and at Oxford, and was returned by Croydon last year after a varied experience in other constituencies. He commands the Queen's Own Oxfordshire Hussars, in which regiment he has served for 30 years, and is a keen sportsman, being for 12 seasons master of hariers, hunting his own hounds in Oxfordshire and Berkshire. Two years ago he was chairman of the National Union of Conservative Associations. He was created a baronet in 1902.

DEPTFORD (15,150).—No change.

*Bowerman, C. W. (Lab.) ..	6,880
Coats, S. A. (U.)	6,358
Labour majority ..	522

1906.—Lab., 6,236; U., 4,977; L., 726—Lab. maj. over U., 1,259.
1900.—U., 6,236; Lab., 3,806—U. maj., 2,430.
1895.—U. maj., 1,229; 1892, U. maj., 565; 1886, U. maj., 627.

Mr. C. W. BOWERMAN was born in 1851, and has been closely connected with trade union movements. He served his apprenticeship as a compositor, and has been a member of the London Society of Compositors since 1873, being elected general secretary in 1892 and Parliamentary Secretary in 1906. In 1901 he was president of the Trade Union Congress at Swansea, and served in the last House of Commons as Labour member for Deptford.

FINSBURY (3).
CENTRAL (8,094).—UNIONIST GAIN.

Archer-Shee, Major M. (U.)	3,559
*Steadman, W. C. (L.) ..	3,187
Unionist majority ..	372

1906.—L., 3,493; U., 2,799—L. maj., 694.
1900.—U., 2,872; L., 2,523—U. maj., 349.
1895, U. maj., 805; 1892, L. maj., 3; 1886, U. maj., 5.

MAJOR MARTIN ARCHER-SHEE was born in 1873, and received his education at the Oratory school, on the Britannia training ship, and at Sandhurst. After two years' service as a midshipman in the Navy he joined the 19th Hussars in 1893. He was severely wounded in the South African campaign, was thrice mentioned in despatches, and gained the Queen's and King's medals, with six clasps, and the Distinguished Service Order.

EAST (4,855).—No change.

*Baker, J. A. (L.)	2,102
Mason, W. J. P. (U.) ..	2,016
Liberal majority ..	86

1906.—L., 2,461; U., 1,772—L. maj., 689.
1900.—U., 2,174; L., 1,827—U. maj., 347.
1895, U. maj., 270; 1892, L. maj., 290; 1886, L. maj., 621.

Mr. J. ALLEN BAKER, who was born in Ontario, Canada, in 1852, came to London in 1876. He is the head of a large engineering business, having branches in Canada, Australia, and the United States. In 1895 he became a member of the London County Council. In the House of Commons he represented East Finsbury from June, 1905, until the dissolution. Mr. Baker is a member of the Society of Friends.

HOLBORN (8,608).—No change.

*Remnant, J. F. (U.) ..	4,847
Stapley, Sir R. (L.) ..	2,262
Unionist majority ..	2,585

1906.—U., 3,881; L., 2,706—U. maj., 1,175.
1900 and 1895.—U. unop.
1892.—U. maj., 2,472; 1886, U. maj., 1,701.

Mr. JAMES FARQUHAR REMNANT was born in 1863, and educated at Harrow and Oxford; called to the Bar, Lincoln's Inn, 1886; has sat for Holborn since 1900; was a member of the Royal Commission on Canals, 1906.

FULHAM (21,000).—UNIONIST GAIN.

Fisher, W. Hayes (U.) ..	9,690
Hemphill, Captain Fitzroy (L.)	7,761
Unionist majority ..	1,929

1906.—L., 8,037; U., 7,407—L. maj., 630.
1900.—U., 6,541; L., 4,247—U. maj., 2,294.
1895.—U. maj. over L., 1,463; 1892, U. maj., 211; 1886, U. maj., 310.

Mr. WILLIAM HAYES FISHER, son of the Rev. Frederick Fisher, rector of Downham, was born in 1853 and educated at Haileybury and University College, Oxford. He was called to the Bar, Inner Temple, in 1879. He was private secretary to Sir Michael Hicks Beach, 1886-7, and to Mr. A. J. Balfour, 1887-92. From 1895 to 1902 he was a Junior Lord of the Treasury, and was Financial Secretary to the Treasury, 1902-3. He is an Alderman of the London County Council and chairman of the Finance Committee, and represented Fulham in Parliament from 1885 to 1906.

GREENWICH (13,153).—UNIONIST GAIN.

Benn, I. H. (U.)	6,284
*Jackson, R. S. (L.) ..	5,083
Unionist majority ..	1,201

1906.—L., 4,906; U., 3,565; U., 2,356; L. maj. over U., 1,341.
1900.—U., 5,454; L., 3,484—U. maj., 1,970.
1895, U. maj., 1,238; 1892, U. maj., 323; 1886, U. maj., 689.

Mr. ION HAMILTON BENN is the third son of late Rev. J. W. Benn, Rector of Carrigaline and Douglas, county Cork. Mr. Benn was born in 1863, and is hon. colonel of the 20th (County of London) Battalion; was Mayor of Greenwich in 1901-2; contested Greenwich in the Tariff Reform interest in 1906; was elected to London County Council, 1907; Metropolitan Water Board, 1903-6; and a member of the first London Port Authority, 1909. He is a director of Price and Peirce (Limited), London; Price Bros. and Co. (Limited), Quebec; and the Canada Iron Corporation (Limited), Montreal.

HACKNEY (3).

CENTRAL (9,343).—No change.

*Spicer, Sir A. (L.)	4,429
Cassel, Felix, K.C. (U.)	3,853
Liberal majority	**576**

1906.—L., 3,998; U., 3,382—L. maj., 616.
1900.—U., 3,747; L., 2,243—U. maj., 1,504.
1895.—U. maj., 312; 1892, U. maj., 285; 1886, U. maj., 1,086.

SIR ALBERT SPICER, a member of a well-known Nonconformist family, was born in 1847, and was educated at Mill Hill School and at Heidelberg. He is a member of the firm of James Spicer and Sons, wholesale stationers. He has taken an active part in the work of the Congregational body, and was the first layman elected Chairman of the Congregational Union of England and Wales in 1893. He was president of the Sunday School Union in 1900, has been treasurer of the London Missionary Society since 1885, and president of the London Chamber of Commerce since 1907. He is also a member of the Commercial Intelligence Advisory Committee of the Board of Trade.

NORTH (11,789).—UNIONIST GAIN.

Greene, Raymond (U.)	5,620
*Hart-Davies, T. (L.)	4,773
Unionist majority	**847**

1906.—L., 4,655; U., 4,431—L., maj., 224.
1900.—U., 5,005; L., 2,437—U. maj., 2,568.
1895.—U. maj., 2,265; 1892, U. maj., 1,519; 1886, U. maj., 1,503.

Mr. RAYMOND GREENE, who was born in 1869, and educated at Eton and Oxford, has always taken a keen interest in politics, and in 1895 was elected as a Unionist for West Cambridgeshire; served in the South African War with the Suffolk Yeomanry, and during his absence, in 1900, was re-elected to Parliament. Sits for North Hackney on the London County Council; is lieutenant-colonel commanding the Suffolk Yeomanry.

SOUTH (14,128).—No change.

*Bottomley, H. (L.)	7,299
Wertheimer, C. (U.)	4,304
Liberal majority	**2,995**

1906.—L., 6,736; U., 3,257; L., 804—L. maj. over U., 3,479.
1900.—U., 4,714; L., 4,376—U. maj., 338.
1895.—U. maj., 319; 1892, L. maj., 1,146; 1886, L. maj., 100.

Mr. HORATIO BOTTOMLEY, financier and journalist; as the one, he is connected with large financial undertakings in the City; as the other, he founded the *Financial Times*, owned the *Sun* (no longer in existence), and started *John Bull*, of which he is proprietor and acting editor; first entered Parliament in 1906, when, as a Liberal, he won South Hackney from the Unionists; a frank, and often a destructive, critic of the Government's proposals.

HAMMERSMITH (14,362).—No change.

*Bull, Sir W. J. (U.)	6,668
Blaiklock, G. (L.)	5,542
Unionist majority	**1,126**

1906.—U., 5,111; L., 4,562; Lab., 885—U. maj. over L., 549.
1900.—U., 5,448; L., 2,166—U. maj., 3,282.
1895.—U. maj., 1,779; 1892, U. maj., 669; 1886, U. maj., 1,629.

SIR WILLIAM J. BULL, born in 1863, is head of the firm of Bull and Bull, solicitors, of Essex-street, Strand, a partner and chairman of J. W. Singer and Sons, bronze founders, of Frome and London, a member of committee of the Birkbeck College, Governor of Latymer Charities, hon. solicitor and vice-president to the Royal Life-Saving Society, and was vice-chairman and chairman of the Bridges Committee of the London County Council during the construction of the Blackwall tunnel.

HAMPSTEAD (12,050).—No change.

*Fletcher, J. S. (U.)	6,228
Howard, F. G. (L.)	3,949
Unionist majority	**2,279**

1906.—U., 4,934; L., 4,461—U. maj., 473.
1900.—U. unop.
1895.—U. unop.; 1892, U. maj., 1,109; 1888, U. maj., 1,762.

Mr. JOHN SAMUEL FLETCHER was born in 1841 at Broomfield, near Manchester, and educated at Harrow and Christ Church, Oxford. He was called to the Bar at Lincoln's Inn in 1868, but does not practise. Interesting himself in the local affairs of Hampstead, he was chairman of the Board of Guardians for eighteen years and served on the London County Council. He has represented the constituency since October, 1905.

ISLINGTON (4).

EAST (11,118).—No change.

*Radford, G. H. (L.)	5,003
Keeves, J. H. T. (U.)	4,674
Liberal majority	**329**

1906.—L., 4,477; U., 3,710—L. maj., 767.
1900.—U., 4,205; L., 2,586—U. maj., 1,619.
1895.—U. maj., 1,224; 1892, U. maj., 465; 1886, U. maj., 1,396.

Mr. GEORGE H. RADFORD is by profession a solicitor, and graduated in laws with honours at the University of London. He was an active Progressive member of the London County Council.

NORTH (12,677).—No change.

*Waterlow, D. S. (L.)	5,543
Touche, G. A. (U.)	5,512
Liberal majority	**31**

1906.—L., 5,284; U., 4,418—L. maj., 866.
1900.—U., 4,881; L., 2,567—U. maj., 2,314.
1895.—U. maj., 1,309; 1892, U. maj., 810; 1886, U. maj., 1,480.

Mr. D. S. WATERLOW, who is the fourth son of Sir Sydney Waterlow, was born in Highgate in 1857 and received his education at Northampton and in Switzerland. After a 12 months' tour of the world he joined the printing firm of Waterlow and Sons, becoming manager and director, but retired in 1898.

SOUTH (8,268).—No change.

*Wiles, T. (L.)	3,918
Faber, D. (U.)	3,187
Liberal majority	731

1906.—L., 3,606; U., 1,991; U., 870—L. maj. over U., 1,615.
1900.—U., 3,881; L., 1,665—U. maj., 2,216.
1895.—U. maj., 1,221 1892, U. maj., 321; 1886, U. maj., 566

Mr. THOMAS WILES, the senior partner in the firm of Joseph Wiles and Sons, Mark-lane, is a grain merchant, and a member of the Corn Exchange and the Baltic Shipping Exchange. Entering the London County Council in 1899 as representative of South-West Bethnal Green, he was for some years Whip to the Progressive Party.

WEST (8,544).—No change.

*Lough, Right Hon. T. (L.)	3,768
Crossley, Right Hon. Sir S., Bt. (U.)	3,514
Liberal majority	254

1906.—L., 4,116; U., 3,618—L. maj., 498.
1900.—L., 3,178; U., 3,159—L. maj., 19.
1895.—L. maj., 463; 1892, L. maj., 730; 1886, U. maj., 1,292.

Mr. T. LOUGH has represented West Islington since 1892. An Irishman by birth, he has always taken an interest in the political and social affairs of his native country; he is the author of "England's Wealth, Ireland's Poverty," and "Ten Years' Tory Rule in Ireland"; the founder of the Home Rule Union and the London Reform Union; was Parliamentary Secretary to the Board of Education from 1905 to 1908, when he was "shed" by Mr. Asquith and made a Privy Councillor; is a wholesale tea merchant in London.

KENSINGTON (2).

NORTH (10,100).—UNIONIST GAIN.

Burgoyne, A. (U.)	4,611
Robson, Sir H. (L.)	4,079
Unionist majority	532

1906.—L., 4,416; U., 3,358—L. maj., 1,058.
1900.—U., 3,257; L., 2,527—U. maj., 730.
1895.—U. maj., 916; 1892, L. maj., 210; 1886, U. maj., 951.

Mr. ALAN BURGOYNE had had previous experience of electioneering at King's Lynn, where he made a strenuous fight against Mr. Gibson Bowles, and had worked untiringly in his present constituency since 1906, greatly strengthening the party organization. He possesses an intimate knowledge of labour conditions in Australia derived as an employer, and is an authority on naval matters.

SOUTH (9,159).—No change.

Hamilton, Lord Claud (U.)	5,771
MacIlwaine, Captain, R.N., (L.)	1,301
Unionist majority	4,470

1906.—U., 4,835; L., 1,624—U. maj., 3,211.
1900.—U. unop.
1895.—U. unop.; 1892, U. unop.; 1886, U. maj., 3,134.

LORD CLAUD HAMILTON entered the House of Commons in 1865 as the representative of Londonderry, and in 1868 was appointed a Lord of the Treasury. He was the member for King's Lynn, 1869-80, and a representative of Liverpool, 1880-88, when he resigned. He is the second son of the first Duke of Abercorn, and was born in 1843, and educated at Harrow. He entered the Grenadier Guards in 1862, and retired in 1867, when he was appointed colonel of the 5th Battalion Royal Inniskilling Fusiliers, of which in 1892 he became hon. colonel. He acted as aide-de-camp to the Queen in 1887. He is chairman of the Great Eastern Railway Company, and High Steward of the Borough of Great Yarmouth.

LAMBETH (4).

BRIXTON (11,442).—UNIONIST GAIN.

Dalziel, D. (U.)	5,465
*Seaverns, J. H. (L.)	4,427
Unionist majority	1,038

1906.—L., 4,521; U., 4,235—L. maj., 286.
1900.—U. unop.
1895.—U. maj., 1,999; 1892, U. maj., 857; 1886, U. maj., 1,414.

Mr. DAVISON DALZIEL contested Brixton four years ago. He is a pioneer of the taxi-cab industry in this country. He is also interested in motor-cab undertakings in Berlin and New York, and for many years has been a director of the International Sleeping Car Company. He is managing director of Dalziel's News Agency.

KENNINGTON (10,088).—No change.

*Collins, S. (L.)	4,246
Lucas, Colonel F. A. (U.)	3,865
Liberal majority	381

1906.—L., 4,639; U., 3,054—L. maj., 1,585.
1900.—U., 4,195; L., 2,309—U. maj., 1,886.
1895.—U. maj., 995; 1892, L. maj., 607; 1886, U. maj., 430.

Mr. STEPHEN COLLINS, born in 1847, began life as a stonemason, and is at present the head of the firm of Stephen Collins (Limited), Vauxhall. He has throughout his career taken a great interest in political and social work; was elected a member of the Wandsworth Vestry and of the District Board of Works, being chosen later as one of the aldermen of Lambeth. From 1901 to 1907 Mr. Collins was a member of the London County Council.

NORTH (6,440).—UNIONIST GAIN.

Gastrell, Major Houghton (U.)	2,947
*Myer, H. (L.)	2,397
Unionist majority	550

1906.—L., 2,162; U., 1,904; L., 733; U., 108.—L. maj. over U., 258.
1900.—U., 2,677; L., 1,795—U. maj., 882.
1895.—U. maj., 405; 1892, L. maj., 130; 1886, U. maj., 412.

MAJOR W. HOUGHTON GASTRELL contested North Lambeth in 1906, when he was defeated by the late member. He is a member of the Grand Council of the Primrose League, of the Council of the National Union of Conservative Associations, and of the Executive Council of the London Municipal Society. He is also the chairman of the Finance Committee and a governor on the Board of Management of the Royal Free Hospital, and a governor of the Royal Eye Hospital. He represented South St. Pancras on the London County Council for three years.

NORWOOD (13,908).—No change.

Samuel, Sir H. S. (U.)	6,958
Lawrence, Sir A., Bt. (L.)	5,180
Unionist majority	1,778

1906.—U., 5,567; L., 4,748—U. maj., 819.
1900.—U., unop.
1895.—U. unop.; 1892, U. maj., 1,563; 1886, U. maj., 1,728.

SIR HARRY SIMON SAMUEL was born in London in 1853 and educated at Eastbourne College and St. John's College, Cambridge. He became a partner in the firm of Montefiore and Co., retiring in 1884. He contested the Limehouse Division of the Tower Hamlets in 1892, and represented that constituency 1895-1906.

LEWISHAM (25,021).—No change.

*Coates, Major E. F. (U.)	12,690
Rosenheim, F. (L.)	8,960
Unionist majority	3,730

1906.—U., 9,689; L., 8,006—U. maj., 1,683.
1900.—U. unop.
1895.—U. unop.; 1892, U. maj., 2,414; 1886, U. unop.

MAJOR EDWARD FEETHAM COATES is a member of the firm of Coates, Son, and Co., stockbrokers, and was born in 1853. He was educated at Marlborough, and has served in the late 3rd Battalion Duke of Wellington's (West Riding Regiment), is a County Alderman for Surrey and chairman of the Surrey County Council, a Deputy-Lieutenant for Surrey, and a J.P. for Surrey and the North Riding of Yorkshire. During the Budget debates in the House of Commons Major Coates presented with conciseness and force the case of the Stock Exchange and other bodies connected with City finance against some of the Government proposals.

MARYLEBONE (2).

EAST (6,759).—No change.

Boyton, J. (U.)	3,134
Moon, Dr. R. O. (L.)	1,905
Jebb, R. (Ind. T.R.)	702
Unionist majority over Lib.	1,229

1906.—U., 2,827; L., 2,167—U. maj., 660.
1900.—U., 3,106; L., 1,126.—U. maj., 1,980.
1895.—U. maj., 1,534; 1892, U. maj., 822; 1886, U. maj., 1,485.

Mr. JAMES BOYTON was born in 1855, and has been for the past 32 years associated with the firm of Messrs. Elliott, Son, and Boyton, auctioneers and estate agents. He served a few years ago on the old vestry of St. Marylebone, and was one of the first members of the Marylebone Borough Council. At the last election for the London County Council he stood for the East Division of Marylebone with Lord Duncannon, and was returned by a large majority. He is a member of the council of the Auctioneers' Institute and was president for the year 1905-6, and he is also a past president of the Estate Agents' Institute.

WEST (8,576).—No change.

*Scott, Sir S. E. (U.)	4,451
Forbes, Capt. the Hon. D. (L.)	2,474
Unionist majority	1,977

1906.—U., 3,446; L., 2,791—U. maj., 655.
1900.—U., 3,487; L., 1,532—U. maj., 1,955.
1895.—U. maj., 1,461; 1892, U. maj., 437; 1886, U. maj., 1,122.

SIR SAMUEL EDWARD SCOTT, son of the 5th Baronet, born in 1873, succeeded his father 1883, was educated at Eton and Sandhurst, and married a daughter of the 5th Earl Cadogan in 1896. He was lieutenant in the Royal Horse Guards, 1894-6, and served in South Africa, 1899-1900, in the Imperial Yeomanry. Late captain in the West Kent Yeomanry. He is a large landowner; he was returned unopposed for West Marylebone at a by-election in February, 1898, and was re-elected in 1900 and 1906.

NEWINGTON (2).

WALWORTH (8,521).—No change.

Dawes, J. A. (L.)	3,509
Belilios, R. E. (U.)	3,319
Liberal majority	190

1906.—L., 3,187; U., 2,418—L. maj., 769.
1900.—U., 3,098; L., 2,233—U. maj., 865.
1895.—U. maj., 553; 1892, L. maj., 296; 1886, U. maj., 235.

Mr. JAMES ARTHUR DAWES, born in 1866, educated at Harrow and at University College, Oxford; admitted a solicitor, 1891; has taken an active part in local affairs and was first Mayor of Southwark, 1900-1; a member of the London County Council since 1906.

WEST (9,635).—No change.

*Norton, Capt. C. (L.)	4,350
Brookes, Warwick (U.)	3,938
Liberal majority	412

1906.—L., 4,446; U., 2,425—L. maj., 2,021.
1900.—L., 3,559; U., 2,403—L. maj., 1,156.
1895.—L. maj., 450; 1892, L. maj., 1,093; 1886, U. maj., 382.

CAPTAIN CECIL NORTON was educated abroad and at Trinity College, Dublin. After serving with the 5th Royal Lancers in India he distinguished himself at the Staff College, and was sent to Italy by the Government to report on the Italian cavalry. He afterwards became a brigade-major at Aldershot. He is now a Junior Lord of the Treasury.

PADDINGTON (2).

NORTH (10,945).—UNIONIST GAIN.

Strauss, A. (U.)	4,892
*Money, L. G. Chiozza (L.)	3,999
Unionist majority	893

1906.—L., 3,825; U., 2,419; U., 817—L. maj., 1,406.
1900.—U., 3,364; L., 1,518—U. maj., 1,846.
1895.—U. maj., 997; 1892, U. maj., 310; 1886, U. maj., 911.

Mr. ARTHUR STRAUSS is 61 years of age, and is a member of the firm of A. Strauss and Company, metal brokers, of Rood-lane, E.C. Of German nationality, he came to England at an early age and was naturalized more than 40 years ago. He represented the Camborne Division of Cornwall in Parliament from 1895 to 1900. He is a large employer of labour. He introduced into mines the tin-ticketing system, the working of which has proved a great boon to miners.

SOUTH (6,415).—No change.

Harris, H. P. (U.)	3,677
Henlé, F. H. (L.)	1,419
Unionist majority	2,258

1906.—U., 2,919 ; L., 1,502—U. maj., 1,417.
1900.—U. unop.
1895.—U. unop. ; 1892, U. unop. ; 1886, U. unop.

Mr. HENRY PERCY HARRIS, who was born in 1856, is a son of the late Sir George David Harris, was educated at Eton and Christ Church, Oxford, and enters Parliament with a ripe experience of the municipal affairs of London, having entered the County Council in 1892 as the representative of Paddington, and held the offices successively since of leader of the Municipal Reform Party, Deputy-Chairman and Chairman of the Council. In 1881 he was called to the Bar by Lincoln's Inn.

ST. GEORGE'S, HANOVER-SQUARE
(8,954).—No change.

*Lyttelton, Rt. Hon. A., K.C. (U.)	5,383
Bell, Mackenzie (L.)	1,469
Unionist majority	3,914

By-election, 1906.—U. unop.
1906.—U., 4,264 ; L., 2,191—U. maj., 2,073.
1900.—U., 3,852 ; L., 1,278 —U. maj., 2,574.
1895, 1892, and 1886.—U. unop.

Mr. ALFRED LYTTELTON, youngest son of the fourth Lord Lyttelton, was born in 1857, and was educated at Eton, and at Trinity College, Cambridge. He is a member of the General Council of the Bar, Deputy High Steward of Cambridge University, Chancellor of the Diocese of Rochester, and a vice-president of the Royal Colonial Institute, and has served as Recorder of Hereford and of Oxford. From 1903 to 1905 he served in Mr. Balfour's Government as Secretary of State for the Colonies. He was Chairman of the Transvaal Concessions Commission, which held its inquiries in South Africa during the latter part of 1900, and in 1901 he was appointed arbitrator in the dispute regarding electric traction between the Metropolitan and the Metropolitan District Railways. Mr. Lyttelton has been Amateur Tennis Champion, and has represented Cambridge University in cricket, football, tennis, racquets, and England in cricket and football.

ST. PANCRAS (4).
EAST (9,487).—No change.

Martin, Hon. J. (L.)	4,276
Preston, W. R. (U.)	3,586
Liberal majority	690

1906.—L., 4,208 ; U., 2,327—L. maj., 1,981.
1900.—U., 3,016 ; L., 2,016—U. maj., 910.
1895.—U. maj., 289 ; 1892, U. maj., 441 ; 1886, U. maj., 501.

Mr. J. MARTIN, K.C., a member of the Canadian Bar, who has now taken up his residence in this country to practise before the Judicial Committee of the Privy Council, has been Attorney-General of Manitoba, Attorney-General and Prime Minister of British Columbia, and for many years sat for Winnipeg in the Dominion Parliament of Canada ; unsuccessfully contested the Stratford-on-Avon Division at the by-election in May, 1909.

NORTH (9,977).—No change.

*Dickinson, W. H. (L.)	4,970
Pakenham, Lt.-Col. H. A. (U.)	3,603
Liberal majority	1,367

1906.—L., 4,094 ; U., 2,643—L. maj., 1,451.
1900.—U., 3,056 ; L., 2,345—U. maj., 711.
1895.—U. maj., 211 ; 1892, L. maj., 60 ; 1886, U. maj., 261.

Mr. W. H. DICKINSON, chairman of the London Liberal Federation, member of the London County Council from 1889 to 1907, deputy chairman 1892-6, and Chairman 1899, fought two unsuccessful Parliamentary contests before his election for North St. Pancras in 1906 ; in the late Parliament he actively identified himself with the woman suffrage movement and introduced a Bill on the subject ; born in 1859, and educated at Eton and at Trinity College, Cambridge ; called to the Bar, 1884, and practises as Parliamentary draftsman.

SOUTH (5,536).—UNIONIST GAIN.

Jessel, Capt. H. (U.)	2,750
*Wilson, P. W. (L.)	1,925
Unionist majority	825

1906.—L, 2,109 ; U., 2,048—L. maj., 61.
1900.—U., 2,273 ; L., 1,113—U. maj., 1,160.
1895.—U. maj.,1,210 ; 1892, U. maj., 437 ; 1886, U. maj., 1,018.

CAPT. HERBERT MERTON JESSEL, the younger son of the late Sir George Jessel, Master of the Rolls, is a member of the council of the city of Westminster, he was mayor in 1903, chairman of the London Municipal Society, and hon. colonel of the 1st (City of London) Battalion, the London Regiment (Royal Fusiliers). He was born in 1866, educated at Brighton and New College, Oxford, and was a captain in the 17th Lancers. He served in India 1887-90. In 1896 he resigned, and contested St. Pancras, South, on the death of his father-in-law, Sir Julian Goldsmid, who had represented the constituency from 1885 up to that time. Capt. Jessel was successful at the by-election and at the next General Election in 1900, and sat as the member for the division until 1906.

WEST (8,589).—No change.

*Collins, Sir W. (L.)	3,553
Dickinson, R. E. (U.)	3,543
Liberal majority	10

1906.—L., 3,230 ; U., 2,545—L. maj., 685.
1900.—U., 3,220 ; L., 1,553—U. maj., 1,667.
1895.—U. maj., 831 ; 1892, U. maj., 42 ;1886, L. maj., 64.

SIR WILLIAM J. COLLINS is an eminent physician and man of science ; born in London, 1859, educated at University College School, London, and St. Bartholomew's Hospital ; Vice-Chancellor, Fellow, scholar, and gold medallist of London University ; has held several important hospital appointments in London ;

served for many years on the London County Council, and was Chairman in 1897-8; knighted in 1902; elected for West St. Pancras in 1906.

SHOREDITCH (2).

HAGGERSTON (7,936).—LIBERAL GAIN.

Chancellor, H. G. (L.)	..	3,041
*Guinness, Hon. R. (U.)	..	2,585
Burrows, H. (Soc.)	..	701

| Liberal majority | .. | 456 |

By-election, 1908.—U., 2,867; L., 1,724; Lab., 986—U. maj. over L., 1,134.
1906.—L., 2,772; U., 2,371—L. maj., 401.
1900.—L., 2,290; U., 2,266—L. maj., 24.
1895.—U. maj., 40; 1892, L. maj., 921; 1886, L. maj., 377.

Mr. H. G. CHANCELLOR was born in 1863 and has long taken a keen interest in social reform; he is vice-president of the Land Values Taxation League and a Nonconformist.

HOXTON (8,530).—LIBERAL GAIN.

| Addison, Dr. C. (L.) .. | .. | 3,736 |
| *Hay, Hon. Claude (U.) | .. | 3,398 |

| Liberal majority | .. | 338 |

1906.—U., 3,489; L., 2,753—U. maj. 736.
1900.—U., 2,866; L., 2,595—U. maj., 271.
1895.—L. maj., 128; 1892, L. maj. over U., 1,296; 1886, L. maj., 245.

Dr. CHRISTOPHER ADDISON was born in Lincolnshire in 1869 and is a lecturer on anatomy in St. Bartholomew's Hospital and examiner in anatomy in the Royal College of Surgeons. As an upholder of the need for home defence he has taken an active share in the Volunteer and Territorial Forces movements.

SOUTHWARK (3).

BERMONDSEY (12,115).—LIBERAL GAIN.

| Glanville, H. J. (L.) .. | .. | 5,477 |
| *Dumphreys, J. (U.) | .. | 4,508 |

| Liberal majority | .. | 969 |

By-election, 1909.—U., 4,278; L, 3,291; Soc., 1,435—U. maj., over L., 987.
1906.—L., 4,775; U., 3,016—L. maj.,·1,759.
1900.—U., 4,017; L., 3,717—U. maj., 300.
1895.—U. maj., 360; 1892, L. maj., 658; 1886, U. maj., 358.

Mr. H. J. GLANVILLE, born in Bermondsey, has been prominently associated with the public life of the borough for about 20 years.

ROTHERHITHE (9,990).—No change.

| *Carr-Gomm, H. (L.) .. | .. | 4,474 |
| Pownall, Assheton (U.) | .. | 3,550 |

| Liberal majority.. | .. | 924 |

1906.—L., 4,192; U., 2,821.—L. maj., 1,371.
1900.—L., 3,938; L., 2,356.—U. maj., 1,582.
1895.—U. maj., 1,846; 1892, U. maj., 1,230; 1886, U. maj., 1,087.

Mr. H. W. CARR-GOMM was born in India in 1879, and was educated at Eton and Oxford. In 1906 he was appointed an assistant private secretary (unpaid) to the late Sir H. Campbell-Bannerman when Prime Minister, and he succeeded Sir J. W. Benn as secretary of the London Liberal Federation.

WEST (8,060).—UNIONIST GAIN.

| Dunn, Sir W. H. (U.).. | .. | 3,387 |
| *Causton, Rt. Hon. R. K.(L.) | | 3,223 |

| Unionist majority | .. | 164 |

1906.—L., 3,057; U., 2,592—L. maj., 465.
1900.—L., 2,893; U., 2,763—L. maj., 130.
1895.—L. maj., 119; 1892, L. maj., 1,239; 1886, L. maj., 113.

SIR WILLIAM HENRY DUNN, who was born in 1865, is a well-known figure in the business and civic life of the City of London; is an auctioneer and surveyor and Fellow of the Surveyors' Institution; an Alderman of the City of London, Sheriff in 1906-7; a Liveryman of several of the City Guilds, associated as an officer with the Territorial Force, and has several foreign decorations.

STRAND (8,019).—No change.

| *Long, Rt. Hon. W. H. (U.).. | | 4,840 |
| Costello, L. W. J. (L.) | .. | 1,627 |

| Unionist majority | .. | 3,213 |

1906.—U., 3,935; L., 1,854—U. maj., 2,081.
1900, 1895, and 1892.—U., unop.
1886.—U. maj., 3,526.

Mr. WALTER LONG, one of the leaders of the Unionist Party in the House of Commons, has filled several important offices of State; has been Parliamentary Secretary to the Local Government Board (1886-92), President of the Board of Agriculture (1895-1900), President of the Local Government Board (1900-05), and Chief Secretary for Ireland (March-December, 1905); was founder and chairman of the Budget Protest League, and one of the most active opponents, especially in the country, of Mr. Lloyd George's proposals; has had a seat in Parliament since 1880, and has successively represented Wiltshire, N., Wiltshire, E., Liverpool (West Derby), Bristol, S., and Dublin County, S.

TOWER HAMLETS (7).

BOW AND BROMLEY (10,330).—UNIONIST GAIN.

Du Cros, Alfred (U.) ..	..	3,695
Lansbury, G. (Lab.)	..	2,955
*Brooke, Stopford W. (L.) ..		2,167

| Unionist majority over Labour | 740 |
| Unionist majority over Liberal | 1,528 |

1906.—L., 4,596; U., 3,974—L. maj., 622.
1900.—U., 4,403; Soc., 2,558—U. maj., 1,845.
1895.—U. maj., 1,161; 1892, L. maj., 423; 1886, U. maj., 571.

Mr. ALFRED DU CROS is 41 years of age, and has had large business experience in America and elsewhere. He has played an important part in the development of the cycle and the motor-car industry. He has held the amateur championship of Ireland for all-round excellence in gymnastics.

LIMEHOUSE (6,405).—No change.

| *Pearce, W. (L.) | .. | .. | 2,826 |
| Borwick, G. O. (U.) | .. | 2,395 |

| Liberal majority | .. | 431 |

1906.—L., 2,981; U., 2,007—L. maj., 974.
1900.—U., 2,608; L., 2,070; U. maj., 538.
1895.—U. maj., 590; 1892, L. maj., 170; 1886, U. maj., 802.

Mr. W. PEARCE, who was born in 1853, is the head

of the firm of William Pearce and Sons, chemical manufacturers, and was educated at the School of Mines and at the Royal College of Science, South Kensington. He is a Fellow of the Chemical Society and manager of the Limehouse Provided Schools, and was a member of the London County Council from 1892 to 1901. He sat on the Technical Education Board from 1895 to 1899, and has been chairman of the Bridges and Main Drainage Committees.

MILE END (5,464).—UNIONIST GAIN.

Lawson, Hon. H. L. W. (U.)..	2,333
*Straus, B. S. (L.)	2,276
Unionist majority ..	57

1906.—L., 2,295 ; U., 2,169—L. maj., 126.
1900.—U., 2,440 ; L., 1,280—U. maj., 1,160.
1895.—U. maj., 867 ; 1892, U. maj., 273 ; 1886, U. maj., 829.

The HON. HARRY LAWSON WEBSTER LAWSON, the eldest son of Lord Burnham, was born in London in 1862, and educated at Eton and Balliol College, Oxford. He was called to the Bar at the Inner Temple in 1891, and commands the Buckinghamshire Yeomanry. He sat as a Liberal for West St. Pancras 1885-92 ; contested East Gloucestershire in 1892, and was elected in a contest held the following year, but was defeated in 1895. He unsuccessfully contested North-East Bethnal Green as a Liberal in 1900 and Bury in 1902 as a Conservative. He was returned for the Mile-end Division in 1905, but was defeated at the General Election. He sat on the London County Council for West St. Pancras, 1889-92, and Whitechapel, 1897-1904, and was Mayor of Stepney, 1908-9.

POPLAR (8,857).—No change.

*Buxton, Rt. Hon. S. (L.) ..	4,172
Wilson, Capt. Leslie (U.) ..	3,115
Liberal majority ..	1,057

1906.—L., 4,546 ; U., 2,235—L. maj., 2,311.
1900.—L., 3,992 ; U., 2,840—L. maj., 1,152.
1895.—L. maj., 829 ; 1892, L. maj., 2,032 ; 1886, L. maj., 76.

Mr. SYDNEY BUXTON was born in 1853 and was educated at Clifton College, and at Trinity College, Cambridge. From 1876 to 1882 he was a member of the London School Board, and from 1892 to 1895 he was Under-Secretary for the Colonies ; is a J.P. for Norfolk, and was appointed Postmaster-General in 1905. In 1908 he established the penny post to America and the Canadian magazine post in 1907.

ST. GEORGE'S (3,133).—No change.

*Benn, W. Wedgwood (L.) ..	1,568
Simmons, P. C. (U.) ..	1,134
Liberal majority ..	434

1906.—L., 1,685 ; U., 1,064—L. maj., 621.
1900.—U., 1,437 ; L., 1,141—U. maj., 296.
1895.—U. maj., 4 ; 1892, L. maj., 398 ; 1886, U. maj., 485.

Mr. W. WEDGWOOD BENN is the son of Sir John W. Benn and was born in 1877. He was educated at the Lycée Condorcet in Paris and at the London University, and acted as Parliamentary Private Secretary (unpaid) to Mr. McKenna when successively at the Treasury, at the Board of Education, and at the Admiralty.

STEPNEY (4,653).—No change.

*Harris, F. Leverton (U.) ..	2,102
Jones, W. S. Glyn (L.) ..	1,866
Unionist majority ..	236

By-election 1907.—U., 2,299 ; Lab., 1,350—U. maj., 949.
1906.—U., 2,490 ; L., 1,853—U. maj., 637.
1900.—U., 2,783 ; L., 1,718—U. maj., 1,065.
1895.—U. maj., 470 ; 1892, U. maj., 89 ; 1886, U. maj., 502.

Mr. F. LEVERTON HARRIS was born in 1864, and was educated at Winchester and Cambridge. He is a member of the London firm of Harris and Dixon, coal factors and insurance agents ; was a member of the Tariff Reform Commission, and takes an active part in the work of the Tariff Reform League ; he served as Parliamentary Private Secretary to the late Mr. Arnold-Forster when at the Admiralty and the War Office, and was a member of the Select Committees on Workmen's Trains and Foreign Shipping. He represents Stepney on the London County Council.

WHITECHAPEL (3,986).—No change.

*Samuel, Stuart (L.) ..	1,963
Greenlees, L. (U.) ..	1,402
Liberal majority ..	561

1906.—L., 1,925 ; U., 1,569—L. maj., 356.
1900.—L., 1,679 ; U., 1,608—L. maj., 71.
1895.—U. maj., 32 ; 1892, L. maj., 527 ; 1886, L. maj., 587.

Mr. STUART MONTAGU SAMUEL was born at Liverpool in 1856 and educated at the Liverpool Institute, and University College School, London. He is a member of Samuel, Montagu, and Co., foreign bankers, and has represented Whitechapel since 1900. He is a member of the United Synagogue and Jewish Board of Guardians, and was a founder of the Whitechapel Picture Gallery.

WANDSWORTH (38,523).—No change.

*Kimber, Sir H. (U.) ..	18,188
Warren, W. (L.) ..	13,749
Unionist majority ..	4,439

1906.—U., 12,433 ; L., 11,888—U. maj., 545.
1900.—U., unop.
1895.—U. maj., 3,239 ; 1892, U. maj., 2,223 ; 1886, U., unop.

SIR HENRY KIMBER, who was created a baronet in 1904, was admitted a solicitor in 1858, and founded the firm of Kimber and Ellis, now Kimbers and Boatman, from which he has retired. He is a director of the Capital and Counties Bank, chairman of the South Indian and Pondicherry Railways, and of the Natal Land and Colonization Co. (Limited), and is the founder or reconstructor of several Colonial and other commercial undertakings.

WEST HAM (2).

NORTH (15,661).—No change.

*Masterman, C. F. G. (L.) ..	7,023
Gray, E. (U.) ..	6,133
Liberal majority ..	890

1906.—L., 6,838 ; U., 5,094—L. maj., 1,744.
1900.—U., 6,613 ; L., 4,133—U. maj., 2,480.
1895.—U. maj., 704 ; 1892, L. maj., 33 ; 1886, U. maj., 727.

Mr. CHARLES FREDERICK GURNEY MASTERMAN, journalist and author ; educated at Weymouth and at Christ's College, Cambridge, where he had a distinguished career and of which he became a Fellow in 1900; has been lecturer for the Cambridge and London University Extension Societies; was appointed Parliamentary Secretary to the Local Government Board in April, 1908, and, in July, 1909, Under-Secretary to the Home Office; has written "Tennyson as a Religious Leader," "The Heart of the Empire," and other works; his wife is a daughter of General the Hon. Sir Neville Lyttelton.

SOUTH (26,682).—No change.

*Thorne, W. (Lab.)	11,791
Grimwood, J. (U.)	6,909
Labour majority	4,882

1906.—Lab., 10,210; U., 4,973.—Lab. maj., 5,237.
1900.—U., 5,615; Lab., 4,439—U. maj., 1,176.
1895.—U. maj., 775; 1892, Lab. maj., 1,232; 1886, U. maj., 303.

Mr. WILLIAM THORNE is a well-known member of the Trade Union Parliamentary Committee. He has taken a prominent part in municipal affairs in West Ham, where in 1898 he filled the office of deputy mayor. In 1889 he established the National Union of Gasworkers and General Labourers, to which he acts as general secretary.

WESTMINSTER (7,284).—No change.

*Burdett-Coutts, W. L. A. B. (U.)	3,917
Hobart, Lieut.-Col. (L.)	1,751
Unionist majority	2,166

1906.—U., 3,167; L., 2,054—U. maj., 1,113.
1900.—U., 2,715; Ind. U., 439—U. maj., 2,276.
1895.—U. unop.; 1892, U., 1,632; 1886, U. unop.

Mr. WILLIAM LEHMAN ASHMEAD BARTLETT-BURDETT-COUTTS was born in the United States in 1851, and married in 1881 Baroness Burdett-Coutts, whose name he assumed. He gained a scholarship at Keble College, Oxford, and graduated M.A. in 1876. In 1877 he acted as Special Commissioner for the Turkish Compassionate Fund during the Russo-Turkish War. He was one of the originators of the Fisheries Exhibition, and has taken interest in matters relating to London food supply and schemes for the benefit of Irish fishermen originated by the late Baroness. He is owner of the Brookfield stud, Governor of Christ's Hospital, and was one of the founders of the British East African Possessions. In 1900 he went to South Africa as *The Times* Correspondent in reference to the sick and wounded, and his statements led to inquiry by Royal Commission, and reforms. He has been member for Westminster since 1885, and carried through the Hampstead Heath Act, 1885, and other Acts.

WOOLWICH (18,536).—UNIONIST GAIN.

Adam, Major W. A. (U.)	8,715
*Crooks, W. (Lab.)	8,420
Unionist majority	295

1906.—Lab., 9,026; U., 6,914—Lab. maj. 2,112.
1900.—U. unop.
1895.—U. maj., 2,805; 1892, U. maj., 1,092; 1886, U. maj., 1,836.

MAJOR W. AUGUSTUS ADAM, of the 5th (Royal Irish) Lancers, was born in 1865, and was educated at Harrow, Dublin University, and Sandhurst, taking first honours in classics and in modern history. He is a senior moderator and gold medallist in modern languages, and an interpreter in Russian, French, and Hindustani. In the South African War he shared in the defence of Ladysmith, was on special service in Japan for two years, and served in 1907 as a General Staff Officer in the War Office.

ENGLAND (BOROUGHS.)

ASHTON-UNDER-LYNE (8,595).—No change.

*Scott, A. H. (L.)	4,039
Whiteley, H. (U.)	3,746
Gee, W. (Soc.)	413
Liberal majority over Unionist	293

1906.—L., 4,310; U., 3,342—L. maj., 968.
1900.—U., 3,545; L., 2,400; Soc., 737—U. maj. over L., 1,445.
1895.—U. maj over L., 754; 1892, U. maj., 135; 1886, U. returned by casting vote of Mayor.

Mr. ALFRED HENRY SCOTT was born at Manchester in 1868, and educated at Tideswell and Lichfield Grammar School. He is a director of Burgons (Limited), wholesale provision dealers, of Manchester, and was a member of the Manchester City Council. He unsuccessfully contested East Manchester in 1900.

ASTON MANOR (11,894).—No change.

*Cecil, E. (U.)	7,369
Allen, J. H. (L.)	1,922
Unionist majority	5,447

1906.—U., 7,134; L., 2,431—U. maj., 4,703.
1900.—U. unop.
1895, U. maj., 3,678; 1892, U. maj., 3,927; 1886, U. maj., 782.

Mr. EVELYN CECIL is the eldest son of Lord Eustace Cecil, and was born in 1865. He was educated at

ENGLAND (BOROUGHS).

Eton and New College, Oxford, and was called to the Bar, Inner Temple, 1889. He acted as assistant private secretary to the late Lord Salisbury, when Prime Minister in 1891-2 and 1895-1902. He represented the Eastern Division of Hertfordshire, 1898-1900, and at the general election in the latter year was elected as the member for Aston Manor. He was the last Englishman to confer with Presidents Kruger and Steyn before the outbreak of the war in South Africa.

BARROW-IN-FURNESS (10,478).—No change.

| *Duncan, C. (Lab.) | .. | .. | 5,304 |
| Meynell, F. (U.) | .. | .. | 4,298 |

| Labour majority | .. | 1,006 |

1906.—Lab., 5,167 ; U., 3,395—Lab. maj., 1,772.
1900.—U. unop.
1895.—U. maj., 837 ; 1892, U. maj., 422 ; 1886, U. maj., 1,330.

Mr. CHARLES DUNCAN is the son of a pilot, and was born in Middlesbrough in 1865. He followed the occupation of an engineer and was employed for some time at the Elswick Ordnance Factory. He has served on the Middlesbrough Town Council, and is general secretary of the Workers' Union. During the last Parliament, to which he was elected to represent Barrow-in-Furness, he acted as one of the Whips of the Labour Party.

BATH (2) (8,144).—Two UNIONIST GAINS.

Thynne, Lord A. (U.)	..	3,961
Hunter, Sir C. (U.)	..	3,889
*Maclean, D. (L.)	..	3,771
*Gooch, G. P. (L.)	..	3,757

| Unionist majority | .. | 118 |

1906.—L., 4,102 ; L., 4,069 ; U., 3,123 ; U., 3,088—L. maj. 946.
1900.—U., 3,486 ; U., 3,439 ; L., 2,605 ; L., 2,549—U. maj., 834.
1895.—U., 3,445 ; U., 3,358 ; L., 2,917 ; L., 2,865—U. maj.,441.
1892.—U., 3,198 ; U., 3,177 ; L., 2,981 ; L., 2,914—U. maj., 196.
1886.—U., 3,309 ; U., 3,244 ; L., 2,588 ; L., 2,529—U. maj., 656.

LORD ALEXANDER GEORGE THYNNE, brother of the fifth Marquis of Bath, was born in 1873, and educated at Eton and Balliol College, Oxford ; unsuccessfully contested the Frome Division of Somerset in 1896 and Bath in 1906 ; served with the 1st Battalion Imperial Yeomanry in South Africa, was on the Staff 1900-02, and gained the Queen's medal with three clasps and the King's medal with two clasps ; acted as secretary to the Lieutenant-Governor of Orange River Colony for a time, and 1903-4 accompanied the Somaliland Field Force as Reuter's special correspondent, and gained another medal with clasp ; is a major in the Royal Wilts Yeomanry and sits on the London County Council.

SIR CHARLES RODERICK HUNTER, who was born in 1858, succeeded his father, the second baronet, in 1890. He was educated at Eton, and has served as a captain in the Rifle Brigade and as a major in the 1st London Rifle Volunteers, and was for a time aide-de-camp to the Lieutenant-General Commanding in Canada, and in 1900 was appointed Inspector of Musketry, Imperial Yeomanry.

BEDFORD (6,063).—UNIONIST GAIN.

| Attenborough, W. A. (U.) | .. | 2,919 |
| *Barlow, P. (L.) | .. | .. | 2,750 |

| Unionist majority | .. | 169 |

1906.—L., 2,771 ; U., 2,278—L. maj., 493.
1900.—U., 2,115 ; L., 1,848—U. maj., 267.
1895.—U. maj., 166 ; 1892, L. maj., 118 ; 1886, L. maj., 23.

Mr. WALTER A. ATTENBOROUGH, M.A., LL.M., Unionist candidate for Bedford, is 59 years of age and was educated at Trinity College, Cambridge ; is a barrister, practising on the Midland Circuit ; he is a J.P. for the Bedford Division of the county.

BIRKENHEAD (18,189).—No change.

| *Vivian, H. (L.) | .. | .. | 8,120 |
| Bigland, A. (U.) | .. | .. | 7,976 |

| Liberal majority | .. | 144 |

1906.—L., 7,074 ; U., 5,271 ; Ind. U., 2,118—L. maj., over U., 1,803.
1900.—U. unop.
1895.—U. maj., 204 ; 1892, U. maj., 604 ; 1886, U. maj., 1,169.

Mr. HENRY VIVIAN, a Labour M.P., who has steadily refused to ally himself with the Independent Labour Party ; by trade a carpenter and joiner, he is strongly in favour of co-partnership ; is secretary of the Labour Co-partnership Association and chairman of Co-partnership Tenants' Housing Council and Co-partnership Tenants, Limited ; has been an active trade union propagandist ; first returned to Parliament in 1906.

BIRMINGHAM (7).

BORDESLEY (17,358).—No change.

| *Collings, Rt. Hon. J. (U.) | .. | 9,021 |
| Hughes, F. (Lab.) | .. | 3,453 |

| Unionist majority* | .. | 5,568 |

1906.—U., 7,763 ; Lab., 3,976—U. maj., 3.787.
1900.—U. unop.
1895.—U. maj., 3,850 ; 1892, U. maj., 3,722 ; 1886, U. maj., 3,435.

Mr. JESSE COLLINGS, who was born in 1831, has been identified during the major portion of his public life with the social and economic policy popularly known as "three acres and a cow." He sat as Radical member for Ipswich, 1880-1885 ; has been member for the Bordesley Division as Liberal Unionist since 1886 ; was Parliamentary Secretary to the Local Government Board 1886 ; and Under-Secretary of the Home Department, 1895-1902. In March last he met with a severe accident at Charing-cross Station, from which he has not yet recovered.

CENTRAL (9,908).—No change.

| *Parkes, E. (U.) | .. | .. | 6,015 |
| Brampton, Arthur (L.) | .. | 1,711 |

| Unionist majority | .. | 4,304 |

1906.—U., 5,684 ; L., 2,075—U. maj., 3,609.
1900 and 1895, U. unop. ; 1892, U. maj., 4,003 ; 1886, U. unop.

Mr. EBENEZER PARKES has represented the Central Division of Birmingham since 1895. In that year and

4—2

again in 1900 he was returned without a contest. He was born in 1848, and educated at Sheffield. He is an ironmaster and a magistrate for Birmingham. For seven years before being elected to Parliament he served on the Birmingham City Council.

East (15,244).—No change.	
Steel-Maitland, A. D. (U.)	8,460
Stephenson, J. J. (Lab.)	3,958
Unionist majority	4,502

1906.—U., 5,928 ; Lab., 5,343—U. maj., 585.
1900.—U., 4,989 ; L., 2,835 ; U. maj., 2,154.
1895.—U. unop. ; 1892, U. maj. over L., 2,209 ; 1886, U. maj., 789.

Mr. ARTHUR HERBERT DRUMMOND RAMSAY STEEL MAITLAND, who was chosen as Unionist candidate on the resignation of Sir B. Stone, the former member, is the second son of the late Colonel Edward Harris Steel, R.A. ; born in India in 1876, and educated at Rugby and at Balliol College, Oxford, where he had a brilliant career, and took a first class in Moderations, a first class in Classics, a first class in Jurisprudence, and won the Eldon Law Scholarship ; rowed for Oxford in the University Boatrace of 1899 ; elected Fellow of All Souls College in 1900 ; assumed the additional surname of Maitland on his marriage in 1901 with Mary, the only surviving child and heir of Sir James Ramsay Gibson Maitland, of Burnton, Mid Lothian ; has been private secretary (unpaid) to Mr. Austen Chamberlain ; at the last election unsuccessfully contested Rugby.

EDGBASTON (13,383).—No change.	
*Lowe, Sir F. W. (U.)	7,951
Morgan, J. H. (L.)	2,850
Unionist majority	5,101

1906.—U., 7,263 ; L., 3,103—U. maj., 4,160.
1900, 1895, 1892, 1886, U. unop.

SIR FRANCIS LOWE, who was born in Edgbaston in 1852, has been the Parliamentary representative of his birthplace since 1898. He was educated at the Birmingham (King Edward's) Grammar School and London University. He contested the Eastern Division of Birmingham in 1885, and the Harborough Division of Leicestershire in 1892. He received the honour of knighthood in 1905.

NORTH (8,542).—No change.	
*Middlemore, J. T. (U.)	5,189
Dawson, Joseph (L.)	988
Unionist majority	4,201

1906.—U., 5,172 ; L., 1,275—U. maj., 3,897.
1900.—U. unop.
1895.—U. maj., 3,334 ; 1892, U. maj., 2,275 ; 1886, U. unop.

Mr. JOHN THROGMORTON MIDDLEMORE, the son of a Birmingham manufacturer, was born in Edgbaston in 1844 ; was a member of the Birmingham City Council from 1883 until 1892, and has represented North Birmingham since 1899 ; has been a munificent contributor to the Birmingham Art Gallery, and founded and has managed for 36 years homes in Birmingham, allied with the Middlemore Homes in Nova Scotia, for the emigration of destitute children and their training in agriculture in Canada.

SOUTH (11,178).—No change.	
*Morpeth, Viscount (U.)	6,207
Butler, A. E. (L.)	2,476
Unionist majority	3,731

1906.—U., 5,541 ; L., 2,641—U. maj., 2,900.
1900.—U. unop.
1895.—U. maj., 3,583 ; 1892, U. maj., 2,923 ; 1886, U. unop.

VISCOUNT MORPETH, the eldest son of the Earl of Carlisle entered Parliament for his present constituency on the death of Mr. Powell Williams in 1904, after unsuccessful contests in Chester-le-Street, Hexham, and Gateshead. He was educated at Rugby and at Balliol College, was a Militia captain, and served in South Africa in 1902. The London School Board formerly provided him with educational interests, and in Cumberland, where he is D.L. and J.P., he has been associated for several years with the county council, and holds office as alderman.

WEST (12,313).—No change.	
*Chamberlain, Rt. Hon. J. (U.)	

1906.—U., 7,173 ; L., 2,094—U. maj., 5,079.
1900.—U. unop.
1895.—U. maj., 4,278 ; 1892, U. maj. over L., 4,418 ; 1886, U. unop.

Mr. JOSEPH CHAMBERLAIN, now in his 74th year, was the representative of Birmingham from 1876 to 1885, and from 1885 onwards he has sat for the West Division of his adopted city. He filled the offices of President of the Board of Trade and President of the Local Government Board before a divergence of views on the Irish policy of Mr. Gladstone caused his resignation in 1886. In 1895 he joined the Government of the late Lord Salisbury as Colonial Secretary, and in 1903 launched his scheme for the revision of the fiscal policy of the country. The resignation of his office was a preliminary step to a campaign in which he personally explained the proposals that are now regarded as the alternative to the Budget.

BLACKBURN (2) (22,572).—ONE LIBERAL GAIN.	
Barclay, Sir T. (L.)	12,064
*Snowden, P. (Lab.)	11,916
†Cecil, Lord R. (U.F.T.)	9,307
†Bowles, G. Stewart (U.F.T.)	9,112
Liberal majority over Unionist	2,757
Labour majority over Unionist	2,609

1906.—U., 10,291 ; Lab., 10,282 ; U., 8,932 ; L., 8,892—Lab. maj. over U., 1,350.
1900.—U., 11,247 ; U., 9,415 ; Soc. 7,096—U. maj., 2,319.
1895.—U., 9,553 ; U., 9,150 ; L., 6,840—U. maj., 2,310.
1892.—U., 9,265 ; U., 9,046 ; L., 7,272 ; L., 6,694—U. maj. 1,774.
1886.—Two Unionists unop.

SIR THOMAS BARCLAY, born in 1853, was educated in Scotland, France, and Germany ; is a barrister and practises as an international lawyer in Paris ; member of the High Court of Appeal at Brussels of the Congo Free State ; president of the British

Chamber of Commerce in Paris (1899-1900); Examiner in International Law and General Jurisprudence at Oxford University, 1900; was for some time a Correspondent of *The Times* in Paris; took a prominent share in the movement to secure a good understanding between Great Britain and France.

Mr. PHILIP SNOWDEN entered the Inland Revenue Department of the Civil Service in 1888, and during enforced leisure, resulting from a bicycle accident, studied social questions. He was elected to the administrative council of the I.L.P. in 1898; he was appointed chairman in 1903. Unsuccessful contests as a Socialist candidate at Blackburn in 1900, and at Wakefield in 1902, preceded his election for Blackburn in 1906.

BOLTON (2) (21,341).—No change.

*Harwood, G. (L.)	12,275
*Gill, A. H. (Lab.)	11,864
Mattinson, W.. K.C. (U.)	7,479
Ashworth, P. (U.)	7,326
Liberal majority	4,796
Labour majority	4,385

1906.—L., 10,953; Lab., 10,416; U., 6,693—Lab. maj. over U., 3,723.
1900.—One U., one L., unop.
1895.—U., 8,494; L., 8,453; U., 7,901; L., 2,694—maj. of L. elected over defeated U., 552.
1892.—U., 8,429; U., 8,140; L., 7,575; L., 7,536—U. maj., 565.
1886.—U., 7,780; U., 7,668; L., 6,452; L., 6,314—U. maj., 1,216.

Mr. G. HARWOOD, born in 1845, and educated at Chorlton High School and Owens College, Manchester, is the chairman of Richard Harwood and Son, Limited, cotton spinners, Bolton. Along with Dean Stanley, Thomas Hughes, and others, he founded the Church Reform Union, the main object of which was to give the laity a larger power in Church control, and has taken an active share in the proceedings of the Church Congress. He is a barrister and was appointed a member of the Royal Commission on Ecclesiastical Discipline in 1904.

Mr. ALFRED HENRY GILL, who entered Parliament in 1906 as Labour member for Bolton, was born in Rochdale in 1856, and began work by selling newspapers at the age of seven years. When ten years old he obtained employment in a cotton mill, and continued in that occupation for 30 years. He was appointed general secretary of the Bolton Operative Spinners' Association in 1897. He is a member of the Bolton and Manchester Chambers of Commerce, the British Cotton Growing Association, and of the Board of Trade Arbitration Court.

BOSTON (4,037).—UNIONIST GAIN.

Dixon, C. H. (U.)	1,975
Lunn, Dr. H. S. (L.)	1,715
Unionist majority	260

1906.—L., 1,801; U., 1,694—L. maj., 107.
1900.—U., 1,710 L., 1,155—U. maj., 555.
1895.—U. maj., 396; 1892, L. maj., 62; 1886, U. maj., 48.

Mr. CHARLES HARVIE DIXON, a younger son of Mr. Henry Dixon, of Watlington, Oxfordshire, is about 42 years of age and was educated privately; has travelled very extensively; has studied medicine, but occupies his time largely in hunting and farming; has fought the Market Harborough Division of Leicestershire on three occasions.

BRADFORD (3).
CENTRAL (9,848).—No change.

*Robertson, Sir G. (L.)	5,249
Howick, Viscount (U.)	3,608
Liberal majority	1,641

1906.—L., 4,954; U., 3,614—L. maj., 1,340.
1900.—U., 4,634; L., 4,007—U. maj., 627.
1895.—U. maj., 41; 1892, L. maj., 465; 1886, L. maj., 459.

SIR GEORGE SCOTT ROBERTSON, born in 1852, has a long record of distinguished service on the Indian frontier. He joined the Indian Medical Service in 1878, and served through the Afghan campaign of 1879-80; he led, in 1895, the Chitral Mission, in the course of which he was besieged in Chitral Fort by the hill tribes, the thrilling story of which he told in his book "Chitral" (1898); he received the K.C.S.I., three war medals, and other distinctions for his services.

EAST (15,879).—No change.

*Priestley, Sir W. E. B. (L.)	7,709
Browne, J. H. Balfour K.C. (U.)	5,014
Hartley, E. R. (Soc.)	1,740
Liberal majority	2,695

1906.—L., 6,185; U., 4,277; Soc., 3,090—L. maj. over U., 1,908.
1900.—U., 6,121; L., 5,514; Lab., 111—U. maj. over L., 607.
1895.—U. maj., 704; 1892, L. maj., 202; 1886, U. maj., 296.

SIR W. E. B. PRIESTLEY is the managing director of a firm of stuff manufacturers in Bradford. He was born in 1859, and his father sat in Parliament for a time as member for the eastern part of the West Riding of Yorkshire. He headed the poll in the East Division of Bradford in 1906, though he was defeated when he stood as the Liberal candidate for the same constituency at the General Election of 1900.

WEST (14,825).—No change.

*Jowett, F. W. (Lab.)	8,880
Flower, Sir E. (U.)	4,461
Labour majority	4,419

1906.—Lab., 4,957; U., 4,147; L., 3,580—Lab. maj. over U., 810.
1900.—U., 4,990; Lab., 4,949—U. maj., 41.
1895.—U. maj. over L., 465; 1892, L. maj. over U., 253; 1886, L. maj., 1,352.

Mr. F. W. JOWETT, described as a journalist and lecturer, is one of the ablest members of the Parliamentary Labour Party; born in 1864, and worked in Bradford as a mill-hand for many years, afterwards becoming a manufacturer's manager; has taken an active part in local affairs; unsuccessfully contested West Bradford in 1900, and successfully in 1906.

BRIGHTON (2) (21,427).—Two UNIONIST GAINS.

Tryon, Captain G. C. (U.) ..	11,625
Rice, Hon. W. F. (U.) ..	11,567
Evatt, Surgeon-Gen. (L.) ..	7,506
Nickalls, M. (L.)	7,472
Unionist majority ..	4,061

1906.—L., 9,062; L., 8,919; U., 8,188; U., 8,176—L. maj. over U., 874.
1900.—U., 7,858; U., 6,626; Ind. U., 4,693—U. maj. over Ind. U., 1,933.
1895.—U., 7,878; U., 7,490; L., 5,082—U. maj., 2,408.
1892.—U., 7,807; U., 7,134; L., 5,448—U. maj., 1,686.
1886.—U., 5,963; U., 5,875; L., 2,633—U. maj., 3,242.

CAPTAIN GEORGE CLEMENT TRYON, the only son of the late Vice-Admiral Tryon, who went down with his flagship, the Victoria, after collision with the Camperdown, was born in 1871 and educated at Sandhurst; joined the Grenadier Guards and served in the South African War; retired with the rank of captain; is an enthusiastic Volunteer and has travelled widely in the Colonies; his wife is a daughter of Lord Swansea.

The HON. WALTER FITZ-URYAN RICE, son and heir of the sixth Lord Dynevor, was born in 1873, educated at Eton and Christ Church, Oxford, and in 1898 married Lady Margaret Villiers, daughter of the seventh Earl of Jersey. He was assistant private secretary to Lord George Hamilton (Secretary of State for India) 1899-1903 and to the Earl of Selborne, First Lord of the Admiralty, 1903-5; formerly in the Carmarthen Artillery, he retired as captain.

BRISTOL (4).
EAST (15,060).—No change.

*Hobhouse, Right Hon. C. (L.)	6,804
Batten, T. H. (U.)	4,033
Sheppard, F. (Lab.) ..	2,255
Liberal majority over Unionist	2,771
Liberal majority over Labour	4,549

1906.—L., 7,935; U., 3,129—L. maj., 4,806.
1900.—L., 4,979; U., 3,848—L. maj., 1,131.
1895.—L. maj., 2,255; 1892, L. unop.; 1886, L. maj. 1,736.

Mr. C. E. HOBHOUSE, who was born in 1862, was educated at Eton, Christ Church, and the Royal Military Academy, Woolwich. He was lieutenant in the 60th Rifles from 1884 to 1890, but retired from the Army and was returned for East Wilts in 1892. In 1906 he became a Church Estates Commissioner, in 1907 he was appointed Under-Secretary for India, going out as chairman of the Royal Commission on Indian Decentralization after the withdrawal of Sir H. Primrose, and in 1908 was appointed Financial Secretary to the Treasury.

NORTH (13,989).—No change.

*Birrell, Right Hon. A. (L.) ..	6,805
Woods, M. H. (U.) ..	5,459
Liberal majority ..	1,346

1906.—L., 6,953; U., 4,011—L. maj., 2,942.
1900.—U., 4,936; L., 4,182—U. maj., 754.
1895.—U. maj., 238; 1892, L. maj., 345; 1886, U. maj., 850.

Mr. BIRRELL, who was successively President of the Board of Education and Chief Secretary to the Lord Lieutenant of Ireland in the course of the last Parliament, was born near Liverpool in 1850. He was educated at Amersham Hall School and Trinity Hall, Cambridge, and was called to the Bar in 1875. He is a brilliant essayist, and is the author of a number of biographical and legal works. In 1889 he was elected member for West Fife, and in the General Election in 1900 was an unsuccessful candidate for North-East Manchester. He re-entered Parliament as the representative of North Bristol in 1906.

SOUTH (16,171).—No change.

*Davies, Sir W. H. (L.) ..	7,281
Chatterton, H. (U.) ..	7,010
Liberal majority ..	271

1906.—L., 7,964; U., 5,272—L. maj., 2,692.
1900.—U., 5,470; L., 4,859—U. maj., 611.
1895.—U. maj., 759; 1892, U. maj., 548; 1886, U. maj., 1,024.

SIR W. HOWELL DAVIES is engaged in the leather trade, and has had much municipal experience. In 1895 he was Mayor of Bristol, and has been president of the local chamber of commerce. He is chairman of the Bristol Docks Committee and of the Bristol Finance Committee, and for more than 20 years he has taken a leading part in the political life of Bristol. He was born in 1851.

WEST (10,127).—No change.

*Gibbs, Lieut.-Col. G. A. (U.)	5,159
Saise, Dr. T. J. (L.) ..	3,881
Unionist majority ..	1,278

1906.—U., 4,267; L., 3,902—U. maj., 365.
1900.—U. unop.
1895.—U. maj., 1,973; 1892, U. unop.; 1886, U. maj., 2,018.

LIEUT.-COLONEL GEORGE A. GIBBS was born in 1873, and educated at Eton and Christ Church, Oxford. He has travelled in Europe and in the East; served in the South African war with the North Somerset Company of Imperial Yeomanry, of which he is

Lieut.-Colonel, and was present at the capture of Pretoria (medal and four clasps). In 1901 he married the eldest daughter of Mr. Walter Long.

BURNLEY (16,992).—Unionist Gain.

Arbuthnot, G. A. (U.)	5,776
*Maddison, F. (L.)..	5,681
Hyndman, H. M. (Soc.) ..	4,948
Unionist majority over Liberal	95

1906.—L., 5,288 ; U., 4,964 ; Lab., 4,932—L. maj. over U., 324.
1900—U., 6,737 ; L., 6,173—U. maj., 564.
1895.—L. maj. over U., 321 ; 1892—L. maj., 1,415 ; 1886— U. maj., 43.

Mr. Gerald Archibald Arbuthnot was born in 1872 and was educated privately and in his Majesty's ship Britannia. From 1887 to 1891 he was a midshipman in the Royal Navy. For nearly 15 years he was private secretary to Mr. Walter Long when he filled the offices of President of the Board of Agriculture, President of the Local Government Board, and Chief Secretary for Ireland.

BURY (LANCS.) (9,657).—No change.

*Toulmin, G. (L.) ..	4,866
Hartley, E. L. (U.) ..	4,258
Liberal majority ..	608

1906.—L., 4,626 ; U., 3,499—L. maj., 1,127.
1900.—U., 4,132 ; L., 3,283—U. maj., 849.
1895.—U. maj., 675 ; 1892—U. maj., 829 ; 1886—U. unop.

Mr. George Toulmin unsuccessfully contested Bury in 1900, but turned the position in 1902 and won again in 1906. He was educated in Preston, in the affairs of which he has taken a prominent part since. He is a newspaper proprietor, and a J.P. for Preston and the county of Lancaster.

BURY ST. EDMUNDS (2,817).—No change.

*Guinness, Hon. W. E. (U.)

By-election, 1907.—U., 1,631 ; L., 741—U. maj., 890.
1906.—U., 1,481 ; L., 1,047—U. maj., 434.
1900.—U. unop.
1895.—U. unop. ; 1892, U. maj., 404 ; 1886, U. maj., 335.

Mr. Walter Edward Guinness, third son of Viscount Iveagh, was born in 1880, and educated at Eton. He served in South Africa as captain in the Imperial Yeomanry, was wounded, and was mentioned in despatches. He contested the Stowmarket Division in the Unionist interest in 1906, and was returned for Bury St. Edmunds in 1907.

CAMBRIDGE (9,392).—Unionist Gain.

Paget, A. H. (U.)	4,667
*Buckmaster, S. O., K.C. (L.)	4,081
Unionist majority ..	586

1906.—L., 4,232 ; U., 3,924—L. maj., 308.
1900.—U. unop.
1895.—U. maj., 654 ; 1892, U. maj., 255 ; 1886, U. maj., 458.

Mr. Almeric Hugh Paget was born in 1861, the youngest son of Lord Alfred Henry Paget ; worked for some years in the fitting shop of the Midland Railway at Derby ; emigrated to the United States and worked as a day labourer, cowboy, and carrier in the Far West ; afterwards engaged in successful railway enterprises and amassed a fortune ; married, in 1895, a daughter of Mr. W. C. Whitney, formerly Secretary of the United States Navy.

CANTERBURY (3,836).—No change.

*Heaton, J. Henniker (U.) ..	1,371
Goldney, F. B. (Ind. U.) ..	1,350
Woodcock, W. D. (L.) ..	815
Unionist majority over Independent Unionist	21
Unionist majority over Liberal	556

1906 —U., 2,210 ; L., 1,262—U. maj., 948.
1900.—1895, 1892, and 1886, U. unop.

Mr. John Henniker Heaton has represented Canterbury since 1885, and is the author of the scheme of Imperial Penny Postage. Numerous other postal reforms stand to his credit. He was born in 1845, and when 17 years of age went to Australia, where he was engaged for some time in pastoral pursuits. He is a landowner in Australia, a part-owner of several Australian newspapers, and the author of " The Australian Dictionary of Dates and Men of the Time," and of a work on " Australian Aborigines." He has been presented with the Freedom of the City of London and of Canterbury.

CARLISLE (7,456).—No change.

Denman, Hon. R. D. (L.) ..	3,270
Walsh, V. Hussey (U.) ..	2,815
Bannington, A. C. (Soc.)	777
Liberal majority ..	455

1906.—L. unop.
By-election, 1905.—L., 3,616 ; U., 2,586—L. maj., 1,030.
1900.—L. unop.
1895.—L. maj., 314 ; 1892, L. maj., 143 ; 1886, L. maj., 293.

The Hon. R. D. Denman, brother of Lord Denman, was born in 1876, and educated at Westminster School, and, after an interval spent in business, at Balliol College, Oxford, where he took honours in history and won two University essay prizes ; leaving the University, he returned to the City and devoted himself to the business of underwriting at Lloyd's ; is a director of the Marine and General Mutual Life Assurance Society ; married, in 1904, the only daughter of Sir Thomas Sutherland, chairman of the P. and O. Steamship Company.

CHATHAM (15,799).—Unionist Gain.

Hohler, G. F., K.C. (U.) ..	7,411
*Jenkins, J. H. (Lab.) ..	6,130
Unionist majority ..	1,281

1903.—Lab., 6,692 ; U., 4,020—Lab. maj., 2,672.
1900.—U., unop.
1895.—U. maj., 583 ; 1892, U. maj., 377 ; 1886, U. maj., 765.

Mr. Gerald Fitzroy Hohler, K.C., is a barrister practising on the South-Eastern Circuit. He was called to the Bar, Inner Temple, 1888, and became K.C. in 1906.

CHELTENHAM (8,353).—UNIONIST GAIN.

Duncannon, Viscount (U.)	3,988
Mathias, R.(L.)	3,850
Unionist majority	138

1906.—L., 3,910; U., 3,509—L. maj., 401.
1900.—U. unop.; 1895, U. maj. over L., 469; 1892, U. maj., 631; 1886, U. maj., 1,063.

VISCOUNT DUNCANNON, son of the Earl of Bessborough, was born in 1880 and educated at Harrow and Trinity College, Cambridge. He was called to the Bar by the Inner Temple in 1903, and has served as lieutenant in the Imperial Yeomanry. In 1906 he contested Carmarthen as a Unionist, and, as a Municipal Reformer, has represented East Marylebone on the London County Council since 1907.

CHESTER (8,102).—UNIONIST GAIN.

Yerburgh, R. (U.)	3,978
Paul, E. (L.)	3,776
Unionist majority	202

1906.—L., 3,524; U., 3,477—L. maj. 47.
1900.—U., 3,303; L., 2,574—U. maj., 729.
1895.—U. unop.; 1892, U. maj., 620; 1886, U. maj., 66.

Mr. ROBERT ARMSTRONG YERBURGH was the Unionist member for Chester from 1886 until 1906, after having contested the borough unsuccessfully in November, 1885. He is the third son of the Rev. Richard Yerburgh, vicar of Sleaford, Lincolnshire, and was born in 1853. He was educated at Rossall, Harrow, and University College, Oxford, and was called to the Bar (Middle Temple) 1880, and went the Northern Circuit. He has been president of the Navy League since 1900, and is president also of the Agricultural Organization Society and the Urban Co-operative Banks Association.

CHRISTCHURCH (10,991).—UNIONIST GAIN.

Croft, H. Page (U.)	5,538
*Allen, A. A. (L.)	4,807
Unionist majority	731

1906.—L., 4,634; U., 4,067—L. maj., 567.
1900.—U., 3,411; L., 3,408—U. maj., 3.
1895.—U. maj., 84; 1892, U. maj., 203; 1886, U. maj., 239.

Mr. HENRY PAGE CROFT, who unsuccessfully contested Lincoln in 1906, is a captain of the 1st Batt. Hertfordshire regiment, and was educated at Eton, Shrewsbury, and Trinity Hall, Cambridge; is a rowing man, and has twice won the Thames Cup at Henley; organized the Tariff Reform movement in Hertfordshire, forming 13 branches, and is on the executive committee of the Tariff Reform League.

COLCHESTER (7,226).—UNIONIST GAIN.

Evans, L. W. (U.)	3,717
Thomson, F. W. (L.)	2,926
Unionist majority	791

1906.—L., 3,122; U., 2,812—L. maj., 310.
1900.—L., 2,548; U., 2,274—L. maj., 274.
1895.—L., 205; 1892, U., 61; 1886, U., 295.

Mr. L. WORTHINGTON EVANS is senior partner of Worthington Evans, Dauncy, and Co., solicitors, London, was appointed by the Court as special manager to "nurse" and realize the assets of the Whitaker Wright companies, after the schemes for which they were promoted had come to grief; was member of the Board of Trade Committee for reform of the Company Law, 1905, and is the author of "Notes on the Companies Act, 1900," and joint author of a larger work on the same subject; born in 1868 and educated at Eastbourne College.

COVENTRY (16,463).—UNIONIST GAIN.

Foster, J. Kenneth (U.)	7,369
Hocking, Silas K. (L.)	7,153
Unionist majority	216

1906.—L., 6,554; U., 5,462—L. maj., 1,092.
1900.—U., 5,257; L., 4,188—U. maj., 1,069.
1895.—U. maj., 350; 1892, L. maj., 143; 1886, U. maj., 405.

Mr. J. KENNETH FOSTER, a cousin of Mr. Philip Foster, who sits for the Stratford-on-Avon Division of Warwickshire, belongs to a West Riding family of woollen manufacturers, is a strong Tariff Reformer, and unsuccessfully contested the city at the last General Election.

DARLINGTON (10,997).—LIBERAL GAIN.

Lincoln, J. T. T. (L.)	4,815
*Pease, H. Pike (U.)	4,786
Liberal majority	29

1906.—U., 4,375; Lab., 4,087—U. maj., 288.
1900.—U. unop.
1895.—U. maj., 657; 1892, L. maj., 56; 1882, L. maj., 57.

Mr. J. T. T. LINCOLN was born at Paka, on the banks of the Danube. In 1892 he removed to Budapest and studied in a Roman Catholic college. In 1898 he went to Montreal, and studied theology in the Presbyterian college there. In 1903 he came to England, and for 13 months acted as curate of the Church of England in a Kentish village. He afterwards gave up his curacy and went to London, where he acted as secretary to Mr. B. Seebohm Rowntree, of York. Mr. Lincoln is a naturalized British subject.

DERBY (2) (20,113).—No change.

*Roe, Sir T. (L.)	10,343
Thomas, J. H. (Lab.)	10,189
Beck, A. E. (U.)	8,038
Page, A. (U.)	7,953
Liberal majority	2,305
Labour majority	2,151

1906.—Lab., 10,361; L., 10,239; U., 6,421; U., 6,409—L. maj. over U., 3,818.
1900.—L., 7,922; Lab., 7,640; U., 7,397; U., 6,775—Lab. maj., 243.
1895.—U., 7,907; U., 7,076; L., 6,785; L., 6,475—U. maj., 291.
1892.—L., 7,507; L., 7,389; U., 5,546; U., 5,363—L. maj., 1,843.
1886.—L., 6,571; L., 6,431; U., 4,346—L. maj., 2,085.

SIR THOMAS ROE has been associated with Derby throughout a long life. He was born there in 1832, educated at local schools, is chairman of Roe's Timber Company (Limited), of Derby, and is an alderman and magistrate for the borough, of which he was mayor in 1867-8 and 1896-7. He sat in Parliament as a representative of Derby from 1883 until 1895, and after having been defeated at the General Election in the latter year was re-elected in 1900 and again in 1906. He received a knighthood in 1894.

Mr. J. H. THOMAS emigrated in early life from Cornwall to Australia, and at the time of the mining strike at Broken Hill in 1890 he was president of the Amalgamated Miners' Association and a member of the Strike Defence Committee. His prominence then led to his selection afterwards as a Labour candidate for the State Parliament of New South Wales, in which he represented Alma from 1894 to 1901. Afterwards, as a member of the House of Representatives, he made a special study of postal and shipping questions; and he established a reputation as a chess player.

DEVONPORT (2) (12,125).—Two UNIONIST GAINS.

Jackson, Sir J. (U.)	5,658
Kinloch-Cooke, Sir C. (U.) ..	5,286
*Benn, Sir J. W. (L.) ..	5,146
Lithgow, S. (L.)	5,140
Unionist majority ..	140

1906.—L., 6,923; L., 6,527; U., 5,239; U., 5,080—L. maj. over U. 1,288.
1900.—L., 3,626; L., 3,538; U., 3,458; U., 3,394—L. maj., 80.
1895.—L., 3,570; L., 3,511; U., 3,303; U., 3,263—L. maj., 208.
1892.—L., 3,354; L., 3,325; U., 3,012; U., 2,972—L. maj., 313.
1886.—U., 2,954; U., 2,943; L., 1,963; L., 1,918—U. maj., 980.

SIR JOHN JACKSON, who was born at York in 1851, and educated in that city and at the University of Edinburgh, is a large contractor for public works. Among his undertakings are the last section of the Manchester Ship Canal, the foundations of the Tower Bridge, Dover Harbour, the Admiralty docks at Devonport, the Admiralty Harbour, Simon's Bay, South Africa, Singapore Harbour, and the Tyne breakwater. He was a member of the Royal Commission to inquire into the war in South Africa, and was knighted in 1895.

SIR CLEMENT KINLOCH-COOKE, who was educated at Brighton College and St. John's College, Cambridge (Mathematical and Law Tripos), was called to the Bar in 1883, and has filled many legal and educational offices. He was legal adviser to the House of Lords' Sweating Commission, private secretary to Lord Dunraven as Under-Secretary for the Colonies, examiner under the Civil Service Commission for factory inspectorships, and has been associated with newspapers and other periodical publications as editor. In the midst of varied duties he has found time for extensive travel and for biographical and other forms of authorship.

DEWSBURY (14,389).—No change.

*Runciman, Rt. Hon. W. (L.)	7,882
Dent, B. (U.)	4,747
Liberal majority ..	3,135

By-election, 1908.—L., 5,594; U., 4,078; Lab., 2,446—L. maj. over U., 1,516.
1906.—L., 6,764; U., 2,959; Lab., 2,629—L. maj. over U., 3,805.
1900.—L., 6,045; U., 3,897—L. maj., 2,148.
1895.—L. maj. over U., 1,504; 1892, L. maj., 2,089; 1886, L. maj., 2,359.

Mr. WALTER RUNCIMAN was born in 1870, and is the only son of Sir Walter Runciman, shipowner, of Newcastle and London. He was educated at Trinity College, Cambridge. He first entered Parliament in 1899 for Oldham, but at the General Election of 1900 Mr. Churchill, now his colleague, won the seat from him. Mr. Runciman returned to the House of Commons in 1902 as member for Dewsbury. On the formation of Sir H. Campbell-Bannerman's Government he was appointed Parliamentary Secretary to the Local Government Board; in 1907 he became Financial Secretary to the Treasury, and in the following year he entered the Cabinet as President of the Board of Education.

DOVER (6,247).—No change.

*Wyndham, Rt. Hon. G. (U.)	3,330
Bradley, A. M. (L.)	1,572
Unionist majority ..	1,758

1906.—U., 3,269; L., 1,705—U. maj., 1,564.
1900.—U. unop.
1895.—U. unop.; 1892, U. maj., 1,253; 1886, U. unop.

Mr. GEORGE WYNDHAM was born in London in 1863, and was educated at Eton and Sandhurst. He was a lieutenant in the 1st Battalion Coldstream Guards, 1883-87, and served in the Suakin campaign and Cyprus. He was private secretary to Mr. A. J. Balfour, 1887-92; was elected member for Dover, 1889, and has represented the borough since; was Under-Secretary for War, 1898-1900, and Chief Secretary for Ireland, 1900-1905. In 1903 he had charge of the Irish Land Act in the Commons.

DUDLEY (17,483).—No change.

*Hooper, A. G. (L.)	8,342
Griffith-Boscawen, Major (U.)	8,155
Liberal majority ..	187

1906.—L., 8,296; U., 7,542—L. maj., 754.
1900.—U., 6,461; L., 5,876—U. maj., 585.
1895.—U. maj., 741; 1892, U. maj., 1,049; 1886, U. maj., 1,930

Mr. ARTHUR GEORGE HOOPER was born in Birmingham in 1857, and, adopting the profession of solicitor, acquired a large practice in his native town and the Midlands. He has served on the Dudley Town Council. He is an ardent supporter of the Congregational Union.

DURHAM (2,601).—No change.

*Hills, J. W. (U.)

1906.—U., 1,313; U.F.T., 880—U. maj., 433.
1900.—U., 1,250; L., 781—U. maj., 469.
1895.—L. maj., 1; 1892, L. maj., 75; 1886, U. maj., 274.

Mr. JOHN WALLER HILLS was born in London in 1867, and educated at Eton and Balliol College, Oxford. He is a solicitor and a member of the firm of Hills, Godfrey, and Halsey.

EXETER (10,383).—UNIONIST GAIN.

Duke, H. E., K.C. (U.) ..	4,902
St. Maur, H. (L.)	4,876
Unionist majority ..	26

1906.—L., 4,469; U., 4,314—L. maj., 85.
1900.—U., 4,001; L., 3,388—U. maj., 613.
1895.—U. maj., 494; 1892, U. maj., 555; 1886, U. maj., 343.

Mr. HENRY EDWARD DUKE, K.C., was born near Plymouth in 1855. He was called to the Bar at Gray's Inn in 1885, joining the Western Circuit. In 1899 he became a Queen's Counsel and was elected a Bencher of his Inn, and was subsequently appointed Recorder of Plymouth and Devonport. He sat for Plymouth from 1900 to 1906.

GATESHEAD (19,138).—LIBERAL GAIN FROM LABOUR.

Elverston, H. (L.)	6,800
Doyle, N. Grattan (U.)	6,323
*Johnson, J. (Lab.)	3,572
Liberal majority over Unionist	477
Liberal majority over Labour	3,228

1906.—Lab., 9,651 ; U., 5,126—Lab. maj., 4,525.
1900.—L., 6,657 ; U., 5,711—L. maj., 946.
1895.—L. maj., 483 ; 1892, L. maj., 293 ; 1886, L. unop.

Mr. HAROLD ELVERSTON, who was born in 1866, is owner and editor of an insurance publication. He is a member of the Manchester City Council, and was a founder of the Liberal Federation. Mr. Elverston unsuccessfully contested Worcester City at the by-election in 1908.

GLOUCESTER (8,475).—UNIONIST GAIN.

Terrell, H., K.C. (U.)	4,109
*Rea, Rt. Hon. Russell (L.)	3,983
Unionist majority	126

1906.—L., 3,921 ; U., 3,619—L. maj., 302.
1900.—L., 3,267 ; U., 3,044—L. maj., 223.
1895.—U. maj., 473 ; 1892, L. maj., 86 ; 1882, L. maj., 195.

Mr. HENRY TERRELL, K.C., was born in 1856 and is a son of the late Judge Terrell. He was called to the Bar at the Middle Temple in 1882, became a Queen's Counsel in 1897, and was made a Bencher in 1904.

GRANTHAM (3,647).—No change.

*Priestley, A. (L.)	1,848
Smyth,Capt. G. H. Skeffington (U.)	1,703
Liberal majority	145

1906.—L., 1,663 ; U., 1,554—L. maj., 109.
1900.—L., 1,347 ; U., 1,309—L. maj., 38.
1895.—U. maj., 340 ; 1892, U. maj., 33 ; 1886, U. maj., 36.

Mr. ARTHUR PRIESTLEY was born in 1864, the son of Mr. Briggs Priestley, of Bradford, who formerly represented the Pudsey Division. He contested the Stamford Division on three occasions and has sat for Grantham since 1900.

GRAVESEND (6,733).—No change.

*Parker, Sir G. (U.)	3,286
Jenkins, S. R. (L.)	2,612
Unionist majority	674

1906.—U., 3,102 ; L., 1,413 ; Lab., 873—U. maj. over L., 1,689.
1900.—U., 2,542 ; L., 1,804—U. maj., 738.
1895.—U. maj., 1,187 ; 1892, U. maj., 751 ; 1886, U. maj., 508.

SIR GILBERT PARKER was born in Canada in 1862, and was educated at Trinity College, Toronto (D.C.L.) ; was associate-editor of the *Sydney Morning Herald*, 1886 ; has travelled extensively, and is known to a wide public as a dramatist and novelist ; since 1900 has represented Gravesend as a Unionist.

GREAT GRIMSBY (18,029).—LIBERAL GAIN.

Wing, T. (L.)	7,772
*Doughty, Sir G. (U.)	7,450
Liberal majority	322

1906.—U., 6,349 ; L., 4,040 ; Lab., 2,248—U. maj over L., 2,309.
1900.—U. unop.
1895.—U. maj., 181 ; 1892, L. maj., 636 ; 1886, U. maj., 333.

Mr. THOMAS HENRY WING, the son of a fancy goods dealer, was born at Hull in 1853 ; first assisted his father in business, and then became a commercial traveller for a firm of printers, stationers, and fancy goods importers in the North of England ; identified himself with the Labour Party, and advocated the municipalization of the Hull tramway and docks systems ; removed to Grimsby, and associated himself with the municipal and social life of the town ; was for 14 years Parliamentary agent of the Commercial Travellers' Association ; now resides at Selby.

GREAT YARMOUTH (9,571).—No change.

*Fell, A. (U.)	4,459
Platt, Major E. (L.)	3,998
Unionist majority	461

1906.—U., 4,071 ; L., 3,835—U. maj., 236.
1900.—U. unop.
1895.—U. maj., 635 ; 1892, L. maj., 268 ; 1886, U. maj., 966.

Mr. ARTHUR FELL was born in New Zealand in 1850, and graduated at St. John's College, Oxford. He was admitted a solicitor in 1874, and was partner in the firm of Hare and Fell, agents to the Treasury solicitors. He is the author of many pamphlets on financial subjects and foreign competition in trade, written from the point of view of a Protectionist.

HALIFAX (2) (15,528).—No change.

*Whitley, J. H. (L.)	9,504
*Parker, J. (Lab.)	9,093
Galbraith, J. F. W. (U.)	4,754
Liberal majority	4,750
Labour majority	4,339

1906.—L., 9,354 ; Lab., 8,937 ; U., 5,041—Lab. maj. over U. 3,896.
1900.—U., 5,931 ; L., 5,543 ; L., 5,325 ; Lab., 3,276—U. maj. over defeated L., 606.
1895.—U., 5,475 ; L., 5,085 ; L., 4,283 ; Lab., 3,818—U. maj. over defeated L., 1,192.
1892.—L., 6,481 ; L., 6,361 ; U., 4,663—L. maj., 1,698.
1886.—L., 5,427 ; L., 5,381 ; U., 3,612—L. maj., 1,769.

Mr. JOHN HENRY WHITLEY has represented Halifax since 1900. Senior partner in the firm of S. Whitley and Co., cotton spinners, he was educated at Clifton College and London University. In 1907 he was appointed a Junior Lord of the Treasury, when he was re-elected for Halifax without opposition.

Mr. JAMES PARKER was born in Lincolnshire in 1863. The greater part of his life has been spent in Yorkshire. He was occupied for some time as a gasworker and general labourer, and later became the paid secretary of a branch of the Independent Labour Party. He has served for nine years as a member of the Halifax Borough Council. He was unsuccessful in his candidature for the representation of the borough in Parliament in 1900, but was elected with Mr. Whitley in 1906.

HANLEY (16,543).—No change.
*Edwards, E (Lab.)	9,199
Rittner, G. H. (U.)	5,202
Labour majority	3,997

1906.—Lab., 9,183 ; U., 4,287—Lab. maj., 4,896.
1900.—U., 6,586 ; L., 5,944—U. maj., 642.
1895.—L. maj., 286 ; 1892, L. maj., 1,832 ; 1886, L. unop.

Mr. ENOCH EDWARDS, who began work as a boy in a coal mine, was appointed treasurer of the North Staffordshire Miners' Association in 1870 and secretary in 1877. Removing to Burslem in 1884 he was there elected to the School Board and the town council, and afterwards became Mayor. He has been president of the Midland Miners' Association, and is president of the Miners' Federation of Great Britain and a member of the Staffordshire County Council.

HARTLEPOOL (13,708).—No change.
*Furness, Sir C. (L.)	6,531
Gritten, W. G. H. (U.)	5,754
Liberal majority	777

1906.—L. unop.
1900.—L., 6,491 ; U., 4,612 —L. maj., 1,879.
1895.—U. maj., 81 ; 1892, L. maj., 76 ; 1886, U. maj., 912.

SIR CHRISTOPHER FURNESS is a great captain of industry in the North of England ; head of Furness, Withy, and Co., and the Furness Line of steamers, and connected with shipbuilding, iron, and colliery works which give employment to thousands of men and boys ; established the " Furness Pension Fund " of £20,000 for aged seamen ; instituted, in 1908, a system of co-partnership in his shipbuilding works ; is also a great landowner, though he disposed of over 10,000 acres in Wiltshire in 1909 ; questions the wisdom of the policy which excludes men of affairs from the headship of State departments ; was knighted in 1895.

HASTINGS (9,027).—No change.
*Du Cros, Arthur (U.)	4,634
Tweedy-Smith, R. (L.)	3,833
Unionist majority	801

By-election, 1908.—U., 4,495 ; L., 3,477—U. maj., 1,018.
1906.—U., 4,348 ; L., 3,935—U. maj., 413.
1900.—L., 3,399 ; U., 3,191—L. maj., 208.
1895.—U. maj., 342 ; 1892, U. maj., 449 ; 1886, U. maj., 535.

Mr. ARTHUR PHILIP DU CROS was born in Dublin in 1871, and is the son of Mr. W. H. Du Cros, whom he succeeded in the representation of Hastings in 1908. He was educated privately, and is managing director of the Dunlop Pneumatic Tyre Company (Limited). He unsuccessfully contested Bow and Bromley in 1906.

HEREFORD (4,066).—No change.
*Arkwright, J. S. (U.)	2,320
Thomas, Lewis, K.C. (L.)	1,533
Unionist majority	787

1906.—U., 1,934 ; L., 1,692—U. maj., 242.
1900.—U. unop.
1895.—U. maj., 340 ; 1892, L. maj., 127 ; 1886, U. maj., 265.

Mr. JOHN STANHOPE ARKWRIGHT has represented Hereford since 1900, and was Parliamentary private secretary to Mr. Gerald Balfour ; born in 1872, educated at Eton and Christ Church, Oxford, and called to the Bar ; is interested in county affairs.

HUDDERSFIELD (19,021).—No change.
*Sherwell, A. J. (L.)	7,158
Snell, H. (Lab.)	5,686
Smith, Harold (U.)	5,153
Liberal majority over Labour	1,472
Liberal majority over Unionist	2,005

By-election, 1906.—L., 5,762 ; Lab., 5,422 ; U., 4,844—L. maj., over U., 918.
1906.—L., 6,302 ; Lab., 5,813 ; U., 4,391—L. maj. over Lab. 489.
1900.—L., 7,896 ; U., 6,831—L. maj., 1,065.
1895.—L. maj. over U., 887 ; 1892, L. maj., 261 ; 1886, L. maj., 184.

Mr. ARTHUR J. SHERWELL is an author who has travelled widely and devoted much attention to the study of social problems. He was associated in investigations which preceded the publication of Mr. Seebohm Rowntree's book on poverty and is hon. secretary of the Temperance Legislation League, a Fellow of the Royal Statistical Society, and a member of the Sociological Society.

HULL (3).
CENTRAL (8,181).—No change.
*King, Sir H. S. (U.)	3,606
Aske, Dr. R. W. (L.)	3,586
Unionist majority	20

1906.—U., 4,345 ; L., 3,167 ; U. maj., 1,178.
1900.—U., 5,257 ; L., 2,465—U. maj., 2,792.
1895.—U. maj., 1,961 ; 1892, U. maj., 476 ; 1886, U. maj., 1,107.

SIR HENRY SEYMOUR KING, K.C.I.E., was born in 1852, and received his education at Charterhouse and Balliol College, Oxford. He is a banker and head of the firm of Henry S. King and Co., London ; King, King, and Co., Bombay ; and King, Hamilton, and Co., Calcutta. He was Mayor of Kensington in 1901 and 1902, and has represented Central Hull since 1885; received a knighthood in 1892.

EAST (14,687).—No change.
*Ferens, T. R. (L.)	7,627
Montefiore, R. M. Sebag (U.)	5,691
Liberal majority	1,936

1906.—L., 6,881 ; U., 4,519—L. maj., 2,362.
1900.—U., 5,264 ; L., 4,428—U. maj., 836.
1895.—U. maj., 153 ; 1892, L. maj., 832 ; 1886, U. maj., 37.

Mr. THOMAS R. FERENS, who won East Hull for the Liberals in 1906, is managing director of Rickett and Sons (Limited), starch and blue manufacturers ; is also director of Star Life Assurance Society ; has been president of Hull Chamber of Commerce, and is a member of the Council of Associated Chambers of Commerce ; finds time, in addition to his business

WEST (22,609).—No change.

*Wilson, Hon. Guy (L.)	..	10,005
Sherburn, Sir J. (U.)	..	8,288
Liberal majority	..	1,717

By-election, 1907.—L., 5,623 ; U., 5,382 ; Lab., 4,512—L. maj. over U., 241.
1906.—L., 8,652 ; U., 6,405—L. maj., 2,247.
1900.—L., 6,364 ; U., 4,419—L. maj., 1,945.
1895.—L. maj., 5,237 ; 1892, L. maj., 2,783 ; 1886, L. maj., 1,578.

The Hon. Guy Greville Wilson, who was born in 1877 and educated at Eton College, is the brother of Lord Nunburnholme. He entered the 11th Hussars in 1898, and during the South African War was employed with Damant's Horse, and took part in operations in the Transvaal, Orange River Colony, and Cape Colony, being mentioned in despatches and receiving the D.S.O. and the Queen's medal with five clasps. He is a director of Earle's Shipbuilding Company, and secured the representation of West Hull at a by-election in 1907.

HYTHE (6,541).—No change.

*Sassoon, Sir E. (U.)	..	3,746
Hall, W. Clarke (L.)	..	1,954
Unionist majority	..	1,792

1906.—U., 3,246 ; L., 2,347—U. maj., 899.
1900.—U. unop.
1895.—U. maj., 463 ; 1892 and 1886, U. unop.

Sir Edward Albert Sassoon, Bt., was born in 1856, and is the second baronet. He is President of the Folkestone Chamber of Commerce and has served in the Middlesex Yeomanry. He has represented Hythe since 1899.

IPSWICH (2) (12,641).—No change.

*Goddard, Sir D. F. (L.)	..	6,120
Horne, C. Silvester (L.)	..	5,958
Churchman, A. C. (U.)	..	5,690
Burton, B. H. (U.)	..	5,645
Liberal majority	..	268

1906.—L., 6,396 ; L., 6,290 ; U., 4,591 ; U., 4,232—L. maj., 1,699.
1900.—L., 4,557 ; U., 4,527 ; L., 4,283 ; U., 4,207—majority of elected U. over L. defeated, 244.
1895.—L., 4,396 ; U., 4,293 ; L., 4,250 ; U., 4,219—majority of elected U. over L. defeated, 43.
1892.—U., 4,350 ; U., 4,277 ; L., 4,054 ; L., 3,888—U. maj., 223.
1886.—U., 3,846 ; U., 3,838 ; L., 3,386 ; L., 3,334—U. maj., 452.

Sir Daniel Ford Goddard has been associated with Ipswich throughout his life, and has represented the borough since 1895. An associate member of the Institute of Civil Engineers, he succeeded his father as engineer and secretary to the Ipswich Gas Company, of which he subsequently became chairman, and was mayor of the city in 1891. He founded and built the Ipswich Social Settlement.

Mr. C. Silvester Horne, who graduated at Glasgow University and afterwards studied theology at Mansfield College, Oxford, is one of the leaders of the Free Churches of the Congregationalist denomination, and in addition to volumes of sermons has published a history of the Free Churches and a story of the London Missionary Society. He is best known for his work in connexion with Whitefield's Mission in Tottenham-court-road, where politics and the discussion of social subjects have been freely mingled with religious activities for some years. He married Miss Katherine Cozens-Hardy, daughter of the Master of the Rolls.

KIDDERMINSTER (4,579).—Unionist Gain.

Knight, Captain E. (U.)	..	2,350
Fraser, Sir E. (L.)	..	1,983
Unionist majority	..	367

1906.—L., 2,354 ; U., 2,083—L. maj., 271.
1900.—U., 1,950 ; L., 1,804—U. maj., 146.
1895.—U. maj., 295 ; 1892, U. maj., 265 ; 1886, U. maj., 285.

Captain Eric Knight, of Wolverley, Kidderminster, is the son of the late Captain Knight, of the 20th Regt. and was born in 1864 ; engaged in early life in ranching in Canada ; on returning to England held a commission in the 1st V.B. Worcestershire Regt., and subsequently joined the Imperial Yeomanry of that county, and served with Lord Methuen's column in Cape Colony, the Orange Free State, and the Transvaal ; succeeded to the property of his late uncle, Colonel Sir F. Wynn Knight, who represented West Worcestershire for many years ; unsuccessfully opposed Mr. C. B. Harmsworth in Mid Worcestershire at the last election.

KING'S LYNN (3,755).—Liberal Gain.

Bowles, T. (L.) G.	..	1,900
Cadogan, Hon. E. (U.)	..	1,638
Liberal majority	..	262

1906.—L., 1,506 ; U.F.T., 1,164 ; U., 772—L. maj. over U.F.T. 342.
1900.—U., 1,499 ; L., 1,332—U. maj., 167.
1895.—U. maj., 69 ; 1892, U. maj., 11 ; 1886, U. maj., 271.

Mr. Thomas Gibson Bowles, who contested King's Lynn as a Liberal while his son, Mr. G. S. Bowles, fought at Blackburn in the Unionist interest, sat for the borough as a Unionist from 1892 to 1906 ; as a Free Trade candidate he opposed Mr. Balfour in the City of London in February, 1906 ; formally seceded from the party, and, as a Liberal, unsuccessfully contested the Central Division of Glasgow at the by-election in March, 1909 ; was at one time in the Civil Service, has been a journalist and newspaper proprietor, and holds a master mariner's certificate ; born in 1843.

LEEDS (5).
CENTRAL (8,369).—No change.

*Armitage, R. (L.)	..	3,987
Gordon, J. (U.)	..	3,366
Liberal majority	..	621

1906.—L., 4,188 ; U., 3,119—L. maj., 1,069.
1900.—U., 4,144 ; L., 3,042—U. maj., 1,102.
1895.—U. maj., 654 ; 1892, U. maj., 113 ; 1886, U. maj., 13.

Mr. Robert Armitage has been associated with municipal administration in Leeds for many years and served as Lord Mayor in 1904-5. Though called to the Bar, he preferred to follow commercial life and occupies a leading position among Leeds manufacturers as head of the Farnley ironworks

He was born in 1866, and was educated at Westminster and Trinity College, Cambridge.

EAST (9,419).—No change.

*O'Grady, J. (Lab.)	5,373
Clarke, W. H. (U.)	2,308
Labour majority	3,065

1906.—Lab., 4,299; U., 2,208—Lab. maj., 2,091.
1900.—U., 3,453; L., 1,586; L., 1,266—U. maj. over L., 1,867.
1895.—L. maj., 710; 1892, L. maj., 827; 1886, L. maj., 1,110.

Mr. J. O'GRADY, organizer of the National Amalgamated Furnishing Trades Association; born in Bristol, 1866, and apprenticed to furniture making; engaged in municipal and Socialistic work in that town; has been president of the Trade Union Congress (1898); first entered Parliament in 1906, and has specialized on Indian questions; vehemently opposed some of the executive and administrative acts of Lord Morley, Secretary of State for India.

NORTH (22,965).—No change.

*Barran, R. H. (L.)	10,775
Birchall, J. D. (U.)	9,164
Liberal majority	1,611

1906.—L., 9,593; U., 7,109—L. maj., 2,484.
1900.—U., 7,512; L., 4,995—U. maj., 2,517.
1895.—U. maj., 1,508; 1892, U. maj., 1,014; 1886, U. maj., 619.

Mr. ROWLAND HIRST BARRAN is director of the firm of John Barran and Sons (Ltd.) merchants, Leeds, and is a Governor of Leeds Grammar School. He was born in 1858 and was educated at a private school. From 1897 to 1902 he was a member of the Leeds School Board, and from 1901 to 1904 a member of the Leeds City Council. He was first returned for North Leeds in 1902.

SOUTH (15,723).—No change.

*Middlebrook, W. (L.)	8,969
Nicholson, W. (U.)	4,366
Liberal majority	4,603

By-election 1908.—L., 5,274; U., 4,915; Lab. 2,451—L. maj. over U., 359.
1906.—L., 6,200; Lab., 4,030; U., 2,126—L. maj. over Lab., 2,170.
1900.—L., 4,952; U., 4,718—L. maj., 234.
1895.—L. maj. over U., 167; 1892, L. maj., 1,535; 1886, L. maj., 1,741.

Mr. WILLIAM MIDDLEBROOK, born at Birstall in 1851, was educated at Huddersfield College and admitted solicitor in 1872. He acted as hon. secretary to the Spen Valley Liberal Association 1885-95, was elected to the Morley Town Council 1892, and was mayor in 1896 and 1904. He is J.P. for the West Riding of Yorkshire, and treasurer of the Wesleyan Methodist General Chapel Committee. He was elected to the last Parliament at a by-election on the death of Sir J. L. Walton in February, 1908.

WEST (18,868).—No change.

Harvey, T. E. (L.)	9,969
Samuel, S. (U.)	6,654
Liberal majority	3,315

1906.—L., 9,258; U., 4,650—L. maj., 4,608.
1900.—L., 7,043; U., 6,522—L. maj., 521.
1895.—L. maj., 96; 1892, L. maj., 353; 1886, L. maj., 2,256.

Mr. T. EDMUND HARVEY has been Warden of Toynbee Hall since 1906; from 1904 to 1907 he was a member of the London County Council, and is a member of the Central (Unemployed)Body for London, and of the Stepney Borough Council. He was born in 1875, and in addition to the educational and University curriculum at home he has studied at the Universities of Berlin and Paris.

LEICESTER (2) (25,336).—No change.

Crawshay-Williams, E. (L.)	14,643
*MacDonald, J. Ramsay (Lab.)	14,337
Fraser, J. Foster (U.)	8,548
Bagley, E. A. (U.)	8,192
Liberal majority over Unionist	6,095
Labour majority over Unionist	5,789

By-election, March, 1906.—L., 10,766; U., 7,206—L. maj., 3,560.
1906.—L., 14,745; Lab. 14,685; U., 7,504—Lab. maj., 7,181.
1900.—L., 10,385; U., 9,066; L., 8,528; Lab., 4,164—Maj. of elected U. over L. defeated, 538.
1895.—L., 9,792; L., 7,753; U., 7,654; Lab., 4,009—L. maj., 99.
1892.—Two L.'s unopposed.
1886.—L., 9,914; L., 9,681; U., 5,686—L. maj., 3,995.

Mr. ELIOT CRAWSHAY-WILLIAMS, born in 1880, the son of Mr. A. J. Williams, formerly Liberal member for South Glamorgan, was educated at Eton and at Trinity College, Oxford. He afterwards served in the Royal Field Artillery at home and in India, accompanying Lord Curzon on his journey to Persia. He returned to England through Persia and Russia, and he has written a book on his travels. At the last election he unsuccessfully contested the Chorley Division of Lancashire, and afterwards he acted as private secretary to Mr. Churchill at the Colonial Office.

Mr. J. RAMSAY MACDONALD, described by an admirer as "the Schnadhorst" of the Labour Party, has held advanced views from his youth up; born in 1866, the son of an Elgin farm labourer, he came to London at the age of 20, worked first as an envelope addresser, afterwards as a clerk; was engaged, from 1887 to 1891, as private secretary; joined the Fabian Society and the Independent Labour Party, took a leading part in the Socialist propaganda, and earned his living as a journalist; is secretary of the Labour Representation Committee, and was secretary of the Parliamentary Labour Party from 1906, when he was returned for Leicester, to 1908; has toured through and given his views about Canada, New Zealand, Australia, and India.

LINCOLN (11,577).—No change.

*Roberts, C. (L.)	5,402
Filmer, Sir R. (U.)	3,236
Seely, C. H. (U.F.T.)	2,129
Liberal majority over Unionist	2,166

1906.—L., 5,110; U.F.T., 3,718; U., 1,162—L. maj. over U.F.T., 1,392.
1900.—U., 4,002; L., 3,935—U. maj., 67.
1895.—U. maj., 218; 1892, L. maj., 224; 1886, U. maj., 308.

Mr. CHARLES HENRY ROBERTS was born in 1865, and educated at Marlborough and Balliol College, Oxford. He is a Commissioner of Lunacy (unpaid)

He unsuccessfully contested Wednesbury in 1895 and Lincoln in 1900, and was elected for the latter constituency in 1906.

LIVERPOOL (9).

ABERCROMBY (6,926).—UNIONIST GAIN.

Chaloner, Col. R. G. W. (U.) ..	3,088
*Seely, Right Hon. Col. (L.)	2,562
Unionist majority ..	526

1906.—L., 2,933 ; U., 2,734—L. maj., 199.
1900 and 1895.—U. unop.
1892.—U. maj., 831 ; 1886, U. maj., 739.

COLONEL RICHARD GODOLPHIN WALMESLEY CHALONER is a brother of Mr. Walter Long, and was born in 1856. He was educated at Winchester, and entered the Army in 1878, serving in India and Afghanistan. From 1888 to 1893 he served as adjutant of the North Somerset Yeomanry Cavalry, and commanded the 1st Battalion of the Imperial Yeomanry in South Africa. By Royal licence he took the name of Chaloner under the will of the late Admiral Chaloner in 1888, and from 1895 to 1900 he represented the Westbury Division of Wilts in the Conservative interest.

EAST TOXTETH (9,514).—UNIONIST GAIN.

Hall, E. Marshall, K.C. (U.) ..	4,037
Lea, John (L.)	3,752
Unionist majority ..	285

[Mr. Austin Taylor, the retiring member, was elected as a Unionist, but seceded to the Liberal Party.]
1906 and 1900.—U. unop.
1895.—U. maj., 1,922 ; 1892, U. maj., 1,507 ; 1886, U. unop.

Mr. EDWARD MARSHALL HALL, K.C., was born at Brighton in 1858 and educated at St. Andrew's College, Chardstock, Rugby, and St. John's College, Cambridge. He was called to the Bar (Inner Temple) in 1883, took silk in 1898, and has practised in London and on the South-Eastern Circuit. He represented the Southport Division of Lancashire from 1900 to 1906.

EVERTON (9,308).—No change.

*Harmood-Banner, J. S. (U.) ..	4,283
Aggs, W. Hanbury (L.) ..	2,577
Unionist majority ..	1,706

1906.—U., 3,949 ; L., 2,884—U. maj., 1,065.
1900 and 1895.—U. unop.
1892.—U. maj., 1,789 ; 1886, U. unop.

Mr. JOHN SUTHERLAND HARMOOD-BANNER has represented the Everton Division of Liverpool since 1905. He is a chartered accountant, a member of the firm of Harmood-Banner and Son, of Liverpool, chairman of the Pearson Knowles Coal and Iron Company (Limited), and auditor of the Lancashire and Yorkshire Railway Company and of the Bank of Liverpool. He has been a member of the Liverpool City Council since 1894, and is chairman of its Finance Committee. In 1904-5 he was President of the Institute of Chartered Accountants, and in 1907 of the Association of Municipal Corporations.

EXCHANGE (5,602).—No change.

Muspratt, Max (L.) ..	2,392
Scott, Leslie, K.C. (U.) ..	2,231
Liberal majority ..	161

1906.—L., 2,291 ; U., 2,170—L. maj., 121.
1900.—U., 2,811 ; L., 1,514—U. maj., 1,297.
1895.—U. maj., 254 ; 1892, L. maj., 66 ; 1886, L. maj., 170.

Mr. MAX MUSPRATT was born in 1872 at Seaforth Hall, near Liverpool, a son of Dr. E. K. Muspratt, the ex-Pro-Chancellor of Liverpool University and president of the Financial Reform Association ; educated at Clifton College, and afterwards at Zurich ; a director of the United Alkali Company and chairman of the Liverpool Rubber Company ; member of the Liverpool City Council and has taken a prominent part in municipal government and educational work, including that of the Liverpool School of Russian Studies which recently arranged the visit of members of the Russian Duma to Liverpool.

KIRKDALE (10,361).—No change.

*McArthur, C. (U.)	4,144
Cameron, A. G. (Lab.) ..	3,921
Unionist majority ..	223

By-election, 1907.—U., 4,000 ; Lab., 3,330—U. maj., 670.
1906.—U., 3,749 ; Lab., 3,157—U. maj., 592.
1900.—U., 4,333 ; L., 1,738—U. maj., 2,595.
1895.—U. maj., 1,350 ; 1892, U. maj., 977 ; 1886, U. maj., 912.

Mr. CHARLES MCARTHUR was born at Kingsdown, near Bristol, in 1844, and educated at Bristol Grammar School. He is an average-adjuster, and was chairman of the Commercial Law Committee 1887, President of the Liverpool Chamber of Commerce 1892-96, a member of the International Law Association, and chairman of the Bill of Lading Committee. From 1897 to 1905 he represented the Exchange Division of Liverpool, was defeated in 1906, and elected for Kirkdale in 1907.

SCOTLAND (5,326).—No change.

*O'Connor, T. P. (Nat.) ..	2,943
Moy, A., jun. (U.)	776
Nationalist majority ..	2,167

1906.—Nat., 2,808 ; U., 1,117—Nat. maj., 1,691.
1900.—Nat., 2,044 ; U., 1,484 ; Nat. maj., 560.
1895.—Nat. maj., 637 ; 1892, Nat. maj., 1,190 ; 1886, Nat. maj., 1,480.

Mr. T. P. O'CONNOR is a well-known author and journalist, and has been in the House of Commons since 1880 as a member of the Irish Nationalist party, first for Galway, and since 1885 for the Scotland Division of Liverpool. He was born in 1848, and was educated at the College of the Immaculate Conception, Athlone, and at Queen's College, Galway. Mr. O'Connor has recently returned from a political tour in the United States, undertaken with the object of obtaining additional funds for furthering the Irish cause in Parliament.

WALTON (15,670).—No change.

*Smith, F. E., K.C. (U.)	6,627
Joseph, F. L. (L.)	5,513
Jellicoe, E. G. (Ind. L.)	481
Unionist majority over Liberal	1,114
Unionist majority over Ind. Liberal	6,146

1906.—U., 5,862 ; L., 5,153—U. maj., 709.
1900 and 1895.—U. unop.
1892.—U. maj., 1,214 ; 1886, U. maj., 1,191.

Mr. F. E. SMITH was born at Birkenhead in 1872, and went to Wadham College, Oxford, with a classical scholarship from Birkenhead Grammar School. At the University he took a first-class in the Final Honour School of Jurisprudence in 1894 and a year later won the Vinerian Scholarship. He was President of the Oxford Union in 1893. In 1896 he was elected a Fellow and lecturer of Merton College, and in 1897 a lecturer of Oriel College. He was called to the Bar in 1895, and had a large practice on the Northern Circuit before becoming a K.C. in 1908. His ability in debate has found opportunities of frequent exercise in the House of Commons, and he is a speaker much sought after on public platforms.

WEST DERBY (11,467).—No change.

*Rutherford, W. Watson (U.)	5,190
Lias, W. J. (L.)	3,682
Unionist majority	1,508

1906.—U., 5,447 ; L., 3,600—U. maj., 1,847.
1900.—U. unop.
1895.—U. maj., 2,936 ; 1892, U. maj., 1,182 ; 1886, U. maj., 1,360.

Mr. W. WATSON RUTHERFORD, a former Lord Mayor of Liverpool, resigned that office in 1903 on the occasion of a vacancy in the West Derby Division, and was elected as its Parliamentary representative ; re-elected in 1906 ; a solicitor (his firm is Messrs. Rutherfords, Liverpool and London), he was one of the most searching and effective critics of the Land Clauses of the Budget ; his knowledge of the legal technicalities of the land question was more than once complimentarily acknowledged by Mr. Lloyd George and the Attorney-General ; has views on certain subjects which, to quote Lord Robert Cecil, " differ completely from those of the average Conservative."

WEST TOXTETH (9,019).—No change.

*Houston, R. P. (U.)	3,928
Sexton, J. (Lab.)	2,909
Unionist majority	1,019

1906.—U., 3,373 ; Lab., 2,592—U. maj., 781.
1900.—U. unop. ; 1895, U. maj., 1,957.
1892.—U. maj., 1,125 ; 1886, U. unop.

Mr. ROBERT PATERSON HOUSTON was born in 1853, and educated at Liverpool College and privately. He is the head of the firm of R. P. Houston and Co., steamship owners and merchants, of Liverpool and London.

MAIDSTONE (6,260).—No change.

*Castlereagh, Viscount (U.)	3,094
Phillips, V. (L.)	2,847
Unionist majority	247

1906.—U., 2,841 ; L., 2,709—U. maj., 132.
1900.—L., 2,201 ; U., 2,163—L. maj., 38.
1895.—U. unop. ; 1892, U. maj., 816 ; 1886, U. maj., 314.

VISCOUNT CASTLEREAGH is the son and heir of the Marquis of Londonderry and the son-in-law of Mr. Chaplin. He was born in 1879, educated at Eton and Sandhurst, and is captain in the Royal Horse Guards.

MANCHESTER (6).

EAST (12,646).—LABOUR GAIN FROM LIBERAL.

Sutton, J. E. (Lab.)	6,110
Robb, E. Elvy (U.)	5,091
Labour majority	1,019

1906.—L., 6,403 ; U., 4,423—L. maj., 1,980.
1900.—U., 5,803 ; L., 3,350—U. maj., 2,453.
1895.—U. maj., 776 ; 1892, U. maj., 398 ; 1886, U. maj., 644.

Mr. JOHN E. SUTTON has represented a part of the division on the City Council for 15 years. He is 47 years of age, and has worked at the Bradford Colliery (Manchester) since he was 14 years old. He has been check-weigher at the colliery for 20 years and Secretary of the Bradford Branch of the Miners' Federation for 14 years. He is a Rechabite and a Socialist.

NORTH (10,284).—No change.

*Schwann, Sir C. E. (L.)	5,210
Howell, H. E. (U.)	3,951
Liberal majority	1,259

1906.—L., 5,716 ; U., 3,262—L. maj., 2,454.
1900.—L., 4,258 ; U., 4,232—L. maj., 26.
1895.—L. maj., 455 ; 1892, L. maj., 305 ; 1886, L. maj., 96.

SIR CHARLES ERNEST SCHWANN, Bt., was born at Huddersfield in 1844 and educated at Huddersfield College and University College, London. He is a vice-president of the Manchester Liberal Four Hundred and president of the Manchester '95 Club, and was created a baronet in 1906. He unsuccessfully contested the Northern Division of the city in 1885, but has represented it since 1886.

NORTH-EAST (9,925).—No change.

*Clynes, J. R. (Lab.)	5,157
Vaudrey, Sir W. H. (U.)	3,679
Labour majority	1,478

1906.—Lab., 5,386 ; U., 2,954—Lab. maj., 2,432.
1900.—U., 4,316 ; L., 3,610—U. maj., 706.
1895.—U. maj. over L., 241 ; 1892, U. maj., 110 ; 1886, U. maj., 327.

Mr. J. R. CLYNES, born in Oldham in 1869, worked as a lad in a cotton mill, became secretary to the Oldham and District Trades Council, is J.P. for Oldham, and takes an active interest in social questions affecting the working classes. As a member of the Labour Party he was elected for the division in 1906.

NORTH-WEST (11,961).—LIBERAL GAIN.

Kemp, Sir G. (L.)	5,930
*Joynson-Hicks, W. (U.)	5,147
Liberal majority	783

By-election, 1908.—U., 5,417 ; L., 4,988 ; Lab., 276—U. maj. over L., 429.
1906.—L., 5,639 ; U., 4,398—L. maj., 1,241.
1900.—U. unop.
1895.—U. maj., 1,471 ; 1892, U. unop. ; 1886, U. maj., 1,036.

LIEUTENANT-COLONEL SIR GEORGE KEMP represented the Heywood Division of Lancashire from 1895 to 1906 ; he left the Liberal Unionist Party on the question of Tariff Reform. Born in 1866, he was educated at Shrewsbury and Trinity College, Cambridge ; is the managing director of Kelsall and Kemp(Limited), woollen manufacturers and merchants, of Rochdale and Manchester. At the time of the South African War he served in the Imperial Yeomanry, his services being mentioned in despatches. In 1896 he married Lady Beatrice Egerton, third daughter of the third Lord Ellesmere.

SOUTH (15,594).—No change.

*Haworth, A. A. (L.)	8,121
Jackson, Capt. C. Ward (U.)	5,669
Liberal majority	2,452

1906.—L., 8,002 ; U., 3,770—L. maj., 4,232.
1900.—U., 5,122 ; L., 3,850—U. maj., 1,272.
1895.—U. maj., 78 ; 1892, L. maj., 181 ; 1886, L. maj., 335.

Mr. ARTHUR ADLINGTON HAWORTH, the son of Mr. Abraham Haworth, J.P., of Altrincham, was born at Eccles in 1865, educated at Rugby, married a daughter of the late John Rigby, of Altrincham, in 1891, and carries on the business of a cotton merchant in Manchester. He is a Governor and Trustee of the Manchester Grammar School, a member of the Council of Mansfield College, and Chairman of the Council of the Congregational Union. He sat as member during the last Parliament, being returned at the General Election, 1906.

SOUTH-WEST (8,180).—UNIONIST GAIN.

Colefax, H. A. (U.)	3,111
Needham, C. T. (L.)	3,004
McLachlan, J. (Lab.)	1,218
Unionist majority over Liberal	107

1906.—Lab., 4,101 ; U., 2,875—Lab. maj., 1,226.
1900.—U., 4,017 ; Lab., 2,398—U. maj., 1,619.
1895.—U. maj., 498 ; 1892, L. maj., 148 ; 1886, L. maj., 111.

Mr. ARTHUR COLEFAX, barrister, had a successful career at Oxford, and afterwards studied in Germany. For some years he was engaged in the woollen trade, but he is now wholly devoted to law practice, and is retained by two of the large railway companies to advise on patent matters. His father was for some years Chairman of the Bradford Central Conservative Association, and contested Dewsbury in 1886.

MIDDLESBROUGH (21,756).—No change.

Williams, Penry (L.)	9,670
Dorman, C. (U.)	6,756
Walls, P. (Lab.)	2,710
Liberal majority over Unionist	2,914
Liberal majority over Labour	6,960

1906.—Lab., 9,271 ; U., 6,864 ; Lab., 1,484—Lab. maj. over U., 2,407.
1900.—U., 6,760 ; Lab., 6,705—U. maj., 55.
1895.—Lab. maj. over U., 2,020 ; 1892, Lab. maj. over L., 629 ; 1886, L. unop.

Mr. PENRY WILLIAMS, a native of Middlesbrough and a son of the late Mr. Edward Williams, one of the pioneers of the Cleveland iron trade, is 44 years of age and joint managing director of the Linthorpe-Dinsdale Iron Company. He served for 20 years in the 1st N.R. Yorkshire Volunteer Artillery, and attained the rank of lieutenant-colonel commanding.

MONMOUTH DISTRICT (12,934).—No change.

*Haslam, L. (L.)	6,496
Cayzer, Sir C. (U.)	5,391
Liberal majority	1,105

1906.—L., 4,531 ; U., 3,939 ; Lab., 1,678—L. maj. over U., 592.
1900.—U., 4,415 ; L., 3,727—U. maj., 688.
1895.—L. maj., 154 ; 1892, L. maj., 293 ; 1886, U. maj., 465.

Mr. LEWIS HASLAM, who was returned for Monmouth Boroughs in 1906 against a Unionist and a Labour candidate, comes from Bolton. He is a J.P. for Lancashire and director of cotton-spinning and manufacturing companies in that county.

MORPETH (10,010).—No change.

*Burt, Rt. Hon. T. (L.)	5,874
Ridley, Hon. Jasper (U.)	3,009
Liberal majority	2,865

1906.—L., 5,518 ; U., 1,919—L. maj., 3,599.
1900.—L., 3,117 ; U., 2,707—L. maj., 410.
1895.—L. maj., 2,169 ; 1892 and 1886, L. unop.

Mr. THOMAS BURT has worked as a miner in the coal mines of Northumberland ; is secretary of the Northumberland Miners' Mutual Provident Association ; was one of the British representatives to the Berlin Labour Conference convened by the German Emperor in 1890, and has taken part in the proceedings of the International Miners' Conferences ; Parliamentary Secretary of the Board of Trade from 1892 to 1895, and is a member of the Board of Trade Arbitration Court ; was born in 1837, and is mainly self-taught ; was made a Privy Councillor in 1905.

NEWCASTLE-ON-TYNE (2) (38,534).—ONE LIBERAL GAIN.

Shortt, E. (L.)	18,779
*Hudson, W. (Lab.)	18,241
Plummer, Sir W. R. (U.)	14,067
*Renwick, G. (U.)	13,928
Liberal majority over Unionist	4,712
Labour majority over Unionist	4,174

By-election, 1908.—U., 13,863; L., 11,720; Lab., 2,971—U. maj. over L., 2,143.
1906.—Lab., 18,869; L., 18,423; U., 11,942; U., 11,223—L. maj., 6,481.
1900.—U., 15,097; U., 14,752; L., 10,488; L., 10,463—U. maj., 4,264.
1895.—U., 12,833; U., 12,170; L., 11,862; L., 11,154; Lab., 2,302—U. maj., 308.
1892.—U., 13,823; L., 10,905; L., 10,686—Maj. of U. over defeated L., 3,137.
1886.—L., 10,681; L., 10,172; U., 9,657; U., 9,580.—L. maj., 515.

Mr. EDWARD SHORTT, barrister-at-law, was born at St. Anthony's, Newcastle, in 1862, the second son of the Rev. Edward Shortt, formerly Vicar of Byker, Newcastle, and educated at Durham; called to the Bar in 1890, and joined the North-Eastern Circuit.

Mr. WALTER HUDSON has represented Newcastle since 1906 as a member of the Labour Party. Born in 1852, he for 26 years served as a main line guard on the North-Eastern Railway: several times he has acted as president at congresses of the Amalgamated Society of Railway Servants, and from 1898 to 1906 was secretary of the Irish branch of that society; president of the Irish Trade Union Congress held in Newry, 1903, and of the Labour Party Congress in Hull, 1908.

NEWCASTLE-UNDER-LYME (10,512).—
No change.

*Wedgwood, J. C. (L.) ..	5,653
Grogan, Capt. E. S. (U.) ..	4,245
Liberal majority ..	1,408

1906.—L., 5,155; U., 2,948—L. maj., 2,207.
1900.—U., 3,750; L., 3,568—U. maj., 182.
1895.—L. maj., 111; 1892, L. maj., 1,088; 1886, U. maj., 124.

Mr. JOSIAH CLEMENT WEDGWOOD, a descendant of the inventor of the famous ware, was born in 1872; he was educated at Clifton College, the Royal Naval College, Greenwich, and later in Germany. He was Assistant Constructor at Portsmouth Dockyard 1895-6; Naval Architect in Elswick Shipyard 1896-1900, and served as captain with the Elswick Battery, South Africa, 1900-1, receiving medal and three clasps, afterwards acting as Resident Magistrate at Ermelo in the Transvaal 1902-4; is president of the League for Taxation of Land Values, and has represented the borough as a Liberal since 1906.

NORTHAMPTON (2) (12,580).—No change.

Smith, H. B. Lees (L.) ..	5,398
McCurdy, C. A. (L.) ..	5,289
Orlebar, R. R. B. (U.) ..	4,569
Barnes, F. Gorell (U.) ..	4,464
Gribble, J. (Soc.) ..	1,792
Quelch, H. (Soc.) ..	1,617
Liberal majority ..	720

1906.—L., 4,479; L., 4,244; U., 4,078; U., 4,000; Lab., 2,544; Lab., 2,366—L. maj. over U., 401.
1900.—L., 5,437; L., 5,281; U., 4,480; U., 4,124—L. maj., 801.
1895.—U., 4,884; U., 3,820; Lab., 3,703; U., 3,394; Soc., 1,216; Ind. L., 1,131—Maj. of U. elected over defeated Lab., 117.
1892.—L., 5,439; L., 5,164; U., 3,651; U., 3,235—L. maj., 1,513.
1886.—L., 4,570; L., 4,353; U., 3,850; U., 3,656—L. maj., 503.

Mr. H. B. LEES SMITH, born in the Himalayas in 1878, the son of a soldier, was first educated for a military life, but, having other tastes, he proceeded to Oxford. He was one of the founders of Ruskin College, of the Executive Council of which he is now chairman, and he is lecturer on Public Administration at the London School of Economics and on Political Science at the University of London, as well as Professor of Public Administration at the University of Bristol. On the invitation of the Government of Bombay, Mr. Lees Smith visited India last winter to advise on economic teaching and to lecture in the University of Bombay.

Mr. CHARLES A. MCCURDY, who was born at Nottingham in 1870, son of a Dissenting minister, is a barrister, practising on the Midland Circuit. At Cambridge he studied both law and medicine. He has had much to do with the development of the garden suburb movement. At the last General Election Mr. McCurdy contested Winchester, where he was beaten by 50 votes, and in the last election for the London County Council he was an unsuccessful candidate for Hampstead.

NORWICH (2) (21,607).—No change.

Low, Sir F., K.C. (L.)	11,257
*Roberts, G. (Lab.) ..	11,119
Hoare, Sir S. (U.) ..	8,480
Snowden, H. G. (U.)	7,981
Liberal majority over Unionist	2,777
Labour majority over Unionist	2,639

1906.—Lab., 11,059; L., 10,972; U., 7,460—L. maj., 3,512.
1900.—Two U.'s unop.
1895.—U., 8,166; U., 8,034; L., 7,330; L., 7,210—L. maj., 704.
1892.—U., 7,718; L., 7,407; L., 6,811—U. maj. over L. defeated, 907.
1886.—L., 6,295; U., 6,156; L., 6,119; U., 5,564—Maj. of U. elected over defeated L., 37.

SIR FREDERICK LOW, K.C., born in 1856, was educated privately and at Westminster, was admitted a solicitor in 1878, and was called to the Bar in 1890, joining the South-Eastern Circuit. He became a recognized authority on all questions connected with licensing and local government. In 1902 Sir F. Low took silk. He was counsel in the Lichfield election petition, in the London General Bank case arising out of the Jabez Balfour frauds, and in the Forwood libel case. He has been Recorder of Ipswich since 1906.

Mr. G. H. ROBERTS was born in 1869, and in 1880 was a monitor in St. Stephen's National School, Norwich, and three years later was apprenticed to the printing trade. Leaving Norwich for London, he joined the Typographical Association, and became organizer in 1904. In 1886 he joined the Independent Labour Party, and was elected a member of the Norwich School Board in 1889.

NOTTINGHAM (3).
EAST (13,218).—UNIONIST GAIN.

Morrison, Capt. J. A. (U.) ..	5,877
*Cotton, Sir H. (L.) ..	5,725
Unionist majority ..	152

1906.—L., 6,020 ; U., 4,290—L. maj., 1,730.
1900.—U., 4,927 ; L., 4,148—U. maj., 779.
1895.—U. maj., 165 ; 1892, L. maj., 577 ; 1886, L. maj., 166.

CAPTAIN JAMES ARCHIBALD MORRISON, late of the Grenadier Guards, is the younger son of the late Mr. Alfred Morrison, of Fonthill, Wilts, and a nephew of the late Mr. Charles Morrison, of Basildon Park, and of Miss Ellen Morrison, who died recently leaving large fortunes. He entered the Army in 1896, served in the Sudan 1898, receiving the British and Egyptian medals, and in South Africa 1899-1900. He sat as member for the Wilton Division of Wiltshire July, 1900, to 1906. Captain Morrison married in 1901 the Hon. Mary Hill-Trevor, sister of Lord Trevor.

SOUTH (14,031).—UNIONIST GAIN.

Cavendish-Bentinck, Lord H. (U.)	6,434
*Richardson, A. (L.)	6,052
Unionist majority	382

1906.—L., 6,314 ; U., 5,514—L. maj., 800.
1900.—U., 5,298 ; L., 3,914—U. maj., 1,384.
1895.—U. maj., 433 ; 1892, U. maj, 83 ; 1886, U. maj., 269.

LORD HENRY CAVENDISH-BENTINCK, who was born in 1863, is half-brother to the present Duke of Portland. He has held commissions in the Reserve Forces, and served in South Africa. He was elected in 1886, by a majority of 20 votes, for North-West Norfolk, a constituency in which he sustained defeats in 1885 and 1892, and sat for his present constituency from 1895 to 1906, when, standing as a Unionist Free-trader, he lost the seat. Marylebone provides him with a seat on the London County Council.

WEST (17,476).—No change.

*Yoxall, Sir J. H. (L.)	8,955
Lygon, Hon. H. (U.)	6,652
Liberal majority	2,303

1906.—L., 8,107 ; U., 5,262—L. maj., 2,845.
1900.—L., 6,023 ; U., 5,639—L. maj., 384.
1895.—L. maj., 513 ; 1892, U. maj., 301 ; 1886, L. maj., 849.

SIR JAMES YOXALL, the general secretary since 1892 of the National Union of Teachers, was born in 1857, and educated at a Wesleyan school in Redditch and at the Westminster Training College. He became a certificated teacher in 1878, was president of the National Union of Teachers in 1891, and in 1894 and 1895 served as a member of the Royal Commission on Secondary Education. He contested the Bassetlaw Division of Nottinghamshire unsuccessfully in 1892 ; was elected for Nottingham (West) in 1895, and has represented that constituency since that date. He received a knighthood last year. He is the author of several novels.

OLDHAM (2) (35,315).—No change.

*Emmott, Rt. Hon. A. (L.)	19,252
Barton, A. W. (L.)	18,840
Hilton, J. (U.)	13,462
Stott, P. S. (U.)	12,577
Liberal majority	5,378

1906.—L., 17,397 ; L., 16,672 ; U., 11,989 ; U., 11,391—L. maj., 4,683.
1900.—L., 12,947 ; U., 12,931 ; L., 12,709 ; U., 12,522—maj. of elected U. over defeated L., 222.
1895.—U., 13,085 ; U., 12,465 ; L., 12,249—U. maj., 216.
1892.—L., 12,619 ; L., 12,541 ; U., 12,205 ; U., 11,952 — L. maj., 336.
1886.—U., 11,606 ; U., 11,484 ; L., 10,921 ; L., 10,891—U. maj., 563.

Mr. ALFRED EMMOTT was Chairman of Committees and Deputy Speaker of the House of Commons throughout the last Parliament, and discharged the arduous duty of presiding over the greater part of the prolonged sittings in Committee when the Budget was before the House. Born in 1858, he was formerly chairman of the cotton-spinning and manufacturing firm of Emmotts and Wallshaw (Limited). At a by-election in 1899 he was returned, with Mr. Runciman, to represent Oldham, and has continued as one of the members for the constituency since that year. He was sworn of the Privy Council in 1908.

Mr. W. BARTON was born in 1862, near Glasgow, the son of a mining engineer. He graduated at Glasgow University, where he specialized in commercial law, political economy, and modern languages. He learned the business of calico printing at Glasgow, and now has a business of his own in Manchester, where he has done public work on the city council. He is a director of the Manchester Athenæum and a vice-president of the Manchester League for the Taxation of Land Values.

OXFORD (9,227).—No change.

*Valentia, Viscount (U.)	4,918
Whale, G. (L.)	3,707
Unionist majority	1,211

1906.—U., 3,910 ; L., 3,810—U. maj., 100.
1900.—U. unop.
1895.—U. maj., 648 ; 1892, U. maj., 120.
1886.—U. unop.

VISCOUNT VALENTIA was born at Inveresk in 1843, and educated at the Royal Military Academy, Woolwich. In 1878 he married the widow of Sir A. W. Peyton. Having entered the 10th Hussars in 1864, he retired as lieutenant in 1872. He is hon. colonel of the Oxfordshire Yeomanry, and served with the Yeomanry Cavalry in South Africa, being mentioned in despatches. He has represented Oxford since 1895, and was Comptroller of the Household from 1898 to 1905, and in the last Parliament acted as Whip to the Unionist Party. He contested Mid Oxfordshire in 1885.

PENRYN AND FALMOUTH (3,215).—UNIONIST GAIN.

Goldman, C. S. (U.)	1,593
*Barker, Sir J. (L.)	1,412
Unionist majority	181

1906.—L., 1,345 ; U., 1,248—L. maj., 97.
1900.—L., 1,184 ; U., 1,164—L. maj., 20.
1895.—L. maj., 49 ; 1892, U. maj., 338 ; 1886, U. maj., 91.

Mr. CHARLES SYDNEY GOLDMAN was born in Cape Colony in 1869, and is the son of a merchant and farmer ; was interested in gold mining in the Transvaal; served as a special correspondent during the Boer War, and subsequently joined the Cavalry in the advance north; the author of "With General French and the Cavalry in South Africa" and "The Cavalry in Future Wars"; interested in military and Imperial affairs, and h s done good work on behalf of the National Service League, the African Society, and similar organizations, and has published several text-books on South African mining; married the Hon. Agnes Mary Peel, second daughter of the first Viscount Peel.

PETERBOROUGH (6,564).—No change.

*Greenwood, G. C. (L.)	3,308
Purvis, Sir R. (U.)	2,875
Liberal majority	433

1906.—L., 3,326; U., 2,167—L. maj., 1,159.
1900.—U., 2,315; L., 2,155—U. maj., 160.
1895.—U. maj., 239; 1892. L. maj., 158; 1886, U. maj., 289.

Mr. GRANVILLE GEORGE GREENWOOD, born in 1850; educated at Eton and Trinity College, Cambridge; called to the Bar, Middle Temple, 1876; unsuccessfully contested Peterborough in 1886 and Central Hull in 1900; was elected for Peterborough in the Liberal interest 1906.

PLYMOUTH (2) (18,085).—No change.

*Mallet, C. E. (L.)	8,091
Williams, A. (L.)	7,961
Astor, Waldorf (U.)	7,650
Durand, Rt. Hon. Sir H. Mortimer (U.)	7,556
Liberal majority	311

1906.—L., 9,021; L., 8,914; U., 6,547; U., 6,234—L. maj., 2,367
1900.—U., 6,009, U.,6,005; L., 5,460, L., 5,264—U. maj., 545.
1895.—U., 5,575; L., 5,482; U., 5,456; L., 5,298—maj. of L. elected over defeated U., 26; 1892, U., 5,081; U., 5,081; L., 4,921; L., 4,861—U. maj., 160; 1886, U., 4,137; U., 4,133; L., 3,255; L., 3,175—U. maj., 878.

Mr. CHARLES EDWARD MALLET was born in 1862, and educated at Harrow and Balliol College, Oxford. He was called to the Bar at the Middle Temple in 1889, and was a lecturer in history for the Oxford University Extension system. He is a director of Nisbet and Co., publishers. Unsuccessfully contested West Salford in 1900, and was elected as junior member for Plymouth in 1906.

Mr. ANEURIN WILLIAMS, son of the late Mr. E. Williams, C.E., of Middlesbrough, was born at Dowlais 1859, and educated at St. John's, Cambridge (M.A. Classical Tripos, 1880); called to the Bar Inner Temple, 1884, and in 1888 married a daughter of Mr. John Pattinson, of Gateshead. He was an acting partner in the Linthorpe Ironworks, Middlesbrough, 1886-1890, and a member of the executive of the Labour Copartnership Association, 1892. He is chairman of the First Garden City (Limited), of the executive of the Land Nationalization Society, and of the International Co-operative Alliance. He was the first editor of *Copartnership*, and has written on the subject of co-operation in The *Encyclopædia Britannica* and elsewhere. He contested Mid Kent in the Liberal interest in 1906.

PONTEFRACT (3,661).—No change.

*Nussey, Sir W., Bt. (L.)	1,924
Shaw, Col. J. R. (U.)	1,515
Liberal majority	409

1906.—L., 1,837; U., 1,030—L. maj., 807.
1900.—L., 1,385; U., 1,269—L. maj., 116.
1895.—L. maj., 57; 1892, U. maj., 40; 1886, U. maj., 209.

SIR THOMAS WILLIAM NUSSEY, J.P., D.L., was born in 1868, the son of Mr. Thomas Nussey, of Bramley Grange, York; was educated at Leamington and Trinity Hall, Cambridge, B.A. 1890, and married, in 1897, a daughter of Dr. E. M. Daniel, of Fleetwood. He was called to the Bar, Inner Temple, 1893; created baronet 1909; contested Maidstone 1892, and has represented Pontefract as a Liberal since June, 1893.

PORTSMOUTH (2) (33,666).—Two UNIONIST GAINS.

Beresford, Admiral Lord C. (U.)	16,777
Falle, B. G. (U.)	15,592
*Bramsdon, Sir T. A. (L.)	12,397
Lambert, R. C. (L.)	9,965
Sanders, W. S. (Lab.)	3,529
Unionist majority over Liberal	3,195
Unionist majority over Labour	12,063

1906.—L., 10,500; L., 10,236; Lab., 8,172; U., 7,970; U., 7,752; Ind., 1,859—L. maj. over Lab., 2,064.
1900.—U., 10,818; U., 10,383; L., 10,214; L. 10,031—U. maj., 169.
1895.—L., 10,451; L., 10,255; U., 9,717; U., 9,567—L. maj., 538.
1892.—L., 9,643; L., 9,448; U., 9,135; U., 9,000—L. maj., 313.
1886.—U., 8,432; U., 8,325; L., 7,196; L., 7,069—U. maj., 1,129.

ADMIRAL LORD CHARLES BERESFORD has had a distinguished career in the Royal Navy, and through the publication of official despatches the attention of the public has been frequently drawn to conspicuous acts of gallantry achieved throughout his career. He has been a Naval Aide-de-Camp, was in command of the Condor at the bombardment of Alexandria, and served on Lord Wolseley's staff in the Nile Expedition, 1884-5; was a Lord Commissioner of the Admiralty in 1886; Commander-in-Chief of the Channel and Mediterranean Fleets; and lately has carried on an active campaign to call public attention to our naval deficiencies.

Mr. BERTRAM GODFRAY FALLE, the only son of the late Mr. J. G. Falle (one of the Judges of the Royal Court of Jersey), is a graduate in mathematics and law honours of the University of Cambridge, and graduate in law of the University of Paris. He was called to the Bar by the Inner Temple in 1885, and held for some years the post of Enroller of Deeds at H.M. Office of Works, and was afterwards, under Lord Cromer, one of the English Judges of the Native Tribunal

Cairo. He contested East Somerset as a "whole-hogger" at the last election.

PRESTON (2) (19,521).—Two UNIONIST GAINS.

Stanley, Capt. the Hon. G. F. (U)	9,526
Tobin, A. A., K.C. (U.)	9,160
*Macpherson, J. T. (Lab.)	7,539
Gorst, Rt. Hon. Sir J. (L.)	6,281
*Cox, Harold (L.)	2,704
Unionist majority over Labour	1,621
Unionist majority over Liberal	2,879

1906.—Lab., 10,181; L., 8,538; U., 7303; U., 6,856—L. maj. over U., 1,235.
1900.—U., 8,944; U., 8,067; Lab., 4,834—U. maj., 3,233.
1895.—U., 8,928; U., 7,622; Lab., 4,781—U. maj., 2,841.
1892.—U., 8,070; U., 7,764; L., 6,182—U. maj., 1,582.
1886.—U., 7,497; U., 7,296; L., 4,982; L., 4,771—U. maj., 2,314.

CAPTAIN GEORGE FREDERICK STANLEY, Royal Horse Artillery, the seventh son of the late Earl of Derby, is 36 years of age; served in the South African war with distinction; was admitted a Guild Burgess of Preston in 1882, in which year his father was Guild Mayor; his wife was Lady Beatrix Taylour, daughter of the Marquis of Headfort.

Mr. ALFRED ASPINALL TOBIN was born in 1855 and educated at Rugby and University College, Oxford. He was called to the Bar by the Middle Temple in 1880, became K.C. in 1903, and Recorder of Salford in 1904. In 1900 he unsuccessfully contested the Scotland Division of Liverpool against Mr. T. P. O'Connor.

READING (11,016).—No change.

*Isaacs, Rufus, K.C. (L.)	5,264
†Renton, Major A. L. (U.)	5,057
Liberal majority	207

1906.—L., 5,407; U., 4,710—L. maj., 697.
1900.—L., 4,592; U., 4,353—L. maj., 239.
1895.—U. maj., 315; 1892, L. maj., 290; 1886, U. maj., 116.

Mr. RUFUS ISAACS, K.C., born in London, 1860; was educated at University College School and in Brussels and Hanover; was for some years on the Stock Exchange, then studied for the Bar and was called at Middle Temple in 1887; has been counsel in many celebrated cases; contested North Kensington in 1900; and has sat as Liberal member for Reading since 1904.

ROCHDALE (14,909).—No change.

*Harvey, A. G. C. (L.)	6,809
Carpenter, W. B. Boyd (U.)	5,381
Irving, D. (Soc.)	1,755
Liberal majority over Unionist	1,428

1906.—L., 5,912; U., 4,449; Lab.,2,506—L. maj. over U ,1,463.
1900.—U., 5,204; L., 5,185; Soc., 901—U. maj. over L., 19.
1895.—U. maj. over L., 442; 1892, L. maj., 980; 1886, L. maj., 1,257.

Mr. A. G. C. HARVEY is a large cotton-mill owner; he is chairman of the Middleton Division Liberal Association, a county alderman for Lancashire, and chairman of the County Elementary Education Committee.

ROCHESTER (5,629).—UNIONIST GAIN.

Ridley, S. F. (U.)	2,675
*Lamb, E. H. (L.)	2,543
Unionist majority	132

1906.—L., 2,967; U., 2,374—L. maj., 593.
1900.—U., unop.; 1895, U. maj., 479; 1892, U. maj., 407; 1886, U. maj., 249.

Mr. SAMUEL FORDE RIDLEY was born in 1864, and educated at Clifton College. He formerly held a commission in the 3rd Middlesex Artillery Volunteers and sat in the 1900-1906 Parliament as the representative of South-West Bethnal Green.

ST. HELENS (13,068).—No change.

*Glover, T. (Lab.)	6,512
Swift, R., K.C. (U.)	5,717
Labour majority	795

1906.—Lab., 6,058; U., 4,647—Lab. maj., 1,411.
1900.—U., 5,300; L., 3,402—U. maj., 1,898.
1895.—U. maj., 609; 1892, U. maj., 59; 1886, U. maj., 217.

Mr. THOMAS GLOVER, one of the founders of the Miners' Federation of Great Britain (1882), began life as a pit boy in Lancashire; worked underground for many years, and afterwards became a miners' agent; treasurer of the Lancashire and Cheshire Miners' Federation, which he established; has done good local work at St. Helens, of which he is a magistrate.

SALFORD (3).

NORTH (9,850).—No change.

*Byles, W. P. (L.)	4,980
Malcolm, Ian (U.)	4,123
Liberal majority	857

1906.—L., 4,915; U., 3,728—L. maj., 1,187.
1900.—U., 4,370; L., 3,487—U. maj., 873.
1895.—U. maj., 6; 1892, L. maj., 287; 1886, U. maj., 157.

Mr. WILLIAM POLLARD BYLES, born in Bradford in 1839, was educated privately; from 1892 to 1895 was member for the Shipley Division of Yorkshire, and as a strong Radical reformer was elected for North Salford in 1906.

SOUTH (8,344).—No change.

*Belloc, H. (L.)	3,952
Barlow, C. Montague (U.)	3,636
Liberal majority	316

1906.—L., 4,230; U., 3,378—L. maj., 852.
1900.—U., 4,207; L., 2,980—U. maj., 1,227.
1895.—U. maj. over L., 74; 1892, U. maj. over L., 37; 1886, U. maj., 126.

Mr. HILAIRE JOSEPH PETER RENÉ BELLOC, one of several authors with political leanings who entered Parliament at the General Election of 1906; born in France in 1870, brought to England as an infant, and educated at the Oratory School, Edgbaston, and at Balliol College, Oxford; has served as a private in a French artillery regiment, and travelled largely; is the author of "The Path to Rome," several historical studies, and other works; holds

ENGLAND (BOROUGHS).

the opinion that corruption is widely prevalent in public and in private life.

WEST (15,083).—No change.

*Agnew, G. W. (L.)	6,216
†Bellairs, C. (U.)	5,238
Purcell, A. A. (Ind. Lab.)	2,396
Liberal majority over Unionist	978

1906.—L., 7,329 ; U., 5,119—L. maj., 2,210.
1900.—U., 5,503 ; L., 4,341—U. maj., 1,162.
1895.—U. maj., 100 ; 1892, U. maj., 40 ; 1886, U. maj., 116.

Mr. G. W. AGNEW was born in 1852 and was educated at Rugby and St. John's College, Cambridge. He was a partner in the firm of Thomas Agnew and Sons, art publishers, and formerly president of the Printsellers' Association ; he is a member of the Court of Governors of Victoria University, Manchester, and has a seat on the board of the Manchester Children's Hospital.

SALISBURY (3,386).—UNIONIST GAIN.

Locker-Lampson, G. (U.)	1,803
*Tennant, Sir E., Bt. (L.)	1,485
Unionist majority	318

1906.—L., 1,646 ; U., 1,605—L. maj., 41.
1900.—U., 1,399 ; L., 1,160—U. maj., 239.
1895.—U. maj., 217 ; 1892, U. maj., 238 ; 1886, U. maj., 349.

Mr. GODFREY LOCKER-LAMPSON was born in 1875, educated at Eton and Trinity College, Cambridge, and subsequently called to the Bar. After a term at the Foreign Office he served in the Diplomatic Service at The Hague and St. Petersburg, and held a commission for three years in the Middlesex Yeomanry. Mr. Locker-Lampson in 1906 unsuccessfully contested the Chesterfield Division of Derbyshire.

SCARBOROUGH (6,166).—No change.

*Rea, W. Russell (L.)	3,011
Monckton-Arundell, Hon. G. V. A. (U.)	2,719
Liberal majority	292

1906.—L., 3,128 ; U., 2,619—L. maj., 509.
1900.—L., 2,548 ; U., 2,441—L. maj., 107.
1895.—L. maj., 24 ; 1892, U. maj., 171 ; 1886, L. maj., 102.

Mr. WALTER RUSSELL REA, eldest son of the Right Hon. Russell Rea, was born in Liverpool in 1873, educated at University College School and abroad, and in 1896 married a daughter of Mr. J. J. Muirhead. He is engaged in business as shipowner and lighterman, and sat as member for Scarborough in the last Parliament, being returned in 1906.

SHEFFIELD (5).

ATTERCLIFFE (16,483).—No change.

*Pointer, J. (Lab.)	7,755
King-Farlow, S. (U.)	6,079
Labour majority	676

By-election, 1909.—Lab., 3,531 ; U., 3,380 ; L., 3,175 ; Ind. U., 2,803—Lab. maj. over U., 151.
1906.—L., 6,523 ; U., 5,736—L. maj., 787.
1900 and 1895.—L. unop.
1892.—L. maj., 1,144 ; 1886, L. maj., 1,407.

Mr. JOSEPH POINTER was born in 1875, and educated at Sheffield Council School, Sheffield Central Higher School, and Ruskin Hall, Oxford. He was apprenticed to engineers' pattern-makers,and has held several unpaid offices under the United Pattern-makers' Association. He is a City Councillor in Sheffield, and was formerly a Methodist local preacher.

BRIGHTSIDE (12,564).—No change.

*Walters, J. T. (L.)	6,156
Vickers, D. (U.)	4,200
Lapworth, C. (Soc.)	510
Liberal majority	1,956

1906.—L., 5,409 ; U., 4,408—L. maj., 1,001.
1900.—U., 4,992 ; L., 4,028—U. maj., 964.
1895.—L. unop. ; 1892, L. maj., 1,277 ; 1886, L. maj., 882.

Mr. JOHN TUDOR WALTERS was born in 1866 and was educated privately and at the Clitheroe Grammar School. He is an architect and surveyor practising in the town ; is a member of the Leicester Town Council and carried out the scheme of municipal housing there ; is chairman of the Borough Education Committee and has been president of the Education Association of England and Wales. During the debates on the Budget he delivered several speeches on the proposals of land valuation and land taxation which earned for him the high commendation of the leaders of both political parties in the House of Commons.

CENTRAL (8,684).—No change.

*Hope, J. F. (U.)	3,829
Bailey, A. J. (L.)	3,440
Unionist majority	389

By-election, 1908.—U. unop.
1906.—U., 4,217 ; L., 3,290—U. maj., 927.
1900 and 1895.—U. unop.
1892.—U. maj., 856 ; 1886. U. maj., 1,196.

Mr. J. F. HOPE, who was born in 1870 and educated at the Oratory School, Birmingham, and at Christ Church, Oxford, is the son of the late Mr. James Robert Hope-Scott, Q.C., leader of the Parliamentary Bar, and of Lady Victoria Howard, eldest daughter of the 14th Duke of Norfolk. He was for some years assistant hon. secretary at the Conservative Central Office and afterwards became private secretary to the Duke of Norfolk as Postmaster-General in 1896, continuing to act in the same capacity to the Marquis of Londonderry.

ECCLESALL (13,961).—No change.

*Roberts, S. (U.)	6,407
Derry, J. (L.)	6,196
Unionist majority	211

1906.—U., 5,856 ; L., 5,392—U. maj., 464.
1900.—U., 5,059 ; L., 3,230—U. maj., 1,829.
1895.—U. unop. ; 1892, U. maj., 840, 1886, U. maj., 1,242.

Mr. SAMUEL ROBERTS, was born in 1852 and was educated at Repton and Trinity College, Cambridge. He was called to the Bar in 1878 and served as Lord Mayor of Sheffield in 1899-1900 ; is deputy-chairman of the West Riding Quarter

Sessions, and unsuccessfully contested the High Peak Division of Derbyshire in 1900.

HALLAM (13,527).—No change.

*Wortley, Rt. Hon. C. B. Stuart (U.)	6,181
Neal, A. (L.)	5,965
Unionist majority	216

1906.—U., 5,546 ; L., 5,465—U. maj., 81.
1900 and 1895.—U. unop.
1892.—U. maj., 643 ; 1886, U. maj., 969.

The Right Hon. Charles Beilby Stuart Wortley, son of the Right Hon. J. Stuart Wortley, Q.C., and grandson of the first Lord Wharncliffe, was born in 1851, educated at Rugby and Balliol College, Oxford (M.A., 1879), and married, first, in 1880, a daughter of Mr. F. A. Trollope, and in 1886 a daughter of the late Sir J. E. Millais, P.R.A. ; called to the Bar at the Inner Temple, 1876, he went the Northern Circuit, and became Q.C. in 1892 ; he was Parliamentary Under-Secretary for the Home Office in 1885 and from 1886 to 1892 ; nominated deputy-chairman of committees in the House of Commons, 1895 ; appointed Ecclesiastical Commissioner 1895 ; and made P.C. in 1896 ; he was Government delegate at International Conferences, Madrid, 1890, and Brussels, 1897 and 1900 ; is a director of the Great Central Railway ; he represented Sheffield from 1880 to 1885, and has represented the Hallam Division since 1885.

SHREWSBURY (4,882).—No change.

*Hill, Sir C. L. (U.)	2,596
Whitworth, J. H. (L.)	1,994
Unionist majority	602

1906.—U., 2,395 ; L., 1,955—U. maj., 440.
1900 and 1895.—U. unop.
1892.—U. maj., 406 ; 1886—U. maj., 557.

Sir Clement Lloyd Hill, a distinguished official of the Foreign Office, from which he retired in 1905, when he was created K.C.B. (is also C.B. and K.C.M.G.) ; born in 1845 and educated at Marlborough ; was secretary to Sir Bartle Frere's Mission to Zanzibar and Muscat, Chargé d'Affaires at Munich, Special Commissioner to Hayti, and Superintendent of African Protectorates under the Foreign Office.

SOUTHAMPTON (2) (20,205).—No change.

*Philipps, Lieut.-Col. Ivor (L.)	8,878
*Ward, Dudley (L.)	8,830
Giles, C. T., K.C. (U.)	7,874
Balfour, Major Kenneth (U.)	7,841
Liberal majority	956

1906.—L., 7,032 ; L., 6,255 ; U., 5,754 ; U., 5,535 ; Soc. 2,146—L. maj., 501.
1900.—U., 6,888 ; U., 6,253 ; L., 5,575 ; L., 4,652—U. maj., 678.
1895.—U., 5,924 ; U., 5,390 ; L., 5,181 ; Lab., 4,178 ; Lab., 867—U. maj., 209.
1892.—U., 5,449 ; L., 5,182 ; L., 5,920 ; U., 4,734—L. maj. over U., 267.
1886.—U., 5,023 ; U., 4,726 ; L., 4,384 ; L., 4,029—U. maj., 342.

Lieut.-Colonel Ivor Philipps, D.S.O., is in command of the Pembroke Yeomanry. Born in 1861, the son of Rev. Sir J. E. Philipps, Bt., he was educated at Felsted School, and in 1891 married a daughter of the late Mr. J. B. Mirrlees, of Glasgow. He served in the Militia, 1881-83, entered the Army as lieutenant 1883, major 1901. He took part in the Burma campaign, 1887-89 ; the Chen Lushai, 1889 ; the Miranzai Expedition, 1891 ; the North-West Frontier of India operations, 1896 ; the Tirah campaign, 1896-97 ; the China Expedition, 1900 (D.S.O.), and has received many decorations. He is a J.P., an Esquire of the Order of St. John of Jerusalem, and an alderman of the Pembroke County Council. He was one of the representatives of the borough through the last Parliament.

Mr. William Dudley Ward, who was born in 1877, is a grandson of the first Lord Esher. He was educated at Eton and Trinity College, Cambridge, and rowed in the Cambridge Eight in the University Boat-race in three years. He was called to the Bar in 1904. Two years later he was returned as one of the Liberal members for Southampton.

SOUTH SHIELDS (18,320).—No change.

*Robson, Sir W., K.C. (L.)	9,090
Williams, R. Vaughan (U.)	4,854
Liberal majority	4,236

1906.—L., 9,717 ; U., 3,431—L. maj., 6,286.
1900.—L., 7,417 ; U., 4,119—L. maj., 3,298.
1895.—L., 5,057 ; U., 4,924—L. maj., 133.
1892.—L., 4,965 ; U., 3,058   L. maj., 1,007.
1886.—L. unop.

Sir William Snowdon Robson, K.C., knighted 1905, was born in 1852 ; is third surviving son of Mr. Robert Robson, J.P. Newcastle ; educated at Gonville and Caius College, Cambridge (M.A.), Moral Science Tripos ; Hon. D.C.L. Durham 1906 ; married, 1887, a daughter of Mr. Charles Burge, of Park-crescent, Portland-place ; was called to the Bar, Inner Temple, 1880, Q.C. 1892, Bencher 1899, was M.P. for Bow and Bromley 1885-86, Recorder of Newcastle 1895-1905 ; in December, 1905, was appointed Solicitor-General, and Attorney-General in January, 1908 ; has sat for South Shields since 1895.

STAFFORD (4,137).—No change.

*Shaw, Sir C. E. (L.)	2,042
Mortimer, R. (U.)	1,957
Liberal majority	85

1906.—L., 1,947 ; U., 1,636—L. maj., 311.
1900.—L., 1,633 ; U., 1,528—L. maj., 105.
1895.—L. maj., 12 ; 1892, L. maj., 362 ; 1886, U. maj., 93.

Sir (Theodore Frederick) Charles Edward Shaw, the first baronet, created 1908, son of the late Mr. E. D. Shaw, of Wolverhampton, was born in 1859, educated at Tettenhall College, Wolverhampton, and Balliol College, Oxford, and in 1900 married a daughter of the late Mr. H. Bursill. He studied for the Bar, but in 1877 entered the firm of John Shaw and Sons, merchants, of Wolverhampton, since converted into a limited liability company, of which he is chairman. He was formerly captain in the 3rd Batt. South Staffordshire Regt., and has been a member of the Wolverhampton Town Council. He was first elected for Stafford in 1892, and represented the borough to the close of the last Parliament.

STALYBRIDGE (7,800).—UNIONIST GAIN.

Wood, J. (U.)	3,736
Bright, Allan (L.)	3,679
Unionist majority	57

1906.—L., 3,836; U., 3,382—L. maj., 454.
1900.—U., 3,321; L., 3,241—U. maj., 80.
1895.—U. maj., 632; 1892, U. maj., 337; 1886, U. maj., 582.

Mr. JOHN WOOD, head of the firm of Messrs. Wood (Limited), cotton spinners, Glossop, was called to the Bar, but never practised. He is a J.P. for three counties—Derbyshire, Cheshire, and Suffolk—and was formerly deputy-lieutenant for Herefordshire. He took great interest in the old Volunteer Force, in which he was for many years colonel.

STOCKPORT (2) (13,002).—No change.

*Wardle, G. J. (Lab.)	6,682
Hughes, S. L. (L.)	6,645
Raine, G. E. (U.)	5,268
Rankin, J. S. (U.)	5,249
Labour majority over Unionist	1,414
Liberal majority over Unionist	1,377

1906.—Lab., 7,299; L., 6,544; U., 4,591; U., 4,064—L. maj., 1,953.
1900.—L., 5,666; U., 5,377; L, 5,200; U., 5,098—maj. of U. elected over defeated L., 177.
1895.—U., 5,410; U., 5,067; L., 4,933; L., 4,562—U. maj., 134.
1892.—L., 5,202; U., 4,986; L., 4,876; U., 4,681—maj. of elected U. over defeated L., 110.
1886.—U., 4,702; U., 4,495; L., 4,184; L., 3,938—U. maj., 311.

Mr. GEORGE J. WARDLE, Labour member for Stockport in the last Parliament, was born in 1855 and was educated at a Wesleyan school, working half-time in a Keighley factory from 8 to 13 years of age. Two years afterwards he entered the service of the Midland Railway Company as clerk, and in 1898 he became editor of the *Railway Review*, in succession to Mr. Maddison. He is described as a "co-operator, trade unionist, and Socialist."

Mr. SPENCER LEIGH HUGHES, a Parliamentary journalist in the Press Gallery of the House of Commons, was born at Trowbridge and was educated at Woodhouse-grove School, near Leeds; he began life as an engineer in the firm of Ransomes, Sims, and Jeffries, of Ipswich; was a special correspondent for the *Morning Leader* during the German Emperor's visit to Palestine. He unsuccessfully contested the Jarrow Division of Durham and Bermondsey at by-elections in 1907 and 1909.

STOCKTON-ON-TEES (11,582).—LIBERAL GAIN.

Samuel, J. (L.)	6,026
Stroyan, J. (U.)	4,913
Liberal majority	1,113

1906.—U., 5,330; L., 3,675; Lab.,2,710—U. maj. over L., 1,655.
1900.—U., 5,262; L., 4,873—U. maj., 389.
1895.—U. maj., 472; 1892, U. maj., 311; 1886, L. maj., 1,002.

Mr. JONATHAN SAMUEL, J.P., Alderman of Durham County Council, manufacturer, was born in 1852, son of the late Mr. F. Samuel, of Tredegar, and married a daughter of the late Mr. Joshua Mellor, of Huddersfield, in 1892. He was Mayor of Stockton, 1894-5 and 1902, and represented the borough in Parliament, 1895-1900.

STOKE-ON-TRENT (15,079).—No change.

*Ward, J. (L.)	7,688
Kyd, D. H. (U.)	5,697
Liberal majority	1,991

1906.—L., 7,660; U., 4,288—L. maj., 3,372.
1900.—U., 4,932; L., 4,732—U. maj., 200.
1895.—U. maj., 200; 1892, L. maj., 1,783; 1886, L. maj., 1,162.

Mr. JOHN WARD worked as a navvy for many years, and founded the Navvies' Union (1889); is a member of the Social Democratic Federation and of the executive council of the National Democratic League; has served in the Sudan, and received the Khedive's Star, medal and clasp; has views on national defence which do not commend themselves to the Labour Party generally; entered the House of Commons in 1906.

SUNDERLAND (2) (27,610).—TWO UNIONIST GAINS.

Storey, S. (Ind. T. R.)	12,334
Knott, J. (U.)	12,270
*Stuart, Rt. Hon. J. (L.)	11,529
*Summerbell, T. (Lab.)	11,058
Unionist majority over Liberal	741
Unionist majority over Lab.	1,212

1906.—L., 13,620; Lab., 13,430; U., 7,879; U., 7,244—Lab. maj. over U., 5,551.
1900.—U., 9,617; U., 9,566; L., 9.370; L., 8,842—U. maj., 196.
1895.—U., 9,833; L.,8,232; L., 8,185—L. maj. over L., 47.
1892.—L., 9,711; L., 9,554; U., 8,394; U., 8,002—L. maj., 1,160.
1886.—L., 6,971; L., 6,840; U., 6,027—L. maj., 813.

Mr. SAMUEL STOREY was born at Sherburn in 1840, educated at Newcastle, and became a newspaper proprietor in Sunderland. Three times he has filled the office of Mayor of Sunderland, 1876, 1877, and 1880. In 1881 he was elected a member for the borough as a Radical and Home Ruler, and retained the seat until 1895, when he was defeated in the election of that year. He now supports the policy of Tariff Reform.

Mr. JAMES KNOTT, who was born in 1854, has been engaged in shipping during the whole of his business career, and is head of the Prince Line, of Newcastle; also a merchant in Newcastle, and colliery owner, with interests in many other industries on the North-East Coast.

TAUNTON (3,814).—No change.

Peel, Hon. W. (U.)	1,906
Addinsell, W. A. (L.)	1,538
Unionist majority	368

By-election, 1909.—U., 1,976; Lab., 1,085 —U. maj., 891.
1906.—U., 1,842; L., 1,503—U., maj., 339.
1900.—U., 1,387; L., 1,024—U. maj., 363.
1895.—U.. unop.; 1892, U. maj., 481; 1886, U. unop.

Mr. W. R. W. PEEL, eldest son of Viscount Peel, formerly Speaker of the House of Commons, sat as member for South Manchester from 1900 to 1905; was defeated in 1906 in the Harrow Division, and returned for Taunton at a by-election in 1909; is the leader of the Municipal Reform Party in the London County Council; acted as war correspondent during the Græco-Turkish war; his wife is the eldest daughter of Lord Ashton.

TYNEMOUTH AND NORTH SHIELDS.
(10,122).—No change.

*Craig, H. J. (L.)	4,487
Churchill, E. G. Spencer (U.)	3,993
Liberal majority	494

1906.—L., 4,286; U., 3,522—L. maj., 764.
1900.—U., 3,501; L., 3,094—U. maj., 407.
1895.—U. maj., 209; 1892, U. maj., 338; 1886, U. maj., 518; 1885, U. maj., 758.

Mr. HERBERT JAMES CRAIG is the son of a former member for Newcastle, the late Mr. James Craig. He was born in 1860 and was educated at Rugby under Dr. Percival, now Bishop of Hereford, and at Trinity College, Cambridge. He was called to the Bar by the Inner Temple and, after practising for some time on the North-Eastern Circuit, he joined the firm of Messrs. Borries, Craig, and Co., export merchants, of Newcastle-on-Tyne.

WAKEFIELD (6,326).—No change.

*Brotherton, E. A. (U.)	3,121
Coit, Dr. Stanton (Lab.)	2,602
Unionist majority	519

1906.—U., 2,285; Lab., 2,068; L., 1,247—U. maj. over Lab. 217.
1900.—U. unop.
1895.—U. maj., 699; 1892, U. maj., 404; 1886, U. maj., 307.

Mr. EDWARD A. BROTHERTON is chairman of Brotherton and Co., of the Calder Vale Ammonia Works, Wakefield. He was born at Manchester in 1856 and educated at Owens College. The council of Wakefield elected him their mayor in 1902.

WALSALL (14,713).—UNIONIST GAIN.

Cooper, R. A. (U.)	7,290
*Dunne, Major E. L.	6,745
Unionist majority	545

1906.—L., 7,092; U., 5,893—L. maj., 1,199.
1900.—L., 5,610; U., 5,285—L. maj., 325.
1895.—U. maj., 317; 1892, U. maj., 237; 1886, L. unop.

Mr. R. A. COOPER, of Ashlyns Hall, Berkhamsted, is the eldest son of Sir Richard Cooper, of Shenstone Court, Lichfield; has great commercial experience and is an ardent Tariff Reformer; is connected with his father's business of Cooper and Nephews, chemical manufacturers; a member of the Herts County Council, and interested in numerous local institutions.

WARRINGTON (10,814).—No change.

*Crosfield, A. H. (L.)	5,256
Pierpoint, R. (U.)	5,103
Liberal majority	153

1906.—L., 5,599; U., 4,099—L. maj., 1,500.
1900.—U., 4,468; L., 3,303—U. maj., 1,165.
1895.—U., maj., 675; 1892, U. maj., 585; 1886, U. maj., 501.

Mr. A. H. CROSFIELD is the head of a firm of soap and chemical manufacturers and is the eldest son of the late Mr. John Crosfield.

WARWICK AND LEAMINGTON (6,642).—
UNIONIST GAIN.

Pollock, E. M., K.C. (U.)	3,605
*Berridge, T. H. (L.)	2,651
Unionist majority	954

1906.—L., 3,011; U., 2,802—L. maj., 209.
1900.—U., 2,785; L., 1,954—U. maj., 831.
1895, 1892, and 1886, U. unop.

Mr. ERNEST MURRAY POLLOCK, who was born in 1861, was educated at Charterhouse and at Trinity College, Cambridge (Classical Tripos, 1883). He was called to the Bar by the Inner Temple in 1885, and contested the Holland Division of Lincolnshire in 1900 and 1906. He became a K.C. in 1905.

WEDNESBURY (13,479).—UNIONIST GAIN.

Griffiths, J. Norton (U.)	6,636
*Hyde, C. G. (L.)	6,040
Unionist majority	596

1906.—L., 6,150; U., 5,206—L. maj., 944.
1900.—U., 4,733; L., 4,558—U. maj., 175.
1895.—U. maj., 191; 1892, U. maj., 60; 1886, L. maj., 662.

Mr. JOHN NORTON GRIFFITHS was born in Somerset in 1871, and is managing director of Griffiths and Co. (Limited), contractors, and senior partner in the firm of Norton Griffiths, Bruce, Marriott, and Co.; has devoted most of his time to the carrying out of various important works connected with civil and mining engineering in Africa and America; a member of the Institute of Mining and Metallurgy and Fellow of the Geological Society; saw active service in the Mashona-Matabele War and in South Africa, where he acted as captain and adjutant of Lord Roberts's bodyguard, and also took part in the Paardeberg, Modder River, and other engagements.

WEST BROMWICH (11,299).—UNIONIST GAIN.

Lewisham, Viscount (U.)	5,672
*Hazel, Dr. A. E. W. (L.)	4,937
Unionist majority	735

1906.—L., 5,475; U., 4,259—L. maj., 1,216.
1900 and 1895.—U. unop.
1892.—U. maj., 1,045; 1886, U. maj., 569.

ENGLAND (BOROUGHS).

VISCOUNT LEWISHAM is the eldest son of the sixth Earl of Dartmouth. He was born in 1881 and married Lady Ruperta Wynn-Carrington, daughter of Earl Carrington. He represents Lewisham on the London County Council and is a lieutenant in the Staffordshire Yeomanry.

WHITEHAVEN (3,050).—UNIONIST GAIN.

Jackson, Lt.-Col. J. A. (U.)..	1,188
Wandless, W. H. (L.) ..	852
Sharp, A. (Lab.)	825
Unionist majority over Liberal	336
Unionist majority over Labour	363

1906.—L., 1,507; U., 1,194—L. maj., 313.
1900.—U., 1,553; L., 876—U. maj., 677.
1895.—U. maj., 266; 1892, L. maj., 218; 1886, U. maj., 106.

LIEUT.-COLONEL J. ARTHUR JACKSON was born in 1873 and educated at St. Peter's, York. He afterwards went into the business of Messrs. J. and W. Jackson, timber merchants, Whitehaven, and is actively associated with the iron and iron ore industries of the district. He is vice-chairman of the Whitehaven Hematite Iron and Steel Company, and a director of various iron ore mining companies. Mr. Jackson has for many years been a member of the Cumberland County Council and of the Whitehaven Harbour Board. He has taken a great interest in the Volunteer movement, is a member of the Cumberland Territorial Force Association, and Lieutenant-Colonel of the 5th Batt. Border Regiment.

WIGAN (9,577).—LABOUR GAIN.

Twist, H. (Lab.)	4,803
Neville, R. J. (U.)	4,293
Labour majority ..	510

1906.—U., 3,573; Lab., 2,205; L., 1,900—U. maj. over Lab., 1,368.
1900.—U., 3,772; L., 3,130—U. maj., 642.
1895.—U. maj., 874; 1892, U. maj., 110; 1886, U. maj., 591.

Mr. HENRY TWIST was born at Platt Bridge, near Wigan, in 1870; at 11 years of age began working in a local mine and has filled every position from door tenter to collier; elected in 1898 president of the local branch of the Lancashire and Cheshire Miners' Federation, and in 1906 succeeded Mr. Sam Woods, ex-Labour M.P., as miners' agent; has taken part in local municipal work.

WINCHESTER (3,200).—No change.

*Baring, Capt. the Hon. G. V. (U.)	1,729
Ricketts, G. W. (L.) ..	1,268
Unionist majority	461

1906.—U., 1,322; L., 1,272—U. maj., 50.
1900.—U., 1,342; L., 846—U. maj., 496.
1895.—U. unop.; 1892, U. maj., 354; 1886, U. maj., 336.

CAPTAIN GUY VICTOR BARING, born 1873, the fourth son of the fourth Lord Ashburton and brother to the present peer; educated at Eton and Sandhurst; Captain 2nd Batt. Coldstream Guards; served in the South African War, and was mentioned in despatches; elected for Winchester in the Unionist interest in 1906.

WINDSOR (3,210).—No change.

*Mason, J. F. (U.)	1,838
Hart, Heber (L.)	1,170
Unionist majority ..	668

1906.—U., 1,594; L., 1,376—U. maj., 123.
1900, 1895, 1892, and 1886.—U. unop.

Mr. JAMES FRANCIS MASON, who succeeded his uncle, Sir Francis Tress Barry, as the Unionist representative of Windsor in 1906, is chairman of the firm of Mason and Barry (Limited), and a director of Alfred Hickman (Limited), Dorman, Long, and Co. (Limited), and the North-Eastern Steel Company (Limited). In a letter addressed to *The Times* in November, 1907, he stated that "It was the cause of Tariff Reform that first dragged me from business into politics, and the success of that cause continues to be my dominant desire." He was born in 1861, educated at Eton, and served in the Oxfordshire Yeomanry.

WOLVERHAMPTON (3).

EAST (10,238).—No change.

*Thorne, G. R. (L.)	5,276
Amery, L. S. (U.)	4,462
Liberal majority ..	814

By-election, 1908.—L., 4,514; U., 4,506—L. maj., 8.
1906.—L., 5,610; U., 2,745—L. maj., 2,865.
1900.—L. unop.
1895.—L. maj., 1,034; 1892, L. unop.; 1886, L. maj., 1,123.

Mr. GEORGE RENNIE THORNE was born in 1853 at Longside, near Peterhead, and educated at Tettenhall College; was admitted a solicitor in 1876, taking honours and receiving the Law Society's prize; is an alderman of Wolverhampton, and was Mayor 1902-3; was a candidate for the West Division of the borough in 1895, and for the South Division in 1898; at the by-election, on Sir Henry Fowler being raised to the peerage, in May, 1908, was returned for Wolverhampton West by a majority of eight votes over Mr. L. S. Amery.

SOUTH (10,253).—UNIONIST GAIN.

Hickman, Col. T. (U.) ..	4,989
*Norman, Sir H. (L.) ..	4,619
Unionist majority ..	370

1906.—L., 4,823; U., 4,137—L. maj., 686.
1900.—L., 3,701; U., 3,532—L. maj., 169.
1895, 1892, 1886, U.—unop.

COL. THOMAS EDGECUMBE HICKMAN, C.B., D.S.O., was born in 1859, a son of Sir A. Hickman, and educated at Cheltenham College; he joined the Worcestershire Regt. in 1881, and saw a good deal of active service in Egypt and the Sudan between the years 1884 and 1900; was on special service in South Africa in 1900-1, served under General French, 1901-2, and commanded in the Middleburg District, Cape Colony, 1902-8.

WEST (13,170).—UNIONIST GAIN.

Bird, A. F. (U.)	6,382
*Richards, T. F. (Lab.) ..	5,790
Unionist majority ..	592

1906.—Lab., 5,756; U., 5,585—Lab. maj., 171.
1900.—U. unop.
1895 – U. maj., 823; 1892, U. maj., 1,116; 1886, L. maj., 123.

Mr. ALFRED FREDERICK BIRD is the chairman of the directors of Alfred Bird and Sons (Limited), analytical chemists, of Deritend, Birmingham. He was born in Birmingham and educated at King Edward's Grammar School in that city. He is a J.P. for Warwickshire.

WORCESTER (8,701).—No change.

*Goulding, E. A. (U.)	4,561
Morgan, J. (L.)	3,405
Unionist majority	156

By-election, 1908.—U., 4,361 ; L., 3,009—U. maj., 1,352.
1906.—U., 3,881 ; L., 3,752—U. maj., 129.
1900.—U. unop.
1895.—U. maj., 1,202 ; 1892, U. maj., over L., 813 ; 1886, U. maj., 143.

Mr. EDWARD ALFRED GOULDING, chairman of the Organization Committee of the Tariff Reform League, sat in the House as member for the Devizes Division of Wiltshire from 1895 to 1906 ; contested Central Finsbury at General Election of 1906, but was defeated ; was returned in February, 1908, for Worcester, which was disfranchised for a period ; born in 1863, educated at St. John's College, Cambridge, and called to the Bar in 1887.

YORK (2) (14,065).—No change.

Rowntree, A. (L.)	6,751
Butcher, J. G., K.C. (U.)	6,741
*Greenwood, Hamar (L.)	6,632
Smith, Riley (U.)	6,495

Liberal majority over defeated Unionist 256
Unionist majority over defeated Liberal 109

1906.—L., 6,413 ; U., 6,108 ; U., 6,094 ; Lab., 4,573—L. maj' over defeated U., 319.
1900.—Two U.'s unop.
1895.—U., 5,516 ; L., 5,309 ; L., 5,214—U. maj. over defeated L., 302.
1892.—U., 5,076 ; L., 5,030 ; L., 4,846—U. maj. over defeated L., 230.
1886.—L., 4,816 ; L., 4,810 ; U., 4,352 ; U., 4,295—L. maj., 458.

Mr. ARNOLD ROWNTREE, son of Mr. John Stephenson Rowntree, Lord Mayor of the city in 1881, was born in 1872, and educated at the Friends' School, Bootham ; began his business career in the establishment which his father then owned, and afterwards became associated with his uncle and cousins in the well-known cocoa firm, being made a director in 1897 ; has taken a great interest in the Adult School movement, and is president of that association ; was for some years on the executive of the National Liberal Federation.

Mr. JOHN GEORGE BUTCHER, K.C., a son of the late Bishop of Meath, was born at Killarney in 1852, and educated at Marlborough College and Trinity College, Cambridge. He graduated eighth classic and Eighth Wrangler at Cambridge, 1874, and was afterwards a Fellow of his College. He was called to the Bar at Lincoln's Inn in 1878 ; took silk in 1897 ; and became a Bencher in 1902. He represented York City from 1892 till 1906, when he was defeated by Mr. Hamar Greenwood. His brother is the senior member for Cambridge University.

ENGLAND (COUNTIES).

BEDFORDSHIRE (2).

NORTH, or BIGGLESWADE (14,031).—No change.

*Black, A. W. (L.)	6,631
Prothero, R. E. (U.)	6,020
Liberal majority	611

1906.—L., 6,902 ; U., 4,298—L. maj., 2,604.
1900.—U. unop.
1895.—U. maj., 267 ; 1892, L. maj., 544 ; 1886, U. maj., 482.

Mr. ARTHUR WILLIAM BLACK is a native of Nottingham and has been connected with that borough throughout his career. Born in 1863, he entered on business as a lace manufacturer in Nottingham in 1888. He was elected to the town council in 1895, was Sheriff in 1898-9, and Mayor in 1902-3. As a member of the Mosely Commission on Education he visited the United States in 1903. In 1900 he contested the Doncaster Division, and was elected for the Biggleswade Division in 1906.

SOUTH, or LUTON (16,564).—No change.

*Ashton, T. G. (L.)	7,946
Elliott, George, K.C. (U.)	7,080
Liberal majority	866

1906.—L., 7,240 ; U., 5,387—L. maj., 1,853.
1900.—L., 5,474 ; U., 5,371—L. maj., 103.
1895.—L. maj., 186 ; 1892, L. maj., 1,019 ; 1886, L. maj., 673.

Mr. T. GAIR ASHTON was born in 1855 and was educated at Rugby, and University College, Oxford. He is a County Councillor for Cheshire, and is a J.P. for Lancashire, Cheshire, and Sussex.

BERKSHIRE (3).

NORTH, or ABINGDON (9,255).—UNIONIST GAIN.

Henderson, Major H. G. (U.)	4,829
*Strauss, E. A. (L.)	3,776
Unionist majority	1,053

1906.—L., 3,943; U., 3,767—L. maj., 176.
1900.—U. unop.
1895.—U. maj., 1,045; 1892, U. maj., 326; 1886, U. maj., 1,989.

MAJOR HENDERSON is the eldest son of Sir Alexander and Lady Henderson, of Buscot Park, near Faringdon, Berks; born at Ealing in 1875 and educated at Eton; joined the Berks Militia and gazetted to the First Life Guards in 1897; served with distinction in the Boer War; retired from the Army in 1906, and joined the Berks Yeomanry with the rank of major; toured round the world in 1908; is president of the Lechlade and president-elect of the Abingdon Agricultural Societies; a J.P. for Berkshire.

SOUTH, or NEWBURY (13,063).—UNIONIST GAIN.

Mount, W. A. (U.)	7,081
Hedderwick, T.C.H., K.C.(L.)	4,723
Unionist majority	2,358

1906.—L., 5,338; U., 4,936—L. maj., 402.
1900.—U. unop.
1895.—U. maj., 1,129; 1892, U. maj., 650; 1886, U. unop.

Mr. WILLIAM ARTHUR MOUNT, son of Mr. W. G. Mount, was born in 1866, was educated at Eton, and New College, Oxford, and called to the Bar, Inner Temple, 1893. In 1899 he married a daughter of Mr. Malcolm Low, of Clatto, Fife. He represented the division from 1900 to 1906 and was private secretary to two Chancellors of the Exchequer—Sir Michael Hicks Beach and Mr. Ritchie.

EAST, or WOKINGHAM (14,327).—No change.

*Gardner, E. (U.)	8,132
Knight, S. Holford (L.)	4,095
Unionist majority	4,037

1906.—U., 6,075; L., 4,750—U. maj., 1,325.
1900.—U. unop.
1895 and 1886.—U. unop. 1892; U. maj., 2,248.

Mr. ERNEST GARDNER was born in 1846 in Essex and succeeded to the Berkshire property of his uncle, John Silvester, in 1864. He is a J.P. and an alderman for the county of Berkshire and has been Mayor of Maidenhead. Having become a Liveryman of the Drapers' Company in 1873 he served as Master in 1901. He was returned unopposed for the Wokingham Division at a by-election in 1901 and held the seat against Lord Haddo in 1906.

BUCKINGHAMSHIRE (3).

MID, or AYLESBURY (12,218).—No change.

Rothschild, Lionel (U.)	6,037
Atkins, R. Wallace (L.)	4,574
Unionist majority	1,463

1906.—U., 5,675; L., 4,463—U. maj., 1,212.
1900 and 1895.—U. unop.
1892.—U. maj., 2,523; 1886, U. maj., 3,043.

Mr. LIONEL NATHAN ROTHSCHILD, the son of Mr. Leopold Rothschild, of Ascott, Bucks, and nephew of Lord Rothschild, was born in 1882 and educated at Cambridge; is a lieutenant in the Bucks Yeomanry and a J.P. for the county.

NORTH, or BUCKINGHAM (13,081).—No change.

*Verney, F. W. (L.)	6,055
Fremantle, Hon. T. F. (U.)	5,944
Liberal majority	111

1906.—L., 6,253; U., 4,673—L. maj., 1,580.
1900.—U., 5,101; L., 4,684—U. maj., 417.
1895.—U. maj., 436; 1892, L. maj., 449; 1886, U. maj., 71.

Mr. FREDERICK WILLIAM VERNEY, a son of the late Sir H. Verney, who formerly sat in the House of Commons, was born in 1846, and educated at Harrow, and Christ Church, Oxford; took Holy Orders, but afterwards relinquished them, and was called to the Bar in 1875; has been secretary to and Councillor of the Siamese Legation; was for nine years a member of the London County Council, and is a member of the Bucks County Council; made three unsuccessful attempts to enter Parliament before his election for North Bucks in 1906.

SOUTH, or WYCOMBE (16,366).—UNIONIST GAIN.

Cripps, Sir C. A., K.C. (U.)	8,690
*Herbert, T. Arnold (L.)	6,134
Unionist majority	2,556

1906.—L., 6,839; U., 5,626—L. maj., 1,213.
1900.—U., 6,111; L., 3,582—U. maj., 2,529.
1895.—U. unop.; 1892, U. maj., 1,042; 1886, U. maj., 1,083.

SIR CHARLES ALFRED CRIPPS was born in 1852, educated at Winchester and Oxford, Fellow of St. John's College, gained the Senior Studentship of the Inns of Court in 1876, and was called to the Bar at the Middle Temple in 1877, becoming Q.C. in 1890. He was Attorney-General to the Prince of Wales, 1895 to 1901, and then reappointed, resigning in 1908; Vicar-General of York, 1900; Vicar-General of Canterbury, 1902. His publications include "The Laws of Church and Clergy," and "Law of Compensation," and he has represented in previous Parliaments the Stroud Division of Gloucestershire and the Stretford Division of Lancashire. In 1908 he was made a K.C.V.O.

CAMBRIDGESHIRE (3).

WEST, or CHESTERTON (10,860).—No change.

*Montagu, Hon. E. S. (L.)	5,240
Morrison-Bell, Capt. E. W. (U.)	4,735
Liberal majority	505

1906.—L., 4,829 ; U., 4,316—L. maj., 513.
1900.—U., 4,190 ; L., 3,961—U. maj., 229.
1895.—U. maj., 420 ; 1892, L. maj., 398 : 1886, U. maj., 976.

Mr. EDWIN SAMUEL MONTAGU is a son of Lord Swaythling. Born in 1879, he received his education at Clifton, and Trinity College, Cambridge, where he was President of the Union. He was appointed Parliamentary private secretary to Mr. Asquith in 1906 and served on the Royal Commission on Electoral Reform in 1908. His present constituency elected him in 1906.

EAST, or NEWMARKET (10,366).—UNIONIST GAIN.

Verrall, G. H. (U.)	4,752
*Rose, Sir C. D. (L.)	4,632
Unionist majority	120

1906.—L., 4,666 ; U., 3,883—L. maj., 783.
1900.—U., 4,295 ; L., 3,218—U. maj., 1,077.
1895.—U. maj., 343 ; 1892, L. maj., 1,223 ; 1886, L. maj. 300.

Mr. GEORGE HENRY VERRALL, of Sussex Lodge, Newmarket, and a member of the well-known racing firm of Messrs. Pratt and Co., is, like Sir Charles D. Rose, keenly interested in racing and the breeding of racehorses, and very popular in the division ; born in 1848, the youngest son of Mr. John Verrall, of Lewes ; a J.P. for Suffolk and Cambridgeshire ; for many years a member of the Cambridge County Council and chairman of the Newmarket Conservative Association.

NORTH, or WISBECH (11,713).—No change.

Primrose, Hon. Neil (L.)	5,279
Garfit, T. Cheney (U.)	5,079
Liberal majority	200

1906.—L., 5,125 ; U., 4,080—L. maj., 1,045.
1900.—L., 4,007 ; U., 3,846—L. maj., 161.
1895.—U. maj., 223 ; 1892, L. maj., 122 ; 1886, U. maj., 1,087.

The HON. NEIL JAMES ARCHIBALD PRIMROSE is the second son of the Earl of Rosebery. He was born in 1882, was educated at Eton and Oxford, and is a second lieutenant in the Buckinghamshire Yeomanry.

CHESHIRE (8).

ALTRINCHAM (18,921).—No change.

*Crossley, Sir W. J. (L.)	8,709
Bury, Viscount (U.)	7,808
Liberal majority	901

1906.—L., 8,321 ; U., 5,672—L. maj., 2,649.
1900.—U., 5,685 ; L., 4,177—U. maj., 1,508.
1895.—U. maj., 1,375 ; 1892, U. maj., 798 ; 1886, U. unop.

SIR WILLIAM CROSSLEY is the chairman of the engineering firm of Crossley Brothers, of Manchester, and the hon. freedom of that city has been conferred upon him. He is a resident in the Altrincham Division, and was returned in 1906 as its representative. He received a knighthood last year.

CREWE (15,866).—No change.

*Tomkinson, Rt. Hon. J. (L.)	7,761
Harrington, Col. Sir J. (U.)	5,419
Rose, F. H. (Lab.)	1,380
Liberal majority	2,342

1906.—L., 7,805 ; U., 5,297—L. maj., 2,508.
1900.—L., 6,120 ; U., 4,921—L. maj., 1,199.
1895.—U. maj., 550 ; 1892, L. maj., 1,568 ; 1886, L. maj., 615.

The RIGHT HON. JAMES TOMKINSON, the son of Lieutenant-Colonel W. Tomkinson, was born at Willington, 1840, educated at Rugby and Balliol College, Oxford (B.A., 1863), and in 1871 married a daughter of Sir G. Hudson Palmer. He was High Sheriff of Cheshire 1887, and was first vice-chairman of the county council. Formerly hon. lieutenant-colonel in the Earl of Chester's Imperial Yeomanry, he retired in 1906. He is J.P. and D.L. for the county of Chester and a director of Lloyds Bank. He has represented the division since his first election in 1900.

EDDISBURY (11,488).—UNIONIST GAIN.

Barnston, H. (U.)	5,664
*Stanley, Hon. A. L. (L.)	4,976
Unionist majority	688

1906.—L., 5,315 ; U., 4,192—L. maj., 1,123.
1900.—U. unop.
1895.—U. maj., 1,805 ; 1892, U. maj., 536 ; 1886, U. maj., 679.

Mr. HARRY BARNSTON, who was born in 1870, is the son of the late Major W. Barnston, of Crewe Hill, Farndon, Cheshire ; was educated at Oxford and called to the Bar in 1898 ; is a county magistrate, lord of the manor of Farndon, and a captain in the Cheshire Imperial Yeomanry.

HYDE (12,166).—No change.

Neilson, F. (L.)	4,476
Eastham, Dr. T. (U.)	4,461
Anderson, W. C. (Lab.)	2,401
Liberal majority over Unionist	15

1906.—L., 5,545 ; U., 4,482—L. maj., 1,063.
1900.—U., 4,774 ; L., 4,195—U. maj., 579.
1895.—U. maj. over L., 891 ; 1892, U. maj., 305 ; 1886, U. maj., 443.

Mr. FRANCIS NEILSON was born at Birkenhead in 1867, and educated at Wellington (Salop), Liverpool High School, and privately by Dr. Finlayson ; is a journalist and author ; founder and editor of the *Democratic Monthly* ; has travelled in America and Canada, Germany, Hungary, and Austria ; is regarded as an authority on the land question ; unsuccessfully contested the Newport Division of Shropshire in 1906-7.

KNUTSFORD (12,142).—UNIONIST GAIN.

Sykes, A. J. (U.)	6,199
*King, A. J. (L.)	5,084
Unionist majority	1,115

1906.—L., 5,296 ; U., 4,596—L. maj., 700.
1900, 1895, and 1886.—U. unop.
1892.—U. maj., 1,962.

Mr. ALAN JOHN SYKES, a son of the late Mr. T. H. Sykes, of Cringle House, Cheshire, was born in 1868; is a magistrate for the county, and was for several years major in the 3rd Volunteer Batt. Cheshire Regiment.

MACCLESFIELD (9,306).—No change.

*Brocklehurst, Col. W. B. (L.)	4,534
Bromley-Davenport, Col. W. (U.)	4,384
Liberal majority	150

1906.—L., 4,251; U., 3,737—L. maj., 514.
1900 and 1895.—U. unop.
1892.—U. maj., 926 ; 1886. U. maj., 527.

Col. WILLIAM BROCKLEHURST, son of the late Mr. W. C. Brocklehurst, M.P. for the division, was born in 1851, and educated at Cheltenham College, and Magdalen College, Oxford. He is senior partner in the firm of Brocklehurst and Son, silk manufacturers, Macclesfield, and is connected with many local offices. He is J.P. for the county, lieutenant-colonel of the Cheshire Yeomanry, and has represented the constituency since 1906.

NORTHWICH (13,389).—No change

†Brunner, J. F. L. (L.)	6,661
Williams, C. (U.)	5,542
Liberal majority	1,119

1906.—L., 6,343 ; U., 4,551—L. maj., 1,792.
1900.—L., 5,377 ; U., 4,678—L. maj., 699.
1895.—L. maj., 1,638 ; 1892, L. maj., 1,255 ; 1886, U. maj., 458.

Mr. J. F. L. BRUNNER is the son of Sir John Brunner, who represented this constituency for nearly a quarter of a century, retiring at the close of the last Parliament. He was born in 1865, and is a director in the firm of Brunner, Mond, and Co., chemical manufacturers, of which his father is chairman, and was educated at Cheltenham College, at the Zurich Polytechnic School, and at Trinity Hall, Cambridge. He was a member of the Cheshire County Council from 1892 to 1895. He was elected for Lancashire (Leigh) in 1906.

WIRRAL (22,330).—UNIONIST GAIN.

Stewart, Gershom (U.)	10,309
Jones, E. Peter (L.)	8,862
Unionist majority	1,447

1906.—L., 8,833 ; U., 7,132—L. maj., 1,701.
1900.—U., 6,084 ; L., 5,079—U. maj., 1,005.
1895 and 1886.—U. unop. ; 1892, U. maj. 2,548.

Mr. GERSHOM STEWART is a native of Birkenhead, where he was born in 1857; served some of his early years in East India houses in Liverpool, and in 1882 went to China in the service of the Hong-kong and Shanghai Bank, from 1889 in business in China on his own account, and was a member of the Hong-kong Legislature ; chairman of the China Association, and represented Hong-kong at the Conference of the Chambers of Commerce of the Empire in London in 1906; has retired from business and resides at Whitehome, Hoylake, Cheshire.

CORNWALL (6).

SOUTH-EAST, or BODMIN (11,553).—No change.

Grenfell, C. A. (L.)	5,133
Pole-Carew, Lt.-Gen. Sir R. (U.)	5,083
Liberal majority	50

By-election, 1906.—L., 4,969 ; U., 3,876—L. maj., 1,093.
1906.—L., 5,201 ; U., 4,029—L. maj., 1,172.
1900.—U., 4,280 ; L., 3,248—U. maj., 1,032.
1895.—U. maj., 543 ; 1892, U. maj., 231 ; 1886, U. maj., 1,662.

Mr. CECIL ALFRED GRENFELL is the second son of the late Mr. Pascoe du Pré Grenfell, and was born in 1864 ; when at school he played in the Eton Eleven, and he has since ridden in the Grand National Steeplechase ; served with the Imperial Yeomanry in South Africa, and is a major in the Buckinghamshire Yeomanry ; unsuccessfully contested Rochester in 1895 against the present Marquis of Salisbury.

NORTH-WEST, or CAMBORNE (9,375).—No change.

*Dunn, A. E. (L.)	5,027
Chamberlain, N. (U.)	2,587
Liberal majority	2,440

1906.—L., 4,614 ; U., 2,384 ; Soc., 109—L. maj. over U., 2,230
1900.—L., 3,101 ; U., 2,993—L. maj., 108.
1895.—U. maj., 462 ; 1892, L. maj., 438 ; 1886, L. maj., 1,187.

Mr. ALBERT EDWARD DUNN is a member of the firm of Dunn and Baker, solicitors, Exeter, and was born in 1864. He was educated at Hallam Hall College, Clevedon, Somerset ; has been a member of the Exeter City Council since 1888, and was Mayor of Exeter in 1900-2, and hon. town clerk in 1905. He took an active part in the reorganization of the Royal Albert Memorial College, and was prominently associated with the erection of the statue in Exeter to General Buller.

LAUNCESTON (9,857).—No change.

*Marks, G. C. (L.)	4,703
Grylls, H. B. (U.)	3,564
Liberal majority	1,139

1906.—L., 4,658 ; U., 2,736—L. maj., 1,922.
1900.—L., 3,831 ; U., 2,737—L. maj., 1,094.
1895.—L. maj., 658 ; 1892, L. maj., 984 ; 1886, L. unop.

Mr. GEORGE CROYDON MARKS is senior partner in the firm of Marks and Clerk, consulting engineers and patent experts, of London, Birmingham, and Manchester. Much of his professional education was acquired at King's College, London, and at Woolwich Arsenal. He has travelled considerably in the course of his profession, and was at one time consulting engineer to the late Duke of Saxe-Coburg-Gotha. He was elected for the division in 1906.

MID, or ST. AUSTELL (10,968).—No change.

*Agar-Robartes, Hon. T. (L.)	6,225
Bernard, F. T. H. (U.)	3,138
Liberal majority	3,087

By-election, 1908.—L. unop.
1906.—L., 5.667 ; U., 2,516—L. maj., 3,151.
1900.—L. unop.
1895.—L. maj., 1,101 ; 1892, L. maj., 1,608 ; 1886, L. unop.

Mr. T. C. R. AGAR-ROBARTES, the eldest son of Viscount Clifden, was born in 1880; takes keen interest in sport and agriculture, and at Oxford was president of the Bullingdon Hunt and Master of the Draghounds; elected for the Bodmin Division of Cornwall in January, 1906, but unseated on petition in the following June; returned for the St. Austell Division at the by-election in February, 1908, occasioned by the retirement of Mr. McArthur, one of the Liberal Whips.

WEST, or ST. IVES (9,411).—No change.
*Cory, Sir C. J. (L.)	4,458
Levita, Major C. B. (U.)	3,586
Liberal majority	872

1906.—L., 4,244; U., 3,052—L. maj., 1,192.
1900, 1895, and 1892.—U. unop.
1886.—U. maj., 2,507.

SIR CLIFFORD CORY is the son of the late Mr. John Cory, a wealthy Glamorgan colliery proprietor, and was born in 1859. He was educated privately and abroad; is a member of the firm of Cory Brothers and Co. (Limited), colliery owners and coal exporters, South Wales, a director of the Barry Railway Company, and since 1892 a member of the Glamorgan County Council and of the South Wales Conciliation Board. He is a J.P. for Glamorgan and Monmouth, and filled the office of High Sheriff of Monmouthshire in 1905.

TRURO (10,162).—No change.
*Morgan, G. Hay (L.)	4,873
Durning-Lawrence, Sir E.(U.)	4,262
Liberal majority	611

1906.—L., 4,187; U., 3,683—L. maj., 504.
1900.—U., 3,869; L., 3,051—U. maj., 818.
1895.—U. maj., 270; 1892, U. maj., 1,511; 1886, U. maj., 1,976.

Mr. GEORGE HAY MORGAN, who was born in 1866, was for some years pastor to Woodberry Down Chapel, Tottenham. Leaving his ministry there, he began to study for the law in 1896 and was called to the Bar in 1899. He was actively engaged on behalf of the Liberal interest at Tottenham in 1895 and was in 1900 an unsuccessful candidate for the division. Truro gave him a seat in the last Parliament.

CUMBERLAND (4).

COCKERMOUTH (11,328).—No change.
*Randles, Sir J. S. (U.)	4,579
Lawson, Sir Wilfrid (L.)	3,638
Whitehead, J. P. (Lab.)	1,909
Unionist majority	941

1906.—U., 4,593; L., 3,903; Lab., 1,436—U. maj. over L., 690.
1900.—U., 4,276; L., 4,067—U. maj., 209.
1895.—L. maj., 241; 1892, L. maj., 770; 1886, L. maj., 1,004.

SIR JOHN SCURRAH RANDLES, knighted in 1905, is a son of the Rev. Dr. M. Randles, was born at Boston in 1857, educated at Woodhouse Grove School, near Leeds, and married a daughter of Mr. R. Spencer, of Bolton. He is chairman and managing director of the Moss Bay Hematite Iron and Steel Company, a director of the Workington Iron Company, and chairman of the West Cumberland Blast Furnacemen's and Masters' Conciliation Board. He represented the division from 1900 to 1906, was defeated at the General Election, but was returned at a by-election on the death of Sir W. Lawson in August of that year.

WEST, or EGREMONT (10,424).—UNIONIST GAIN.
Grant, J. A. (U.)	4,060
*Fullerton, H. (L.)	3,949
Unionist majority	111

1906.—L., 4,067; U., 3,255—L. maj., 812.
1900.—U., 3,917; L., 3,377—U. maj., 540.
1895.—U. maj., 131; 1892, L. maj., 471; 1886, U. maj., 164.

Mr. JAMES AUGUSTUS GRANT, son of the late Colonel Grant, C.B., was born in 1867 and educated at Oxford; travelled with Mr. Cecil Rhodes in South Africa; private secretary to Mr. Gerald Balfour when he was Chief Secretary for Ireland; was Registrar of the Royal College of Art under the Board of Education from 1899 to 1904; unsuccessfully contested Banffshire in 1892 and 1895; a good all-round sportsman, and very popular with the iron ore miners in the division.

NORTH, or ESKDALE (11,014).—No change.
*Howard, Hon. Geoffrey (L.)	4,504
Lowther, Claude (U.)	4,470
Liberal majority	34

1906.—L., 4,467; U., 4,230—L. maj., 237.
1900.—U., 4,052; L., 3,349—U. maj., 703.
1895.—L. maj., 147; 1892, L. maj., 813; 1886, L. maj., 886.

Mr. GEOFFREY WILLIAM ALGERNON HOWARD is a son of the Earl of Carlisle and brother to Viscount Morpeth, the Unionist member for East Birmingham; introduced in March, 1909, a Representation of the People Bill; the second reading was carried by a majority of 35, but the Bill did not proceed further; born in 1877, and educated at Trinity College, Cambridge.

PENRITH (8,907).—No change.
*Lowther, Right Hon. J. W. (U.)

1906.—U. unop.
1900.—U. unop.
1895.—U. maj., 600: 1892, U. maj., 125; 1886, U. maj., 644.

The RIGHT HON. JAMES WILLIAM LOWTHER, J.P., LL.M., D.L., D.C.L. (Oxford), has been Speaker of the House of Commons since June, 1905. Born in London in 1855, the son of the Hon. William Lowther, he was educated at Eton, King's College, London, and Trinity College, Cambridge; graduated LL.M. 1882 (honours in Classical and Law Tripos), became Fellow of King's College, London, and D.C.L., Oxford, 1907. In 1886 he married a daughter of the late Right Hon. A. J. B. Beresford-Hope. Called to the Bar at the Inner Temple, 1879, he was Bencher in 1906. From August, 1883, to November, 1885, he represented Rutland in Parliament, and was unsuccessful in a contest for Mid Cumberland in 1885. In 1886 he was elected for the division which he has represented since, being returned without opposition in 1900 and 1906. In 1891-2 he was Under-Secretary for Foreign Affairs, and in 1892 was representative of this country at the International Conference held in Venice. From 1895 to 1905 he was Chairman of Committee of Ways and Means and Deputy-Speaker.

DERBYSHIRE (7).
CHESTERFIELD (16,248).—No change.

*Haslam, J. (Lab.)	8,234
Radford, G. W. (U.)	5,693
Labour majority	2,541

1906.—Lab., 7,254; U., 5,590—Lab. maj., 1,664.
1900.—L., 5,418; U., 4,729—L. maj., 689.
1895.—L. maj., 247; 1892., L. maj., 180; 1886., U. maj., 114.

Mr. JAMES HASLAM, the secretary of the Derbyshire Miners' Association, was born in 1842, and was educated at a colliery school. He was a member of the Chesterfield Town Council from 1896 to 1905, and is a member of the Parliamentary Committee of the Trade Union Congress. He is a J.P. for Chesterfield.

HIGH PEAK (12,412).—No change.

*Partington, O. (L.)	5,912
Hill-Wood, S. (U.)	5,806
Liberal majority	106

By-election, July, 1909.—L., 5,619; U., 5,272—L. maj., 347.
1906.—L., 5,450; U., 4,662—L. maj., 788.
1900.—L., 4,591; U., 4,432—L. maj., 159.
1895.—U. maj., 507; 1892, U. maj., 366; 1886, U. maj., 161.

Mr. OSWALD PARTINGTON, who was born in 1873 and educated at Rossall, is a director of the Kellner-Partington Paper Pulp Company, of Manchester, and a member of the firm of Messrs. Olive and Partington, Glossop; first elected for the division in 1900; was appointed Junior Lord of the Treasury (unpaid) in July, 1909.

ILKESTON (19,467).—No change.

*Foster, Rt. Hon. Sir W. (L.)	10,632
Morrow, F. St. John (U.)	6,432
Liberal majority	4,200

1906.—L., 9,655; U., 5,358—L. maj., 4,297.
1900.—L., 6,633; U., 5,698—L. maj., 935.
1895.—L. maj., 961; 1892, L. maj., 1,783; 1886, L. maj., 828.

SIR B. WALTER FOSTER first entered Parliament for Chester City in 1885, but was defeated in the following year. In 1887 he was returned by the Ilkeston Division, which he has since represented. Born at Cambridge and educated at Drogheda Grammar School, and Trinity College, Dublin, he became Professor of Medicine at Queen's College, Birmingham, in 1868, and occupied that post until 1892. After achieving various medical distinctions he entered politics and became chairman of the National Liberal Federation, president of the Allotments and Small Holdings Association, president of the Land Law Reform Association, and held office from 1892 to 1895 as Parliamentary Secretary to the Local Government Board.

MID (13,660).—No change.

*Hancock, J. G. (Lab.)	7,557
Francis, F. (U.)	4,268
Labour majority	3,289

By-election, July, 1909.—Lab., 6,735; U., 4,392—Lab. maj., 2,343.
1906.—L., 7,065; U., 3,475—L. maj., 3,590.
1900.—L., 5,323; U., 4,094—L. maj., 1,229.
1895.—L. maj., 575; 1892, L. maj., 992; 1886, L. maj., 863.

Mr. JOHN GEORGE HANCOCK, who was returned as Labour member for Mid Derbyshire at a by-election in July, 1909, was born in the colliery village of Pinxton in 1858; is self-educated, and has worked as a collier; after filling several offices under the Notts Miners' Association he was appointed agent 13 years ago, and went to live in Nottingham, where he became a member of the town council; is a local preacher of the United Methodist Free Church, and an active temperance worker.

NORTH-EAST (17,701).—No change.

*Harvey, W. E. (Lab.)	8,715
Court, Dr. J. (U.)	6,411
Labour majority	2,304

By-election, 1907.—Lab., 6,644; U., 5,915—Lab. maj., 729.
1906.—L., 7,665; U., 5,896—L. maj., 1,769.
1900.—L., 5,251; U., 4,983—L. maj., 268.
1895.—L. maj., 527; 1892, L. maj., 2,172; 1886, L. maj., 721.

Mr. WILLIAM EDWIN HARVEY, born in 1852 at Hasland, near Chesterfield, began work in the pits as a boy. He continued work as a miner until 1881, and then became agent for the Derbyshire Miners' Association. He is a member of the Chesterfield Town Council and of the Education Committee, a J.P., and an executive member of the Miners' Federation of Great Britain and of the Conciliation Board. He was elected for the Parliamentary division at a by-election in 1907.

SOUTH (17,368).—No change.

*Raphael, H. H. (L.)	8,259
Marsden-Smedley, J. B. (U.)	7,473
Liberal majority	786

1906.—L., 7,961; U., 6,468—L. maj., 1,493.
1900.—U., 6,073; L., 5,707—U. maj., 366.
1895.—U. maj., 887; 1892, L. unop.; 1886, L. maj., 1,153.

Mr. HERBERT HENRY RAPHAEL fought four Parliamentary contests without success before he secured election as the representative of South Derbyshire in 1906. He was born in 1862, educated in Germany and France and at Trinity Hall, Cambridge. Having practised at the Bar for some years, he abandoned the pursuit of his profession in order to take up public work, and served for a time as a member of the London School Board, the first London County Council, and the Essex County Council.

WEST (11,962).—No change.

*Kerry, the Earl of (U.)	5,974
Hinmers, E. (L.)	4,925
Unionist majority	1,049

By-election, 1908.—U. unop.
1906.—U., 5,283; L., 4,724—U. maj., 559.
1900, 1895, and 1888, U. unop.
1892.—U. maj., 3,193.

The EARL of KERRY, the eldest son of the Marquis of Lansdowne, was born in 1872 and educated at Eton and Balliol College, Oxford; entered the Grenadier Guards in 1895, and, five years later, transferred to the Irish Guards; served in the South African War (1899-

1900), and retired with the rank of major in 1906; contested the Appleby Division of Westmorland in 1906, when he was beaten by three votes by Mr. Leif Jones, who was himself defeated in the same constituency in 1910; returned, unopposed, for West Derbyshire in April, 1908, on the succession of Mr. Victor Cavendish to the dukedom of Devonshire.

DEVONSHIRE (8).
Mid, or Ashburton (11,976).—Liberal Gain.

Buxton, C. R. (L.)	5,668
*Morrison-Bell,Capt.E.F.(U.)	5,421
Liberal majority	247

By-election, 1908.—U., 5,191; L., 4,632—U. maj., 559.
1906.—L., 5,079; U., 3,790—L. maj., 1,289.
1900.—L., 4,487; U., 3,716—L. maj., 771.

Mr. CHARLES RODEN BUXTON is a son of Sir Thomas Fowell Buxton and is 34 years of age. He was educated at Harrow, and Trinity College, Cambridge, and took a first class in the Classical Tripos, 1897. Mr. Buxton acted as secretary to his father when Sir Thomas Fowell Buxton was Governor of South Australia. He has visited South Africa, had ranching experience in Canada, and at home has interested himself in social and educational work in connexion with Morley College and in the promotion of small holdings. He is a member of the Balkan Committee, and as an outcome of a visit to Turkey wrote a book on " Turkey in Revolution."

North-West, or Barnstaple (13,126).— No change.

*Soares, E. J. (L.)	6,236
Borwick, G. (U.)	5,354
Liberal majority	882

1906.—L., 6,510; U., 4,465—L. maj., 2,045.
1900.—L., 5,007; U., 4,660—L. maj., 347.
1895.—U. maj., 232; 1892, L. maj., 147; 1886, U. maj., 1,262.

Mr. ERNEST JOSEPH SOARES, born in 1864, was an exhibitioner at St. John's College, Cambridge, and first-class prizeman, graduated B.A. and LL.B. (with honours in law), and subsequently M.A. and LL.D. In 1893 he married a daughter of the late Samuel Lord, of Ashton-on-Mersey. He was admitted solicitor in 1888, and was for some time partner in the firm of Allen, Prestage, and Soares, in Manchester; has acted as private secretary to Mr. H. Gladstone. He was elected for the division in 1900 and 1906.

East, or Honiton (10,522).—No change.

Morrison-Bell, Major Clive (U.)	5,604
Luke, W. B. (L.)	3,733
Unionist majority	1,871

1906.—U., 4,854; L., 3,711—U. maj., 1,143.
1900 and 1895.—U. unop.
1892.—U. maj., 2,026; 1886, U. unop.

MAJOR A. C. MORRISON-BELL is a son of Sir Charles Morrison-Bell, of Otterburn Hall, Northumberland, and brother of the late member for the Tavistock Division of Devonshire; born in 1871, he got his commission in the Scots Guards in 1890, and his majority in 1906, retiring from the Army two years later; served in the South African War with the Canadian contingent, and took part in the operations at Paardeberg, Poplar Grove, and Dreifontein.

North, or South Molton (8,700).—No change.

*Lambert, G. (L.)	4,419
Perowne, Col. (U.)	3,398
Liberal majority	1,021

1906 and 1900.—L. unop.
1895.—L. maj., 1,360; 1892, L. maj., 1,339; 1886, U. maj., 1,689.

Mr. GEORGE LAMBERT, Civil Lord of the Admiralty since 1905 in the late Government, was born 1866 at South Taunton, and educated in the Grammar School there. He is a farmer and lord of the manor of Spreyton, J.P., county councillor, and was formerly Captain in the 3rd Batt. of the Devonshire Regiment. He served on the Royal Commission on Agriculture, 1893, and on the Committee on Preferential Railway Rates. In 1904 he married a daughter of the late Mr. G. Stavers, of Morpeth, and has represented the division since 1891.

West, or Tavistock (15,063).—No change.

*Luttrell, H. C. F. (L.)	6,570
Spear, J. W. (U.)	6,343
Liberal majority	227

1906.—L., 6,405; U., 5,196—L. maj., 1,209.
1900.—U., 4,746; L., 4,731—U. maj., 15.
1895.—L. maj., 373; 1892, L. maj., 217; 1886, U. maj., 1,195.

Mr. HUGH COURTNEY FOWNES LUTTRELL, who sat for the division from 1892 to 1900, and again from 1906, was formerly captain in the Rifle Brigade, and acted as A.D.C. to Lord Cowper and Lord Spencer, Viceroys of Ireland, and to General Sir John Adye, Governor of Gibraltar; born in 1857 and educated at Cheltenham College.

North-East, or Tiverton (9,660).—No change.

*Walrond, Hon. W. L. C. (U.)	4,945
Heathcoat-Amory, I. (L.)	4,153
Unionist majority	792

1906.—U., 4,455; L., 3,970—U. maj., 485.
1900 and 1895.—U. unop.
1892.—U. maj., 1,332; 1886, U. unop.

The HON. WILLIAM LIONEL WALROND, eldest son of Lord Waleran, was born in 1876, and in 1904 married a daughter of Mr. G. Coats, of Ayr, N.B. He acted as private secretary to his father when Sir W. Walrond was Whip to the Unionist Party and to Sir A. Acland-Hood. He was elected for the division in 1906.

Torquay (11,241).—No change.

*Layland-Barratt, Sir F. (L.)	5,104
Lopes, Sir H. Buller (U.)	5,093
Liberal majority	11

1906.—L., 4,856; U., 4,396—L. maj., 460.
1900.—L., 4,020; U., 3,891—L. maj., 129.
1895.—U. maj., 175; 1892, U. maj., 394; 1886, U. maj., 80.

SIR FRANCIS LAYLAND-BARRATT, son of the late Francis Barratt, of St. Austell, Cornwall, was born in 1860 and educated at Trinity Hall, Cambridge;

assumed by Royal licence the additional name of Layland; High Sheriff of Cornwall in 1897; an unsuccessful candidate for the division in 1895, and was returned in 1900 and again in 1906; chairman of the Local Legislation Committee of the House of Commons last Session.

TOTNES (10,107).—No change.

*Mildmay, F. B. (U.)	.. ..	5,505
Foot, I. (L.)	.. ..	3,578
Unionist majority	..	1,927

1906.—U., 5,226; L., 2,998—U. maj., 2,228.
1900.—U. unop.
1895.—U. maj., 2,366 · 1892, U. maj., 2,431; 1886, U. maj., 3,511.

Mr. FRANCIS BINGHAM MILDMAY, son of Mr. H. B. Mildmay, of Shoreham and Flete, S. Devon, his mother being a grand-daughter of the second Earl Grey, was born in London, 1861, educated at Eton and Trinity College, Cambridge (B.A. 1884), and in 1906 married a daughter of Mr. Seymour Grenfell. He is a J.P., lieutenant-colonel of the West Kent Imperial Yeomanry, and served in South Africa. He has represented the division since 1885, and won the House of Commons Steeplechase, 1892.

DORSET (4).
EAST (14,794).—No change.

Guest, Capt. the Hon. F. (L.)	6,957
Nicholson, Col. J. S. (U.) ..	6,531
Liberal majority ..	426

1906.—L., 6,104; U., 6,083—L. maj., 21.
1900.—U., 4,776; L., 4,680—U. maj., 96.
1895 and 1892.—U. unop.; 1886, U. maj., 655.

CAPTAIN the HON. FREDERICK EDWARD GUEST is the third son of Lord Wimborne, and was born in 1875. He joined the 1st Life Guards, and served on the White Nile in 1900 and in South Africa 1901-2. He also held an appointment as A.D.C. in India, and was attached to the Egyptian Army. He has since acted as assistant secretary (unpaid) to the President of the Board of Trade.

NORTH (8,616).—UNIONIST GAIN.

Baker, Sir Randolf (U.)	..	4,093
*Wills, A. W. (L.)..	..	3,944
Unionist majority	..	149

1906.—L., 4,153; U., 3,508—L. maj., 645.
1900.—U., 3,705; L., 3,165—U. maj., 540.
1895.—U. unop.; 1892, U. maj., 525; 1886, L. maj., 235.

SIR RANDOLF LITTLEHALES BAKER, of Ranston, Blandford, Dorset, was born in 1879, the only son of Canon Sir T. H. Baker, whom he succeeded in the baronetcy in 1900; is a lieutenant in the Dorset Yeomanry and a county magistrate; unsuccessfully contested the division at the by-election in 1905, on the death of Mr. Wingfield-Digby, and again at the General Election of 1906.

SOUTH (11,440).—UNIONIST GAIN.

Hambro, Angus V. (U.)	..	5,811
*Scarisbrick, Sir T. L. (L.)	..	4,379
Unionist majority	..	˙1,432

1906.—L., 5,035; U., 4,411—L. maj., 624.
1900.—U., 3,884; L., 3,519—U. maj., 364.
1895.—U. unop.; 1892, U. maj., 168; 1886, U., maj., 991.

Mr. ANGUS V. HAMBRO, who was born in 1883, is the third son of Sir Everard Alexander Hambro, of Milton Abbey, Blandford, Dorset, and brother of Mr. Eric Hambro, who sat for the Wimbledon Division of Surrey from 1900 to 1907.

WEST (7,576).—No change.

*Williams, Col. R. (U.)	..	4,011
Edwards, W. S. (L.)	..	2,759
Unionist majority..		1,252

1906.—U., 3,671; L., 2,834—U. maj., 837.
1900 and 1895.—U. unop.
1892.—U. maj., 878; 1886, U. maj., 1,205.

COLONEL ROBERT WILLIAMS, son of the late Mr. R. Williams, of Dorchester, was born in London, 1848; educated at Eton, and Christ Church, Oxford, and in 1869 married a daughter of Mr. N. P. Simes, of Strood Park, Sussex. He is a director of the Williams Deacon's Bank, of the Wilts and Dorset Bank (Limited), and of the London and South-Western Railway; D.L. for the county, Lieutenant of the City of London, and Hon. Colonel 4th Batt. Dorset Regiment. He has represented the division since his return at a by-election in May, 1895.

DURHAM (8).
BARNARD CASTLE (12,212).—No change.

*Henderson, A. (Lab.)..	..	6,136
Stobart, H. G. (U.)	..	4,646
Labour majority	...	1,490

1906.—Lab., 5,540; U., 3,888—Lab. maj., 1,652.
1900.—L., 5,036; U., 3,545—L. maj., 1,491.
1895.—L. maj., 1,076; 1892, L. maj., 2,413; 1886, L. unop.

Mr. ARTHUR HENDERSON, who has represented the division since 1903, is a native of Glasgow. He was born in 1863, and educated at St. Mary's School, Newcastle-on-Tyne. In 1888 he married a daughter of Mr. W. Watson, of Forest Row, Sussex. He served an apprenticeship as moulder in the works of Robert Stephenson and Co., Newcastle. He has been a member of the town council of Newcastle and of Darlington, and was Mayor of Darlington in 1903. He has held various official positions in relation to his trade union, that of ironfounders, and was chairman of the Labour Party in the House of Commons, 1908-9.

BISHOP AUCKLAND (14,552).—No change.

Havelock-Allan, Sir H. (L.)..		5,391
Chaytor, Sir W. C. (U.)	..	3,841
House, Ald. W. (Lab.)	..	3,579
Liberal majority	..	1,550

1906.—L., 7,430; U., 3,056—L. maj., 4,374.
1900.—L., 4,872; U., 3,641—L. maj., 1,231.
1895.—L. maj., 1,297; 1892, L. maj., 3,177; 1886, L. unop.

SIR HENRY SPENCER MORETON HAVELOCK-ALLAN, second baronet, was born in 1872, a son of the first baronet, who received the honour intended for his father, Major-General Sir Henry Havelock, whose name is associated with the heroic relief and defence of Lucknow, but who died before the completion of the patent. Sir H. S. M. Havelock-Allan, D.L., J.P., succeeded his father in 1897, married in 1903 a daughter of Mr. T. C. J. Sowerby, and is captain in the 4th Batt. Durham Light Infantry (Special Reserve).

Chester-le-Street (23,906).—No change.

*Taylor, J. W. (Lab.)	12,684
Shafto, A. Duncombe (U.)	6,891
Labour majority	5,793

1906.—Lab., 8,085 ; U., 4,985 ; L., 4,660—Lab. maj. over U., 3,100.
1900.—L., 5,830 ; U., 5,391—L. maj., 439.
1895.—L. maj., 3,257 ; 1892, L. maj., 2,387 ; 1886, L. unop.

Mr. J. W. Taylor, a member of the Labour Party, was born in 1861, and started work when nine years old, being apprenticed to a blacksmith at 12, and working afterwards in a colliery. He is secretary of the Durham Mechanics' Association. At the General Election of 1906 Mr. Taylor succeeded to the seat which had been hitherto held in the Liberal interest by Sir James Joicey before his elevation to the Peerage.

Houghton-le-Spring (17,504).—No change.

*Cameron, R. (L.)	10,393
Streatfeild, Major H. (U.)	4,382
Liberal majority	6,011

1906.—L., 9,429 ; U., 3,639—L. maj., 5,790.
1900.—L., 6,865 ; U., 4,917—L. maj., 1,948.
1895.—L. maj., 881 ; 1892, L. maj., 1,433 ; 1886, U. maj., 811.

Mr. Robert Cameron became a teacher in 1846, at the age of 21 years, and for many years he took an active part in the public life of Sunderland. He is the son of the late Rev. Duncan Cameron, a Baptist minister. After an unsuccessful contest in the Central Division of Sheffield in 1892, he was elected for the Houghton-le-Spring Division of Durham in 1895, and has represented it continuously since that year.

Jarrow (18,292).—Liberal Gain from Labour.

Palmer, G. (L.)	4,885
*Curran, P. (Lab.)	4,818
Kirkley, J. (U.)	4,668
Liberal majority over Labour	67
Liberal majority over Unionist	217

By-election, 1907.—Lab., 4,698 ; U., 3,930 ; L., 3,474 ; Nat., 2,124—Lab. maj., 768.
1906.—L., 8,047 ; Lab., 5,093—L. maj., 2,954.
1900 and 1895.—L. unop.
1892.—L. maj., 4,927 ; 1886, L. unop.

Mr. Godfrey Mark Palmer is the youngest son of the late Sir Charles Mark Palmer, who represented Jarrow in Parliament for many years ; born in 1878, he was educated at Eton and Paris ; is a director of a large shipping business in London and interested also in several large works upon Tyneside.

Mid (15,832).—No change.

*Wilson, John (L.).

1906.—L. unop.
1900.—L., 5,565 ; U., 4,105—L. maj., 1,460.
1895.—L. maj., 1,642 ; 1892, L. maj., 1,992 ; 1886, L. unop.

Mr. John Wilson, born at Greatham in 1837, married in 1863 a daughter of Mr. George Forth, a coalminer of Sherburn Hill. At a very early age he began work at Stanhope Quarries, and at the age of 13 worked in the pit at Ludworth Colliery. At 19 he went to sea for a few years, and afterwards worked in the Haswell Colliery, and from 1863 to 1867 in collieries in the United States. In 1869 he assisted in establishing the Durham Miners' Association ; in 1882 he was elected treasurer of the Miners' Association, and became financial secretary and corresponding secretary in 1890 and 1896. In 1885 he was elected for the Houghton-le-Spring Division, was defeated at the election in the following year, returned for Mid Durham in 1890, and has represented the constituency since.

North-West (18,361).—No change.

*Atherley-Jones, L., K.C. (L.)	10,497
Knott, J. Leadbitter (U.)	5,227
Liberal majority	5,270

1906.—L., 9,146 ; U., 3,999—L. maj., 5,147.
1900.—L., 5,158 ; U., 5,137—L. maj., 21.
1895.—L. maj., 1,559 ; 1892, L. maj., 2,230 ; 1886, L. unop.

Mr. Llewellyn Archer Atherley-Jones was born in 1851, and educated at Manchester Grammar School, and Brasenose College, Oxford. He was called to the Bar at the Inner Temple in 1875, and joined the North-Eastern Circuit ; became a Queen's Counsel in 1896 and Bencher in 1907 ; and was appointed Recorder for Newcastle-on-Tyne in 1906. He has written treatises on International Law and the law of mining, a political novel, and other works.

South-East (18,880).—Liberal Gain.

Hayward, Evan (L.)	9,298
*Lambton, Hon. F. W. (U.)	6,860
Liberal majority	2,438

1906.—U. unop.
1900.—U., 6,198 ; L., 5,524—U. maj., 674.
1895.—U. maj., 114 ; 1892, L. maj., 164 ; 1886, U. maj., 939.

Mr. Evan Hayward, born at Wotton-under-Edge, Gloucestershire, was educated at Bristol School and Katherine Lady Berkeley's Grammar School. He spent two years as a pupil teacher at Ipswich, becoming articled later with Messrs. Charter and Co., of Wotton-under-Edge, passing his final examination with honours in 1900, and receiving the prize awarded by the Gloucestershire and Wiltshire Law Society. He went to West Hartlepool in 1901, and began practice on his own account.

ESSEX (8).

Mid, or Chelmsford (13,314).—No change.

*Pretyman, Captain E. G. (U.)	6,816
Cuthbertson, T. (L.)	4,271
Unionist majority	2,545

By-election, 1908.—U., 6,152 ; L., 3,587—U. maj., 2,565.
1906.—U., 4,915 ; L., 4,461—U. maj., 454.
1900.—U., 4,978 ; L., 1,849—U. maj., 3,129.
1895.—U. unop. ; 1892, U. maj., 1,369 ; 1886, U. unop.

Mr. Ernest George Pretyman is one of the small band of Unionists who throughout the prolonged all-night sittings of the Budget debates last Session were able to wring concessions from Mr. Lloyd George, and to win the admiration even of their political opponents for their stubborn tenacity. He was born in 1859, and was educated at Eton and the Royal Military Academy, Woolwich, and served in the Royal Artillery from 1880 until 1889. He sat for the Woodbridge Division of Suffolk from 1895 to 1905, and was first returned for his present constituency in December, 1908. For three years after 1900 he was Civil Lord of the Admiralty, and from 1903 to 1905 he was Secretary to the Admiralty.

WEST, or EPPING (12,164). —No change.

*Lockwood, Right Hon. Lieut.-Col. A. R. M. (U.)	6,578
Symmons, I. A. (L.)	3,845
Unionist majority	2,733

1906.—U., 5,204 ; L., 4,030—U. maj., 1,174.
1900, 1895, and 1886—U. unop.
1892.—U. maj., 1,798.

LIEUTENANT-COLONEL AMELIUS RICHARD MARK LOCKWOOD, C.V.O., was born in 1847 and was educated at Eton. In 1866 he entered the Coldstream Guards and retired with the rank of lieutenant-colonel in 1883. He was made a Privy Councillor in 1905, and received the C.V.O. the same year. He has sat for the division since 1892.

HARWICH (14,285).—UNIONIST GAIN.

Newton, H. K. (U.)	6,757
*Lever, A. Levy (L.)	5,608
Unionist majority	1,149

1906.—L., 5,650 ; U., 5,308—L. maj., 342.
1900.—U. unop.
1895.—U. maj., 1881 ; 1892, U. maj., 305 ; 1886, U. maj., 2,301.

Mr. HARRY KOTTINGHAM NEWTON was born in 1875, the only son of Sir Alfred J. Newton, a former Lord Mayor of London, and educated at Rugby, and New College, Oxford ; was hon. secretary to the C.I.V.'s Organization, raised by the City of London for the South African War, and accompanied the C.I.V.'s to South Africa ; is one of H.M.'s Lieutenants for the City of London, and a barrister (called 1889).

EAST, or MALDON (11,517).—UNIONIST GAIN.

Flannery, Sir F. (U.)	5,691
*Bethell, T. R. (L.)	4,822
Unionist majority	869

1906.—L., 4,773 ; U., 4,624—L. maj., 149.
1900.—U., 4,649 ; L., 3,301—U. maj., 1,348.
1895.—U. maj., 612 ; 1892, L. maj., 168 ; 1886, U. maj., 457.

SIR J. FORTESCUE FLANNERY is a consulting engineer and was born in 1851. He was educated at the Liverpool School of Science and became a pupil at the Britannia Engine Works, Birkenhead. Later he was an inspecting engineer under the late Sir E. J. Reed ; is an ex-president of the Institution of Marine Engineers and an Associate of Lloyd's ; represented the Shipley Division of Yorkshire from 1895 to 1906, when he stood for Cardiff and was defeated.

SOUTH, or ROMFORD (52,984).—No change.

*Bethell, Sir J. H. (L.)	23,181
Williamson, G. H. (U.)	21,224
Liberal majority	1,957

1906.—L., 21,534 ; U., 12,679—L. maj., 8,855.
1900.—U., 10,450 ; L., 7,338—U. maj., 3,962.
1895.—U. maj., 1,327 ; 1892, U. maj., 1,182 ; 1886, U. maj. over L., 2,478.

SIR JOHN HENRY BETHELL, who has been prominently identified with municipal and local affairs in the East-end of London, is a land agent and auctioneer ; fought three unsuccessful Parliamentary contests before his return for this division in 1906 ; was knighted in November, 1906.

SAFFRON WALDEN (9,187).—UNIONIST GAIN.

Proby, Lieut.-Col. D. J. (U.)	4,283
*Pease, Rt. Hon. J. A. (L.)	4,011
Unionist majority	272

1906.—L., 4,203 ; U., 2,935—L. maj., 1,268.
1900.—L., 3,247 ; U., 3,137—L. maj., 110.
1895.—U. maj., 425 ; 1892, L. maj., 1,881 ; 1886, L. maj., 740

LIEUT.-COLONEL DOUGLAS JAMES PROBY, born in 1856, is the only son of the late Lord Claud Hamilton. He assumed by Royal licence in 1904 the surname of Proby, his mother's maiden name, in lieu of his patronymic. After his education at Eton and Christ Church, Oxford, he joined the Coldstream Guards, serving with the 2nd Battalion in the Egyptian campaign of 1882, and with the 1st Battalion in the Suakin expedition of 1885. He retired with the rank of lieutenant-colonel in 1908.

SOUTH-EAST (24,645).—UNIONIST GAIN.

Kirkwood, J. H. Morrison (U.)	11,199
*Whitehead, R. (L.)	9,288
Unionist majority	1,911

1906.—L., 9,230 ; U., 7,170—L. maj., 2,060.
1900.—U., 5,815 ; L., 4,461—U. maj., 1,354.
1895.—U. maj., 1,940 ; 1892, U. maj., 542 ; 1886, U. maj., 842.

Mr. JOHN HENDLEY MORRISON KIRKWOOD was born in 1877, the only son of the late Major J. Morrison Kirkwood ; was formerly a lieutenant in the 7th Dragoon Guards, and served in the South African War ; is now a captain in the Royal North Devon Yeomanry, a J.P. for Devon, and lives at Yeo Vale, Fairy Cross, North Devon.

SOUTH-WEST, or WALTHAMSTOW (39,117).— No change.

*Simon, J. A., K.C. (L.)	17,726
Johnson, J. Stanley (U.)	15,531
Liberal majority	2,195

1906.—L., 15,011 ; U., 11,074—L. maj., 3,937.
1900.—U., 9,807 ; L., 7,342—U. maj., 2,465.
1895.—U. maj., 2,353 ; 1892, U. maj., 1,150 ; 1886, U. maj., 1,822.

Mr. JOHN ALLSEBROOK SIMON, who was born in 1873, is the son of the Rev. E. Simon, a Congregationalist minister at Bath. He was educated at Fettes College, Edinburgh, and Wadham College, Oxford, and was President of the Oxford Union Society in 1896. He was called to the Bar in 1899, and was one of the counsel engaged on behalf of the British Government before the Alaska Boundary Commission. He was returned as the representative of Walthamstow in 1906.

GLOUCESTERSHIRE (5).

East, or Cirencester (9,934).—Unionist Gain.

Bathurst, Lieut.-Col. the Hon. A. B. (U.)	5,091
*Essex, R. W. (L.)	4,108
Unionist majority	983

1906.—L., 4,517 ; U., 4,011—L. maj., 506.
1900.—U. unop.
1895.—U. maj., 215 ; 1892, L. maj., 153 ; 1886, L. unop.

Lieut.-Colonel Allen Benjamin Bathurst represented the Cirencester Division from 1895 until 1906. He is the youngest son of the 6th Earl Bathurst by his first wife, and was born in 1872. He was educated at Eton and the Royal Agricultural College, Cirencester. He served in the 4th Battalion Gloucester Regiment Militia, and retired as major in 1908, and in that year was appointed Lieut.-Col. of the 5th Battalion Gloucester Regiment.

Forest of Dean (10,881).—No change.

*Dilke, Rt. Hon. Sir C. W. (L.)	6,141
Renton, J. H. (U.)	3,279
Liberal majority	2,862

1906.—L. unop.
1900.—L., 4,972 ; U., 2,520—L. maj., 2,452.
1895.—L. unop. ; 1892, L. maj., 2,418 ; 1886, L. maj., 1,407.

Sir Charles Wentworth Dilke was born in 1843 and was educated at Trinity Hall, Cambridge. In 1866 he was called to the Bar by the Middle Temple, and from 1880 to 1882 was Under-Secretary for Foreign Affairs ; he held the office of President of the Local Government Board from the last mentioned year until 1885. He represented Chelsea from 1868 to 1886, and has sat for the Forest of Dean Division of Gloucestershire since 1892. Sir Charles Dilke speaks with authority on subjects connected with Imperial defence, foreign affairs, local government administration, and factory legislation. He is the author of several books, among them being " Greater Britain," " The Present Position of European Politics," " The British Army," and " Problems of Greater Britain."

Mid, or Stroud (10,992).—No change.

*Allen, C. P. (L.)	5,285
Clifford, A. W. (U.)	4,962
Liberal majority	323

1906.—L, 5,401 ; U., 4,221—L. maj., 1,180.
1900.—L., 4,692 ; U., 4,379—L. maj., 313.
1895.—U. maj., 661 ; 1892, L. maj., 201 ; 1886, U. maj., 709.

Mr. Charles Peter Allen, who is a newspaper proprietor and barrister, was born in 1861, and educated at Rugby, and University College, Oxford ; has travelled in Bulgaria, Turkey, and Russia ; and has sat for the division since 1900.

North, or Tewkesbury (13,155).—No change.

*Beach, Hon. M. Hicks (U.)	6,050
Lister, R. A. (L.)	5,088
Fox, C. (Lab.)	238
Unionist majority	962

1906.—U., 5,321 ; L., 5,194—U. maj., 127.
1900 and 1895.—U. unop.
1892.—U. maj., 903 ; 1886, U. unop.

The Hon. Michael Hugh Hicks Beach, who has represented the division since 1906, is the son of Viscount St. Aldwyn, and was born in 1877. He was educated at Eton, and Christ Church, Oxford. In 1908 he transferred as second lieutenant to the Royal Gloucestershire Yeomanry from the 4th (Militia) Batt. of the Gloucestershire Regiment, where he had been captain, and during the South African War he served at St. Helena. He acted as assistant private secretary to his father, then Chancellor of the Exchequer, in 1901-2, and afterwards to Sir Alexander Acland-Hood.

South, or Thornbury (14,742).—No change.

*Rendall, A. (L.)	7,270
Ward, Hon. Cyril A. (U.)	6,251
Liberal majority	1,019

1906.—L., 7,370 ; U., 5,240—L. maj., 2,130.
1900.—U. unop.
1895.—U. maj., 1,089 ; 1892, U. maj., 224 ; 1886, U. maj., 881.

Mr. Athelstan Rendall, a practising solicitor at Yeovil, was born in 1871 and educated at University College School, London, and at Lancaster ; his membership of the Fabian Society and the Cobden Club indicates the character of his Liberalism ; his return in 1906 meant the loss of a Unionist seat.

HAMPSHIRE (6).

West, or Andover (11,370).—No change.

*Faber, Capt. W. V. (U.)	6,127
Wodehouse, Hon. P. (L.)	3,723
Unionist majority	2,404

1906.—U., 4,603 ; L., 4,524—U. maj., 79.
1900, 1895, 1892, 1886, U. unop.

Captain Walter Vavasour Faber is a son of Mr. Charles Wilson Faber, of Northaw, Herts, and a younger brother of Lord Faber, who, before being raised to the Peerage, represented this constituency in the House of Commons from 1901 to 1905. Born in 1857, he was educated at Cheam School, and the Royal Military Academy, Woolwich. He retired from the Royal Artillery with the rank of captain in 1885, and is now on the Reserve List of Officers.

North, or Basingstoke (13,136).—No change.

*Salter, A. C., K.C. (U.)	7,506
Wallis, J. E. (L.)	3,821
Unionist majority	3,685

1906.—U., 4,825 ; L., 4,705—U. maj., 120.
1900, 1895, and 1886.—U. unop.
1892.—U. maj., 1,491.

Mr. Arthur Clavell Salter, K.C., born in 1859, was educated at King's College, London, took B.A. and LL.B. at London University, was called to the Bar by the Middle Temple, 1885, and joined the Western Circuit. In 1894, he married a daughter of the late Major J. H. Lloyd, became K.C. in 1904, and from that date has been Recorder of Poole. He was returned for the division at a by-election in March, 1906.

SOUTH, or FAREHAM (18,695).—No change.

*Lee, A. H. (U.)	.. ..	10,117
Sandy, J. (L.)	.. ..	5,763
Unionist majority	..	4,354

1906.—U., 7,683 ; L., 6,331—U. maj., 1,352.
1900.—U., 7,375 ; L., 3,828—U. maj., 3,547.
1895.—U. unop. ; 1892, U. maj., 1,539 ; 1886, U. unop.

Mr. ARTHUR HAMILTON LEE has represented the Fareham Division since 1900. Having passed through Cheltenham College and the Royal Military Academy at Woolwich, he joined the Royal Garrison Artillery when 20 years of age. In the course of his military career he acted as a professor in the Royal Military College of Canada, and served as British military attaché with the United States Army during the Spanish-American War, and at the Embassy in Washington. In 1903 he was appointed Civil Lord of the Admiralty, and in the last Parliament was a strenuous critic of the administration of the Navy. Last Session he was selected to move the vote of censure on the naval policy of the Liberal Government.

ISLE OF WIGHT (15,969).—UNIONIST GAIN.

Hall, Douglas B. (U.)	..	7,414
*Baring, Godfrey (L.)	..	7,123
Unionist majority	..	291

1906.—L., 7,453 ; U., 5,892—L. maj., 1,561.
1900.—U. unop.
1895.—U. maj., 446 ; 1892, U. maj., 461 ; 1886, U. maj., 1,258.

Mr. DOUGLAS BERNARD HALL, a son of Mr. Bernard Hall, J.P., of Burton Park, Petworth, Sussex, was born in 1867, and educated at Charterhouse, and Christ Church, Oxford ; is the owner of the Burton Park estates, Sussex, and lord of the manor of Burton and Barlavington ; has taken an active part in county and local affairs ; was Unionist candidate for Penryn and Falmouth in 1906, but was defeated by 97 votes.

NEW FOREST (12,118).—UNIONIST GAIN.

Perkins, W. F. (U.)..	..	6,516
*Hobart, Sir R. (L.)	..	4,423
Unionist majority	..	2,093

1906.—L., 4,949 ; U., 4,901—L. maj., 48.
1900.—U. unop.
1895 and 1886, U. unop. ; 1892, U. maj., 755.

Mr. WALTER FRANK PERKINS, of Boldre Bridge House, Lymington, Hants, the son of the late Mr. Walter Perkins, of Portswood, Southampton, was born at Southampton in 1865 ; is a consulting surveyor, and well known throughout the South of England as an agriculturist ; studied at the Royal Agricultural College, Cirencester, and is a member of the Royal Agricultural Society of England and the Highland Agricultural Society.

EAST, or PETERSFIELD (11,110).—No change.

*Nicholson, W. G. (U.)	..	6,279
Baker, H. A. (L.) ..	..	3,594
Unionist majority	..	2,685

1906.—U., 4,349 ; L., 4,253—U. maj., 96.
1900 and 1895.—U. unop.
1892.—U. maj., 904 ; 1886, U. maj., 111.

Mr. WILLIAM GRAHAM NICHOLSON, son of Mr. W. Nicholson, J.P., some time member for the division, was born in London in 1862, and educated at Harrow, and Trinity College, Cambridge (B.A., 1884) ; is a director of J. and W. Nicholson and Co. (Limited), distillers, of Clerkenwell, an alderman of the Hants County Council, and Lieutenant-Colonel (hon. Colonel) commanding the 3rd Battalion of the Hampshire Regiment ; was first elected for the division at a by-election in June, 1897, and has represented the constituency since.

HEREFORDSHIRE (2).

NORTH, or LEOMINSTER (9,689).—UNIONIST GAIN.

Rankin, Sir J. (U.)	.. ..	4,822
*Lamb, E. (L.)	.. ..	3,991
Unionist majority	..	831

1906.—L., 3,892 ; U., 3 864—L. maj., 28.
1900 and 1895.—U. unop.
1892.—U. maj., 1,400 : 1886. U. maj., 1,893.

SIR JAMES RANKIN was born in 1842 and educated at Trinity College, Cambridge. He represented Leominster Borough, 1880-85, and, on the disfranchisement of the borough under the Redistribution Act, the Leominster Division from 1886 to 1906. He is a landowner and was created a baronet in 1898.

SOUTH, or ROSS (10,946).—No change.

*Clive, Capt. P. A. (U.)	..	5,073
Webb, H. (L.)	.. ..	4,678
Unionist majority	..	395

By-election, 1908.—U., 4,947 ; L., 3,928—U. maj., 1,019.
1906.—L., 4,497 ; U., 4,185—L. maj., 312.
1900.—U. unop.
1895.—U. maj., 1,745 ; 1892, U. maj., 457 ; 1886, U. maj., 2,298.

CAPTAIN PERCY ARCHER CLIVE represented the Ross Division of Herefordshire from 1900 until 1906, and, after two years' absence from Westminster, was re-elected in January, 1908. Born in 1873, he was educated at Eton and Sandhurst, entered the Grenadier Guards in 1891, and became a captain eight years later. He served with the West African Frontier Force in 1898, and in South Africa 1899-1901. He acted as private secretary (unpaid) to Lord George Hamilton when Secretary of State for India and to Mr. Austen Chamberlain when Chancellor of the Exchequer in 1905.

HERTFORDSHIRE (4).

EAST, or HERTFORD (11,838).—No change.

Rolleston, Sir J. (U.)..	..	6,147
†Barnard, E. B. (L.)	..	4,455
Unionist majority	..	1,692

1906.—U., 4,836 ; L., 4,756—U maj., 80.
1900 and 1895. U. unop.
1892.—U. maj., 1,458 ; 1886, U. unop.

SIR JOHN ROLLESTON, who sat in the Parliament of 1900-6 as Conservative member for Leicester, has a remarkable record of contests in that borough, which he fought in 1894, 1895, 1900, and twice in 1906. Born in 1848, the eldest son of the Rev. W. Lancelot Rolleston, he was educated at Repton School and King's College, London. He attained a foremost place in his profession as a surveyor, and was president of the Surveyors' Institution in 1901. He received a knighthood in 1897. In recognition of his 20 years' service to the Conservative cause the Unionists of Leicester presented him with a silver cup last November.

NORTH, or HITCHIN (10,885).—UNIONIST GAIN.

Hillier, Dr. A. (U.)	5,761
Fox-Pitt, St. G. L. (L.)	3,877
Unionist majority	1,884

1906.—L., 4,157; U., 4,081—L. maj., 76.
1900 and 1895.—U. unop.
1892.—U. maj., 1,459; 1886, U. unop.

Dr. ALFRED PETER HILLIER, B.A., M.D., C.M., a retired physician, was born in 1858, the son of Mr. P. P. Hillier, of Shortwood, Gloucestershire; was educated at Edinburgh University, B.A. Cape University, M.D. and C.M. Edinburgh University, and married a daughter of Mr. F. B. Brown. He served as a trooper with the Colonial Forces in the Kaffir War, 1878-9, and received medal and clasp; presided at the South African Medical Congress, 1893; was a member of the Reform Committee, Johannesburg, and was a political prisoner in Pretoria, 1895-6; was a delegate at the Berlin Tuberculosis Congress, 1899. He contested Stockport in 1900 and South Bedfordshire in 1906.

MID, or ST. ALBANS (13,929).—No change.

*Carlile, E. H. (U.)	7,323
Beddoes, Lieut.-Col. H. (L.)	5,271
Unionist majority	2,052

1906.—U., 5,856; L., 5,304—U. maj., 552.
1900.—U. maj.
1895 and 1886, U. unop.; 1892, U. maj. over L., 844.

Mr. E. H. CARLILE was born in 1852 and was educated privately in England and in Switzerland. He was formerly a partner in J. Brook and Brothers, Meltham Mills, Yorks, and is a director of J. and P. Coats (Limited); captain of the 2nd West Yorks Yeomanry, and lieutenant-colonel 2nd V.B. West Riding Regiment. Since 1906 Mr. Carlile has been hon. colonel of the battalion.

WEST, or WATFORD (17,710).—UNIONIST GAIN.

Ward, Arnold S. (U.)	8,782
*Micklem, N., K.C. (L.)	7,231
Unionist majority	1,551

1906.—L., 7,612; U., 6,136—L. maj., 1,476.
1900 and 1895.—U. unop.
1892.—U. maj., 1,175; 1886, U. unop.

Mr. ARNOLD SANDWITH WARD, son of Mr. and Mrs. Humphry Ward, was born in 1876. He was educated at Eton, where he obtained the Newcastle Scholarship and played against Harrow at Lord's, and at Oxford, where he was a scholar of Balliol, Craven scholar, and winner of the Chancellor's prize for Latin verse. He also obtained a first class in Moderations and in the final classical school. He travelled in the Sudan and spent a year and a half in India (1900-02), acting as Special Correspondent of *The Times*. Mr. Ward was called to the Bar in 1903 and was for some years in the Chambers of Sir Charles Mathews. He is an officer in the Herts Imperial Yeomanry. He unsuccessfully contested the Cricklade Division of Wiltshire as a Unionist at the last election.

HUNTINGDONSHIRE (2).

SOUTH, or HUNTINGDON (5,175).—UNIONIST GAIN.

Cator, J. (U.)	2,466
Brett, Hon. O. (L.)	2,099
Unionist majority	367

1906.—L., 2,426; U., 1,957—L. maj., 469.
1900.—U., 2,118; L., 1,838—U. maj., 280.
1895.—U. maj., 351; 1892, U. maj., 22; 1886, U. maj., 161.

Mr. JOHN CATOR is the eldest son of the late Mr. Cator, D.L., of Woodbastwick Hall, Norwich. He was born in 1863 and was educated at Eton and Christ Church, Oxford. In 1895 he married Maud, younger daughter of the late Mr. H. J. Adeane, of Babraham, Cambridge. He was at one time a director of the Alliance Insurance Company, a member of the London School Board, and was private secretary to Mr. Chaplin when the latter was President of the Local Government Board. He contested North Norfolk unsuccessfully in 1892 and South Hunts at the last election.

NORTH, or RAMSEY (7,034).—UNIONIST GAIN.

Locker-Lampson, O. (U.)	3,350
*Boulton, A. C. F. (L.)	2,915
Unionist majority	435

1906.—L., 3,184; U. 2,803—L. maj., 381.
1900.—U., 2,893; L., 1,742—U. maj., 1,151.
1895.—U. maj., 949; 1892, U. maj., 397; 1886, U. unop.

Mr. OLIVER LOCKER-LAMPSON is the son of Mr. Frederick Locker, poet and author; his mother was a daughter of Sir Curtis Lampson, a native of Vermont, and on her inheriting her father's estate at Rowfant, Sussex, Mr. Locker added the name Lampson to his own; born in 1880, educated at Eton and at Trinity College, Cambridge, and called to the Bar.

KENT (8).

SOUTH, or ASHFORD (14,202).—No change.

*Hardy, L. (U.)	7,966
Farrer, R. (L.)	4,422
Unionist majority	3,544

1906.—U., 5,994; L., 5,614—U. maj., 380.
1900.—U., 5,898; Ind. U., 2,343—U. maj., 3,555.
1895 and 1886.—U. unop.
1892.—U. maj., 1,231.

Mr. LAURENCE HARDY is a son of Sir John Hardy, and was educated at Eton, and Christ Church, Oxford. He was Deputy-Chairman of Committees in the House of Commons in 1905, and has been one of the Chairman's Panel for Grand Committees since 1899. After an unsuccessful fight in the Shipley Division of Yorks in 1885, he contested his present constituency in 1892, and has sat for it uninterruptedly from then until now.

NORTH-WEST, or DARTFORD (21,398).—UNIONIST GAIN.

Mitchell, W. Foot (U.)	9,807
*Rowlands, J. (L.)	8,990
Unionist majority	817

1906.—L., 9,532 ; U., 6,728—L. maj., 2,804.
1900.—U. unop.
1895.—U. maj., 1,142 ; 1892, U. maj., 572 ; 1886, U. maj., 1,233

Mr. WILLIAM FOOT MITCHELL was born in London in 1859, and educated privately in London, Glasgow, and Paris ; went in 1886 to Japan as principal in the East of Messrs. Samuel, Samuel, and Co., and for two years was chairman of the Yokohama Foreign Chamber of Commerce ; was a few years ago decorated by the Emperor with the Order of the Sacred Treasure, in recognition of services rendered to the Japanese Government ; is a director of the Shell Transport Company, in which the business of Samuel, Samuel, and Co. has been merged.

NORTH-EAST, or FAVERSHAM (14,649).—
UNIONIST GAIN.

Wheler, G. C. H. (U.)	7,438
*Napier, T. B. (L.)	5,394
Unionist majority	2,044

1906.—L., 6,925 ; U., 5,091—L. maj., 1,834.
1900.—U. unop.
1895.—U. maj., 1,181 ; 1892, U. maj., 206 ; 1886, U. unop.

Mr. GRANVILLE CHARLES HASTINGS WHELER, born in 1872, is the son of the late Mr. Charles Wheler Wheler, of Faversham, and of Castleford, Yorkshire. He was called to the Bar in 1898 and is a magistrate. He unsuccessfully stood for Osgoldcross, in the West Riding, at the last General Election, and in 1907 he contested the Colne Valley by-election at very short notice against Mr. Grayson. Mr. Wheler became a member of the West Riding County Council in 1907.

ISLE OF THANET (12,588).—No change.

Craig, Norman C., K.C. (U.)	6,892
Weigall, J. W. W. (L.)	3,410
Unionist majority	3,482

1906.—U., 5,154 ; L., 3,961 ; U., 925—U. maj., 1,193.
1900 and 1895.—U. unop.
1892.—U. maj., 1,044 ; 1886, U. maj., 2,088.

Mr. NORMAN CARLYLE CRAIG, who was born in 1868, was educated at Bedford and Cambridge ; Classical Tripos, 1890. He was called to the Bar in 1892 and took silk in 1909.

MID, or MEDWAY (15,181).—No change.

*Warde, Col. C. E. (U.)	8,093
Cairns, A. (L.)	5,285
Unionist majority	2,808

1906.—U., 6,167 ; L., 6,061—U. maj., 106.
1900 and 1895.—U. unop.
1892.—U. maj., 1,964 ; 1886, U., unop.

COLONEL CHARLES EDWARD WARDE, son of the late General Sir Edward Warde, was born in Limerick in 1845, and in 1890 married a daughter of the late Viscount de Stern. He is D.L. and J.P. for Kent and lately colonel commanding the West Kent Yeomanry. For 23 years he served in the 19th and the 4th Hussars ; was A.D.C. to the Governor of Gibraltar 1873-6, and General Commanding the Northern District of Ireland 1884-6. He has represented Mid Kent since 1892.

EAST, or ST. AUGUSTINE'S (16,614).—No change.

*Akers-Douglas, Rt. Hon. A. (U.)	9,500
Lang, R. T. (L.)	4,114
Unionist majority	5,386

1906.—U., 7,655 ; L., 4,794—U. maj., 2,861.
1900, 1895, 1892, and 1886.—U. unop.

Mr. ARETAS AKERS-DOUGLAS, who has been one of the members for Kent since 1880, is the eldest son of the late Rev. Aretas Akers, born in 1851, and assumed the name of Douglas in 1875 ; was educated at Eton and University College, Oxford, and called to the Bar in 1875 ; was Chief Conservative Whip for many years, and afterwards First Commissioner of Works and Home Secretary.

WEST, or SEVENOAKS (19,035).—No change.

*Forster, H. W. (U.)	10,421
Lely, Sir F. (L.)	6,351
Unionist majority	4,070

1906.—U., 7,219 ; L., 6,855 ; Ind. Lib., 44—U. maj. over L., 364.
1900.—U., 6,604 ; L., 1,792—U. maj., 4,812.
1895.—U., unop. ; 1892. U. maj., 2,128 ; 1886, U. unop.

Mr. HENRY WILLIAM FORSTER has represented Sevenoaks since 1892. Born in 1866, he was educated at Eton, and New College, Oxford. He played in both his school and University elevens and for Gentlemen v. Players. He was a Junior Lord of the Treasury from 1902 to 1905 and acted as an Opposition Whip during the recent Administration.

SOUTH-WEST, or TUNBRIDGE (17,116).—
UNIONIST GAIN.

Clay, Captain H. Spender (U.)	9,240
*Hedges, A. P. (L.)	6,030
Unionist majority	3,210

1906.—L., 7,170 ; U., 5,887—L. maj., 1,283.
1900.—U., 5,576 ; L., 3,494—U. maj., 2,082.
1895.—U. unop. ; 1892, U. maj., 933 ; 1886, U. unop.

CAPT. H. H. SPENDER CLAY, of Ford Manor, Lingfield, Surrey, was born in 1875 and educated at Eton and Sandhurst ; held a commission for six years in the Life Guards, and served in the South African war, receiving the medal and six clasps ; is a practical agriculturist, farming a large acreage himself.

LANCASHIRE (NORTH) (4).
BLACKPOOL (22,360).—No change.

*Ashley, W. W. (U.)	11,567
Hodgkinson, S. (L.)	7,943
Unionist majority	3,624

1906.—U., 10,139 ; L., 7,078—U. maj., 3,061.
1900, 1895, and 1886.—U. unop.
1892.—U. maj., 3,049.

Mr. WILFRID W. ASHLEY is the eldest son of the late Mr. Evelyn Ashley and grandson of the seventh Earl of Shaftesbury. He was born in 1867 and was educated at Harrow and Magdalen College, Oxford, entered the Grenadier Guards in 1889, and retired as lieutenant in 1898. He has travelled in Africa and America. In 1901 he married the only daughter of Sir Ernest Cassel. He was first elected for the Blackpool Division in 1906.

CHORLEY (14,347).—No change.
*Balcarres, Lord (U.).. .. 7,735
Blease, W. L. (L.).. .. 5,523

Unionist majority .. 2,212
1906.—U., 6,803 ; L., 5,419—U. maj., 1,384.
1900, 1895, 1892, and 1886, U. unop.

LORD BALCARRES is the eldest son of the Earl of Crawford and was born in 1871 ; educated at Eton, and Magdalen College, Oxford ; a Junior Lord of the Treasury from 1903 to 1905 ; a Trustee of the National Portrait Gallery, hon. secretary to the Society for the Protection of Ancient Buildings, vice-chairman of the National Trust, and Chairman of the National Art Collections Fund, which has been instrumental in securing many valuable works of art for the nation.

LANCASTER (14,797).—No change.
*Helme, N. W. (L.) 7,132
Russell-Taylor, E. (U.) .. 6,048

Liberal majority .. 1,084
1906.—L., 6,524 ; U., 5,640—L. maj., 884.
1900.—L., 5,113 ; U., 5,069—L. maj., 44.
1895.—U., 5,028 ; L., 4,394—U. maj., 634.
1892.—L., 4,755 ; U., 4,075—L. maj., 680.
1886.—L., 3,886 ; U., 3,691—L. maj., 195.

Mr. NORVAL WATSON HELME, who has represented the Lancaster Division of Lancashire since 1900, is the senior partner in the firm of Messrs. James Helme and Co., of Halton Mills, Lancaster. He has taken an active part in the public life of the town and county, and is a magistrate and county alderman of Lancashire, chairman of the County Asylums Board, an alderman of the borough of Lancaster (of which he was Mayor in 1896-7), and president of the Lancaster and District Chamber of Commerce. He was born in 1849.

NORTH LONSDALE (9,702).—No change.
*Haddock, G. B. (U.) .. 4,281
Bliss, J. (L.) 4,212

Unionist majority .. 69
1906.—U., 4,121 ; L., 3,942—U. maj., 179.
1900.—U. unop.
1895.—U. maj., 703 ; 1892, L. maj., 777 ; 1886, U. maj., 800.

Mr. GEORGE B. HADDOCK is a shipowner and a director of Harrison, Ainslie, and Co., owners of the Lindal Moor Mines, in Furness; born in 1863 and educated at Clifton College.

LANCASHIRE (NORTH-EAST) (4).
ACCRINGTON (16,297).—No change.
Baker, Harold (L.) 8,968
Jessel, A. H., K.C. (U.) .. 6,455

Liberal majority .. 2,513
1906.—L., 7,209 ; Lab., 4,852 ; Lab., 619—L. maj. over Lab., 2,357.
1900.—L., 6,585 ; U., 5,993 ; Soc., 433—L. maj. over U., 592.
1895.—L. maj., 340 ; 1892, L. maj., 547 ; 1886, U. maj., 220.

Mr. HAROLD BAKER, barrister, is the son of the late Sir John Baker, member for Portsmouth, and is 32 years of age. At Oxford he was President of the Union.

CLITHEROE (22,368).—No change.
*Shackleton, D. J. (Lab.) .. 13,873
Smith, T. (U.) 6,727

Labour majority .. 7,146
1906.—Lab., 12,035 ; Ind, U., 3,828—Lab. maj., 8,207.
1900 and 1895.—L. unop.
1892.—L. maj., 2,151 ; 1886, L. unop.

Mr. DAVID JAMES SHACKLETON, who was born in 1863, was for many years a Lancashire cotton operative ; has been closely associated with the trade union movement amongst the textile workers of that county, and is now chairman of the Northern Counties' Weavers' Association ; is a member of the Parliamentary Committee of the Trade Union Congress and has been twice President of the Congress ; was for a time vice-chairman of the Parliamentary Labour Party, and had charge of the Trade Disputes Bill in the House of Commons.

DARWEN (17,734).—LIBERAL GAIN.
Hindle, F. G. (L.).. .. 8,639
*Rutherford, J. (U.) .. 8,428

Liberal majority .. 211
1906.—U., 7,792 ; L., 7,767—U. maj., 25.
1900.—U., 7,228 ; L., 6,758—U. maj., 470.
1895.—U. maj., 841 ; 1892, L. maj., 214 ; 1886, U. maj., 726.

Mr. FREDERICK GEORGE HINDLE, a native of Darwen, was born in 1848 and educated at the Queen Elizabeth Grammar School, Blackburn ; admitted a solicitor in 1870, and has a large professional connexion ; unsuccessfully contested the Darwen Division in the Liberal interest in 1906.

ROSSENDALE (13,217).—No change.
*Harcourt, Rt. Hon. Lewis (L.) 7,185
Kebty-Fletcher, J. R. (U.) 4,695
Bulley, A. K. (Wom. Suf.) 639

Liberal majority .. 2,490
1906.—L., 6,881 ; U., 4,662—L. maj., 2,219.
1900 and 1895.—L. unop.
1892.—L. maj., 1,724 ; 1886, U. maj., 1,450.

Mr. LEWIS HARCOURT, who was born in 1863, began his political career in the capacity of private secretary to Sir William Harcourt, his father, and has represented the Rossendale Division of Lancashire since 1904. He was appointed First Commissioner of Works in 1905, an office for which he showed great fitness and in which he found sufficient leisure occasionally to undertake other duties, discharged alike with ease and tact. He obtained a seat in the Cabinet in 1905.

LANCASHIRE (SOUTH-EAST) (8).
ECCLES (18,786).—No change.
*Pollard, Sir G. H. (L.) .. 7,093
Assinder, G. F. (U.) .. 6,682
Stuart, G. H. (Lab.) .. 3,511

Liberal majority .. 411
1906.—L., 5,841 ; U., 5,246 ; Lab., 3,985—L. maj. over U. 595.
1900.—U., 6,153 ; L., 5,934—U. maj., 219.
1895.—U., 5,722 ; L., 5,302—U. maj., 420.
1892.—L., 5,340 ; U., 5,071—L. maj., 269.
1886.—U., 4,277 ; L., 3,985—U. maj., **292**.

ENGLAND (COUNTIES).

SIR GEORGE HERBERT POLLARD was born in 1864, and was educated at Edinburgh and Oxford Universities. He has served on the Lancashire County Council and the Southport Town Council, and was Mayor of Southport in 1897. In 1893 he was called to the Bar by the Inner Temple. He unsuccessfully contested the Southport Division of South-West Lancashire in 1892, and the Radcliffe Division of South-East Lancashire in 1895. He is M.D. of Edinburgh (honours, 1890) and M.B., C.M., of Edinburgh and Oxford, 1886.

GORTON (18,175).—No change.

*Hodge, J. (Lab.)	7,807
White, H. (U.)	7,334
Labour majority	473

1906.—Lab., 8,566 ; U., 4,341—Lab. maj., 4,225.
1900.—U., 5,761 ; L., 5,241—U. maj., 520.
1895.—U. maj., 1,604 ; 1892, L. maj., 222 ; 1886, L. maj., 457.

Mr. JOHN HODGE was born at Muirkirk, Ayrshire, in 1855. On the formation of the Steel Smelters' Association in 1886 he became secretary and in 1892 he was president of the Glasgow Trades Council. In 1898 he was elected to the Manchester Town Council. He was an unsuccessful candidate for the Gower Division of Glamorganshire in 1900 and again for Preston in 1903, but won his present seat for the Labour Party from the Unionists in 1906.

HEYWOOD (11,339).—No change.

Cawley, H. T. (L.)	5,809
Manningham-Buller, Capt. (U.)	4,750
Liberal majority	1,059

1906.—L., 5,351 ; U., 4,245—L. maj., 1,106.
1900.—U., 4,657 ; L., 4,431—U. maj., 226.
1895.—U. maj., 556 ; 1892, L. maj., 621 ; 1886, L. maj., 444.

Mr. HAROLD THOMAS CAWLEY is the second son of Sir Frederick Cawley, who has represented the Prestwich Division for many years ; was born in 1878 and educated at Rossall Preparatory School, Rugby, and New College, Oxford ; called to the Bar (Inner Temple) in 1902 and goes the Northern Circuit ; a lieutenant in the 6th Battalion Manchester Regiment (T.).

MIDDLETON (15,391).—No change.

*Adkins, W. R. (L.)	7,669
Rose-Innes, P., K.C. (U.)	6,266
Liberal majority	1,403

1906.—L., 7,018 ; U., 5,485—L. maj., 1,533.
1900.—U., 6,147 ; L., 6,011—U. maj., 136.
1895.—U. maj., 865 ; 1892, L. maj., 116 ; 1886, U. maj., 318.

Mr. W. RYLAND ADKINS, who was born in 1862, was educated at Mill Hill School, University College, London, and Balliol College, Oxford, where he was history exhibitioner in 1882. He was called to the Bar in 1890. He is a member of the Northamptonshire County Council, and a Justice of the Peace.

PRESTWICH (22,123).—No change.

*Cawley, Sir F., Bt. (L.)	11,564
Potter, C. H. (U.)	8,180
Liberal majority	3,384

1906.—L., 10,186 ; U., 6,024—L. maj., 4,163.
1900.—L., 7,127 ; U., 6,406—L. maj., 721.
1895.—L. maj., 101 ; 1892, U. maj., 155 ; 1886, U. maj., 139.

SIR FREDERICK CAWLEY, who was born in 1850, makes his fourth appearance in Parliament as the representative of Prestwich. He is in business in Lancashire as a bleacher, dyer, and calico printer, and is also a landowner in Cheshire and Herefordshire. He is a J.P. for the county of Lancaster, and has been a member of the Manchester City Council. His baronetcy was among the Birthday honours of 1906.

RADCLIFFE-CUM-FARNWORTH (14,046).—No change.

*Taylor, T. C. (L.)	7,367
White, E. (U.)	5,827
Liberal majority	1,540

1906.—L., 6,719 ; U., 5,117—L. maj., 1,602.
1900.—L. 5,497 ; U., 5,437—L. maj., 60.
1895.—U. maj., 600 ; 1892, L. maj., 95 ; 1886, L. maj., 136.

Mr. THEODORE COOKE TAYLOR, who was born in 1850, and educated at Batley Grammar School and the Northern Congregational School, Silcoates, is a spinner and woollen manufacturer at Batley, and in connexion with his business carried out an experiment in profit sharing, which developed into a limited liability company. He is a J.P. for Batley, has been president of the Batley Chamber of Commerce, and a county councillor for the West Riding of Yorks, and has represented his present constituency in Parliament since 1900.

STRETFORD (27,629).—No change.

*Nuttall, H. (L.)	12,917
Samuel, A. M. (U.)	10,626
Liberal majority	2,291

1906.—L., 11,131 ; U., 8,307—L. maj., 2,824.
1900.—U., 7,591 ; L., 4,938—U. maj., 2,563.
1895.—U. unop. ; 1892, U. maj., 1,345 ; 1886, U. maj., 739.

Mr. HARRY NUTTALL, born in Manchester in 1849, was educated at Owens College, and married, in 1886, a daughter of Mr. W. Smith, of Bolton-le-Moors. He is an export and import merchant in Manchester, a J.P., F.R.G.S., and in 1905 was president of the Manchester Chamber of Commerce. After being unsuccessful in the election of 1900 he was returned for the Stretford Division in 1906.

WESTHOUGHTON (19,751).—No change.

*Wilson, W. T. (Lab.)	10,141
Byrne, H. Morgan (U.)	7,709
Labour majority	2,432

1906.—Lab., 9,262 ; U., 6,134—Lab. maj., 3,128.
1900.—U., 7,989 ; L., 4,949 ; U. maj., 3,040.
1895.—U. unop.
1892.—U., 6,711 ; L., 4,871 —U. maj., 1,840.
1886.—U. unop.

Mr. WILLIAM TYSON WILSON was born in Westmorland in 1855. He has taken a leading part in organizing the union of workers in the building trades. From 1898 to 1906 he was chairman of the General and Executive Councils of the Amalgamated Society of Carpenters and Joiners and was one of the founders of the Bolton Building Trades' Federation. He represented the division in the last Parliament.

LANCASHIRE (SOUTH-WEST) (7).

BOOTLE (23,903).—No change.

*Sandys, Colonel T. M. (U.)	9,954
Permewan, Dr. (L.) ..	8,869
Unionist majority ..	1,085

1906.—U., 7,821 ; L., 7,481—U. maj., 340.
1900 and 1895.—U. unop.
1892.—U. maj., 2,072 ; 1886, U. unop.

COLONEL THOMAS MYLES SANDYS, who has represented Bootle since 1885, was born at Blackheath in 1837, and educated at Shrewsbury School. Entering the service of the East India Company, he served in Bengal throughout the Sepoy Mutiny, and afterwards joined the Punjab Frontier Force. He exchanged to the 7th Royal Fusiliers, selling out as captain after 20 years' service, and after commanding the 3rd Loyal North Lancashire Regiment for eight years retired in 1897 as honorary colonel.

INCE (14,107).—No change.

*Walsh, S. (Lab.)	7,723
Lord, W. G. (U.)	5,029
Labour majority ..	2,694

1906.—Lab., 8,046 ; U., 3,410—Lab. maj., 4,636.
1900.—U. unop.
1895.—U. maj., 445 ; 1892, L. maj., 227 ; 1886, U. maj., 1,080.

Mr. STEPHEN WALSH is one of the ablest of the miners' representatives in the House ; born in 1859 and educated at Kirkdale (Liverpool) Industrial School, he worked for many years in the coalpits of Lancashire ; is a member of the Miners' Conciliation Board and agent, at Wigan, of the Lancashire and Cheshire Miners' Federation.

LEIGH (14,150).—No change.

Raffan, P. W. (L.)	5,325
Smith, F. Cuthbert (U.) ..	4,646
Greenall, T. (Lab.) ..	3,268
Liberal majority ..	679

1906.—L., 7,175 ; U., 5,169—L. maj., 2,006.
1900.—L., 5,239 ; U., 5,119—L. maj., 120.
1895.—L. maj., 677 ; 1892, L. maj., 904 ; 1886, L. maj., 1,163.

ALDERMAN PETER WELSAR RAFFAN was born in Aberdeen 46 years ago, but as a young man went to Monmouth. He is chairman of the Monmouthshire County Council and of the Western Valleys Sewerage Board ; a member of the Council of the South Wales and Monmouthshire University College, Cardiff ; of the Court of Governors of the University of Wales ; and of the Aberdeen District Council. He is vice-chairman of the South Monmouthshire Liberal Association, and a member of the Executive of the Welsh National Liberal Council.

NEWTON (14,803).—No change.

*Seddon, J. A. (Lab.) ..	7,256
Wolmer, Viscount (U.) ..	6,504
Labour majority ..	752

1906.—Lab., 6,434 ; U., 5,893—Lab. maj., 541.
1900.—U. unop.
1895.—U., 5,358 ; L., 3,854—U. maj., 1,504.
1892.—U., 4,713 ; L., 3,819—U. maj., 894.
1886.—U., 4,302 ; L., 3,486—U. maj., 816.

Mr. JAMES SEDDON, who entered Parliament in 1906 as the Labour member for the Newton Division, was born in Lancashire in 1868. Apprenticed to the grocery trade, he served behind the counter for 16 years and for ten years afterwards was a commercial traveller. As a trade unionist he engaged in the work of organizing shop assistants. He is a past president of the Shop Assistants' Union and the St. Helens Labour Council.

ORMSKIRK (13,511).—No change.

*Stanley, Hon. A. (U.) ..	6,919
†Lever, W. H. (L.) ..	4,679
Unionist majority ..	2,240

1906.—U., 6,207 ; L., 3,891—U. maj., 2,316.
1900.—U. unop.
1895.—U. maj., 2,895 ; 1892, U. maj., 2,517 ; 1886, U. unop.

The HON. ARTHUR STANLEY is third son of the 16th Earl of Derby. Born in 1869, he was educated at Wellington College and became Attaché in the Diplomatic Service, clerk in the Foreign Office, and private secretary to Mr. A. J. Balfour when First Lord of the Treasury in 1892. He was also in the Diplomatic Service under the Earl of Cromer at Cairo 1895-98. He has represented the Ormskirk Division since 1898.

SOUTHPORT (16,660).—UNIONIST GAIN.

White, Major Dalrymple (U.)	7,637
de Forest, Baron (L.) ..	7,218
Unionist majority ..	419

1906.—L., 6,607 ; U., 6,367—L. maj., 240.
1900.—U., 5,522 ; L., 5,313—U. maj., 209.
1895.—U. maj., 763 ; 1892—U. maj., 604 ; 1886—U. maj., 461.

MAJOR GODFREY DALRYMPLE WHITE, who was born in 1866, is a son of the late General Sir H. Dalrymple White, who commanded the 5th Inniskilling Dragoons throughout the Crimean War and was later Inspector-General of Cavalry in Great Britain ; served in the Grenadier Guards from 1885 to 1903, and went through two years of the South African War, and was mentioned in despatches ; has had Staff service in Canada and elsewhere ; unsuccessfully contested East Wilts in 1906.

WIDNES (11,780).—No change.

*Walker, Col. W. H. (U.) ..	5,758
Bernacchi, L. G. (L.) ..	4,666
Unionist majority ..	1,092

1906.—U., 5,017 ; L., 4,165—U. maj., 852.
1900.—U., 4,716 ; L., 2,062—U. maj., 2,654.
1895.—U. maj., 517 ; 1892, U. maj., 205 ; 1886, U. maj., 792.

COLONEL WILLIAM HALL WALKER, son of Sir Andrew Barclay Walker, of Osmaston, born in 1856 and educated at Harrow, married in 1896 a great-granddaughter of Richard Brinsley Sheridan. He is managing director of Peter Walker and Sons (Limited), brewers, and Hon. Colonel of the Second Brigade, Lancashire Artillery. He is owner of racehorses and has written books on horse breeding. Has represented the Widnes Division since 1900.

LEICESTERSHIRE (4).

WEST, or BOSWORTH (13,681).—No change.

*McLaren, Rt.Hon.Sir C.,K.C. (L.)	7,709
Fraser, Capt. Sir Keith (U.)	4,427
Liberal majority ..	3,282

1906.—L., 7,678; U., 3,627—L. maj., 4,051.
1900.—L. unop.
1895.—L. maj., 1,120; 1892, L. maj., 1,524; 1886, L. maj., 1,292.

SIR CHARLES MCLAREN, who was born in 1850, is the son of the late Mr. Duncan McLaren, formerly M.P. for Edinburgh, who married the sister of Mr. John Bright. His career has been one of prolific achievement. After education at the Universities of Edinburgh, Bonn, and Heidelberg he became a barrister and Q.C., but left a large practice in order to devote himself to the development of various companies in which he was interested as a shareholder. He is now officially connected with some of the most representative of undertakings engaged in the building of ships and in the production of machinery and engineering material, and many valuable articles on financial and commercial topics bear his name as author. His baronetcy came in 1902 and he was made a Privy Councillor in 1908.

SOUTH, or HARBOROUGH (17,921).—No change.

*Lehmann, R. C. (L.).. ..	8,632
Marshall, Sir H. (U.) ..	7,561
Liberal majority ..	1,071

1906.—L., 8,380; U., 6,382—L. maj., 1,998.
1900.—L., 7,269; U., 5,946—L. maj., 1,323.
1895.—L. maj., 1,026; 1892, L. maj., 656; 1886, U. maj., 1,138

Mr. RUDOLPH CHAMBERS LEHMANN is a barrister and journalist, a well-known contributor to *Punch*, and was in 1901 editor of the *Daily News*. Born in 1856, he was educated at Highgate School and Trinity College, Cambridge, and was called to the Bar in 1880. He is an authority on rowing and a well-known coach at Oxford and Cambridge. In 1901 he was High Sheriff of Buckinghamshire, and is the author of many books.

MID, or LOUGHBOROUGH (13,754).—No change.

*Levy, Sir M. (L.)	6,760
Smith-Carington, N. W. (U.)	6,007
Liberal majority ..	753

1906.—L., 6,803; U., 5,023—L. maj., 1,780.
1900.—L., 4,897; U., 4,830—L. maj., 67.
1895.—L. maj., 372; 1892, L. maj., 721; 1886, U. maj., 135.

SIR MAURICE LEVY has represented the Loughborough division of Leicestershire since 1900. He was born in Leicester in 1859, and educated privately and at London University. He entered into partnership with Sir Israel Hart, and is a life director of Hart and Levy (Limited), manufacturers and wholesale merchants. He is on the Commission of the Peace for Leicestershire.

EAST, or MELTON (16,873).—No change.

*Walker, H. de R. (L.)	..	7,748
Yate, Col. C. (U.) ..	..	7,625
Liberal majority	..	123

1906.—L., 7,800; U., 6,033; L. maj., 1,767.
1900.—U., 5,585; L., 5,193; U. maj., 392.
1895.—U. maj., 1,353; 1892 and 1886, U. unop.

Mr. HENRY DE ROSENBACH WALKER, who was elected to represent the Melton Division in 1906, after having unsuccessfully contested the Stowmarket Division of Suffolk in 1895 and Plymouth in 1900, was born in 1867, and educated at Winchester and Trinity College, Cambridge. He was a clerk in the Foreign Office from 1889 until 1892. He has travelled in Russia, Central Asia, the Far East, North America, the West Indies, and the Antipodes, and is the author of works on "Australasian Democracy" and "The West Indies and the Empire."

LINCOLNSHIRE (7).

NORTH LINDSEY, or BRIGG (14,048).— LIBERAL GAIN.

Gelder, Sir W. A. (L.)	..	6,548
*Sheffield, Sir Berkeley, Bt.(U.)		6,311
Liberal majority	..	237

By-election, Feb., 1907.—U., 5,389; L., 5,273—U. maj., 116.
1906.—L., 5,753; U., 4,027—L. maj., 1,726.
1900.—L., 4,899; U., 4,077—L. maj., 822.
1895.—L. maj., 776; 1892, L. maj., 427; 1886, L. maj., 165.

SIR WILLIAM ALFRED GELDER, who was born in 1855, has taken a prominent part in municipal and public affairs in Hull. He was Mayor of that city from 1899 to 1903, in which year he received a knighthood.

WEST LINDSEY, or GAINSBOROUGH (13,164).— LIBERAL GAIN.

Bentham, G. J. (L.) ..	..	6,178
Henderson, Capt. R. R. (U.)		5,663
Liberal majority	..	515

1906.—L., 5,922; U., 5,071—L. maj., 851.
1900.—U., 4,661; L., 4,624—U. maj., 37.
1895.—L. maj., 776; 1892, L. maj., 908; 1886, U. maj., 85.

Mr. G. J. BENTHAM is a native of Hull, and has served on the Municipal Council for many years. At the last General Election he stood unsuccessfully for the Central Division of Hull.

[Major Leslie Renton, the late representative of this division in the House of Commons, was returned as a Liberal at the General Election of 1906; but subsequently he crossed the floor of the House and supported the Unionist Party until the Dissolution.]

SOUTH LINDSEY, or HORNCASTLE (10,508).—
No change.
*de Eresby, Lord Willoughby
(U.) 5,162
Conybeare, C. A. V. (L.).. 4,292

Unionist majority .. 870
1906.—U., 4,250; L., 4,100—U. maj., 150.
1900.—U., 4,302; L., 2,962—U. maj., 1,340.
1895.—U., maj., 1,541; 1892, U. maj., 738; 1886, U. unop.

LORD WILLOUGHBY DE ERESBY is the eldest son of the Earl of Ancaster and was born in 1867 and educated at Eton and Trinity College, Cambridge. Since 1894 he has represented this division in the House of Commons. He is a J.P. for the Kesteven Division of Lincolnshire and for Rutland, Hon. Lieut.-Col. in the Lincolnshire Yeomanry, and chairman of the Primrose League.

EAST LINDSEY, or LOUTH (10,315).—
UNIONIST GAIN.
Brackenbury, Capt. H. L. (U.) 4,433
†Davies, T. (L.) 4,275

Unionist majority .. 158
1906.—L., 4,551; U., 3,572—L. maj., 979.
1900.—L., 4,188; U., 3,286—L. maj., 902.
1895.—L., 4,191; U., 3,779—L. maj., 412.
1892.—L., 4,284; U., 3,445—L. maj., 839.
1886.—U. unop.

Mr. H. LANGTON BRACKENBURY, who is a native of Lincolnshire, and resides at Thorpe Hall, near Louth, was born in 1868, a son of the late Major Henry Brackenbury, of his Majesty's Bodyguard; is a county magistrate, and succeeds Sir R. W. Perks (L.) in the representation of the division.

NORTH KESTEVEN, or SLEAFORD (10,389).—
UNIONIST GAIN.
Royds, E. (U.) 5,265
*Lupton, A. (L.) 4,000

Unionist majority .. 1,265
1906.—L., 4,355; U., 4,062—L. maj., 293.
1900.—U., 4,228; L., 2,785—U. maj., 1,443.
1895.—U., 4,653; L., 2,687—U. maj., 1,966.
1892.—U., 4,157; L., 3,250—U. maj., 907.
1886.—U. unop.

Mr. EDMUND ROYDS, who resides at Caythorpe, in the division, is a solicitor, a director of the Stamford, Spalding, and Boston Banking Company, and holds a commission in the Lincolnshire Yeomanry. He is a keen sportsman, a vice-president of the Lincolnshire Agricultural Society, and a member of the Lincolnshire Farmers' Union and the Lincolnshire Chamber of Agriculture.

HOLLAND, or SPALDING (14,846).—No change.
McLaren, F. (L.) 5,527
Royce, W. S. (U.) 5,148

Liberal majority .. 379
1906.—L., 5,800; U., 4,180—L. maj., 1,620.
1900.—L., 4,352; U., 4,295—L. maj., 57.
1895.—U. maj., 349; 1892, L. maj., 326; 1886, U. maj., 288.

Mr. FRANCIS WALTER STAFFORD MCLAREN, a younger son of the Rt. Hon. Sir Charles McLaren, who has represented the Bosworth Division of Leicestershire since 1892, was born in 1886, and educated at Eton and Oxford University.

SOUTH KESTEVEN, or STAMFORD (10,056).—No change.
Willoughby, Major the
Hon. C. (U.) 4,666
Parkin, G. H. (L.) 4,310

Unionist majority .. 356
1906.—U., 4,559; L., 4,018—U. maj., 541.
1900.—U., 4,292; L., 3,395—U. maj., 897.
1895.—U. maj., 389; 1892, U. maj., 124; 1886, U. unop.

MAJOR the HON. CLAUD HEATHCOTE-DRUMMOND WILLOUGHBY, who was born in 1872, is the third son of the first Earl of Ancaster. Entering the Coldstream Guards in 1891 he became captain in 1900 and major in 1908. He served in South Africa from 1899 to 1902, and holds the Queen's medal with five clasps and the King's with two.

MIDDLESEX (7).

BRENTFORD (20,701).—UNIONIST GAIN.
Compton, Lord A. F. (U.) .. 10,675
*Rutherford, Dr. V. H. (L.) 6,819

Unionist majority .. 3,856
1906.—L., 6,506; U., 6,053—L. maj., 453.
1900.—U. unop.; 1895, U. unop.
1892.—U., 4,417; L., 2,625—U. maj., 1,792.
1886.—U., 3,043; L., 1,409—U. maj., 1,634.

LORD ALWYNE FREDERICK COMPTON, D.S.O., the second surviving son of the fourth Marquis of Northampton, was born in 1855. He was educated at Eton, and joined the Grenadier Guards in 1874, transferring to the 10th Royal Hussars in 1879. He served as A.D.C. to the Marquis of Ripon, Viceroy of India, 1882-84, and in the Sudan Expeditions, 1884-85. He retired from the Army in 1887, and raised a body of Horse for South Africa and saw further service with the Imperial Yeomanry, 1899-1902. He represented North Bedfordshire as a Liberal Unionist from 1895 to 1906.

EALING (25,073).—No change.
*Nield, H. (U.).. 12,916
Hulbert, M. B. (L.) .. 8,210

Unionist majority .. 4,706
1906.—U., 8,261; L., 6,982—U. maj., 1,279.
1900 and 1895.—U. unop.
1892.—U. maj., 3,435; 1886, U. unop.

Mr. HERBERT NIELD, who was elected by the Ealing Division in 1906, is a barrister of the Inner Temple. He was returned to the Middlesex County Council in 1895, is a J.P., and represented the county on the Lea Conservancy Board. He has been active for many years in Conservative organization in the Ealing, Tottenham, and neighbouring districts.

ENFIELD (28,571).—UNIONIST GAIN.

Newman, J. R. Pretyman (U.)	12,625
*Branch, J. (L.)	11,383
Unionist majority	**1,242**

1906.—L., 9,790; U., 7,674—L. maj., 2,116.
1900.—U., 6,923; L., 3,655—U. maj., 3,268.
1895.—U. unop.; 1892, U. maj., 1,831; 1886, U. maj., 2,220.

Mr. J. R. PRETYMAN NEWMAN is the son of the late Mr. J. A. R. Newman, of Newberry Manor, county Cork, and was born in 1871. He was educated at Charterhouse School, and Trinity College, Cambridge; and was formerly captain 5th Batt. Royal Fusiliers. Is D.L. for county Cork and was High Sheriff of the county in 1898. He contested South-East Essex as a Unionist in 1906.

HARROW (35,379).—UNIONIST GAIN.

Mallaby-Deeley, H. C. (U.)	16,761
Harris, P. (L.)	13,575
Unionist majority	**3,186**

1906.—L., 11,393; U., 10,977—L. maj., 416.
1900, 1895, and 1886.—U. unop.
1892.—U. maj., 2,619.

Mr. HARRY MALLABY-DEELEY, of Mitcham Court, Surrey, was born in Cheshire in 1863; graduated at Trinity College, Cambridge, and was called to the Bar, but does not practise; formerly private secretary to Mr. Henry Chaplin, and is well versed in economic and political questions; a director of the Norwich Union, and recently acquired the Piccadilly Hotel, one of the chief promoters of the Prince's Golf Club, Mitcham, and the Prince's Club, Sandwich.

HORNSEY (23,450).—No change.

*Ronaldshay, The Earl of (U.)	12,014
Dummett, R. E. (L.)	8,633
Unionist majority	**3,381**

By-election. 1907.—U. unop.
1906.—U., 8,859; L., 7,289—U. maj., 1,570.
1900 and 1895.—U. unop.
1892.—U. maj., 3,279; 1886, U. unop.

The EARL OF RONALDSHAY, the eldest surviving son of the Marquis of Zetland, was born in 1876, and educated at Harrow, and Trinity College, Cambridge. He has travelled extensively in Central Asia and the Far East, and was A.D.C. on the Viceroy's Staff, India, in 1900. He is the author of several books of travel.

TOTTENHAM (29,260).—No change.

*Alden, Percy (L.)	12,302
Sturdy, E. V. (U.)	11,787
Liberal majority	**515**

1906.—L., 9,956; U., 7,009—L. maj., 2,947.
1900.—U., 6,721; L., 4,009—U. maj., 2,712.
1895.—U. maj., 2,571; 1892.—U. maj., 1,720; 1886—U. maj., 1,879.

Mr. PERCY ALDEN, born in 1865, and educated at Balliol College, Oxford, is a journalist and lecturer; social and labour problems, on which he has lectured here and in the United States, New Zealand, and Australia, specially interest him; was for many years Warden of Mansfield House University Settlement and a member of the West Ham Borough Council.

UXBRIDGE (17,634).—No change.

Mills, Hon. C. T. (U.)	10,116
Pocock, S. J. (L.)	5,408
Unionist majority	**4,708**

1906.—U., 6,429; L., 6,284—U. maj., 145.
1900 and 1895.—U. unop.
1892.—U. maj., 3,143; 1886, U. unop

The HON. CHARLES THOMAS MILLS, who was born in 1887, is the son and heir of Lord Hillingdon. He is a lieutenant in the West Kent Yeomanry.

MONMOUTHSHIRE (3).

NORTH (15,711).—No change.

*McKenna, Rt. Hon. R. (L.)	8,596
Carmichael, E. G. M. (U.)	4,335
Liberal majority	**4,261**

1906.—L., 7,730; U., 3,155—L. maj., 4,575.
1900.—L., 5,139; U., 3,740—L. maj., 1,399.
1895.—L. maj.. 762; 1892, L. maj., 1,157; 1886. L. maj., 1,403.

Mr. REGINALD MCKENNA, who was born in 1863, was in earlier years a great rowing man. He was bow in the Cambridge boat during his University career, and won the Grand and Stewards' cups at Henley. The General Election of 1895 gave him his seat in Parliament, and he was appointed Financial Secretary to the Treasury in 1905. The period following was one of quick change, for in 1907 he succeeded Mr. Birrell as President of the Board of Education, only to transfer his attention the next year to the Admiralty as First Lord.

SOUTH (19,134).—No change.

*Herbert, Col. Sir I. (L.)	9,738
Forestier-Walker, L. (U.)	6,910
Liberal majority	**2,828**

1906.—L., 7,503; U., 6,216—L. maj., 1,287.
1900.—U. unop.
1895.—U. maj., 612; 1892, U. maj., 721; 1886, U. maj., 2,285.

COLONEL SIR IVOR JOHN CARADOC HERBERT was born in 1851 and was educated at St. Mary's Roman Catholic College, Oscott. In 1870 he entered the Grenadier Guards, and became colonel in 1899; local major-general (Canada) from 1890 to 1895; brigade major of Guards in 1882-3; and commandant of the School of Instruction for Auxiliary Forces in 1886. From 1886 to 1890 he acted as military attaché at St. Petersburg and commanded the Canadian local forces from 1890 to 1895. In 1882 he served in Egypt, in the Sudan in 1884-5, and was Assistant Adjutant-General in South Africa from 1889 to 1901. He has the Orders of the Red Eagle, the Crown of Italy, the Legion of Honour, and the Medjidieh.

WEST (20,399).—No change.

*Richards, T. (Lab.)	13,295
Cameron, J. (U.)	3,045
Labour majority	**10,250**

1906.—Lab. unop.
1900.—L., 5,976; U., 2,401—L. maj., 3,575.
1895.—L. maj., 5,287; 1892, L. maj., 5,319; 1886, L. unop.

Mr. THOMAS RICHARDS, who succeeded Sir William Harcourt in the representation of West Monmouthshire in 1904, was born in Ebbw Vale in 1859 and began work in a mine when 12 years old. On the formation of the Miners' Federation after the strike of 1898 he was appointed general secretary of that organization, and in 1901 he became its chairman. He has been a member of several local government authorities and is an alderman of the Monmouthshire County Council and a magistrate for two counties.

NORFOLK (6).

EAST (11,560).—No change.

*Price, Sir R. J. (L.)	.. ..	5,592
Fitch, Cecil (U.)	.. ..	4,348
Liberal majority	..	1,244

1906.—L., 5,631 ; U., 3,435—L. maj., 2,196.
1900.—L., 4,563 ; U., 3,733—L. maj., 830.
1895.—L. maj., 198 ; 1892, L. maj., 440 ; 1886, U. maj., 578.

SIR ROBERT JOHN PRICE, who was born in 1854, is a member of the Royal College of Surgeons, was called to the Bar by the Middle Temple, and is a director of many limited liability companies. He has represented East Norfolk since 1892, defeating Mr. Rider Haggard in 1895, and was knighted in June, 1908.

MID (9,984).—UNIONIST GAIN.

Boyle, W. L. (U.)	.. ..	4,724
Lester, W. R. (L.)	.. ..	4,265
Unionist majority	..	459

1906.—L., 4,197 ; U., 4,170—L. maj., 27.
1900.—L., 3,993 ; U., 3,422—L. maj., 574.
1895.—L. maj., 134 ; 1892, L. maj., 470 ; 1886, U. maj., 407.

Mr. WILLIAM LEWIS BOYLE was born in 1859 at the Cape, where his father at that time held an appointment in the Diplomatic Service. He spent some years in Canada and British Columbia before settling down in England. He has lived in Norfolk for some years past.

NORTH (11,169).—No change.

Buxton, Noel (L.)	.. ..	5,189
King, H. D. (U.)	.. ..	4,604
Liberal majority	..	585

1906.—L., 5,155 ; U., 3,628—L. maj., 1,527.
1900.—L., 4,490 ; U., 3,493—L. maj., 997.
1895.—L. maj., 526 ; 1892, L. maj., 1,283 ; 1886, L. maj., 760.

Mr. NOEL BUXTON, the second son of Sir T. Fowell Buxton, was born in 1869 and educated at Trinity College, Cambridge (History Honours 1889, M.A. 1894). In 1896 he acted as A.D.C. to his father, then Governor of South Australia. He has travelled in the Near East, and has interested himself in the condition of the Turkish Empire in Europe and in social reforms at home. Was a member of the Departmental Committee on Lead Poisoning and was formerly a major in the Volunteers. In 1900 he contested Ipswich, and from June, 1905, to the General Election of 1906 sat as member for the Whitby Division of Yorkshire (N.R.).

NORTH-WEST (11,613).—No change.

*White, Sir G. (L.)	.. ..	5,596
Jodrell, N. P. (U.)	.. ..	4,388
Liberal majority	..	1,208

1906.—L., 5,772 ; U., 2,972—L. maj., 2,800.
1900.—L., 4,287 ; U., 3,811—L. maj., 476.
1895.—L. maj., 1,297 ; 1892, L. maj., 1,089 ; 1886, U. maj., 20.

SIR GEORGE WHITE, who was born in 1840, is a well-known Nonconformist, and has been President of the Baptist Union. He is alderman and J.P., and has been High Sheriff of Norwich, presides over the Education Committee, and was knighted in 1907. In business he is chairman and managing director of Howlett and White, shoe manufacturers, and chairman of the Rotary Machine Company. He held his present seat in the Parliaments of 1900 and 1906.

SOUTH (9,779).—No change.

*Soames, A. W. (L.)	.. ..	4,781
Kerrison, Col. E. R. (U.)	..	3,694
Liberal majority	..	1,087

1906.—L., 4,677 ; U., 3,519—L. maj., 1,158.
1900.—L., 3,986 ; U., 3,566—L. maj., 420.
1895.—U. maj., 836 ; 1892, U. maj., 753 ; 1886, U. unop.

Mr. ARTHUR WELLESLEY SOAMES, born at Brighton in 1852, was educated at Trinity College, Cambridge, graduated B.A., 1876, M.A., 1880, and married in 1876 a daughter of Mr. T. H. Coles, of Ore, Sussex. From 1882 to 1898 he practised as an architect. In 1892 and again in 1895 he unsuccessfully contested Ipswich. At a by-election in May, 1898, he was elected for South Norfolk, and continued to represent the constituency to the end of the last Parliament.

SOUTH-WEST (9,045).—No change.

*Winfrey, R. (L.)	.. ..	4,239
Hare, Sir T. L. (U.)	.. ..	4,000
Liberal majority	..	239

1906.—L., 4,416 ; U., 3,513—L. maj., 903.
1900.—U., 3,702 ; L., 3,636—U. maj., 66.
1895.—U., 3,968 ; L., 3,762—U. maj., 206.
1892.—U., 4,077 ; L., 3,739 U. maj, 338.
1886.—U. unop.

Mr. RICHARD WINFREY was born in 1858 and educated at Croad's School, King's Lynn. He is the manager of various newspaper companies in the Eastern Counties, and has taken an active part in local life, having served on the city council of Peterborough, the Soke of Peterborough County Council, and the local Citizens' League. He is chairman of the South Lincolnshire and Norfolk Small Holdings Association and an ex-president of the Peterborough and District Free Church Council. Having unsuccessfully contested South-West Norfolk in 1895 and 1900, he was returned in 1906 and was an assistant private secretary (unpaid) to Earl Carrington at the Board of Agriculture in the last Parliament.

NORTHAMPTONSHIRE (4).

EAST (17,470).—No change.

*Channing, Sir F. A. (L.)	8,679
Brooke, Sir A. De-Capell- (U.)	6,802
Liberal majority	1,877

1906.—L., 9,017; U., 5,414—L. maj., 3,603.
1900.—L., 7,003; U., 5,563; L. maj., 1,440.
1895.—L. maj., 1,216; 1892, L. maj., 1,484; 1886, L. maj., 1,416.

SIR FRANCIS ALLSTON CHANNING was educated at Liverpool and at Exeter College, Oxford, and was formerly Fellow and Lecturer in Philosophy of University College. He has taken an active part in the promotion of labour, educational, and agricultural reforms, and was a member of the Royal Commission on Agricultural Depression and of the Small Holdings Committee. He was made a baronet in 1906.

MID (14,189).—No change.

*Manfield, H. (L.)	6,559
Paget, T. G. F. (U.)	6,003
Liberal majority	556

1906.—L., 6,307; U., 5,067—L. maj., 1,240.
1900.—L., 5,399; U., 4,605—L. maj., 794.
1895.—U. maj., 282; 1892, L. maj., 431; 1886, L. maj., 956.

Mr. HARRY MANFIELD is the elder son of the late Sir Philip Manfield, some time colleague with Mr. Labouchere in the representation of Northampton. He was born in 1855, and is senior partner in the firm of Manfield and Sons, boot manufacturers, Northampton. He has long been associated with Liberal politics in the Midlands and, as a member, with the Northamptonshire County Council.

NORTH (10,767).—UNIONIST GAIN.

Brassey, H. L. C. (U.)	5,520
*Nicholls, G. (L.)	4,429
Unionist majority	1,091

1906.—L., 4,880; U., 4,195—L. maj., 685.
1900.—U., 4,559; L., 3,303—U. maj., 1,256.
1895.—U. unop.; 1892, U. maj., 669; 1886, U. unop.

Mr. HENRY LEONARD CAMPBELL BRASSEY is the second son of the late Henry Arthur Brassey, brother of Lord Brassey, and was born in 1870. In 1894 he married a daughter of the Duke of Richmond. He is a large landowner, until lately was major in the West Kent Yeomanry, and is a member of the Jockey Club.

SOUTH (9,290).—UNIONIST GAIN.

Fitzroy, E. A. (U.)	4,565
Kellaway, F. (L.)	3,955
Unionist majority	610

1906.—L., 4,136; U., 3,814—L. maj., 322.
1900.—U., 4,174; L., 3,166—U. maj., 1,088.
1895.—U. maj., 1,229; 1892, L. maj., 48; 1886, U. maj., 316.

The HON. EDWARD ALGERNON FITZROY, D.L., born in 1869, younger son of the third Lord Southampton, was educated at Sandhurst, and in 1891 married a daughter of the late Lieutenant-Colonel Douglas-Pennant. He was formerly Page of Honour to the Queen, and late lieutenant in the 1st Life Guards. He was member for the constituency from 1900 to 1906.

NORTHUMBERLAND (4).

BERWICK-UPON-TWEED (9,420).—No change.

*Grey, Rt. Hon. Sir Edward (L.)	5,010
Inskip, T. W. H. (U.)	3,327
Liberal majority	1,683

1906.—L., 5,102; U., 2,862—L. maj., 2,240.
1900.—L. unop.
1895.—L. maj., 785; 1892, L. maj., 442; 1886, L. maj., 724.

SIR EDWARD GREY, who was born in 1862, has represented the Berwick-on-Tweed Division of Northumberland since 1885. His only stepping-stone to the high office of Secretary of State for Foreign Affairs, to which he was appointed in 1905, was his connexion as Under-Secretary with the Foreign Office during the Gladstone-Rosebery Government. His conduct of the affairs of his department for the last four years has won general confidence and added considerably to his personal influence. He is a J.P. and D.L. for Northumberland, and was made a Privy Councillor in 1902.

HEXHAM (11,151).—No change.

*Holt, R. D. (L.)	5,478
Bates, Col. C. L. (U.)	4,417
Liberal majority	1,061

By-election, 1907.—L., 5,401; U., 4,244—L. maj., 1,157.
1906.—L., 5,632; U., 3,547—L. maj., 2,085.
1900.—L., 4,197; U., 4,011—L. maj., 186.
1895.—L. maj., 435; 1892, U. maj., 82; 1886, L. maj., 957.

Mr. RICHARD DURNING HOLT was born in Liverpool in 1868 and educated at Winchester College and New College, Oxford. He entered the shipowning firm of his father, the late Mr. R. D. Holt, who was the first Lord Mayor of Liverpool, and is a partner of Alfred Holt and Co. and a member of the Mersey Docks and Harbour Board. He unsuccessfully contested the West Derby Division of Liverpool in 1903 and 1906.

TYNESIDE (25,667).—No change.

*Robertson, J. M. (L.)	13,158
Cochrane, A. H. J. (U.)	7,807
Liberal majority	5,351

1906.—L., 11,496; U., 6,885—L. maj., 4,611.
1900.—U., 7,093; L., 6,730—U. maj., 363.
1895.—L. maj., 435; 1892, L. maj., 450; 1886, L. maj., 122.

Mr. JOHN MACKINNON ROBERTSON, born in 1856 and educated at Stirling, is a journalist, and the author of a number of books and criticisms on religious, literary, historical, political, and social subjects; has lectured in the United States and acted as a special correspondent in South Africa; a severe critic of the late Government's policy in Egypt and India.

WANSBECK (18,959).—No change.

| *Fenwick, C. (L.) | .. | .. | 10,872 |
| Percy, C. (U.) | .. | .. | 4,650 |

| Liberal majority | .. | 6,222 |

1906.—L., 10,386 ; U., 3,210—L. maj., 7,176.
1900.—L., 5,474 ; U., 4,283—L. maj., 1,191.
1895.—L. maj., 3,207 ; 1892, L. maj., 2,776 ; 1886, L. maj., 3,525.

Mr. CHARLES FENWICK began life as a pit boy at the age of nine, and was working in Bebside Colliery, Northumberland, when he was first invited, in 1885, to contest the Wansbeck Division, which he has since represented in Parliament. He succeeded in 1890 Mr. Broadhurst as Parliamentary Secretary to the Trade Union Congress, and held that position for four years, when he was replaced by Mr. Sam Woods ; was consistently opposed to the Eight Hours (Mines) Bill, and, in company with Mr. Thomas Burt, declined to subscribe to the constitution of the Independent Labour Party ; has actively promoted the University Extension system in the mining districts, and is a Methodist local preacher.

NOTTINGHAMSHIRE (4).

BASSETLAW (12,012).—UNIONIST GAIN.

| Hume-Williams, K.C. (U.) | .. | 5,631 |
| *Newnes, F. (L.) | .. | .. | 5,290 |

| Unionist majority | .. | 341 |

1906.—L., 5,365 ; U., 4,834—L. maj., 531.
1900.—U. unop.
1895.—U. maj., 1,253 ; 1892—U. maj., 402 ; 1886—U. unop.

Mr. WILLIAM ELLIS HUME-WILLIAMS contested North Monmouthshire in 1895, the Frome Division of Somerset in 1900, and North Kensington in 1906. The son of a barrister, he was called to the Bar in 1881, after having graduated at Trinity Hall, Cambridge. He took silk in 1899, was Recorder of Bury St. Edmunds 1901-5, and became Recorder of Norwich in 1905. He has written on " The Taking of Evidence on Commission " and " The Irish Parliament from 1782 to 1800," and has edited the tenth edition of " Taylor on Evidence."

MANSFIELD (21,075).—No change.

| *Markham, A. B. (L.) | .. | 12,622 |
| Campbell, J. G. D. (U.) .. | 4,382 |

| Liberal majority | .. | 8,240 |

1906.—L. unop.
1900.—L., 6,496 ; U., 4,127—L. maj., 2,369.
1895.—L. maj., 1,385 ; 1892 L. maj., 2,496 ; 1886, L. maj., 2,044.

Mr. ARTHUR BASIL MARKHAM has represented Mansfield since 1900. He was born in 1866, and educated at Rugby, and is a director of several colliery companies.

NEWARK (11,320).—No change.

| *Starkey, J. R. (U.) | .. | .. | 5,497 |
| Wallis, R. B. (L.) | .. | .. | 4,618 |

| Unionist majority | 879 |

1906.—U., 4,772 ; L., 4,444—U. maj., 328.
1900, 1895, 1892, and 1886.—U. unop.

Mr. JOHN RALPH STARKEY was born in 1859 and educated at Eton, and Christ Church, Oxford ; married in 1888 a daughter of Sir Charles Seely ; is a J.P. and D.L., and has been captain in the South Notts Yeomanry ; was elected for the division in 1906.

RUSHCLIFFE (19,640).—No change.

| *Ellis, Rt. Hon. J. E. (L.) | .. | 9,942 |
| Disraeli, Coningsby (U.) .. | 7,098 |

| Liberal majority | .. | 2,844 |

1906.—L., 9,094 ; U., 5,460—L. maj., 3,634.
1900.—L., 6,359 ; U., 5,913—L. maj., 446.
1895.—L. maj., 633 ; 1892, L. maj., 792 ; 1886, L. maj., 1,447.

Mr. JOHN EDWARD ELLIS has sat for the division since 1885, and is regarded as an authority on the rules and the procedure of the House ; takes a special interest in the work of Grand Committees and Private Bill Committees ; was Under-Secretary for India for a year (1905-6), when he resigned office ; is a member of the Privy Council ; born at Leicester in 1841, and educated at the Friends' School, Kendal.

OXFORDSHIRE (3).

NORTH, or BANBURY (8,021).—UNIONIST GAIN.

| Brassey, Capt. R. B. (U.) | .. | 3,831 |
| *Fiennes, Hon. Eustace (L.) | 3,516 |

| Unionist majority | .. | 315 |

1906.—L., 3,992 ; U., 2,796—L. maj., 1,196.
1900.—U., 3,632 ; L., 2,821—U. maj., 811.
1895.—U. maj., 983 ; 1892, L., 187 ; 1886, L. maj., 493.

CAPTAIN ROBERT B. BRASSEY, the eldest son of Mr. Albert Brassey, of Heythrop, Chipping Norton, was born at Heythrop in 1878 ; served in the 17th Lancers from 1897 to 1905, and went through the South African War ; served also as A.D.C. to Major-General Sir J. R. Slade, K.C.B., in Egypt, 1903-4 ; a keen agriculturist ; his father represented the division in the Unionist interest from 1895 to 1906.

SOUTH, or HENLEY (10,536).—UNIONIST GAIN.

| Fleming, V. (U.) | .. | .. | 5,649 |
| *Morrell, P. (L.) | .. | .. | 4,046 |

| Unionist majority | .. | 1,603 |

1906.—L., 4,562 ; U., 4,050—L. maj., 512.
1900.—U., 3,622 ; L., 3,450—U. maj., 172.
1895.—U. maj., 361 ; 1892, U. maj., 419 ; 1886, U. maj., 1,074

Mr. VALENTINE FLEMING was born in 1882, and educated at Eton, and Magdalen College, Oxford ; is a barrister-at-law, but principally engaged in business in the City of London ; is a lieutenant in the Oxfordshire Yeomanry, and has travelled extensively ; was a member of the winning crew in the Ladies' Plate at Henley Regatta.

MID, or WOODSTOCK (10,525).— UNIONIST GAIN.

| Hamersley, A. St. G. (U.) | .. | 5,098 |
| *Bennett, E. N. (L.) | .. | .. | 4,378 |

| Unionist majority | .. | 720 |

1906.—L., 4,585 ; U., 4,144—L. maj., 441.
1900.—U. unop.
1895.—U. maj., 929 ; 1892, L. maj., 111 ; 1886, U. unop.

Mr. ALFRED ST. GEORGE HAMERSLEY, K.C., born in 1848, is the son of Mr. Hugh Hamersley, J.P., D.L., of Pyrton Manor, Oxfordshire, who was chairman of Quarter Sessions for the county for many years; educated at Marlborough and called to the Bar; went to New Zealand and practised at the Bar there; took an active part in military affairs in the colony, commanding the Militia Artillery, and was in command of a contingent against the Maoris at Parihaka; returned to England, but subsequently went to Canada and there practised at the Bar; took great interest in public affairs and the commercial development of Vancouver; acted as chairman of several companies interested in the development of British Columbia; keenly interested in sports generally; founded the New Zealand Grand National Steeplechase Club, and started the Amateur Athletic Club of British Columbia, of which he was president; has two sons in the British Army and is a keen Imperialist.

RUTLANDSHIRE (4,128).—No change.
*Gretton, J. (U.) 2,235
Emery, J. N. (L.) .. 1,531

Unionist majority .. 704
By-election, June, 1907.—U., 2,213; L., 1,362—U. maj., 852.
1906.—U., 2,047; L., 1,564—U. maj., 483.
1900, 1895, 1892, and 1886.—U. unop.

Mr. JOHN GRETTON is a director of the great brewing firm of Bass, Ratcliff, and Gretton, Burton-on-Trent. He was born in 1867 and educated at Harrow, entering Parliament in 1895 as member for South Derbyshire. During the debates on the Licensing and Finance Bills he proved an untiring critic of the Ministerial proposals.

SHROPSHIRE (4).

LUDLOW (10,530).—No change.
*Hunt, R. (U.).. 5,769
Forsdike, P. F. (L.) .. 3,365

Unionist majority .. 2,404
1906.—U., 4,978; L., 4,218—U. maj., 760.
1900 and 1895.—U. unop.
1892.—U. maj., 3,819; 1886, U. unop.

Mr. ROWLAND HUNT has represented Ludlow since 1903. He comes of a family well known in the political world before he entered the House of Commons, for his uncle, Mr. G. Ward Hunt, was Financial Secretary to the Treasury in 1866 and 1867, Chancellor of the Exchequer in 1868, and First Lord of the Admiralty 1874-7. Mr. Rowland Hunt was born in 1858, and educated at Eton, and Magdalene College, Cambridge. He volunteered for service with Lovat's Scouts during the war in South Africa. He has been an outspoken advocate of Tariff Reform from the start of the movement, and as a Roman Catholic is a strong supporter of denominational religious education. His speeches in the House frequently contribute humour to the debates.

NORTH, or NEWPORT (10,886).—No change.
*Stanier, Beville (U.) 5,570
Moulsdale, W. E. (L.) .. 4,324

Unionist majority .. 1,246
By-election, 1908.—U., 5,328; L., 4,377—U. maj., 951.
1906.—U., 4,853; L., 4,677—U. maj., 176.
1900 and 1895, U. unop.
1892.—U. maj., 1,285; 1886, U. maj., 1,576.

Mr. BEVILLE STANIER, born in 1867, has shown a great interest throughout his career in agricultural and archæological pursuits, and has been a successful breeder of cattle and Shropshire sheep. He was educated privately and at the Royal Agricultural College, Cirencester; spent three years on Lord Dudley's estate at Whitley, afterwards going to South Africa to manage a stock farm. He is a tenant farmer on his own account. In 1901 he succeeded to the Peplow estates, and is lord of the manor of Peplow and High Hatton and patron of the livings of Stanton, Salop, and Knutton, Staffordshire.

WEST, or OSWESTRY (10,151).—No change.
*Bridgeman, W. C. (U.) .. 5,003
Powell, E. (L.) 4,379

Unionist majority .. 624
1906.—U., 5,011; L., 4,508—U. maj., 503.
1900.—U. unop.
1895.—U. maj., 1,007; 1892 and 1886, U. unop.

Mr. WILLIAM CLIVE BRIDGEMAN, who fought three Parliamentary contests before his return in 1906, was born in 1864 and educated at Eton, and Trinity College, Cambridge; has travelled widely; was private secretary to Viscount Knutsford at the Colonial Office and to Viscount St. Aldwyn when, as Sir M. Hicks Beach, he was Chancellor of the Exchequer; sat on the London School Board (1897-1904), and has served on the County Council; is specially interested in rural education.

MID, or WELLINGTON (8,751).—No change.
*Henry, C. S. (L.) 4,673
Wood, Capt. C. P. B. (U.) 3,484

Liberal majority .. 1,189
1906.—L., 4,806; U., 3,114—L. maj., 1,692.
1900.—U., 3,480; L., 2,318—U. maj., 1,162.
1895.—U. unop.; 1892, U. maj., 1,283; 1886, U. unop.

Mr. CHARLES SOLOMON HENRY is managing director of the firm of C. S. Henry and Co. (Limited), metal merchants, of London. He was born in 1860, and was educated at St. Marylebone and All Souls Grammar School (in connexion with King's College, London), and at Göttingen University.

SOMERSET (7).

BRIDGWATER (10,341).—UNIONIST GAIN.
Sanders, R. A. (U.) 5,575
Hicks, Harold (L.).. .. 3,896

Unionist majority .. 1,679
1906.—L., 4,422; U., 4,405—L. maj., 17.
1900.—U. unop.; 1895, U. unop.
1892.—U., 4,555; L., 3,362—U. maj., 1,193.
1886.—U. unop.

Mr. ROBERT ARTHUR SANDERS, born in 1867, was educated at Harrow, and Balliol College, Oxford, M.A., first class Honour School of Jurisprudence, called to the Bar, Inner Temple, 1891, and in 1893 married a daughter of Mr. W. H. Halliday, of Lynton. He is J.P., alderman of the Somerset County Council, major in the Royal North Devon Imperial Yeomanry, and was master of the Devon and Somerset Staghounds, 1895-1907.

EAST (9,791).—UNIONIST GAIN.
Jardine, E. (U.) 4,997
*Thompson, J. W. H. (L.) .. 3,970

Unionist majority .. 1,027
1906.—L., 4,553 ; U., 3,890—L. maj., 663.
1900.—U. unop.
1895.—U. maj., 1,074 ; 1892, U. maj., 755 ; 1886, U. unop.

Mr. ERNEST JARDINE is a lace manufacturer of Nottingham who has taken up his residence in Glastonbury ; became prominent in the Eastern Division of Somerset shortly after the last General Election, and has identified himself with its interests in the most practical manner ; advanced £30,000 for the purchase of the ruins of Glastonbury Abbey for the Church of England and the nation, and when the Abbey was handed over to the Church he and Mrs. Jardine entertained the Prince and Princess of Wales and suite at the Abbey House ; has started a model factory at Shepton Mallet ; is president of the County Agricultural Show, and has given great encouragement to agriculture.

FROME (13,168).—No change.
*Barlow, Sir J. E. (L.).. .. 6,248
Foxcroft, C. T. (U.) .. 5,469

Liberal majority .. 779
1906.—L., 6,297 ; U., 4,552—L. maj., 1,745.
1900.—L., 5,066 ; U., 4,708—L. maj., 358.
1895.—U. maj., 383 ; 1892, L. maj., 487 ; 1886, U. maj., 703.

SIR JOHN EMMOTT BARLOW sat in the House of Commons as member for the Frome Division from 1892 until 1895, when he was defeated by Lord Weymouth, but he secured re-election in the following year, and has retained the seat from that time. His earlier attempts to enter Parliament, made in the Knutsford Division of Cheshire in 1885 and the Denbigh Boroughs in 1886, proved unsuccessful. He is the senior partner in the firm of Thomas Barlow and Brother, of Manchester and London, and Barlow and Co., of Calcutta, Shanghai, and Singapore. He was born in 1857, and received a baronetcy 50 years later.

NORTH (13,492).—No change.
King, J. (L.) 6,568
Beauchamp, F. B. (U.) .. 5,768

Liberal majority .. 800
1906.—L., 6,626 ; U., 4,380—L. maj., 2,246.
1900.—U., 4,530 ; L., 4,014—U. maj., 516.
1895.—U. maj., 686 ; 1892, L. maj., 19 ; 1886, U. maj., 2,165.

Mr. JOSEPH KING, of Witley, Surrey, is M.A. of Oxford, a member of the Eighty Club, and the author of a number of books on political topics ; unsuccessfully contested the New Forest Division of Hampshire in 1892 and the Isle of Thanet Division of Kent in 1900 and 1906.

SOUTH (10,164).—No change.
*Strachey, Sir E. (L.) 4,955
Herbert, Hon. Aubrey (U.) 4,444

Liberal majority .. 511
1906.—L., 5,164 ; U., 3,247—L. maj., 1,917.
1900.—L., 4,349 ; U., 3,671—L. maj., 678.
1895.—L. maj., 340 ; 1892, L. maj., 405 ; 1886, L. maj., 227.

SIR EDWARD STRACHEY was born at Clifton in 1858 and educated at Christ Church, Oxford ; a member of the Somerset County Council, and a past Chairman of the Central Chamber of Agriculture ; contested North Somerset in 1885, Plymouth in 1886, and has represented South Somerset since 1892 ; in the last Parliament was Treasurer of the Household, and represented the Board of Agriculture in the House of Commons ; was appointed, under a Bill passed towards the close of the Session, Parliamentary Secretary to the Board of Agriculture.

WEST, or WELLINGTON (10,209).—No change.
*Acland-Hood, Rt. Hon. Sir
A. F. (U.) 5,216
King, W. (L.). 4,150

Unionist majority .. 1,066
1906.—U., 4,558 ; L., 4,286—U. maj., 272.
1900 and 1895.—U. unop.
1892.—U. maj., 885 ; 1886, U. maj., 897.

The RIGHT HON. SIR ALEXANDER FULLER ACLAND-HOOD, Bt., was born at St. Audries, Bridgwater, in 1853, and educated at Eton, and Balliol College, Oxford. He entered the Grenadier Guards in 1875, and took part in the Egyptian campaign 1882, retiring in 1892. From 1889 to 1891 he was A.D.C. to the Governor of Victoria. Elected for West Somerset in 1892, he acted as Vice-Chamberlain of the Household 1900-2, was Patronage Secretary to the Treasury 1902-5, and is Chief Conservative Whip.

WELLS (12,642).—UNIONIST GAIN.
Sandys, G. J. (U.) 6,167
*Silcock, T. B. (L.) .. 4,871

Unionist majority.. 1,296
1906.—L., 5,146 ; U., 4,765—L. maj., 385.
1900.—U. unop.
1895.—U. maj., 1,410 ; 1892, U. maj., 940 ; 1886, U. unop.

Mr. G. J. SANDYS, late a lieutenant in the 2nd Life Guards, is now a captain in the Glamorganshire Yeomanry ; was defeated at the last General Election, when he contested a Cornish seat, and about six months later, when Mr. Agar-Robartes was unseated on petition, unsuccessfully contested the Bodmin Division of Cornwall.

STAFFORDSHIRE (7).
BURTON (11,878).—No change.
*Ratcliff, R. F. (U.).
1906.—U., 5,613 ; L., 4,572—U. maj., 1,041.
1900.—U. maj., 2,171.
1895.—L., unop. ; 1892, L. unop. ; 1886, L. unop.

Mr. ROBERT F. RATCLIFF, born in 1867, was educated at Rossall and Jesus College, Cambridge (B.A.). He is director of Bass, Ratcliff, and Gretton (Limited) and Major and Hon. Lieut.-Col. of 6th Battalion North Staffordshire Regiment. He was first elected for the division in 1900.

HANDSWORTH (28,937).—No change.
*Meysey-Thompson, E. C. (U.) 14,594
Jackson, G. (L.) 9,488

Unionist majority .. 5,106
1906.—U., 13,407 ; L., 8,636—U. maj., 4,771.
1900 and 1895.—U. unop.
1892.—U. maj., 1,937 ; 1886, U. unop.

Mr. ERNEST CLAUDE MEYSEY-THOMPSON is the sixth son of the late Sir Harry Stephen Meysey-Thompson and brother to Lord Knaresborough. He was born in 1859, educated at Eton and Oxford, and is a J.P. for the North and West Ridings of Yorkshire. He spent several years in New Zealand, and has devoted much time to the study and improvement of agriculture. In 1900 he was a candidate for the Buckrose Division of the East Riding of Yorkshire, and was returned for his present constituency four years ago.

KINGSWINFORD (14,076).—No change.

*Staveley-Hill, H. (U.)	7,267
Coysh, F. (L.)	5,226
Unionist majority	2,041

1906.—U., 6,311; L., 5,470—U. maj., 841.
1900 and 1895, U. unop.
1892.—U. maj., 1,571; 1886, U. unop.

Mr. HENRY STAVELEY STAVELEY-HILL was born in 1865, and educated at Westminster and St. John's College, Oxford. He was called to the Bar at the Inner Temple in 1891, and practises on the Oxford Circuit. He was appointed Recorder of Banbury in 1903, and is a member of the Cannock Rural District Council and Board of Guardians.

LEEK (12,079).—UNIONIST GAIN.

Heath, Col. A. H. (U.)	5,463
*Pearce, R. (L.)	5,453
Unionist majority	10

1906.—L., 5,749; U., 4,275—L. maj., 1,474.
1900.—U., 4,800; L., 4,041—U. maj., 759.
1895.—U., 4,705; L., 4,091—U. maj., 614.
1892.—U., 4,576; L., 4,213—U. maj., 363.
1886.—U., 4,324; L., 3,669—U. maj., 655.

Mr. ARTHUR HOWARD HEATH contested Hanley in 1892 and 1895, before securing election as its representative in 1900. In 1906 he fought that borough once more. He was born in 1856, and educated at Clifton, and Brasenose College, Oxford. He is colonel of the Staffordshire Imperial Yeomanry.

LICHFIELD (10,703).— No change.

*Warner, T. C. (L.)	5,220
Coates, Dr. G. (U.)	4,353
Liberal majority	867

1906.—L., 5,421; U., 2,991—L. maj., 2,430.
1900.—L., 4,300; U., 3,485—L. maj., 815.
1895.—L. maj., 44; 1892, U. maj., 4; 1886, L. maj., 633.

Mr. THOMAS COURTENAY THEYDON WARNER has sat for the Lichfield Division since 1896, when Mr. Fulford was unseated, and had previously represented North Somerset. He was born in 1857, educated at Eton and Oxford, is a J.P. for Somerset and Suffolk, and has been a county councillor and high sheriff of Essex. He is chairman of the Warner Estate Company and Tottenham and Forest Gate Railway Company, a director of the Law Land Company, and owns about 4,000 acres. In 1906 he was elected president of the Central Chamber of Agriculture.

NORTH-WEST (6,498).—No change.

*Stanley, A. (Lab.)	8,566
Nugent, G. (U.)	5,754
Labour majority	2,812

By-election, 1907.—Lab., 7,396; U., 5,047—Lab. maj., 2,349.
1906.—L., 7,667; U., 5,557—L. maj., 2,110.
1900.—U., 6,205; L., 4,594—U. maj., 1,611.
1895.—U. maj., 668; 1892, U. maj., 232; 1886, U. maj., 793.

Mr. ALBERT STANLEY, who was born in 1862, worked in a coal-pit and afterwards in colliery offices. He has been miners' agent for the Cannock Chase Miners' Association since 1886, and is secretary to the Midland Miners' Federation and a member of the Joint Conciliation Board of Coalowners and Miners. He has been a member of the Staffordshire County Council since its formation, and is a J.P. for the county.

WEST (12,197).—UNIONIST GAIN.

Lloyd, G. A. (U.)	5,892
*McLaren, H. D. (L.)	5,327
Unionist majority	565

1906.—L., 5,586; U., 4,708—L. maj., 878.
1900 and 1895.—U. unop.
1892.—U. maj., 2,348; 1886, U. unop.

Mr. GEORGE A. LLOYD, the son of the late Mr. S. S. Lloyd, of Dolobran, Montgomeryshire, was born in 1879 and educated at Eton and Cambridge; began his business career as director of the family business; as Government Special Commissioner inquired into and reported upon the prospects of British trade in Mesopotamia and Eastern Asiatic Turkey; his grandfather, Mr. Sampson Lloyd, formerly M.P. for Plymouth, fought Mr. John Bright on the fiscal question at Birmingham.

SUFFOLK (5).

NORTH-EAST, or EYE (10,621).—No change.

*Pearson, W. H. M. (L.)	4,991
Graham, Lord (U.)	4,614
Liberal majority	377

By-election, 1906.—L., 4,568; U., 4,371—L. maj., 197.
1906.—L. unop.
1900.—L., 4,664; U., 2,947—L. maj., 1,717.
1895.—L. maj., 834; 1892, L. maj., 1,270; 1886, L. maj., 1,606.

Mr. WEETMAN HAROLD MILLER PEARSON, the son of Sir Weetman Pearson, M.P. for Colchester from 1895 to 1906, was born in 1882, and educated at Rugby, and Christ Church, Oxford; married in 1905 a daughter of Lord Edward Spencer Churchill; is a lieutenant in the Sussex Yeomanry; contested Rutland in 1906, and was elected for the Eye Division at a by-election in April of the same year.

NORTH, or LOWESTOFT (15,084).—UNIONIST GAIN.

Foster, H. S. (U.)	6,530
*Beauchamp, E. (L.)	6,294
Unionist majority	236

1906.—L., 6,510; U., 4,905—L. maj., 1,605.
1900.—U., 5,077; L., 3,348—U. maj., 1,729.
1895.—U. maj., 1,379; 1892, U. maj., 1,190; 1886, U. unop.

Mr. Harry Seymour Foster, who sat for this division from 1892 to 1900, was born in 1855 and educated at Margate and City of London School; formerly a chartered accountant, and interested in various phases of London life; was at one time Consul-General of Persia, and is the author of a work on the gold standard of currency.

Stowmarket (11,190).—Unionist Gain.
Goldsmith, F. (U.)	5,311
*Hardy, G. A. (L.) ..	4,666
Unionist majority ..	645

1906.—L., 4,801; U., 4,588—L., maj., 213.
1900.—U., 4,431; L., 3,068—U. maj., 1,363.
1895.—U. maj, 1,443; 1892, L. maj., 144; 1886, U. maj., 543.

Mr. Frank Goldsmith, who lives at Cavenham Park, Mildenhall, is 31 years of age, and was educated at Cheltenham, and Magdalen College, Oxford; called to the Bar (Inner Temple) in 1902, but has devoted himself to public work; was for four years a member of the Westminster City Council, and sits on the London County Council, where he acts as Whip to the Municipal Reform Party; is captain in the Suffolk Yeomanry.

South, or Sudbury (10,036).—Unionist Gain.
Quilter, W. E. C. (U.) ..	5,026
Hirst, F. W. (L.)	3,958
Unionist majority ..	1,068

1906.—L., 4,201; U., 4,065—L. maj., 136.
1900 and 1895.—U. unop.; 1892, U. maj., 2,206; 1886, U. unop.

Mr. W. Eley Cuthbert Quilter, of Methersgate Hall, Woodbridge, who is 36, is the eldest son of Sir W. Cuthbert Quilter, M.P. for the division from 1885 to 1906, and was educated at Harrow and Trinity College, Cambridge; his wife was the Hon. Gwynedd Douglas-Pennant, daughter of the second Lord Penrhyn; is a captain in the Suffolk Imperial Yeomanry.

South-East, or Woodbridge (12,808).—Unionist Gain.
Peel, Captain R. F. (U.) ..	6,120
Buxton, C. S. (L.)	5,226
Unionist majority..	894

1906.—L., 5,527; U., 5,348—L. maj., 179.
1900.—U., 5,089; L., 4,437—U. maj., 652.
1895.—U. maj., 632; 1892, L. maj., 733; 1886, U. maj., 313.

Captain Robert Peel, a grandson of the Right Hon. William Yates Peel, was born in 1874, and received a special education in agriculture. He joined the Coldstream Guards in February, 1898, and served through the South African War, being mentioned in despatches. Captain Peel unsuccessfully contested Mid Northants against Mr. Manfield at the last election.

SURREY (6).

North-West, or Chertsey (16,723).—Unionist Gain.
Macmaster, D., K.C. (U.) ..	9,672
Newbolt, Francis G. (L.) ..	5,059
Unionist majority ..	4,613

1906.—L., 6,365; U., 6,266—L. maj., 99.
1900.—U., 5,367; L., 3,080—U. maj., 2,287.
1895, 1892, and 1886.—U. unop.

Mr. Donald Macmaster, K.C., was born at Williamstown, Ontario, in 1846, and educated at Williamstown and the M'Gill University, Montreal; has acted as Crown Prosecutor in Canada, as arbitrator between the Newfoundland Government and the Reid-Newfoundland Railway 1904-5, and as counsel in important Privy Council appeals; has been a member of the Ontario Legislature and of the Canadian House of Commons; contested the Leigh Division of Lancashire in 1906.

Mid, or Epsom (18,821).—No change.
*Keswick, W. (U.)	10,919
Rollit, Sir A. (L.)	5,232
Unionist majority ..	5,687

1906.—U., 7,316; L., 6,221—U. maj., 1,095.
1900.—U. unop.; 1895, U. unop.
1892.—U., 5,123; L., 2,720—U. maj., 2,403.
1886.—U. unop.

Mr. William Keswick, born in 1835, is a member of Jardine and Co., China merchants, and of Matheson and Co., London, a director of the Indo-China Steam Navigation Company, and was formerly a member of the Legislative Council of Hong Kong; has represented the division since 1900.

South-West, or Guildford (16,020).—Unionist Gain.
Horne, W. E. (U.)	9,264
Methuen, A. M. S. (L.) ..	5,033
Unionist majority ..	4,231

1906.—L., 6,430; U., 5,630—L. maj., 800.
1900.—U., 5,816; L., 3,609—U. maj., 2,207.
1895.—U. unop.; 1892, U. maj., 1,471; 1886, U. unop.

Mr. William Edgar Horne is the eldest son of the late Mr. Edgar Horne, for many years head of the Prudential Assurance Company. He was educated at Westminster School and entered his father's firm, Messrs. Horne and Co., auctioneers and surveyors. He is a director of the Prudential Assurance Company, a vice-president of the Surveyors' Institution, a vice-president of the National Service League, and has been chairman of the Guildford and West Surrey Agricultural Association. Mr. Horne was formerly chairman of the united vestries of St. Margaret's and St. John's, Westminster, and subsequently became a member of the Westminster County Council, being offered the Mayoralty five or six years ago. In 1906 he unsuccessfully contested the Barnstaple Division in the Unionist interest.

Kingston (19,647).—No change.
*Cave, G., K.C. (U.)	10,918
Holzapfel, A. G. (L.) ..	5,814
Unionist majority ..	5,104

1906.—U., 7,656; L., 6,637—U. maj., 1,019.
1900.—U. unop.
1895.—U. maj., 2,145; 1892, U. maj., 743; 1886, U. unop.

Mr. George Cave, K.C., was born in 1856, and was educated at the Merchant Taylors' School and St. John's College, Oxford. He has been Chairman of the Surrey Quarter Sessions since 1894 and Recorder of Guildford since 1904, and is an alderman of the Surrey County Council. He is a J.P. and Deputy-Lieutenant for Surrey. During the recent debates in the House of Commons on the Budget Mr. Cave gave invaluable aid to the Opposition by the searching legal criticisms to which he subjected the Government proposals in respect of land taxation and licensing, and also by the interesting debates raised on the amendments which stood in his name.

SOUTH-EAST, or REIGATE (15,636).— UNIONIST GAIN.

Rawson, Col. R. H. (U.) ..	8,339
*Brodie, H. C. (L.) ..	5,715
Unionist majority ..	2,624

1906.—L., 6,067 ; U., 5,848—L. maj., 219.
1900.—U. unop.
1895 and 1836.—U. unop. ; 1892, U. maj., 1,689.

COLONEL RICHARD HAMILTON RAWSON was born in 1863, and after education at Eton and Oxford he served for nine years in the 1st Life Guards and retired with the rank of captain in 1892. He has been colonel commanding the Sussex Yeomanry since 1908, was high sheriff of Sussex in 1899, and contested his present constituency in 1896.

WIMBLEDON (27,810).—No change.

*Chaplin, Rt. Hon. H. (U.) ..	14,445
Holland, A. L.	8,930
Unionist majority..	5,515

By-election, May, 1907.—U., 10,263 ; Woman Suffrage, 3,299— U. maj., 6,964.
1906.—U., 9,523 ; L., 7,409—U. maj., 2,114.
1900 and 1895.—U. unop.
1892.—U. maj., 4,795 ; 1886, U. unop.

Mr. HENRY CHAPLIN, who is one of the most popular and picturesque figures in political life, entered Parliament for Mid Lincolnshire in 1868, and through his long career in the House of Commons has been a faithful advocate of the cause of Protection and given unremitting attention to the welfare of the agricultural industry. He was appointed Chancellor of the Duchy of Lancaster in 1885, First President of the Board of Agriculture in 1889, and President of the Local Government Board in 1895. After representing the Sleaford Division of Lincolnshire for over 20 years he was defeated in 1906, but was returned in 1907 by the electors of Wimbledon.

SUSSEX (6).

SOUTH-WEST, or CHICHESTER (12,147).— No change.

*Talbot, Lord E. (U.).. ..	6,589
Reiss, R. (L.)	3,338
Unionist majority ..	3,251

1906.—U., 5,197 ; L., 4,023—U. maj., 1,174.
1900.—U. unop.
1895 and 1886.—U. unop. ; 1892, U. maj., 1,875.

LORD EDMUND BERNARD TALBOT, brother of the present Duke of Norfolk, was born in 1855 and educated at the Oratory School, Edgbaston ; took the name of Talbot in lieu of Howard in 1876 ; joined 11th Hussars in 1875 and retired with the rank of lieutenant-colonel in 1900 ; served in South Africa 1900-1901, and received the D.S.O. ; contested Burnley in 1880 and Sheffield (Brightside) in 1885 and 1886 ; has represented the Chichester Division since 1894.

EASTBOURNE (14,172).—UNIONIST GAIN.

Gwynne, R. S. (U.)	7,553
Morison, H. (L.)	5,249
Unionist majority..	2,304

1906.—L., 5,933 ; U., 5,303—L. maj., 630.
1900.—U., 4,948 ; L., 4,245—U. maj., 703.
1895.—U. maj., 60 ; 1892, U. maj., 363 ; 1886, U. maj., 1,259.

Mr. RUPERT SACKVILLE GWYNNE, born in 1873, is a younger son of Mr. J. E. A. Gwynne, of Folkington Manor, one of the largest landowners in East Sussex. In 1898 Mr. R. Gwynne was called to the Bar, and, taking an active interest in local affairs, he has served for some time as a member of the Eastbourne Board of Guardians and as chairman of the Eastbourne Rural District Council. He has won the Bar Point-to-Point Steeplechase on three occasions.

NORTH, or EAST GRINSTEAD (11,562).—UNIONIST GAIN.

Cautley, H. S. (U.)	6,563
*Corbett, C. H. (L.)	3,660
Unionist majority ..	2,903

1906.—L., 4,793 ; U., 4,531—L. maj., 262.
1900.—U., 3,890 ; L., 3,003—U. maj., 887.
1895.—U. maj., 857 ; 1892, U. maj., 1,638 ; 1886, U. maj., 1,412.

Mr. HENRY STROTHER CAUTLEY sat in the Parliament of 1900-6 as the member for East Leeds, after having contested Dewsbury in 1892 and 1895. He owns about 1,000 acres in Yorkshire. Born in 1863, he was educated at Charterhouse, and King's College, Cambridge, and was called to the Bar in 1886. He goes on the North-Eastern Circuit.

HORSHAM (11,484).—No change.

*Winterton, Earl (U.) ..	6,324
Outhwaite, R. L. (L.) ..	3,534
Unionist majority ..	2,790

1906.—U., 4,093 ; L., 4,286—U. maj., 617.
1900 and 1895.—U. unop.
1892.—U. maj., 2,035 ; 1886, U. unop.

EARL WINTERTON, who was born in 1883, was first elected for Horsham when only 21 years of age at a by-election and re-elected in 1906. He succeeded to his present title in 1907 but, the Peerage being an Irish one, he had not to resign his seat. From 1904 to 1906 he was private secretary to Mr. Pretyman, Financial Secretary to the Admiralty. He is controlling editor of the *World*.

MID, or LEWES (17,277).—No change.

*Aubrey-Fletcher, Rt. Hon. Sir H. (U.)..	9,168
Williams, Basil (L.) ..	4,572
Unionist majority ..	4,596

1906.—U., 7,172 ; L., 5,458—U. maj., 1,714.
1900 and 1895.—U. unop.
1892.—U. maj., 3,299 ; 1886, U. unop.

Sir Henry Aubrey-Fletcher, C.B., has been in the House of Commons since 1880, first for Horsham, and since 1885 for Mid Sussex. He was born in 1835, was educated at Eton, and entered the Army in 1853 as Ensign 69th Foot, and in 1855 became Lieutenant in the Grenadier Guards. In 1885 he was a Parliamentary Groom-in-Waiting, is a magistrate for Surrey and Sussex, a Deputy-Lieutenant for the last-named county, a J.P. for Bucks, and a Privy Councillor (1901).

East, or Rye (13,746).—No change.

*Courthope, G. L. (U.)	7,352
Hutchinson, St. J. (L.)	4,750
Unionist majority	2,602

1906.—U., 6,122 ; L., 4,964—U. maj., 1,158.
1900.—U., 5,376 ; L., 2,887—U. maj., 2,489.
1895.—U. unop ; 1892, U. maj., 711 ; 1886, U. maj., 1,498.

Mr. George Loyd Courthope, who gained the seat for the Unionists in 1906, was born in 1877, educated at Eton, and Christ Church, Oxford, and called to the Bar, Inner Temple, in 1901. He is a captain in the 5th Batt. (Cinque Ports) Royal Sussex Regt., and chairman of the Central Chamber of Agriculture, of the National Rifle Assciation, and of the United Club. He has served on the committees of Lady Henry Somerset's Inebriates' Home and the Duxhurst Farm Colony.

WARWICKSHIRE (4).

North-East, or Nuneaton (17,451).—No change.

*Johnson, W. (Lab.)	8,154
Maddocks, H. (U.)	7,893
Labour majority	261

1906.—Labour, 7,677. ; U., 5,849 ; Lab. maj., 1,828.
1900.—U., 5,736 ; Lab., 4,432 ; U. maj., 1,304.
1895.—U. maj., 1,397 ; 1892, U. maj., 641 ; 1886, U. maj., 1,018.

Mr. William Johnson entered Parliament for Nuneaton in 1906, after a defeat in the same division in 1900. He was born at Chilvers Coton, Warwickshire, in 1849, and in early life worked both in factory and colliery. Since 1885 he has been secretary of the Warwickshire Miners' Association. After election to other local bodies he obtained a seat on the Warwickshire County Council, to which he has been returned several times without opposition.

Rugby (12,275).—Unionist Gain.

Baird, J. L. (U.)	6,191
Clonmell, the Earl of (L.)	4,986
Unionist majority	1,205

1906.—L., 5,181 ; U., 4,909—L. maj., 272.
1900.—L., 4,349 ; U., 4,130—L. maj., 219.
1895.—U., maj., 284 ; 1892, L. maj., 688 ; 1886, L. maj., 478.

Mr. John Lawrence Baird, who was born in 1874, the eldest son of Sir Alexander Baird, has spent many years in the Diplomatic Service ; has held appointments in Vienna, Cairo, Abyssinia, where he was Acting Agent and Consul-General, and Paris.

South-West, or Stratford-on-Avon (10,835).—No change.

*Foster, P. S. (U.)	5,505
Bowen, Oscar (L.)	3,838
Unionist majority	1,667

By-election, 1909.—U., 5,374 ; L., 2,747 ; Ind., 479—U. maj. over L., 2,627.
1906.—L., 4,321 ; U., 4,173—L. maj., 148.
1900.—U. unop.
1895.—U. maj., 1,771 ; 1892, U. maj., 864 ; 1886, U. maj., 489.

Mr. Philip Staveley Foster, son of the late Mr. A. B. Foster, of Sutton Coldfield, was born in 1865, educated at Eton, and Magdalen College, Oxford (B.A.), and in 1890 married a daughter of the late Colonel Wemyss, of his Majesty's Royal Bodyguard. He was formerly in the 6th West Yorks Militia, and lately hon. major of the Staffordshire Yeomanry. He is J.P. for Staffordshire and Warwickshire. He contested the Elland Division (West Riding) in 1899, represented the Stratford Division of Warwickshire from 1901 to 1906, and was elected for the latter again in May, 1909. He is a director of William Foster and Son (Limited), worsted spinners and manufacturers, Queensbury, Yorks.

Tamworth (18,228).—No change.

*Newdigate-Newdegate, F. A. (U.)	10,313
Brampton, C. H. (L.)	4,799
Unionist majority	5,514

By-election, Jan., 1909—U. unop.
1906.—U., 7,561 ; L., 4,842—U. maj., 2,719.
1900 and 1895.—U. unop.
1892.—U. maj., 2,426 ; 1886, U. unop.

Mr. Francis Alexander Newdigate-Newdegate was born in 1862, and was educated at Eton and Sandhurst. He served in the Coldstream Guards 1883-85 ; is a Governor of Rugby School, and an Alderman of the Warwickshire County Council. He represented the Nuneaton Division of Warwickshire 1892-1906, and was returned at a by-election for Tamworth in 1909.

WESTMORLAND (2).

North, or Appleby (6,656).—Unionist Gain.

Sanderson, L., K.C. (U.)	3,335
*Jones, Leif (L.)	2,868
Unionist majority	467

1906.—L., 2,894 ; U., 2,891—L. maj., 3.
1900.—L., 2,835 ; U., 2,256—L. maj., 579.
1895.—U. maj., 873 ; 1892, U. maj., 707 ; 1886, U. maj., 186.

Mr. Lancelot Sanderson, K.C., born in 1863, was educated at Elstree, Harrow, and Trinity College, Cambridge, M.A. 1895 ; was called to the Bar, Inner Temple, 1886, K.C. 1903, and went the Northern Circuit. In 1891 he married a daughter of Dr. A. Fletcher, of Allerton, and since 1901 has been Recorder of Wigan. In July, 1905, upon Mr. Gully being raised to the peerage, Mr. Sanderson was a candidate for the representation of Carlisle.

South. or Kendal (6,546).—Unionist Gain.

Bagot, Lt.-Col. J. F. (U.)	3,278
*Stewart-Smith, D., K.C. (L.)	2,726
Unionist majority	552

1906.—L., 2,899 ; U., 2,647—L. maj., 252.
1900.—U. unop.
1895.—U. maj., 722 ; 1892, U. maj., 629 ; 1886, U. unop.

Lieutenant-Colonel Josceline FitzRoy Bagot, son of the late Colonel C. Bagot, of the Grenadier Guards, was born at Epsom in 1854, and educated at Eton ; joined the Grenadier Guards in 1874, and retired as captain in 1886 ; was A.D.C. to the Governor-General of Canada (the Marquis of Lorne) 1882-3 ; a retired lieut.-colonel of the Westmorland and Cumberland Yeomanry, and a member of the Westmorland Territorial Force Association ; represented the Kendal Division from 1892 to 1906.

WILTSHIRE (5).

North-West, or Chippenham (9,175).—Unionist Gain.

Terrell, G. (U.)	4,408
†Beck, Cecil (L.)	4,120
Unionist majority	288

1906.—L., 4,937 ; U., 2,971—L. maj., 1,966.
1900.—U., 3,863 ; L., 3,278—U. maj., 585.
1895.—U. maj., 508 ; 1892, U. maj., 229 ; 1886, U. maj., 537.

Mr. George Terrell was born at Croydon in 1862, the third son of his Honour Judge Terrell ; served in his early years in the Mercantile Marine, but afterwards studied law and was admitted a solicitor ; then turned his attention to business, and is now director of the firm of Saxby and Farmer, which has railway signal manufacturing works at Chippenham ; he is also a director of other industrial companies ; prominent in the yachting world, and is commodore of the Eastern Yacht Club of London and member of the council of the Yacht Racing Association.

North, or Cricklade (15,203).—Unionist Gain.

Calley, Col. T. C. P. (U.)	7,389
*Massie, J. (L.)	6,754
Unionist majority	635

1906.—L., 7,294 ; U., 5,716—L. maj., 1,578.
1900.—L., 5,754 ; U., 4,920—L. maj., 834.
1895.—U. maj., 99 ; 1892, L. maj., 998 ; 1886, U. maj., 1,718.

Colonel Thomas Charles Pleydell Calley, C.B., M.V.O., who was born in 1856, was educated at Harrow, and Christ Church, Oxford. In 1876 he joined the 1st Life Guards, and served in Egypt, 1882, and South Africa, 1899-1900. In 1908 he was appointed to the command of the London Territorial Mounted Brigade.

East, or Devizes (9,277).—Unionist Gain.

Peto, B. E. (U.)	4,709
*Rogers, F. N. (L.)	3,742
Unionist majority	967

1906.—L., 4,247 ; U., 3,633—L. maj., 614.
1900.—U., 3,738 ; L., 3,111—U. maj., 627.
1895.—U. maj., 477 ; 1892, L. maj., 138 ; 1886, U. maj., 1,726.

Mr. Basil F. Peto, who was born in 1862 and educated at Harrow, is the youngest of seven sons of the late Sir Samuel Morton Peto, M.P. for Finsbury, Norwich, and Bristol, one of the firm which built the Houses of Parliament and himself the constructor of the railway from Balaclava to Sebastopol in the Crimean War ; first joined his brother Herbert in business as builder and contractor, but later became a director of the Morgan Crucible Company, which has works at Battersea.

West, or Westbury (10,411).—No change.

*Fuller, J. M. F. (L.)	5,279
Long, R. C. C. (U.)	4,525
Liberal majority	754

1906.—L., 5,264 ; U., 3,788—L. maj., 1,476.
1900.—L., 4,520 ; U., 3,961—L. maj., 559.
1895.—U. maj., 166 ; 1892, L. maj., 624 ; 1886, L. maj., 993.

Mr. John Michael Fleetwood Fuller served as a Junior Lord of the Treasury (unpaid) in 1906, and has been Vice-Chamberlain in his Majesty's Household since February, 1907. He was born in 1864, and was educated at Winchester and Christ Church, Oxford. In 1894-5 he fulfilled the duties of aide-de-camp to the Viceroy of India. He has been an alderman of the Wilts County Council since 1888, and is a major of the Royal Wilts Yeomanry. In the last Parliament he acted as a Liberal Whip.

Wilton (9,072).—Unionist Gain.

Bathurst, C. (U.)	4,541
Verney, H. C. (L.)	3,894
Unionist majority	647

1906.—L., 4,272 ; U., 3,548—L. maj., 724.
1900.—U., 3,733 ; L., 2,892—U. maj., 841.
1895.—U. maj., 263 ; 1892, U. maj., 407 ; 1886, U. unop.

Mr. Charles Bathurst, who was born in 1867, was educated at Eton and Oxford, and was called to the Bar at the Inner Temple in 1890. He is an active member of the Central Chamber of Agriculture and of many other agricultural organizations, and a director of Richard Thomas and Co. (Limited), tinplate manufacturers.

WORCESTERSHIRE (5).

Bewdley (10,638).—No change.

*Baldwin, S. (U.)	6,618
Brooks, J. L. (L.)	2,370
Unionist majority	4,248

By-election, Feb., 1908, U. unop.
1906.—U., 5,912 ; L., 2,718—U. maj., 3,194.
1900, 1895, 1892, and 1886.—U. unop.

Mr. Stanley Baldwin, who is an ironmaster, was returned unopposed in February, 1908, as the member for the Bewdley Division, in succession to his father, the late Mr. Alfred Baldwin, who had represented the constituency for 16 years. Born in 1867 at Bewdley, Mr. Stanley Baldwin was educated at Harrow, and Trinity College, Cambridge. He is the vice-chairman of Baldwins (Limited) and a director of the Great Western Railway. He contested Kidderminster unsuccessfully at the General Election in 1906.

MID, or DROITWICH (11,200).—UNIONIST GAIN.

Lyttelton, Hon. J. C. (U.) ..	5,078
*Harmsworth, Cecil (L.) ..	4,973
Unionist majority ..	105

1906.—L., 5,165 ; U., 4,611—L. maj., 554.
1900.—U., 4,020 ; L., 3,752—U. maj., 268.
1895.—U. unop. ; 1892, U. maj., 570 ; 1886, U. maj., 1,270.

The HON. JOHN CAVENDISH LYTTELTON is the eldest son of the eighth Viscount Cobham, and was born in 1881 ; was a lieutenant in the Rifle Brigade, 1901-8, and served in South Africa ; A.D.C. and assistant private secretary to the High Commissioner of South Africa from 1905 to 1908 ; a captain in the Worcestershire Yeomanry.

EAST (23,269).—No change.

*Chamberlain, Rt. Hon. Austen (U.)	12,644
Young, Hilton (L.) ..	6,955
Unionist majority ..	5,689

1906.—U., 10,129 ; L., 5,763—U. maj., 4,366.
1900.—U. unop.
1895 and 1886.—U. unop. ; 1892, U. maj., 2,594.

Mr. AUSTEN CHAMBERLAIN, who has represented East Worcestershire since 1892, is the eldest son of Mr. Chamberlain by his first wife. Born in Birmingham in 1863, he studied at Rugby, Trinity College, the École des Sciences Politiques in Paris, and in Berlin. In 1895 he was appointed Civil Lord of the Admiralty, and later held successively the offices of Financial Secretary to the Treasury, Postmaster-General, and Chancellor of the Exchequer. He introduced the Budgets of 1904 and 1905. In the last Parliament he was active as one of the leading members of the Opposition, and in the discussion of Mr. Lloyd George's Budget, in particular, he added greatly to his reputation by the display of debating power and critical acumen.

EVESHAM (10,416).—No change.

Eyres-Monsell, B. M. (U.) ..	5,416
Burt, W. (L.)	3,998
Unionist majority ..	1,418

1906.—U., 4,385 ; L., 4,293—U. maj., 92.
1900 and 1895.—U. unop.
1892.—U. maj., 580 ; 1886, U. maj., 1,736.

Mr. BOLTON M. EYRES-MONSELL, R.N., of Dumbleton Hall, Evesham, the son of Lieutenant-Colonel Bolton J. Monsell, of London, was born in Hampshire in 1880, and educated at Stubbington House, Fareham ; joined the Britannia in 1894, and passed for lieutenant with five first-class certificates ; specialized in torpedo work and became an instructor on the Vernon, afterwards serving on the Majestic ; resigned in 1906, after 11 years' service, but has since had his commission restored and his name placed on the emergency list ; assumed the name of Eyres on marrying Miss Eyres, of Dumbleton Hall, in 1904 ; interested in agriculture and sport.

NORTH (18,200).—No change.

*Wilson, J. W. (L.)	8,272
Campion, W. R. (U.) ..	7,953
Liberal majority ..	319

1906.—L., 6,908 ; U., 6,429—L. maj., 479.
1900.—U. unop.
1895.—U. maj., 988 ; 1892, L. maj., 2,158 ; 1886, U. unop.

Mr. JOHN WILLIAM WILSON, born at Edgbaston in 1858, received his education at Grove House, Tottenham, and in Germany ; is a partner in the firm of Albright and Wilson, chemical manufacturers, Oldbury, and a director of the Great Western Railway ; has represented the division since 1895, when he was returned as a Liberal Unionist ; stood as a Liberal in 1906.

YORKSHIRE (EAST RIDING) (3).

BUCKROSE (10,652).—No change.

*White, Sir Luke (L.) ..	4,957
Sykes, Major Mark (U.) ..	4,739
Liberal majority ..	218

1906.—L., 5,236 ; U., 3,634—L. maj., 1,602.
1900.—L., 4,083 ; U., 3,992—L. maj., 91.
1895.—L. maj., 90 ; 1892, L. maj., 652 ; 1886, U. maj., 6.

SIR LUKE WHITE was born at Deighton, near York, in 1845, and educated at Foss Bridge School, York. He was admitted a solicitor in 1874, and is one of his Majesty's coroners for Yorkshire, East Riding District. He has served as chairman of Select Committees and was knighted in 1908.

HOLDERNESS (10,850).—No change.

*Wilson, Major Stanley (U.)	5,046
Bethell, Commander, R.N. (I.F.T.)	4,661
Unionist majority ..	385

1906.—U., 4,441 ; L., 4,411—U. maj., 30.
1900.—U., 4,597 ; L., 2,810—U. maj., 1,787.
1895.—U. maj., 1,027 ; 1892, U. maj., 465 ; 1886. U., unop.

Mr. ARTHUR STANLEY WILSON was born in 1868, and educated at Eton and Cambridge. He is a J.P. for the East Riding, and has sat for the Holderness Division since 1900.

HOWDENSHIRE (10,597).—No change.

*Harrison-Broadley, Col. H. B. (U.)	5,423
Norris, F. (L.)	4,186
Unionist majority ..	1,237

1906.—U., 4,763 ; L., 4,150—U. maj., 613.
1900 and 1895.—U. unop.
1892.—U. maj., 350 ; 1886, U. unop.

COLONEL HENRY BROADLEY HARRISON-BROADLEY was born in 1853 and was educated at Brackenbury's, Wimbledon, assuming the addition of Broadley to his name in 1896. He is a J.P. for the East Riding and since 1899 has been honorary colonel of the 1st Volunteer Battalion of the East Yorkshire Regiment.

YORKSHIRE (NORTH RIDING) (4).

CLEVELAND (14,811).—No change.
*Samuel, Rt. Hon. H. (L.) ..	7,384
Lewis, J. Windsor (U.) ..	5,491
Liberal majority ..	1,893

By-election, 1909.—L., 6,296 ; U., 5,325—L. maj., 971.
1906 and 1900.—L. unop. ; 1895, L. maj., 587 ; 1892, L. maj., 348 ; 1886, L. unop.

Mr. HERBERT LOUIS SAMUEL, the son of a Liverpool banker and nephew of Lord Swaythling, head of the banking firm of Samuel Montagu and Co., London, was born in 1870, and educated at University College School, London, and Balliol College, Oxford ; was twice unsuccessful in South Oxfordshire, but was returned for the Cleveland Division in 1902 ; was appointed Under-Secretary to the Home Office in 1905, and had the conduct of the Children Bill, and was promoted to the Cabinet as Chancellor of the Duchy of Lancaster in 1909 ; is governor of the London School of Economics and Political Science.

RICHMOND (10,485).—UNIONIST GAIN.
Orde-Powlett, Hon. W. G. A. (U.)	5,246
*Acland, F. D. (L.) ..	4,163
Unionist majority ..	1,083

1906.—L., 4,470 ; U., 4,368—L. maj., 102.
1900.—U., 4,573 ; L., 3,117—U. maj., 1,456.
1895.—U. maj., 584 ; 1892, U. maj., 159 ; 1886, U. maj., 951.

The HON. WILLIAM GEORGE ALGAR ORDE-POWLETT is the eldest son of the fourth Lord Bolton. He was born in 1869, and was a lieutenant in the King's Royal Rifle Corps. After serving with the Yorkshire Yeomanry he became a major in the 4th (Territorial) Battalion the Yorkshire Regiment.

THIRSK AND MALTON (13,363).—No change.
*Helmsley, Viscount (U.) ..	6,382
Brigg, J. J. (L.) ..	5,197
Unionist majority ..	1,185

1906.—U., 5,848 ; L., 5,044—U. maj., 804.
1900 and 1895.—U. unop. ; 1892, U. maj., 2,349 ; 1886, U. unop.

VISCOUNT HELMSLEY, grandson and heir of the Earl of Feversham, was born in 1879, and educated at Eton, and Christ Church, Oxford. From 1902 to 1904 he was assistant private secretary to the Earl of Selborne when First Lord of the Admiralty ; is a major in the Yorkshire Hussars, Imperial Yeomanry, and a Master of Hounds. In 1904 he married Lady Margaret Greville, daughter of the Earl of Warwick.

WHITBY (11,200).—No change.
*Beckett, Hon. Gervase (U.)	5,161
Jardine, W. (L.) ..	4,602
Unionist majority ..	559

1906.—U., 4,780 ; L., 4,709—U. maj., 71.
1900.—U. unop. ; 1895, U. unop.
1892.—U., 4,909 ; L., 3,826—U. maj., 1,083.
1886.—U., 5,078 ; L., 3,940—U. maj., 1,138.

The HON. WILLIAM GERVASE BECKETT was returned to Parliament as the representative of the Whitby Division at the General Election in 1906, after having unsuccessfully contested the seat at the by-election in 1905 caused by the succession of his elder brother, the former member, to the Peerage as Lord Grimthorpe. Born in 1866 at Meanwood, near Leeds, the second son of the late Mr. W. Beckett, M.P., he was educated at Eton, and married, in 1896, the Hon Mabel Theresa Duncombe, daughter of the late Viscount Helmsley. He is a partner in the banking firm of Beckett and Co., and is the principal proprietor of the *Saturday Review*. He was formerly captain in the Yorkshire Hussars Imperial Yeomanry.

YORKSHIRE (WEST RIDING) (19).

BARKSTON ASH (10,871).—No change.
*Lane-Fox, G. R. (U.) ..	5,299
Horne, F. (L.)	4,546
Unionist majority ..	753

1906.—U., 4,894 ; L., 4,246—U. maj., 648.
1900 and 1895.—U. unop.
1892.—U. maj., 1,241 ; 1886, U. unop.

Mr. GEORGE RICHARD LANE-FOX was educated at Eton, and New College, Oxford, where he took his degree with second class honours in the Classical and History schools, and was called to the Bar in 1896, but has not practised as a barrister. He is J.P. and a member of the West Riding County Council. He was returned for the constituency in 1906 after a defeat at a by-election there the previous year.

BARNSLEY (20,861).—No change.
*Walton, J. (L.)	12,425
Groser, A. W. (U.) ..	5,053
Liberal majority	7,372

1906.—L., unop.
1900.—L., 7,549 ; U., 4,356—L. maj., 3,193.
1895.—L., 6,820 ; U., 4,653—L. maj., 2,167.
1892.—L., 6,739 ; U., 3,498—L. maj., 3,241.
1886.—L., 5,425 ; U., 2,917—L. maj., 2,508.

Mr. JOSEPH WALTON was born in 1849, and after being educated privately began his commercial career in Middlesbrough in the coal and allied trades in 1870. He is F.R.G.S., and has travelled much in the Colonies, America, Persia, India, and Burma, and in 1899-1900 in China and Japan with a view to the promotion of British trade. In 1900 he published " China and the Present Crisis." He is J.P. for Middlesbrough, J.P. and D.L. for the North Riding of Yorkshire, and found his seat at Barnsley at a by-election in 1897, after unsuccessfully contesting Doncaster in 1895. His recreation is Alpine climbing.

COLNE VALLEY (12,489).—LIBERAL GAIN OVER SOCIALIST.
Leach, C. (L.)	4,741
Carpenter, Captain A. Boyd (U.)	3,750
*Grayson, A. Victor (Soc.)	3,149
Liberal majority over Unionist	991
Liberal majority over Socialist	1,592

By-election, July, 1907.—Soc., 3,648 ; L., 3,495 ; U., 3,227—Soc. maj. over L., 153.
1906.—L. unop.
1900.—L., 4,699 ; U., 4,176—L. maj., 523.
1895.—L., 4,276 ; U., 3,737 ; Lab., 1,245—L. maj. over U., 539.
1892.—L., 4,987 ; U., 4,281—L. maj., 706.
1886.—U. unop.

Mr. CHARLES LEACH was born at Illingworth, near Halifax, and when quite young he was employed in a worsted factory. When in his teens he began business as a boot, shoe, and clog maker in Halifax. Mr. Leach at the age of 26 disposed of his business, and went to college and was ordained for the ministry, and spent most of his ministerial life in such large centres of population as Sheffield, Birmingham, Manchester, and London. When in Birmingham Mr. Leach was elected a member of the School Board, and on removal to London he was a member of Chelsea Vestry and manager of two large Board schools. He founded a day college of secondary education, and an evening educational institute under the London County Council. He is a founder, director, and vice-chairman of the Abstainers and General Insurance Company, and a member of the London Chamber of Commerce.

DONCASTER (21,511).—No change.

*Nicholson, C. N. (L.)	..	10,654
Whitworth, C. W. (U.)	..	7,085
Liberal majority	..	3,569

1906.—L., 9,315 ; U., 5,646—L. maj., 3,669.
1900.—U., 6,512 ; L., 6,147—U. maj., 365.
1895.—U., 6,098 ; L., 5,959—U. maj., 141.
1892.—L., 5,831 ; U., 5,552—L. maj., 279.
1886.—L., 5,060 ; U., 4.792—L. maj., 268.

Mr. CHARLES NICHOLSON was born in 1857, and was educated at Charterhouse, and Trinity College, Cambridge, where he took the LL.B. degree, and was called to the Bar by Lincoln's Inn in 1880, but does not practise. For some years he was employed in the Lunacy Office. Subsequently he interested himself in Poor Law administration, and acted as chairman of the Shoreditch Board of Guardians and of the Poor Law Schools Committee.

ELLAND (13,956).—No change.

*Trevelyan, C. P. (L.)	..	7,469
Ramsden, G. T. (U.)	..	4,686
Liberal majority	..	2,783

1906.—L., 7,609 ; U., 3,962—L. maj., 3,647.
1900.—L., 6,154 ; U., 4,512—L. maj., 1,642.
1895.—L. maj., 306 ; 1892, L. maj., 1,821 ; 1886, L. unop.

Mr. CHARLES PHILIPS TREVELYAN, who has represented the Elland Division since 1899, is the eldest son of Sir George Trevelyan. He was born in 1870, and educated at Harrow, and Trinity College, Cambridge. He acted as private secretary to the Earl of Crewe when he was Lord Lieutenant of Ireland in 1893, and for a short time he was a member of the London School Board. In 1895 he contested North Lambeth. He was appointed a Charity Commissioner in 1906, and in October, 1908, became Parliamentary Secretary to the Board of Education.

HALLAMSHIRE (19,935).—No change.

*Wadsworth, J. (Lab.)	..	10,193
Timmis, S. (U.)	..	6,185
Labour majority	..	4,008

1906.—Lab., 8,375 ; U., 6,807—Lab. maj., 1,568.
1900.—L., 6,688 ; U., 4,938—L. maj., 1,750.
1895.—L., 5,949 ; U., 5,054—L. maj., 1,895.
1892.—L. unop. ; 1886, L. unop.

Mr. JOHN WADSWORTH, secretary of the Yorkshire Miners' Association, was born in 1850, and worked in the coal pits of South Yorkshire until he became a trade union official ; is a member of the Parliamentary Labour Party.

HOLMFIRTH (12,788).—No change.

*Wilson, H. J. (L.)	..	6,339
Ellis, R. Geoffrey (U.)	..	3,043
Pickles, W. (Lab.)	..	1,643
Liberal majority over Unionist		3,296

1906.—L., 6,850 ; U., 2,677—L. maj., 4,173.
1900.—L., 4,505 ; U., 3,738—L. maj., 767.
1895.—L. maj., 1,542 ; 1892, L. maj., 2,323 ; 1886, L. maj., 2,542.

Mr. HENRY JOSEPH WILSON, born in 1833, was educated at the West of England Dissenters' Proprietary School, Taunton, and University College, London. He is largely interested in the Sheffield Smelting Company, is a magistrate for the West Riding and for the City of Sheffield. For 15 years he was a member of the Sheffield School Board, and has served on the India Office Committee, on the Regulation of Prostitution in India, and the Royal Commission on Opium. Last year he gave £10,000 towards the purchase of a public garden in the east end of Sheffield.

KEIGHLEY (13,373).—No change.

*Brigg, Sir J. (L.)	..	7,768
Acworth, W. M. (U.)	..	4,132
Liberal majority	..	3,636

1906.—L., 5,322 ; U., 3,229 ; Soc., 3,102—L. maj. over U., 2,093.
1900.—L., 5,432 ; U., 4,792—L. maj., 640.
1895.—L. maj., 840 ; 1892 and 1886, L. unop.

SIR JOHN BRIGG, son of the late Mr. John Brigg, J.P., of Keighley, was born in 1834, married in 1860 a daughter of Mr. W. Anderton, of Bingley, and engaged in the worsted trade till 1890. Was knighted in 1909. He is J.P. and D.L., was co-opted member of the Education Committee of the West Riding County Council, and is on the council of several educational and other local institutions. He is a director of the Leeds and Liverpool Canal Company and is on the board of the United Counties Bank. He has sat as member for the Keighley Division since 1895.

MORLEY (15,823).—No change.

France, G. (L.)	..	8,026
Charlesworth, J. S. (U.)	..	3,395
Smith, H. (Lab.)	..	2,191
Liberal majority	..	4,631

1906.—L. unop.
1900.—L., 6,428 ; U., 3,888—L. maj., 2,540.
1895.—L. maj., 1,668 ; 1892, L. maj., 2,162 ; 1886, L. unop.

Mr. GERALD ASHBURNER FRANCE resides at Newbiggen Hill, Newcastle-on-Tyne, and is an agent and importer ; is about 37 years of age, and was educated at a private school ; elected six years ago by the miners of Prudhoe as their representative on the Northumberland County Council, and was the principal mover in the agitation which resulted in the appointment of a commission of inquiry into the housing conditions in the mining villages ; chairman of the old-age pensions committee of the county and president of the Gladstone Club.

NORMANTON (16,466).—No change.
*Hall, F. (Lab.)	9,172
Bartlett, E. Ashmead (U.)	3,540
Labour majority	5,632

1906.—Lab. unop.
1900.—L., 5,025 ; U., 3,606—L. maj., 1,419.
1895.—L. maj., 1,558 ; 1892, L. maj., 2,331 ; 1886, L. maj., 1,047.

Mr. FRED HALL was born in Staffordshire in 1855, and worked as a miner for some years in a Rotherham colliery. In 1878 he was appointed local secretary of the Ardwarkle branch of the Yorkshire Miners' Association, and he is now agent of the association for the whole county. He has been a member of the West Riding County Council for 12 years, and was returned unopposed to Parliament by Normanton both in 1905 and 1906.

OSGOLDCROSS (18,286).—No change.
*Compton-Rickett. Sir J. (L.)	9,517
Hargreaves, G. de la P. (U.)	4,840
Liberal majority	4,677

1906.—L., 8,482 ; U., 4,358—L. maj., 4,124.
1900.—I.L., 5,609 ; L., 3,025—I.L. maj., 2,584.
1895.—L. maj., 1,065 ; 1892, L. maj., 1,876 ; 1886, L. maj., 998.

SIR JOSEPH COMPTON-RICKETT was born in London in 1847, and educated at King Edward VI. Grammar School, Bath, and privately. He was formerly chairman of Rickett, Cockerell, and Co. (Limited), and of other companies ; was chairman of the Congregational Union of England and Wales in 1907-8, and is co-treasurer of the National Council of the Evangelical Free Churches. He represented Scarborough 1895-1905, and was elected for Osgoldcross in 1906.

OTLEY (13,397).—No change.
*Duncan, J. H. (L.)	6,911
Thompson, W. W. (U.)	5,010
Liberal majority	1,901

1906.—L., 6,307 ; U., 4,658—L. maj., 1,649.
1900.—L., 5,327 ; U., 4,747—L. maj., 580.
1895.—U. maj., 48 ; 1892, L. maj., 690 ; 1886, L. maj., 884.

Mr. JAMES HASTINGS DUNCAN was elected in 1900 for his native place, and has continued to represent it. He is 55 years of age, a partner in the firm of William Ackroyd and Co., worsted spinners, and in Duncan, Barraclough, and Co., a director of the Otley Gas Company and of Waite and Saville (Ltd.), and an alderman of the West Riding County Council.

PUDSEY (15,071).—LIBERAL GAIN.
Ogden, F. (L.)	7,358
*Oddy, J. J. (U.)	5,934
Liberal majority	1,424

By-election, June, 1903, U., 5,444 ; L., 5,331 ; Lab., 1,291—U. maj. over L., 113.
1906.—L., 7,043 ; U., 3,541—L. maj., 3,502.
1900.—L., 5,973 ; U., 5,424—L. maj., 549.
1895.—L. maj., 470 ; 1892, L. maj., 603 ; 1886, L. maj., 1,171.

Mr. FRED OGDEN is a native of Leeds, and was born in 1871. He carries on the business of a boot factor. For some time he was on the city council as chairman of the waterworks committee. Mr. Ogden is a Primitive Methodist, and was for some time a local preacher in the body.

RIPON (12,860).—UNIONIST GAIN.
Wood, Hon. E. (U.)	6,363
*Lynch, H. F. B. (L.)	5,119
Unionist majority	1,244

1906.—L., 5,645 ; U., 5,332—L. maj. 313.
1900.—U. unop.
1895.—U. maj., 702 ; 1892 U. maj., 611 ; 1886, U. maj. 988.

The HON. EDWARD FREDERICK LINDLEY WOOD, son of Viscount Halifax, was born in 1881, and educated at Christ Church and All Souls, Oxford ; a lieutenant in the Yorkshire Dragoons, and greatly interested in agriculture and in county affairs ; married in 1909 Lady Dorothy Evelyn Augusta, younger daughter of the Earl of Onslow ; resides at the historic mansion of Temple Newsam, near Leeds, Park House, Harrogate, and 88, Eaton-square, S.W.

ROTHERHAM (20,487).—No change.
*Holland, Sir W. H. (L.)	12,225
Dransfield, J. H. (U.)	4,667
Liberal majority	7,558

1906.—L. unop.
1900.—L., 6,926 ; U., 5,021—L maj., 1,905.
1895.—L. unop.
1892.—L., 6,567 ; U., 2,839—L maj., 3,728.
1886.—L., 5,155 ; U., 2,070—L. maj., 3,085.

SIR WILLIAM HENRY HOLLAND, whose Parliamentary career began in 1892 and has been divided between the representation of the Northern Division of Salford and his present constituency, is an authority on questions of British trade and industry ; is chairman of the Fine Cotton Spinners' and Doublers' Association, and a bank director; was president in 1896 of the Manchester Chamber of Commerce and of the Associated Chambers of Commerce from 1904 to 1907 ; was a Commissioner of the Paris, Brussels, and Milan Exhibitions ; created a knight in 1902 and a baronet in 1907.

SHIPLEY (16,329).—No change.
*Illingworth, P. H. (L.)	9,144
Hewins, Prof. W. A. S. (U.)	5,369
Liberal majority	3,775

1906.—L. unop.
1900.—U., 6,284 ; L., 6,223—U. maj., 61.
1895.—U. maj., 78 ; 1892, L. maj., 282 ; 1886, L. unop.

Mr. PERCY HOLDEN ILLINGWORTH, who contested the Shipley Division unsuccessfully in 1900, and was returned unopposed as its representative in 1906, was born in Bradford in 1869, educated at Jesus College, Cambridge. He served with the Yorkshire Yeomanry in South Africa, and is a barrister and a captain of the Westminster Dragoons Imperial Yeomanry. He has acted as an unpaid private secretary to Mr. Birrell.

SKIPTON (13,864).—No change.

*Clough, W. (L.)	6,579
Roundell, R. F. (U.)	6,071
Liberal majority	508

1906.—L., 5,834 ; U., 5,601—L. maj., 233.
1900.—L., 5,139 ; U., 5,007—L. maj., 132.
1895.—U. maj., 139 ; 1892, L. maj., 92 ; 1886, U. maj., 134.

Mr. WILLIAM CLOUGH was born in 1862 and was educated at the Steeton Provident School, Keighley Trade School, and Pannal College, Harrogate. He has always been an energetic supporter of the Liberal Party in the North of England, and has been a member of the West Riding County Council since 1903.

SOWERBY (12,805).—No change.

*Higham, J. S. (L.)	6,811
Hinchliffe, W. A. S. (U.)	4,781
Liberal majority	2,030

1906.—L., 6,482 ; U., 4,034—L. maj., 2,448.
1900.—L., 5,528 ; U., 4,067—L. maj., 1,461.
1895.—L. maj., 1,575 ; 1892, L. maj., 2,430 ; 1886, L. unop.

Mr. JOHN SHARP HIGHAM was born at Sabden, Lancashire, in 1857 and privately educated. He is a cotton spinner and manufacturer, and head of the firm of Highams (Limited), of Accrington and Manchester. He has been a member of the Lancashire County Council for 12 years, and of the Accrington Town Council for 15, and was Mayor of Accrington from 1898 till 1900. He was first elected for the Sowerby Division in 1904.

SPEN VALLEY (11,631).—No change.

*Whittaker, Rt. Hon. Sir T. P. (L.)	4,817
Kelly, F. (U.)	3,439
Williams, J. R. (Lab.)	2,514
Liberal majority	1,378

1906.—L., 5,956 ; U., 3,092—L. maj., 2,864.
1900.—L., 5,068 ; U., 3,653—L. maj., 1,415.
1895.—L. maj., 821 ; 1892. L. maj., 1,478 ; 1886. L. maj., 2,342.

SIR THOMAS WHITTAKER, who has represented the Spen Valley Division since 1892, and is known in Parliament chiefly as an advocate of moderate temperance legislation, was born in Scarborough in 1850, and educated at Huddersfield College. He has had a varied business career in the hardware trade, as an editor and a newspaper proprietor, and as chairman and managing director of a life insurance institution. He was a member of the Royal Commission on the Licensing Laws, and an active supporter of the Licensing Bill of 1908. To the land clauses of the Finance Bill of last year he expressed hostility, and pointed out that they would inflict hardship upon thrifty persons of small means whose savings, deposited in industrial and insurance societies, had been invested in land.

WALES (BOROUGHS).

CARDIFF DISTRICT (28,723).—No change.

†Thomas, D. A. (L.)	13,207
Crichton-Stuart, Lord N. (U.)	11,652
Liberal majority	1,555

1906.—L., 12,434 ; U., 9,429—L. maj., 3,005.
1900.—L., 9,342 ; U., 8,541—L. maj., 801.
1895.—U. maj., 824 ; 1892, L. maj., 686 ; 1886, L. maj., 342.

Mr. DAVID ALFRED THOMAS, senior partner in the firm of Thomas and Davey, coal-shippers, Cardiff, was born in 1856, and educated at Gonville and Caius College, Cambridge ; takes, naturally, a great interest in the coal trade and was awarded in 1904 the Guy Silver Medal of the Royal Statistical Society for a paper on " The Growth and Direction of our Foreign Trade in Coal during the last Half Century " ; sat as member for Merthyr Tydvil from 1888 to 1910 ; acts, occasionally, independently of his party, and was in temporary revolt against the Government in 1909 owing to the withdrawal of the Welsh Disestablishment Bill.

CARMARTHEN DISTRICT (6,772).—No change.

*Williams, W. Llewellyn (L.)	4,197
Tiverton, Viscount (U.)	1,965
Liberal majority	2,232

1906.—L., 3,902 ; U., 1,808 —L. maj., 2,094.
1900.—L., 2,837 ; U., 2,047 —L. maj., 790.
1895.—U. maj., 52 ; 1892, L. maj., 225 ; 1886, L. maj., 222.

Mr. WILLIAM LLEWELLYN WILLIAMS is a barrister ; was born in Carmarthenshire in 1867, educated at Llandovery College, and Brasenose College, Oxford. He is prosecuting counsel to the Post Office on the South Wales Circuit and is the author of several essays on Welsh history and literature, two Welsh novels, and a work on " Welsh Catholics on the Continent." He was elected member for the Carmarthen boroughs in 1906.

CARNARVON DISTRICT (5,717).—
No change.

*Lloyd George, Rt. Hon. D. (L.)	3,183
Vincent, H. C. (U.)	2,105
Liberal majority	1,078

1906.—L., 3,221 ; U., 1,997—L. maj., 1,224.
1900.—L., 2,412 ; U., 2,116—L. maj., 298.
1895.—L. maj., 194 ; 1892, L. maj., 196 ; 1886, U. maj., 136.

Mr. DAVID LLOYD GEORGE, the Chancellor of the Exchequer, was born in Manchester in 1863, and was educated at the Llanystumdwy Church Schools and privately. Admitted a solicitor in 1884, he became a member of the firms of Lloyd George and George, of Criccieth, and of Lloyd George, Roberts, and Co., London. From 1905 to 1908 he was President of the Board of Trade, and was appointed Chancellor of the Exchequer in 1908 in succession to Mr. Asquith on the reconstruction of the Ministry after the death of Sir H. Campbell-Bannerman. In the same year he was appointed Constable of Carnarvon Castle ; is Hon. D.C.L. of Oxford and Hon. LL.D. of the University of Wales, and is a county alderman for Carnarvonshire. He has sat for the Carnarvon District since 1890, and his political creed is defined as being that of a Liberal and Welsh Nationalist, supporting Home Rule, Temperance, Disestablishment, and other items in the programme of the advanced Liberal Party.

DENBIGH DISTRICT (5,130).—UNIONIST GAIN.

Ormsby-Gore, Hon. W. (U.)	2,438
*Edwards, A. C. (L.)	2,430
Unionist majority	8

1906.—L. 2,533 ; U., 1,960—L. maj., 573.
1900.—U., 1,862 ; L., 1,752—U. maj., 110.
1895.—U. maj., 229 ; 1892, U. maj., 98 ; 1886, U. maj., 211.

The HON. WILLIAM GEORGE ARTHUR ORMSBY-GORE, born in 1885, only son of the third Lord Harlech ; was educated at Eton, and New College, Oxford. He travelled on the Continent, making a study of social and political conditions. He rendered good service to the Unionist cause in the Oswestry Division in 1906, and when he returned to Oxford he distinguished himself in history and political economy.

FLINT DISTRICT (4,060).—No change.

Summers, J. W. (L.)	2,150
Tilby, H. A. (U.)	1,723
Liberal majority	427

1906.—L., 1,899 ; U., 1,523 ; L. maj., 376.
1900.—L., 1,760 ; U., 1,413—L. maj., 347.
1895.—L. maj., 165 ; 1892, L. maj., 359 ; 1886, L. maj., 424.

Mr. J. W. SUMMERS, who was born at Dukinfield in 1849, is connected with the firm of Messrs. John Summers and Sons, who carry on a great iron works industry at Hawarden-bridge, Flintshire, and are the largest employers of labour in the county ; has taken a considerable part in county affairs, and has been chairman of the Flintshire County Council since March, 1904 ; is a magistrate for Lancashire, Denbighshire, and Flintshi.e.

MERTHYR TYDVIL (2) (23,219).- No change.

Jones, Edgar (L.)	15,448
*Hardie, Keir (Lab.)	13,841
Davies, A. C. Fox (U.)	4,756
Morgan, W. Pritchard (Ind. L.)	3,639
Liberal majority over Unionist	10,692
Labour majority over Unionist	9,085

1906.—L., 13,971 ; Lab., 10,187 ; L., 7,776—Lab. maj. over defeated L., 2,411.
1900.—L., 8,598 ; Lab., 5,745 ; L., 4,004—Lab. maj. over defeated L., 1,741.
1895.—L., 9,250 ; L., 8,554 ; U., 6,525 ; Lab., 659—L. maj., 2,029.
1892.—L., 11,948 ; L., 11,756 ; U., 2,304—L. maj., 9,452
1886.—Two L.'s unop.

Mr. EDGAR JONES, M.A., a lecturer to the Welsh National Liberal Council, is a son of the Rev. M. H. Jones, Baptist minister, of Ystrad, Rhondda ; was formerly a member of the scholastic profession ; qualified for his M.A. degree with a thesis on " Political Theories in England in the Seventeenth Century " ; came into prominence during Mr. Lloyd George's education revolt campaign in 1903.

Mr. J. KEIR HARDIE, who has been described by an admirer as " the most remarkable man the British democracy has produced during the last 50 years," has declared that his object is " to make his own class the ruling class " ; born in Lanarkshire in 1856, and worked from his seventh to his 24th year in the mines ; afterwards acted as a miners' union secretary and then as a journalist ; first elected to Parliament in 1892, and endeavoured to enter Palace-yard in circumstances which necessitated the interference of the police ; was the first member to wear a tweed cap in the House ; was chairman of the Independent Labour Party from 1893 to 1900 and of the Parliamentary Labour group from 1906 to 1908 ; visited India in 1907, and made a number of speeches which, in the conditions of unrest then prevailing, were regarded as mischievous.

MONTGOMERY DISTRICT (3,354).—No change.

*Rees, J. D. (L.)	1,539
Pryce-Jones, Col. E. (U.)	1,526
Liberal majority	13

1906.—L., 1,541 ; U., 1,458 ; L. maj., 83.
1900.—U., 1,478 ; L., 1,309—U. maj., 169.
1895.—U. maj., 84 ; 1892, U. maj., 118 ; 1886, L. maj., 173.

Mr. JOHN DAVID REES, who was born in 1854 and educated at Cheltenham College, is a distinguished member of the Indian Civil Service (retired), in which for 26 years he filled important judicial and administrative positions ; holds strong Imperial views, the expression of which proved distasteful to many of his Radical colleagues in the late Parliament ; is interested in a number of commercial undertakings and the author of " The Real India " and other works.

PEMBROKE AND HAVERFORDWEST DISTRICT (7,338).—No change.

*Philipps, Sir O. C. (L.)	3,582
Armstrong, Sir G., Bt. (U.)	2,877
Liberal majority	705

1906.—L., 3,576 ; U., 2,527—L. maj., 1,049.
1900.—U., 2,679 ; L., 2,667—U. maj., 12.
1895.—U. maj., 169 ; 1892, L. maj., 195 ; 1886, U. maj., 272.

SIR OWEN COSBY PHILIPPS, one of the leading men in the shipping world, is chairman of the Royal Mail Steam Packet Company, vice-chairman of the Port of London Authority, director of the Thames Haven Oil Wharves Company, and chairman of the King Line of steamers. He was a member of the Royal Commission on Shipping Rings in 1906-8, and of the Executive Committee of King Edward VII. Hospital Fund. In 1904 he served as High Sheriff of Pembrokeshire. Sir Owen Philipps was born in 1863, and was educated at Newton College, South Devon. He unsuccessfully contested Montgomery in 1895 and Darlington in 1898.

SWANSEA DISTRICT (12,983).—No change.

*Jones, Sir D. Brynmor, K.C. (L.)	8,488
Campbell, R. (U.)	2,415
Liberal majority	6,073

1906 and 1900.—L., unop.
1895.—L. maj., 1,832 ; 1892, L. maj., 5,023 ; 1883, L., unop.

SIR DAVID BRYNMOR JONES was born in 1852, and educated privately and at University College School and University College, London. He was called to the Bar at the Middle Temple in 1876. He was a County Court Judge for Mid Wales and Gloucestershire from 1885 till 1892, when he resigned and was elected by the Stroud Division of Gloucestershire. Since 1895 he has represented the Swansea District. He served on the Welsh Land Commission, 1894-96, and the Welsh Church Commission, 1907. He was chairman of the Metropolitan Police Commission, 1906, in which year he was knighted, and is one of the hon. secretaries to the Welsh Liberal Parliamentary Party.

SWANSEA TOWN (12,935).—No change.

†Mond, A. (L.)	6,020
Wright, Col. J. R. (U.)	4,375
Tillett, Ben (Soc.)	1,451
Liberal majority	1,645

1906.—L., 5,535 ; U., 4,081 —L. maj., 1,454.
1900.—L., 4,318 ; U., 3,203—L. maj., 1,115.
1895.—U. maj., 421 ; 1892, L. maj., 722 ; 1886, L. maj., 1,300.

Mr. ALFRED MOND, who sat in the last Parliament for Chester, is managing director in the firm of Brunner, Mond, and Co., chemical manufacturers, of Northwich, and the son of the late Dr. Ludwig Mond, F.R.S., who recently bequeathed a large collection of pictures to the nation. He was educated at Cheltenham College, St. John's College, Cambridge, and Edinburgh University, and is a barrister of the Inner Temple.

WALES (COUNTIES)

ANGLESEY (10,341).—No change.

*Griffith, Ellis (L.)	5,888
Roberts, R. O. (U.)	2,436
Liberal majority	3,452

By-election, Aug., 1907.—L. unop.
1906.—L., 5,356 ; U., 2,638—L. maj., 2,718.
1900.—L. unop.
1895.—L. maj., 1,027 ; 1892, L. maj., 1,718 ; 1886, L. maj., 306.

Mr. ELLIS JONES GRIFFITH has sat for Anglesey since 1895, after having unsuccessfully contested the Toxteth Division of Liverpool in 1892. Born in 1860, he received his education at the University College of Wales, Aberystwith, and Downing College, Cambridge ; was President of the Union in 1886 ; called to the Bar in 1887, and appointed Recorder of Birkenhead in 1907.

BRECKNOCKSHIRE (13,432).—No change.

*Robinson, S. (L.)	6,335
Devereux, Hon. R. C. (U.)	3,865
Liberal majority	2,470

1906.—L., 5,776 ; U., 3,499—L. maj., 2,277.
1900.—L. unop.
1895.—L. maj., 963 ; 1892, L. maj., 1,258 ; 1886, L. unop.

Mr. SIDNEY ROBINSON, who was born in 1863 and educated at Mill Hill School, has been engaged in the timber trade as a partner in a Cardiff firm, and served for many years as a member of the Cardiff Corporation. He is a Nonconformist. He entered Parliament in 1906 as the member for Brecknockshire.

CARDIGANSHIRE (13,333).—No change.

*Vaughan-Davies, M. L. (L.)	6,348
Roberts, Capt. G. Fossett (U.)	2,943
Liberal majority	3,405

1906.—L., 5,829 ; U., 2,960 ;—L. maj., 2,869.
1900.—L., 4,568 ; U., 3,787—L. maj., 781.
1895.—L. maj., 1,179 ; 1892, L. maj., 196 ; 1886, L. maj., 9.

Mr. MATTHEW LEWIS VAUGHAN-DAVIES, who was born in 1840 and educated at Harrow, has represented Cardinganshire since 1895. He was High Sheriff of the county in 1875.

CARMARTHENSHIRE (2).

East (12,268).—No change.

*Thomas, Abel, K.C. (L.)	7,619
Peel, Mervyn (U.)	2,451
Liberal majority	5,168

1906.—L. unop.
1900.—L., 4,337 ; U., 2,155—L. maj., 2,182.
1895.—L., 4,471 ; U., 2,466—L. maj., 2,005.
1892.—L., 4,439 ; U., 1,223 ; L. maj., 3,216.
1886.—L. unop.

Mr. ABEL THOMAS, K.C., son of the Rev. T. E. Thomas, J.P. of Pembroke, was born at Trahale. 1848, educated at Clifton College and University of London (B.A.), and married a daughter of Mr. S. Polak in 1875. Called to the Bar at the Middle Temple, 1875, he practised on the South Wales and Chester Circuits, and became Q.C. in 1892. He is chairman of the Pembrokeshire Quarter Sessions, and represented the Eastern Division of Carmarthen from his unopposed return at a by-election in 1890 to the close of the last Parliament.

West (9,433).—No change.

*Morgan, J. Lloyd, K.C. (L.)	5,684
Cremlyn, W. J. (U.)	2,059
Liberal majority	3,625

1906.—L., 3,902 ; U., 1,808—L. maj., 2,094.
1900.—L., 2,837 ; U., 2,047—L. maj., 790.
1895.—U. maj., 52 ; 1892, L. maj., 225 ; 1886, L. maj., 222.

Mr. JOHN LLOYD MORGAN, who was born in 1861, was called to the Bar at the Inner Temple in 1884 and became K.C. in 1906. He was appointed Recorder of Swansea at the beginning of 1908 in the place of Sir S. T. Evans, who had resigned on his appointment as Solicitor-General. He has sat for the Western Division of Carmarthenshire since 1889.

CARNARVONSHIRE (2).

North, or Arfon (10,153).—No change.

*Jones, W. (L.)	6,223
Hughes, A. E. (U.)	2,629
Liberal majority	3,594

1906.—L., 5,945 ; U., 2,533—L. maj., 3,412.
1900.—L. unop.
1895.—L. maj., 1,628 ; 1892, L. unop. ; 1886, L. maj., 1,122.

Mr. WILLIAM JONES was born in Anglesey in 1860, and was educated at Bangor Normal College, Aberystwith University College, and at Oxford. He was a private tutor at Oxford, and became an assistant schoolmaster in Anglesey and subsequently at Holloway under the London School Board. He has represented the Arfon Division since 1895.

South, or Eifion (9,455).— No change.

*Davies, Ellis W. (L.)	6,118
Priestley, C. F. Lloyd (U.)	1,700
Liberal majority	4,418

By-election, June, 1906.—L. unop.
1906, 1900, and 1895.—L. unop.
1892.—L. maj., 2,594 ; 1886, L. maj., 2,977.

Mr. ELLIS WILLIAM DAVIES, who was born in 1871, was a clerk in an insurance office, but at the age of 23 was articled to a solicitor and passed the final examination of the Law Society with first-class honours, winning the Law Society Prize in 1899. He is partner in the firm of Ellis Davies, Jones and Jones, has a seat on the Carnarvon County Council, and is a Governor of North Wales University College and of University College of Wales.

DENBIGHSHIRE (2).

East (11,911).—No change.

*Hemmerde, E. G., K.C. (L.)	6,865
Rhys, D. (U.)	3,321
Liberal majority	3,544

By-election, Aug., 1906.—L., 5,917 ; U., 3,126—L. maj., 2,791.
1906 and 1900.—L. unop.
1895.—L. maj., 1,784 ; 1892, L. maj., 766 ; 1886, L. maj., 26.

Mr. EDWARD GEORGE HEMMERDE, K.C., was born in 1871 and educated at Winchester, and University College, Oxford ; called to the Bar in 1897, and joined the Northern Circuit ; took silk in 1908, and was appointed Recorder of Liverpool last year ; unsuccessfully contested Winchester in 1900 and Shrewsbury at the General Election in 1906, and was elected for East Denbigh at a by-election in August, 1906.

West (9,920).—No change.

*Roberts, Sir J. H. (L.)	5,854
Thompson, S. (U.)	2,829
Liberal majority	3,025

1906 and 1900.—L. unop.
1895.—L. maj., 1,603 ; 1892, L. maj., 2,333 ; 1886, U. unop

SIR JOHN HERBERT ROBERTS, who was born in 1863, was educated privately, and at Trinity College, Cambridge. He has represented West Denbighshire since 1892, and is one of the hon. secretaries to the Welsh Liberal Parliamentary Party in the House of Commons. The baronetcy was created in 1908.

FLINTSHIRE (12,774).—No change.

*Lewis, J. H. (L.)	6,610
Howard, Col. H. R. Lloyd (U.)	4,454
Liberal majority	2,156

1906.—L., 6,294 ; U., 3,572—L. maj., 2,722.
1900.—L., 4,528 ; U., 3,922—L. maj., 606.
1895.—L. maj., 451 ; 1892, L. maj., 1,452 ; 1886, L. unop.

Mr. JOHN HERBERT LEWIS, who formerly represented Flint District, and was elected for Flintshire in 1906, was born in 1858 and educated at Denbigh Grammar School, the University of Montreal, and Exeter College, Oxford. He is a solicitor and shipowner, and interested in the development of technical instruction. He became a Junior Lord of the Treasury in 1905, and was appointed Parliamentary Secretary to the Local Government Board last Session.

GLAMORGANSHIRE (5).

East (23,979).—No change.

*Thomas, Sir A. (L.)	..	14,721
Gaskell, F. H. (U.)	..	5,727
Liberal majority	..	8,994

1906.—L. unopposed.
1900.—L., 6,994 ; U., 4,080—L. maj., 2,914.
1895.—L. maj., 2,146 ; 1892, L. maj., 2,967 ; 1886, L. unop.

Sir Alfred Thomas, who was born in 1840, was a merchant of Cardiff, and five years after his election as Mayor in 1882 he received the freedom of the city. He has been President of the Baptist Union of Wales and of University College of South Wales, and his part in the national affairs of Wales has been conspicuous. From 1885 East Glamorganshire has provided him with a seat in Parliament, and since 1898 he has led the Welsh Parliamentary Party.

West, or Gower (14,712).—No change.

*Williams, J. (Lab.)	..	9,312
Simner, P. (U.)	..	2,532
Labour majority	..	6,780

1906.—Lab., 4,841 ; L., 4,522 ; U., 1,939—Lab. maj. over L. 319.
1900.—L., 4,276 ; Lab., 3,853—L. maj., 423.
1895.—L., 6,074 ; U., 2,256—L. maj., 3,818.
1892.—L. unop. ; 1886, L. unop.

Mr. John Williams, born in 1861, is a miners' representative who began life as a boy in the coal pits ; at the age of 27 he was appointed agent for the Western District Miners' Association ; is now the chief agent of the organization as well as general secretary of the Amalgamated Society of South Wales Colliery Workers ; actively concerned in the municipal and local life of the Mountain Ash district.

Mid (20,017).—No change.

*Evans, Sir S. T., K.C. (L.)	..	13,175
Williams, G. H. (U.)	..	3,382
Liberal majority	..	9,793

By-election, Oct., 1906.—L. unop.
1906.—L. unop.
1900.—L., 7,027 ; U., 2,244—L. maj., 4,783.
1895.—L. maj., 2,677 ; 1892, L. maj., 4,216 ; 1886, L. unop.

Sir Samuel Evans first practised as a solicitor, but was called to the Bar in 1891 and took silk in 1901 ; entered Parliament in 1890 ; was made Recorder of Swansea in September, 1906, but resigned the position in 1908 on his appointment as Solicitor-General ; in that capacity he was largely responsible for the conduct through the Commons of the Licensing Bill of 1908 ; is very popular with all sections of the House.

Rhondda (17,640).—No change.

*Abraham, Rt. Hon. W. (Lab.)		12,436
Lloyd, Harold (U.)	..	3,471
Labour majority	..	8,965

1906.—L. unop.
1900.—L., 8,383 ; U., 1,874—L. maj., 6,509.
1895, 1892, and 1886—L. unop.

Mr. William Abraham (" Mabon ") is the son of a working collier and copper smelter, and worked in the mines at 10 years of age. Since 1873 he has been a miners' agent, and he is the vice-president of the Monmouthshire and South Wales Conciliation Board, president of the South Wales Miners' Federation, and treasurer of the Miners' Federation of Great Britain. He was sworn of the Privy Council last year.

South (22,953).—No change.

*Brace, W. (Lab.)	..	11,612
Morgan, L. (U.)	..	7,411
Labour majority	..	4,201

1906.—Lab., 10,514 ; U., 6,096—Lab. maj., 4,418.
1900.—U., 6,841 ; L., 6,322—U. maj., 519.
1895.—U. maj., 825 ; 1892, L. maj., 918 ; 1886, L. maj., 1,320.

Mr. William Brace, like most of the miners representatives in Parliament, began life as a pit boy ; is now agent and vice-president of the South Wales Miners' Federation ; was a member of the Royal Commission on the Coal Resources of the United Kingdom, and serves on the Monmouthshire County Council.

MERIONETHSHIRE (9,305).—No change.

Jones, Haydn (L.)	..	6,065
Jones-Morris, R. (U.)	..	1,873
Liberal majority	..	4,192

1906 and 1900.—L. unop.
1895.—L. maj., 2,941 ; 1892, L. maj., 3,238 ; 1886, L. maj.,1,267.

Mr. H. Haydn Jones has been a member of the Merionethshire County Council from its establishment and was made an alderman 10 years ago ; he is a member of the Welsh Central Board and of the Court of Governors of the University College of Wales, while as unpaid secretary to the County Education Committee he took a leading share in the agitation against the Education Act of 1902. In business he is an ironmonger.

MONTGOMERYSHIRE (7,928).—No change.

*Davies, D. (L.)	..	4,369
Wynn, A. W. W. (U.)	..	2,697
Liberal majority	..	1,672

1906.—L. unop.
1900.—L., 3,482 ; U., 3.218 ; L. maj., 264.
1895.—L. maj., 27 ; 1892, L. maj., 815 ; 1886, L. maj., 579.

Mr. David Davies is a landed proprietor and director of the Cambrian Railways and Barry Railway Company ; a generous supporter of the Calvinistic Methodist Church in Wales, and of Welsh denominational colleges ; a member of the Court of the University of Wales ; born in 1880 and educated at

Merchiston Castle School, Edinburgh, and King's College, Cambridge.

PEMBROKESHIRE (11,750).—No change.

*Roch, W. F. (L.)	6,135
Samson, E. M. (U.) ..	3,291
Liberal majority ..	2,844

By-election, July, 1908.—L., 5,460 ; U., 3,286 —L. maj., 2,174
1906.—L., 5,886 ; U., 2,606—L. maj., 3,280.
1900.—L. unop.
1895.—L. maj., 580 ; 1892, L. maj., 1,099 ; 1886, L. maj., 116.

Mr. WALTER FRANCIS ROCH, who describes himself as an advanced Radical and Social Reformer, comes of a Pembrokeshire family, several members of which belong to the Unionist Party; was born in 1881 and educated at Harrow, was admitted a solicitor in 1904, and is now entered as a student at the Middle Temple.

RADNORSHIRE (5,971).—UNIONIST GAIN.

Venables-Llewelyn, C. (U.)..	2,222
*Edwards, Sir F. (L.) ..	2,208
Unionist majority ..	14

1906.—L., 2,186 ; U., 2,011—L. maj., 175.
1900.—L., 2,082 ; U., 1,916 ; L. maj., 166.
1895.—U. maj., 79 ; 1892. L. maj.. 233 ; 1886, U. maj., 242.

Mr. CHARLES DILLWYN VENABLES-LLEWELYN is the only surviving son of Sir J. T. Dillwyn Llewelyn ; has twice before unsuccessfully contested Radnorshire ; is J.P. for Radnorshire, a member of the Joint Standing Committee for the county, and a keen agriculturist.

SCOTLAND (BURGHS).

ABERDEEN (2).
NORTH (10,331).—No change.

*Pirie, D. V. (L.)	4,297
Scott-Brown, R. (U.) ..	2,314
Kennedy, T. (Soc.) ..	1,344
Liberal majority ..	1,983

1906.—L., 4,852 ; Soc., 1,935 ; U., 931—L. maj. over Soc., 2,917.
1900.—L., 4,238 ; U., 2,251—L. maj., 1,987.
1895.—L. maj., over Lab., 3,548 ; 1892, L. maj., 3,592 ; 1886, L. unop.

Mr. DUNCAN VERNON PIRIE was born at Aberdeen in 1858 and educated at Glenalmond and Clifton College. Entering the Army in 1879 he retired as captain in the 3rd Hussars in 1898, having served in the campaigns of Egypt, 1882, the Sudan, 1884, and the Nile, 1884-5. He was A.D.C. to the Governor of Ceylon 1890-93, and served in South Africa 1899-1902. He is a director of Alexander Pirie and Sons (Limited), of Aberdeen. Unsuccessfully contested West Renfrewshire in 1895; has sat for North Aberdeen since May, 1896.

SOUTH (13,496).—No change.

*Esslemont, G. B. (L.) ..	6,749
McNeill, R. (U.)	4,433
Liberal majority ..	2,316

By-election, 1907.—L., 3,779 ; U., 3,412 ; Soc., 1,740—L. maj. over U., 367.
1906.—L., 6,780 ; U., 2,332—L. maj., 4,448.
1900.—L., 4,238 ; U., 3,830—L. maj., 408.
1895.—L. maj., 864 ; 1892, L. maj. over U., 1,745 ; 1886, L. unop.

Mr. GEORGE BIRNIE ESSLEMONT was elected for South Aberdeen in 1907 in succession to Mr. James Bryce, who was appointed Ambassador to the United States. Born in 1860, he was educated privately and at Aberdeen Grammar School, and entered business in 1876. He has served on many local boards in his native city, and became its senior magistrate in 1905-6.

AYR BURGHS (8,067).—No change.

*Younger, G. (U.)	3,647
Robertson, W. (L.) ..	3,594
Unionist majority ..	53

1906.—U., 3,766 ; L., 3,505—U. maj., 261.
1900.—U., 3,101 ; L., 2,511—U. maj., 590.
1895.—U., 3,057 ; L., 2,722—U. maj., 335.
1892.—L., 2,780 ; U., 2,753—L. maj., 7.
1886.—U., 2,673 ; L., 1,498—U. maj., 1,175.

Mr. GEORGE YOUNGER is the chairman of the firm of George Younger and Co. (Limited), brewers, at Alloa ; born in 1851, and educated at the Edinburgh Academy ; a member of the Royal Commission on Licensing, President of the County Councils Association of Scotland, 1902-4, and of the National Union of Conservative Associations in Scotland in 1904 ; contested Clackmannan and Kinross in 1895, 1899, and 1900, and the Ayr Burghs in 1904 before he secured election for the latter constituency in 1906.

DUMFRIES BURGHS (4,307).—No change.

*Gulland, J. W. (L.).. ..	2,303
Duncan, J. Bryce (U.) ..	1,730
Liberal majority ..	573

By-election, July, 1909, L., 1,877 ; U., 1,585—L. maj., 292.
1906.—L., 2,035 ; U., 1,402—L. maj., 633.
1900.—L., 1,847 ; U., 1,300—L. maj., 547.
1895.—L. maj., 600 ; 1892, L. maj., 532 ; 1886, L. maj., 330.

Mr. J. W. GULLAND is a graduate of Edinburgh University and first entered Parliament in 1906 as the successor in the representation of Dumfries

Burghs of the Lord Chancellor. During his career in Edinburgh as a corn merchant he has taken a keen interest in local affairs. He was recently appointed a Lord of the Treasury.

DUNDEE (2) (19,374).—No change.

*Churchill, Rt. Hon. W. S. (L.)	10,747
*Wilkie, A. (Lab.)	10,365
Lloyd, J. S. (U.)	4,552
Glass, J. (U.)	4,339
Scrymgeour, E. (Prohibitionist)	1,512
Liberal majority over Unionist	6,195
Labour majority over Unionist	5,813

By-election, 1908.—L., 7,079 ; U., 4,370 ; Lab., 4,014 ; Ind. 655—L. maj. over U., 2,709 ; U. maj. over Lab., 356.
1906.—L., 9,276 ; Lab., 6,833 ; L., 6,122 ; U., 3,865 ; U., 3,183—L. maj. over Lab., 2,443 ; L. maj. over U., 5,411.
1900.—L., 7,777 ; L., 7,650 ; U., 5,181 ; U., 5,152—L. maj., 2,469.
1895.—L., 7,602 ; L., 7,592 ; U., 5,390 ; U., 4,318 ; Lab., 1,313—L. maj. over U., 2,202.
1892.—L., 8,484 ; L., 8,191 ; U., 5,659 ; U., 5,066 ; Lab., 354—L. maj. over U., 2,532.
1886.—L., 8,236 ; L., 8,216 ; U., 3,545 ; U., 3,346—L. maj., 4,671.

Mr. WINSTON LEONARD SPENCER CHURCHILL, born in 1874, son of Lord Randolph Churchill, has been an English cavalry officer, has fought for the Spaniards in Cuba, and seen active service on the Indian frontier, in Egypt, and South Africa ; has practised journalism, and engaged in literature, his principal books being the " Life " of his father (1906) and " My African Journey " (1908) ; entered Parliament as Unionist member for Oldham in 1900 ; appointed Under-Secretary for the Colonies in the Liberal Government in 1905, and returned at the General Election for North-West Manchester ; was promoted to the Cabinet as President of the Board of Trade in April, 1908, when he failed to secure re-election, but was found a seat at Dundee.

Mr. ALEXANDER WILKIE is a ship carpenter, and was born in Fife in 1850. He is general secretary of the Ship Constructive and Shipwrights' Association. As a member of the Trade Union Congress Committee he had a share in instituting the General Federation of Trades. He also assisted in forming the Labour Representation Committee, and in 1902 visited America as a member of the Mosely Commission.

EDINBURGH (4).

CENTRAL (7,005).—No change.

*Price, C. E. (L.)	3,965
Scott, D. A. (U.)	1,980
Liberal majority	1,985

1906.—L., 3,935 ; U., 1,857—L. maj., 2,078.
1900.—L., 3,028 ; U., 2,459—L. maj., 569.
1895.—L. unop.
1892.—L., 3,733 ; U., 1,758 ; Lab., 434—L. maj. over U., 1,975
1886.—L., 3,760 ; U., 2,236—L. maj., 1,524.

Mr. CHARLES E. PRICE, born in 1857, comes of a Shropshire family, and has long been settled in Edinburgh. In 1888 he founded the firm of McVitie and Price, biscuit manufacturers, of Edinburgh and London, and retired from business in 1901.

EAST (12,544).—No change.

*Gibson, Sir J. (L.)	6,760
Ford, P. J. (U.)	4,273
Liberal majority	2,487

By-election, 1909.—L., 4,527 ; U., 4,069—L. maj., 458.
1906.—L., 6,606 ; U., 2,432—L. maj., 4,174.
1900.—L., 4,461 ; U., 3,170—L. maj., 1,291.
1895.—L., 3,499 ; U., 3,050—L. maj., 449
1892.—L., 3,069 ; U., 2,809—L. maj., 1,160.
1886.—L., 3,694 ; U., 2,253—L. maj., 1,441.

SIR JAMES PUCKERING GIBSON is head of the firm of Messrs. R. and T. Gibson, provision merchants, Edinburgh, and has taken a large and active part in the municipal life of the city. He served as Lord Provost from 1906 to 1909, and at the close of his term of office a baronetcy was conferred upon him. He was born in 1849, and was educated at the Edinburgh Institution and the University.

SOUTH (20,433).—No change.

*Dewar, A., K.C. (L.)	10,235
Cox, H. B. (U.)	7,901
Liberal majority	2,334

By-election, 1909, L., 8,185 ; U., 6,964—L. maj., 1,221.
1906.—L., 8,945 ; U., 5,085—L. maj., 3,860.
1900.—U., 5,766 ; L., 5,655—U. maj., 111.
1895.—U., 4,802 ; L., 4,708—U. maj., 94.
1892.—L., 4,692 ; U., 4,261—L. maj., 431.
1886.—L., 3,778 ; U., 2,191—L. maj., 1,587.

Mr. ARTHUR DEWAR, born in 1860, the son of Mr. John Dewar, distiller, and educated at Perth and at Edinburgh University, is a member of the Faculty of Advocates and a K.C. ; was appointed Solicitor-General for Scotland in March, 1909.

WEST (9,758).—No change.

*Clyde, J. A., K.C. (U.)	4,683
†Lyell, C. H. (L.)	4,233
Unionist majority	450

By-election, 1909.—U. unop.
1906.—U., 3,949 ; L., 3,643—U. maj., 306.
1900.—U., 4,180 ; L., 2,645—U. maj., 1,535.
1895.—U. unop.
1892.—U., 3,728 ; L., 3,216—U. maj., 512.
1886.—U., 3,083 ; L., 2,393—U. maj., 690.

Mr. J. A. CLYDE, K.C., is a son of Dr. James Clyde, formerly Rector of Edinburgh Academy. He was born in 1863, and was educated at Edinburgh Academy and at the University, being one of the founders of the University Union. Called to the Bar in 1887, he became a King's Counsel in 1901, and was appointed Solicitor-General for Scotland towards the close of the Unionist Administration in 1905.

ELGIN BURGHS (5,301).—No change.

*Sutherland, J. E. (L.)	3,031
Black, W. G. (U.)	1,201
Liberal majority	1,830

1906.—L., 2,742 ; U., 786—L. maj., 1,956.
1900.—L., 1,744 ; U., 1,187—L. maj., 557.
1895 —L. maj., 692 : 1892, L. maj., 541 : 1886, L. unop.

Mr. JOHN EBENEZER SUTHERLAND, born in 1854, and educated at Aberdeen University, is a partner in the firm of J. and P. Sutherland, Portsoy, J.P. for Banffshire, member of the Banffshire County Council, and was for many years chairman of the Fordyce School Board and of the Scottish Temperance and Social Reform Association. He has represented the Elgin Burghs since his return at a by-election in September, 1905.

FALKIRK BURGHS (12,889).—No change.

*Macdonald, J. A. M. (L.)	6,524
Keith, H. S. (U.)	4,375
Liberal majority	2,149

1906.—L., 5,158; U., 3,176; Lab., 1,763—Lib. maj. over U., 1,982.
1900.—U., 4,222; L., 4,022—U. maj., 200.
1895.—U. maj., 253; 1892, L. maj., 639; 1886, U. maj., 19.

Mr. JOHN ARCHIBALD MURRAY MACDONALD is secretary to the Cobden Club; sat for Bow and Bromley from 1892 to 1895, and was elected for Falkirk in 1906, after a failure in 1900; is a prominent member of what is generally spoken of as the "Little Navy" group in the House; born in 1854, and educated at Glasgow High School and Glasgow and Edinburgh Universities.

GLASGOW (7).

BLACKFRIARS (8,481).—No change.

*Barnes, G. N. (Lab.)	4,496
Constable, A. H. B., K.C. (U.)	2,796
Labour majority	1,700

1906.—Lab., 3,284; U., 2,974; L., 2,058—Lab. maj., 310.
1900.—U., 4,130; L., 3,140—U. maj., 990.
1895.—L. maj. over U., 381; 1892, L. maj., 1,081; 1886, L. maj., 864.

Mr. GEORGE N. BARNES is an engineer, born at Lochee, Forfar, in 1859, and was apprenticed in Dundee. He was general secretary of the Amalgamated Society of Engineers from 1896 to 1908. He is president of the National Committee of Organized Labour on Old-Age Pensions, and as an expert in labour questions he went with the Mosely Commission to the United States in 1902. He is vice-chairman of the Labour Party in the House of Commons.

BRIDGETON (10,144).—No change.

*Cleland, J. W. (L.)	5,336
Lang, P. K. (U.)	3,539
Liberal majority	1,797

1906.—L., 5,585; U., 4,019—L. maj., 1,566.
1900.—U., 5,032; L., 4,041—U. maj., 991.
1895, L, maj. over U., 442; 1892, L. maj., 1,378; 1886, L. maj., 797.

Mr. J. W. CLELAND is a barrister, and was a member of the London County Council for Lewisham from 1904 to 1907. He was born in Glasgow in 1874, and was educated at the Academy and University there, and thence went to Balliol College, Oxford. He takes part in the social work of the Passmore Edwards Settlement.

CAMLACHIE (9,661).—UNIONIST GAIN.

Mackinder, H. J. (U.)	3,227
*Cross, A. (L.)	2,793
Kessack, J. O'C. (Lab.)	2,443
Unionist majority over Liberal	434

1906.—U., 3,119; L., 2,871; Lab., 2,568—U. maj. over L., 248.
1900.—U., 4,345; Lab., 3,107—U. maj., 1,238.
1895.—U. maj. over L., 701; 1892; U. maj. over L., 371; 1886, L. maj., 159.

Mr. HAROLD JOHN MACKINDER, though not a stranger to politics, is much better known as an authority on geographical and economical subjects; born in 1861, educated at Epsom College and Christ Church, Oxford, where he was president of the Union, and called to the Bar; is at present Reader in Geography in the University of London, and was previously Reader in Geography at Oxford University, Principal of University College, Reading, and Director of the London School of Economics and Political Science.

[Mr. A. Cross was returned as a Liberal Unionist in 1892, but he seceded from the Party towards the close of the last Parliament.]

CENTRAL (14,768).—No change.

*Scott Dickson, Right Hon. C., K.C. (U.)	6,713
Murison, Prof.	6,058
Unionist majority	655

By-election, 1909.—U., 7,298; L., 5,185—U. maj., 2,113.
1906.—L., 6,720; U., 6,289—L. maj., 431.
1900.—U. unop.
1895.—U. maj., 1,829; 1892, U. maj., 876; 1886, U. maj., 1,357.

Mr. CHARLES SCOTT DICKSON, K.C., was born in 1850, and was educated at the Glasgow High School and at the University of that city. In 1877 he was admitted to the Faculty of Advocates, and was lecturer on Constitutional Law at Glasgow University in the same year. Appointed Advocate-Depute in 1892, 1895, and 1896, he was Solicitor-General for Scotland from 1896 to 1903, and succeeded Mr. Graham Murray (Lord Dunedin) as Lord Advocate in 1903.

COLLEGE (14,208).—No change.

*Watt, H. A. (L.)	6,525
Maxwell, Sir J. Stirling (U.)	5,823
Liberal majority	702

1906.—L., 7,359; U., 5,676—L. maj., 1,683.
1900.—U., 6,629; L., 5,160—U. maj., 1,469.
1895.—U. maj., 1,145; 1892, L. maj. over U., 1,046; 1886, L. maj., 655.

Mr. HARRY ANDERSON WATT is a native of Glasgow, and was educated at the High School and the University in that city. By his prowess as an athlete he gained more than 100 prizes, and for three years he held the championship of Scotland in hurdle racing. He was called to the Bar at Gray's Inn in 1895, but did not practise. For some time he followed his father's business of a yarn merchant, but retired before he was returned to Parliament as the representative of the College Division in 1906.

St. Rollox (19,581).—No change.

*Wood, T. McKinnon (L.)	10,019
Chamberlayne, A. R. (U.)	6,821
Liberal majority	3,198

1906.—L., 9,453 U., 6,048—L. maj., 3,405.
1900.—U., 6,232; L., 6,049—U. maj., 183.
1895.—U. maj. over L., 361; 1892, L. maj., 1,356; 1886, U. maj., 119.

Mr. Thomas McKinnon Wood was born in London in 1855, and educated at Mill Hill School and University College, London. Identifying himself with the Progressive Party on the London County Council, he represented Central Hackney on that body from 1892 to 1907, when he was elected an alderman. He served as chairman of the Parliamentary Committee from 1896 to 1898, was leader of the Progressive Party, and in 1898-9 was Chairman of the Council. After contesting East Islington in 1895, the St. Rollox Division in 1900, and Orkney and Shetland in 1902, Mr. McKinnon Wood entered Parliament in 1906. He was Parliamentary Secretary to the Board of Education from April to October, 1908, when he was appointed Under-Secretary for Foreign Affairs. He is a D.L. for London and LL.D. of St. Andrews University.

Tradeston (9,664).—No change.

*Corbett, A. Cameron (Ind. L.)	2,966
Main, A. P. (U.)	2,773
Mason, D. M. (L.)	2,673
Ind. Liberal majority over Unionist	193

1906.—U., 4,416; L., 4,063; U., 245—U. maj. over L., 353.
1900.—U., 4,389; L., 2,785—U. maj., 1,604.
1895.—U. maj. over L., 805; 1892, U. maj. over L., 169; 1886, U. maj., 704.

Mr. A. Cameron Corbett, who represented the division from 1885 to the dissolution, was elected as a Liberal, but joined the Liberal Unionists when the split came on the Home Rule question; seceded from the Unionist Party during the Session of 1909, principally on the question of licensing legislation; born in 1856 and educated privately.

Greenock (7,853).—No change.

Collins, G. P. (L.)	4,253
Smith, Rt. Hon. J. Parker (U.)	2,632
Liberal majority	1,601

1906.—L., 3,596; U., 3,254—L. maj., 342.
1900.—U., 3,165; L., 2,886—U. maj., 279.
1895.—U. maj., 818; 1892, U. maj., 55; 1886, U. maj., 697.

Mr. Godfrey P. Collins is a comparatively young man. He is a partner of the printing and publishing firm of Messrs. William Collins and Sons (Limited), Glasgow. He served for a period as an officer in the Navy, but retired from the service some years ago to enter business. This is the first time he has stood for Parliament.

Hawick Burghs (6,030).—No change.

*Barran, Sir J., Bt. (L.)	3,261
Graham, J. E., K.C. (U.)	2,268
Liberal majority	993

By-election, 1909.—L., 3,028; U., 2,508—L. maj., 520.
1906.—L., 3,125; U., 2,444—L. maj., 681.
1900.—L., 2,611; U., 2,386—L. maj., 225.
1895.—L. maj., 502; 1892, L. maj., 365; 1886, L. maj., 30.

Sir John Nicholson Barran, who was elected for the Hawick Burghs in March, 1909, for the vacancy created by the elevation of the Lord Advocate (Mr. Thomas Shaw) to the Peerage, was born in 1872, and educated at Winchester, and Trinity College, Cambridge; is director of John Barran and Sons (Limited), Leeds.

Inverness Burghs (4,547).—No change.

*Bryce, J. A. (L.)	2,440
McMicking, T. (U.)	1,650
Liberal majority	790

1906.—L., 2,304; U., 1,746—L. maj., 558.
1900.—U., 1,829; L., 1,469—U. maj., 360.
1895.—U. maj., 250; 1892, L. maj., 53; 1886, U. maj., 273.

Mr. John Annan Bryce, brother of Mr. James Bryce, British Ambassador in Washington, has represented Inverness Burghs since 1906; educated at the High School and University of Glasgow, Edinburgh University, and Balliol College, Oxford (Brackenbury History Scholar and First-class Honours in Classics); formerly an East India merchant, and member of the Legislative Council of Burma; a director of the London and County Bank, the Atlas Assurance Company, and the Bombay-Baroda Railway Company, and member of the Council of the Royal Geographical Society.

Kilmarnock Burghs (16,467).—No change.

*Rainy, A. R. (L.)	8,937
Bell, J., Jr. (U.)	5,701
Liberal majority	3,236

1906.—L., 8,268; U., 5,743—L. maj., 2,525.
1900.—U., 6,076; L., 5,692—U. maj., 384.
1895.—U. maj., 381; 1892, L. maj., 775; 1886, L. maj., 884.

Dr. Adam Rolland Rainy, the eldest son of the late Principal Rainy, was born in 1862 and educated at the Edinburgh, Vienna, and Berlin Universities; practised for some years in London as a surgeon oculist, and then gave himself up to political work; unsuccessfully contested the Burghs in 1900.

Kirkcaldy Burghs (8,425).—No change.

*Dalziel, Sir J. H. (L.)	5,035
Baumann, A. A. (U.)	1,659
Liberal majority	3,376

1906.—L., 4,659; U., 1,410—L. maj., 3,249.
1900.—L., 3,354; U., 2,013—L. maj., 1,341.
1895.—L., 3,078; U., 1,122—L. maj., 1,956.
1892.—L., 2,741; U., 939—L. maj., 1,802.
1886.—L., 2,014; U., 911—L. maj., 1,103.

Sir James Henry Dalziel, who was born in 1868 and educated at Shrewsbury High School and King's

College, London, is a journalist and newspaper director. Since his election to Parliament in 1892 he has held his present seat against all comers. He was knighted for his political services in 1908.

LEITH BURGHS (17,351).—No change.

*Munro-Ferguson, R. C. (L.)	7,146
Cranston, Sir R. (U.)	4,540
Walker, W. (Lab.)	2,724
Liberal majority	2,606

1906.—L., 7,677 ; U., 4,865—L. maj., 2,812.
1900.—L., 6,043 ; U., 5,226—L. maj., 817.
1895.—L. maj., 1,325 ; 1892, L. maj., 1,643 ; 1886, L. unop.

Mr. RONALD CRAUFURD MUNRO-FERGUSON, born in 1860, is the eldest son of the late Col. R. Munro-Ferguson, some time member for Kirkcaldy. He was educated at Sandhurst, and in 1889 married Lady Helen Hermione Blackwood, daughter of the first Marquis of Dufferin and Ava. He was formerly lieutenant in the Grenadier Guards, has been private secretary to Lord Rosebery, and in 1894-5 was a Lord of the Treasury. In 1884-5 he represented Ross and Cromarty and was elected for Leith Burghs in 1886, and continued to represent the constituency to the close of the last Parliament.

MONTROSE BURGHS (8,414).—No change.

*Harcourt, R. V. (L.)	3,606
Burgess, J. (Ind. Lab.)	1,888
Low, W. (U.)	1,592
Liberal majority over Labour	1,718
Liberal majority over Unionist	2,014

By-election, May, 1908.—L., 3,083 ; Lab., 1,937 ; U., 1,576— L. maj. over Lab., 1,146.
1906.—L., 4,416 ; U., 1,922—L. maj., 2,494.
1900.—L., 3,960 ; U., 2,390—L. maj., 1,570.
1895.—L., 3,594 ; U., 2,462—L. maj., 1,132.
1892.—L., 3,941 ; U., 2,090—L. maj., 1,851.
1886.—L., 3,357 ; U., 2,088—L. maj., 1,269.

Mr. ROBERT VERNON HARCOURT, who entered Parliament in 1908 at a by-election caused by the elevation of Lord Morley of Blackburn to the Peerage, is a son of the late Sir William Harcourt. He was born in 1878 and was educated at Eton, and Trinity College, Cambridge, where he secured honours in the History Tripos. For five years he was on the diplomatic establishment of the Foreign Office, and has engaged in journalism. He successfully agitated for the appointment of a Parliamentary inquiry into the Censorship of Plays and was a member of the Joint Committee on the subject. Contested Hastings at a by-election in 1908.

PAISLEY (12,331).—No change.

*McCallum, J. (L.)	6,812
Campbell, Capt. D. (U.)	3,891
Liberal majority	2,921

1906.—L., 5,664 ; U., 2,594 ; Lab., 2,482—L. maj. over U., 3,070.
1900.—L., 4,532 ; U., 3,474—L. maj., 1,058.
1895.—L. maj., 1,342 ; 1892, L. maj., 1,821 ; 1886, L. maj., 566.

Mr. JOHN MILLS MCCALLUM, born in 1847 in Paisley, and educated there, married in 1875 a daughter of Mr. Stephen Oates, J.P., of Grimsby. He is J.P. for Renfrewshire, a member of the Scottish Liberal Association, and in business as a soap manufacturer. He represented the burgh in the last Parliament.

PERTH (5,433).—No change.

Whyte, A. F. (L.)	2,841
Chapman, S. (U.)	2,103
Liberal majority	738

By-election, 1907.—L. unop.
1906.—L., 2,875 ; U., 1,867— L. maj., 1,008.
1900.—L., 2,171 ; U., 1,827— L. maj., 344.
1895.—L. maj., 374 ; 1892, U. maj. over L., 227 ; 1886, L. maj., 453.

Mr. A. F. WHYTE has acted as political secretary since January, 1909, to Lord Lucas, Under-Secretary for War. Mr. Whyte is the son of the Rev. Principal Whyte, United Free Church College, Edinburgh, is 26 years of age, and was educated in Edinburgh. He was president of Edinburgh University Union and warden of the University Settlement in 1907-8.

ST. ANDREWS BURGHS (3,206).—LIBERAL GAIN.

Millar, J. D. (L.)	1,507
*Anstruther-Gray, Major W. (U.)	1,469
Liberal majority	38

1906.—U., 1,495 ; L., 1,472—U. maj., 23.
1900.—U., 1,148 ; L., 1,094—U. maj., 54.
1895.—U. maj., 196 ; 1892, U. maj., 112 ; 1886, U. maj., 416.

Mr. J. DUNCAN MILLAR is a member of the Faculty of Advocates and was called to the Bar in 1896. He has a family connexion with the late Mr. Duncan M'Laren, for many years M.P. for Edinburgh, and also with Mr. John Bright.

STIRLING BURGHS (8,147).—No change.

*Ponsonby, A. (L.)	4,471
Cochran-Patrick, N. K. (U.)	2,419
Liberal majority	2,052

By-election, 1908.—L., 3,873 U., 2,512—L. maj., 1,361.
1906.—L. unop.
1900.—L., 2,715 ; U., 2,085—L. maj., 630.
1895.—L. maj., 1,127 ; 1892, L. maj., 1,096 ; 1886, L. maj., 989.

Mr. ARTHUR AUGUSTUS WILLIAM HARRY PONSONBY, private secretary to the late Sir H. Campbell-Bannerman for three years, is a son of the late General Sir Henry Ponsonby, for many years private secretary to Queen Victoria. He was born in 1871 and was educated at Eton, and Balliol College, Oxford. From 1882 to 1887 he was a page of honour to Queen Victoria, and afterwards served for nine years in the Diplomatic Service. He unsuccessfully contested Taunton in 1906.

WICK BURGHS (3,018).—LIBERAL GAIN.

Munro, R. (L.)	1,537
*Bignold, Sir A. (U.)	1,262
Liberal majority	275

1906.—U., 1,362 ; L., 1,266—U. maj., 96.
1900.—U., 1,154 ; L., 1,041—U. maj., 113.
1895.—U. maj., 24 ; 1892, U. maj., 127 ; 1886, L. maj., 224.

Mr. ROBERT MUNRO, born in 1868, is the son of a Free Church minister in Ross-shire ; called to the Bar in 1895, and has now one of the largest junior practices in Parliament House ; junior counsel for the United Free Church in the Church case ; appointed Advocate Depute about a year ago.

SCOTLAND (COUNTIES).

ABERDEENSHIRE (2).
East (12,635).—No change.
†Cowan, W. H. (L.)	..	6,600
Burn, Col. C. R. (U.)	..	3,962

Liberal majority	..	2,638

By-election, 1906—L. unop.
1906.—L., 6,149 ; U., 4,319—L. maj., 1,830.
1900.—U., 4,173 ; L., 4,100—U. maj., 73.
1895.—L. maj., 1,415 ; 1892, L. maj., 1,624 ; 1886, L. maj., 2,408.

Mr. WILLIAM HENRY COWAN, who is a director of W. and B Cowan (Limited), manufacturers, was born in Edinburgh in 1862, and was educated at Merchiston Castle and at the Collegiate School and University of Edinburgh. He has travelled extensively, paying repeated visits to the Colonies, and sat in the last Parliament as the representative of the Guildford Division of Surrey.

West (10,898).—No change.
*Henderson, J. M. (L.)	..	5,901
Smith, G. (U.)	..	3,194

Liberal majority	..	2.707

1906.—L., 5,949 ; U., 2,791—L. maj., 3,158.
1900.—L., 4,352 ; U., 3,213—L. maj., 1,139.
1895.—L., 4,187 ; U., 3,967—L. maj., 220.
1892.—L., 3,720 ; U., 3,640—L. maj., 80.
1886.—L., 3,854 ; U., 1,657—L. maj., 2,197.

Mr. JOHN MCDONALD HENDERSON, who has represented West Aberdeen since 1906, is a chartered accountant and barrister. Born in 1846, he was educated at Gordon College and Marischal College, Aberdeen, and in 1872 married a daughter of Mr. T. F. Robins. He is a director of Thomas Bolton and Son (Limited), the Lancashire United Tramways Company, and other companies.

ARGYLLSHIRE (11,025).—No change.
*Ainsworth, J. S. (L.)	..	4,443
Clark-Hutchinson, G.A.(U.)		3,617

Liberal majority	..	826

1906.—L., 4,507 ; U., 3,012—L. maj., 1,495.
1900.—L., 3,834 ; L., 3,234—L. maj., 600.
1895.—U. maj., 135 ; 1892, L. maj., 80 ; 1886, U. maj., 613.

Mr. JOHN STIRLING AINSWORTH, who was first elected for the county in 1903, was born in 1844 and educated at University College School and University College, London ; is interested in the iron mines and other industries of Cumberland, chairman of the Cleator and Workington Junction Railway, and a director of the Whitehaven Joint Stock Bank.

AYRSHIRE (2).
North (16,458).—LIBERAL GAIN.
Anderson, A. (L.)	..	6,189
*Cochrane, Hon. T. (U.)		5,951
Brown, J. (Lab.)	..	1,801

Liberal majority	..	238

1906.—U., 5,603 ; L., 4,587 ; Lab., 2,683—U. maj. over L., 716.
1900.—U., 5,985 ; L., 4,791—U. maj., 1,194.
1895.—U. maj., 710 ; 1892, U. maj., 448 ; 1886, U. unop.

Mr. A. M. ANDERSON was born at Coupar Angus in 1862. He was educated at the High School, Dundee, and afterwards at the University of Edinburgh, where he graduated M.A., LL.B., with distinction, and was awarded the Forensic Prize as the most distinguished law graduate of his year. He was called to the Bar in 1889. In 1906 Mr. Anderson was appointed an advocate depute, an office he still holds. In 1905 he published a book on the Criminal Law of Scotland, and he also wrote most of the criminal articles in Green's Encyclopædia. He is an adviser on registration questions to the Scottish Liberal Association. In 1906 he unsuccessfully contested North Ayrshire.

South (18,272).—No change.
*Beale, W. P. (L.)	..	8,833
McIntyre, T. W. (U.)	..	6,793

Liberal majority	..	2,040

1906.—L., 7,853 ; U., 6,611—L. maj., 1,242.
1900.—U., 6,615 ; L., 5,753—U. maj., 862.
1895.—U. maj., 550 ; 1892, L. maj., 197 ; 1886, U. maj., 5.

Mr. W. P. BEALE was educated at Heidelberg and Paris, called to the Bar at Lincoln's Inn in 1867, became a Bencher in 1892, and is an F.G.S. and F.C.S. as well as a K.C. Since retiring from regular practice he has devoted much time to geological and chemical investigations. Before his election for South Ayrshire he unsuccessfully contested North Warwickshire, Central Birmingham, and Aston Manor.

BANFFSHIRE (8,181).—No change.
*Waring, Capt. W. (L.)	..	4,066
Crabb-Watt, J. (U.)	..	2,053

Liberal majority	..	2,013

By-election, Feb., 1907, L., 3,901 ; U., 1,892—L. maj., 2,009.
1906.—L., 4,101 ; U., 1,901—L. maj., 2,200.
1900.—L., 2,768 ; U., 2,470—L. maj., 298.
1895.—L. maj., 510 ; 1892, L. maj., 869 ; 1886, L. maj., 1,189.

CAPTAIN WALTER WARING, son of the late Mr. C. Waring, M.P. for Poole, was born in London in 1876, educated at Eton, and in 1901 married a daughter of the 10th Marquis of Tweeddale. He joined the 1st Life Guards, 1897, was captain in 1904, and retired in 1906 ; served in South Africa, 1899-1900, and was mentioned in despatches ; and was Master of the Horse to the Lord Lieutenant of Ireland, 1906-7. He is J.P. for Berwickshire and captain of the Lothians and Border Horse. In 1906 he contested Wigtownshire and was elected for Banffshire at a by-election in 1907.

BERWICKSHIRE (5,674).—No change.
*Tennant, H. J. (L.)	..	2,992
Seton-Karr, Sir H. (U.)	..	2,060

Liberal majority	..	932

1906.—L., 2,975 ; U., 1,624—L. maj., 1,351.
1900.—L., 2,518 ; U., 1,968—L. maj., 550.
1895.—L., 2,673 ; U., 2,166—L. maj., 507.
1892.—L., 2,704 ; U., 1,956—L. maj., 748.
1886.—L., 2,778 ; U., 1,177—L. maj., 1,601.

Mr. HAROLD JOHN TENNANT, who has represented Berwickshire since 1894, is the youngest son of the late Sir Charles Tennant and brother-in-law of Mr. Asquith; born in 1865 and educated at Eton, and Trinity College, Cambridge, was appointed Parliamentary Secretary to the Board of Trade in January, 1909, and has always been specially interested in questions relating to factory and workshop administration and inspection; his wife was Miss Margaret Edith Abraham, formerly H.M. Superintendent Inspector of Factories.

BUTESHIRE (3,562).—UNIONIST GAIN.

Hope, H. (U.)	1,531
*Lamont, N. (L.)	1,372
Unionist majority	159

1906.—L., 1,637 ; U., 1,517—L. maj., 120.
1900.—U., 1,241 ; L., 1,046—U. maj., 195.
1895.—U. unop. ; 1892, U. maj., 453 ; 1886, U. maj., 545.

Mr. HARRY HOPE, of Barney Hill, Dunbar, eldest son of Mr. James Hope, Eastbarns, was born in 1865, and was educated at Edinburgh University. He has taken an active part in county administration, and is a member of Dunbar Town Council. The candidate is himself the tenant of two farms, and as an agricultural authority he has occupied several important positions. He is a member of the Scottish Chamber of Agriculture, and acted as president of that body in 1908 ; he was a member of the Scottish Agricultural Commission which visited Canada, and at present he is a member of a Departmental Committee on Agriculture appointed by the Secretary for Scotland.

CAITHNESS-SHIRE (3,944).—No change.

*Harmsworth, R. Leicester (L.)	2,643
Strain, L. H. (U.)	590
Liberal majority	2,053

1906.—L., 2,686 ; U., 483—L. maj., 2,203.
1900.—L., 1,189 ; U., 1,161 ; L., 673 ; L., 141—maj. of successful L. over U., 28.
1895.—L. maj., 1,300 ; 1892, L. maj., 1,441 ; 1886, L. maj., 1,450.

Mr. ROBERT LEICESTER HARMSWORTH, who was born in 1870, is the fourth son of the late Mr. Alfred Harmsworth, and brother of Lord Northcliffe. He was at one time a director of the Amalgamated Press (Limited), and some years ago travelled round the world, visiting the principal British Colonies. His representation of Caithness dates from 1900, and he was actively associated with the formation of the Liberal League.

CLACKMANNAN AND KINROSS (8,103).—No change.

*Wason, Rt. Hon. E. (L.)	3,971
Constable, N. B. (U.)	2,703
Liberal majority	1,268

1906.—L., 4,027 ; U., 2,648—L. maj., 1,379.
1900.—L., 3,284 ; U., 2,933—L. maj., 351.
1895.—L. maj., 545 ; 1892, L. maj., 1,614 ; 1886, L. maj., 1,315.

Mr. EUGENE WASON, born in 1846, is the son of Mr. Rigby Wason, formerly M.P. for Ipswich, He was educated at Rugby, and Wadham College, Oxford (M.A. 1870), was called to the Bar by the Middle Temple 1870, and went the Northern Circuit. In 1876 he was admitted solicitor, and until 1885 was partner in the firm of Williams, James, and Wason. For four years he was assistant examiner in common law to the Law Society. In 1885 he was elected for South Ayrshire, but was defeated at the election in the following year. He was again elected in 1892 and defeated in 1895. He has represented Clackmannan and Kinross since December, 1899.

DUMBARTONSHIRE (18,399).—No change.

*White. J. D. (L.)	8,640
Brock, H. (U.)	7,607
Liberal majority	1,033

1906.—L., 7,404 ; U., 6,937—L. maj., 467.
1900.—U., 6,083 ; L., 5,393—U. maj., 690.
1895.—U. maj., 33 ; 1892, L. maj., 293 ; 1886, U. maj., 32.

Mr. JAMES DUNDAS WHITE was born in 1866 and was educated at Rugby, and Trinity College, Cambridge ; is a barrister (called in 1891), and the author of works on the Merchant Shipping and Marine Insurance Acts and on economic and legal subjects.

DUMFRIESSHIRE (9,651).—No change.

*Molteno, P. A. (L.)	4,666
Murray, W. (U.)	4,091
Liberal majority	575

1906.—L., 4,814 ; U., 3,431—L. maj., 1,383.
1900.—U., 4,124 ; L., 3,675—U. maj., 449.
1895.—L., 3,965 ; U., 3,952—L. maj., 13.
1892.—U., 4,123 ; L., 3,849—U. maj., 274.
1886.—U., 4,106 ; L., 3,252—U. maj., 854.

Mr. PERCY ALPORT MOLTENO is the second son of Sir John Charles Molteno, the first Premier of Cape Colony. Born in Edinburgh in 1861, he was educated at the Cape of Good Hope University and at Trinity College, Cambridge. He married a daughter of Sir Donald Currie, and is a member of the ship-owning firm of Donald Currie and Co. He was called to the Bar by the Inner Temple in 1886.

EDINBURGHSHIRE.

MID LOTHIAN (17,141).—No change.

†Elibank, Master of (L.)	9,062
Elphinstone, Hon. M. W. (U.)	5,427
Liberal majority	3,635

1906.—L., 8,348 ; U., 5,131—L. maj., 3,217.
1900.—L., 5,804 ; U., 5,490—L. maj., 314.
1895, L. maj., 459 ; 1892, L. maj., 690 ; 1886, L. unop.

The Hon. ALEXANDER WILLIAM CHARLES OLIPHANT MURRAY, Master of Elibank, who represented Peebles and Selkirk in the last Parliament, is the eldest son of Lord Elibank, and was born in 1870, and educated at Cheltenham. From 1892 to 1895 he was assistant private secretary at the Colonial Office, and has served as Comptroller to his Majesty's Household and as Scottish Liberal Whip. Last year he was appointed Under Secretary for India. He has served as lieutenant in the Lothians and Berwickshire Yeomanry Cavalry.

ELGIN AND NAIRN (5,748).—No change.

| *Williamson, Sir A. (L.) | .. | 2,917 |
| Glyn, R. G. C. (U.) | .. | 1,734 |

| Liberal majority | .. | 1,183 |

1906.—L., 3,006 ; U., 1,546—L. maj., 1,460.
1900.—U., 2,334 ; L., 2,159—U. maj., 175.
1895.—U. maj., 128 ; 1892, L. maj., 545 ; 1886, L. maj., 119.

SIR ARCHIBALD WILLIAMSON is a partner in the firm of Balfour, Williamson, and Co., merchants and shipowners, of London and Liverpool. He is the eldest son of the late Mr. Stephen Williamson, who sat in the House of Commons as a Scottish Liberal member, and a grandson of Thomas Guthrie, the eminent Free Church divine. He contested Elgin and Nairn unsuccessfully in 1900, and was elected in 1906. He received a baronetcy last year.

FIFE (2).
EAST (10,372).—No change.

| *Asquith, Right Hon. H. H. (L.) | .. | .. | 5,242 |
| Sprot, Col. A. (U.).. | .. | 3,183 |

| Liberal majority | .. | 2,059 |

1906.—L., 4,723 ; U., 3,279—L. maj., 1,444.
1900.—L., 4,141 ; U., 2,710—L. maj., 1,431.
1895.—L. maj., 716 ; 1892, L. maj., 294 ; 1886, L. maj., 374.

Mr. HERBERT HENRY ASQUITH has sat in the House of Commons since 1886, and has there realized the prophecy of his contemporaries at the City of London School and at Balliol, where he had a distinguished career, that he would "go far"; in the Liberal Administration of 1892-95 he was Home Secretary ; after ten years in the political "wilderness" became Chancellor of the Exchequer in December, 1905, and, in his Budget of 1908, made provision for the inauguration of old-age pensions ; in April of the same year took office as Prime Minister, on the retirement of Sir H. Campbell-Bannerman ; a brilliant debater and speaker, with unsurpassed powers of lucid expression and exposition.

WEST (17,267).—No change.

*Hope, J. D. (L.)	..	..	6,159
Adamson, R. (Lab.)	..	4,736
Ralston, Gavin W. (U.)	..	1,994

| Liberal majority over Labour | 1,423 |

1906.—L., 6,692 ; U., 1,776—L. maj., 4,916.
1900.—L. 4,352 ; U., 2,374—L. maj., 1,978.
1895.—L. maj., 1,754 ; 1892, L. maj., 3,582 ; 1886, L. unop.

Mr. JOHN DEANS HOPE was born at Duddington, Mid Lothian, in 1860 and was educated at Fettes College and Edinburgh University. He is a chartered accountant and stockbroker. He unsuccessfully contested West Perthshire in 1895.

FORFARSHIRE (13,175).—No change.

| *Falconer, J. (L.) | .. | .. | 6,789 |
| Blackburn, R. F. L. (U.).. | 4,284 |

| Liberal majority | .. | 2,505 |

By-election, March, 1909, L., 6,422 ; U., 3,970—L. maj., 2,452.
1906.—L., 6,796 ; U., 3,277—L. maj., 3,159.
1900.—L., 4,962 ; U., 4,714—L. maj., 248.
1895.—L. maj., 441 ; 1892, L. maj., 866 ; 1886, U. maj., 407.

Mr. JAMES FALCONER, Writer to the Signet, was born in Forfarshire in 1856, and was educated at Arbroath High School and Edinburgh University. He was returned for this constituency on the elevation of Lord Pentland to the Peerage in 1909.

HADDINGTONSHIRE (7,961).—No change.

| *Haldane, Right Hon. R. B. (L.) | .. | .. | .. | 3,771 |
| Blyth, B. H. (U.) .. | .. | 3,026 |

| Liberal majority | .. | 745 |

1906.—L., 3,469 ; U., 2,289—L. maj., 1,180.
1900.—L., 2,668 ; U., 2,290—L. maj., 378.
1895.—L. maj., 580 ; 1892, L. maj., 293 ; 1886, L. maj., 963.

Mr. RICHARD BURDON HALDANE is one of the most gifted and versatile members of the House of Commons ; he is a lawyer, philosopher, theologian, man of science, educationist, and military expert ; can discourse learnedly, eloquently, and lengthily on these and all other phases of human thought and effort ; Lord Rosebery has described him as "the brain of the Empire," and others, with perhaps just a touch of envy, as "omniscient"; a Liberal Imperialist, out of sympathy with the bulk of his party on the South African War and the policy of Mr. Balfour's Education Bill of 1902, his inclusion in 1905 in Sir H. Campbell-Bannerman's Cabinet as Secretary of State for War came as a surprise ; his policy at the War Office, of which the most striking feature has been the creation of the Territorial Force, has given him a high place among military reformers and administrators ; his watchwords are "clear thinking" and "efficiency."

INVERNESS-SHIRE (9,951).—No change.

| *Dewar, Sir J. A. (L.) .. | .. | 4,599 |
| Macleod, Sir R. (U.) | .. | 2,774 |

| Liberal majority | .. | 1,825 |

1906.—L., 3,918 ; U., 1,810—L. maj., 2,108.
1900.—L., 3,168 ; U., 2,867—L. maj., 301.
1895.—U. maj., 100 ; 1892, L. maj., 329 ; 1886, U. unop.

SIR JOHN ALEXANDER DEWAR, the first baronet, created 1907, was born in Perth in 1856, and in 1884 married, first, a daughter of Mr. Dod, of Gospetry, and, secondly, in 1905, a daughter of the late Mr. Henry Holland. He is chairman of John Dewar and Sons (Limited), distillers, Perth, and was Lord Provost of the City in 1893-9. Has represented the county in Parliament since 1900.

KINCARDINESHIRE (7,179).—No change.

| *Murray, Capt. the Hon. A. C. (L.) | .. | .. | 3,926 |
| Pearson, R. B. (U.) | .. | 1,891 |

| Liberal majority | .. | 2,035 |

By-election, April, 1908, L., 3,661 ; U., 1,963—L. maj., 1,698.
1906.—L., 3,877 ; U., 1,524—L. maj., 2,253.
1900.—L., 3,092 ; U., 1,536—L. maj., 1,556.
1895.—L. maj., 563 ; 1892, L. maj., 1,068 ; 1886, L. unop.

CAPTAIN ARTHUR CECIL MURRAY is the fourth son of Lord Elibank and brother of the Master of Elibank. Born in 1879, he entered the Army in 1898 and received the China medal for service with the expeditionary force in 1900. He has also seen service on the Indian frontier.

KIRKCUDBRIGHTSHIRE (5,878).—
Unionist Gain.

Stewart, Sir M. J. McT. (U.)	2,661
*McMicking, Major (L.) ..	2,620
Unionist majority ..	41

1906.—L., 2,715 ; U., 2,418—L. maj., 297.
1900.—U., 2,784 ; L., 2,181—U. maj., 603.
1895.—U. maj., 170 ; 1892, U. maj., 31 ; 1886, U. maj., 65.

Sir Mark John MacTaggart Stewart was born in 1834, and educated at Winchester College and Oxford. He was called to the Bar by the Inner Temple in 1862, and his connexion with Westminster goes back to 1874. In that year he was returned by Wigtown Burghs, a constituency which gave him a strangely varied experience in 1880, when after a defeat by 12 votes, he in turn beat his opponent on his appointment as Lord Advocate, only to be unseated later on petition. At each of the five contests preceding 1906 he was faithfully retained as the representative of his present constituency. He has travelled all over the world, and is a large landowner.

LANARKSHIRE (6).
Govan (17,994).—Liberal Gain.

Hunter, W. (L.)	6,556
*Duncan, R. (U.)	5,127
Brownlie, J. T. (Lab.) ..	3,545
Liberal majority ..	1,429

1906.—U., 5,224 ; L., 5,096 ; Lab., 4,212—U. maj. over L., 128.
1900.—L., 5,744 ; U., 5,580—L. maj., 164.
1895.—L. maj. over U., 261 ; 1892, L. maj., 1,000 ; 1886, U. maj., 362.

Mr. William Hunter is a native of Ayrshire and was educated at Ayr Academy ; admitted a member of the Faculty of Advocates in 1889 and took silk in 1905 ; has one of the largest practices at the Scottish Bar.

Mid (17,803).—No change.

Whitehouse, J. H. (L.) ..	5,792
Pickering, J. J. (U.) ..	5,401
Smillie, R. (Lab.)	3,864
Liberal majority ..	391

1906.—L., 7,246 ; U., 4,470 ; Ind., 758—L. maj. over U., 2,776.
1900.—L., 5,267 ; U., 5,075—L. maj., 192.
1895.—L. maj., 71 ; 1892, L. maj., 1,122 ; 1886, L. maj., 870.

Mr. John Howard Whitehouse, after a University career, was for a time engaged in organizing social schemes on behalf of Messrs. Cadbury ; later he was secretary of the Carnegie Dunfermline Trust and was brought into close touch with the problems of mining and other industries in the East of Scotland ; for some two years was resident in East London as secretary of Toynbee Hall, a secretary of the Ruskin Union, and editor of the *Saint George Quarterly Review* ; well known for his interest in boys, being hon. secretary of the National League of Workers among Boys, and a member of the Departmental Committee on Child Labour ; recently appointed Warden of the Manchester University Society, which he resigned in January, 1910, in view of his candidature.

North-East (21,811).—No change.

Wilson, T. F. (L.)	9,105
Wilson, J. R. (U.)	7,012
Sullivan, J. (Lab.).. ..	2,160
Liberal majority ..	2,093

1906.—L., 6,436 ; U., 4,838 ; Lab., 4,658—L. maj. over U., 1,598.
1900.—L., 7,120 ; U., 5,567—L. maj., 1,553.
1895.—L. maj., 537 ; 1892, L. maj., 97 ; 1886, L. maj., 279.

Mr. T. F. Wilson is a member of the firm of Wilson and Chalmers, writers, Glasgow ; has taken an active interest in county affairs and for 15 years has represented the Uddingston district on Lanark County Council ; was for many years Liberal election agent for the Camlachie Division of Glasgow, and acted in a similar capacity in the Central Division of Glasgow for the late Sir A. M. Torrance and for Mr. Gibson Bowles at the by-election in March last.

North-West (20,274).—Liberal Gain.

Pringle, W. M. R. (L.) ..	8,422
*Mitchell-Thomson, W. (U.)	7,528
Small, R. (Lab.)	1,718
Liberal majority ..	894

1906.—U., 5,588 ; L., 4913 ; Lab., 3,291—U. maj., over L., 675.
1900.—L., 5,505 ; U., 5,214—L. maj., 291.
1895.—L. maj., 97 ; 1892, U. maj., 81 ; 1886, L. maj., 332.

Mr. W. M. R. Pringle was born at Gordon, Berwickshire, in 1874, and educated at Garnethill School and Glasgow University, where he graduated with first-class honours in classics and history ; called to the Bar by the Middle Temple in 1904 ; has been a member of the executive of the Scottish Liberal Council and president of the Glasgow Students' Representative Council, the Dialectic Society, and the University Liberal Club.

Partick (23,300).—No change.

*Balfour, R. (L.)	10,093
Maconochie, A. W. (U.)..	9,522
Liberal majority ..	571

1906.—L., 9,477 ; U., 7,960—L. maj., 1,517.
1900.—U., 6,950 ; L., 4,717—U. maj., 2,233.
1895.—U. maj., 1,207 ; 1892, U. maj., 727 ; 1886, U. maj., 801.

Mr. Robert Balfour is a partner in the firm of Balfour, Williamson, and Co., foreign merchants, of Liverpool and London. Born in Largo, Fifeshire, in 1844, educated at Madras College, St. Andrews, he entered in 1863 the office of the firm with which he is associated. From 1869 until 1893 he represented the firm in San Francisco ; he passed the ensuing six years in Liverpool, and then came to London.

He defeated Mr. J. Parker Smith in the Partick Division at the General Election in 1906.

SOUTH (10,618).—No change.

*Menzies, Sir W. (L.) ..	5,346
Mitchell, J. D. (U.) ..	3,715
Liberal majority ..	1,631

1906.—L., 4,816 ; U., 3,541—L. maj., 1,275.
1900.—U., 3,968 ; L., 3,516—U. maj., 452.
1895.—U. maj., 230 ; 1892, U. maj., 368 ; 1886, U. maj., 18.

SIR WALTER MENZIES is the eldest son of the late Mr. James Menzies, who founded the Phœnix Tube Works at Rutherglen, Glasgow. He was engaged in the business of the firm of James Menzies and Co. until 1898 and had occasion in connexion with it to travel extensively in Europe and America. He was candidate for the Central Division of Glasgow in 1892 and unsuccessfully contested his present constituency in 1900. He was knighted last June.

LINLITHGOWSHIRE (11,810).—No change.

*Ure, Rt. Hon. A., K.C., (L.)..	6,451
Smith, W. C., K.C., (U.) ..	3,536
Liberal majority ..	2,915

1906.—L., 5,282 ; U., 2,761—L. maj., 2,521.
1900.—L. 3,827 ; U., 3,034—L. maj., 793.
1895.—L. maj., 607 ; 1892, L. maj., 161 ; 1886, L. maj., 733.

Mr. ALEXANDER URE, K.C., the Lord Advocate in the last Administration, has been more active than any other politician during the past few months in carrying on the propaganda work of his party from public platforms throughout the country. His name, indeed, bids fair to pass into political nomenclature in connexion with the Budget controversy and the bitterness engendered by what is known as " the old-age pension lie," arising from a declaration made by Mr. Ure in one of his speeches that the aged poor were nervous and apprehensive lest they should lose their pensions if the Budget were thrown out and there was a change of Government. He was born in 1853 and was educated at Glasgow and Edinburgh Universities. Generally, it may be said that he holds advanced political views, being especially interested in the subject of and values. He was made a Privy Councillor in 1909.

ORKNEY AND SHETLAND (7,115).—No change.

*Wason, J. C. (L.)	4,117
Hemsley, T. W. (U.) ..	994
Liberal majority ..	3,123

1906.—L., 3,837 ; U., 1,021—L. maj., 2,816.
1900.—U., 2,057 ; L., 2,017—U. maj., 40.
1895.—L. maj., 781 ; 1892, L. maj., 1,007 ; 1886, L. maj., 97.

Mr. JOHN CATHCART WASON, who was born in 1848, and educated at Laleham and Rugby, was called to the Bar by the Middle Temple. For a number of years he was engaged in sheep-farming in New Zealand, and held a seat in the New Zealand House of Representatives. He was elected as a Liberal Unionist for his present constituency in 1900, but resigned in 1902, and was re-elected then, and again in 1906, as a Liberal.

PEEBLES AND SELKIRK (4,032).—No change.

Younger, W. (L.)	1,941
Steel, S. Strang (U.) ..	1,735
Liberal majority ..	206

1906.—L., 1,955 ; U., 1,549—L. maj., 406.
1900.—U., 1,598 ; L.,*1,387—U. maj., 211.
1895.—U., 1,563 ; L., 1,509—U. maj., 54.
1892.—U., 1,603 ; L., 1,367—U. maj., 236.
1886.—U., 1,375 ; L., 1,325—U. maj., 50.

Mr. WILLIAM YOUNGER contested Orkney and Shetland in 1892, and sat for Stamford, Lincs, as a Unionist from 1895 until 1906. He resides at Auchen Castle, Dumfries.

PERTHSHIRE (2).

EAST (7,902).—No change.

Young, W. (L.)	3,884
Murray, Hon. A. D. (U.)..	2,703
Liberal majority ..	1,181

1906.—L., 3,738 ; U., 2,648—L. maj., 1,090.
1900.—L., 3,185 ; U., 2,143—L. maj., 1,042.
1895.—L. maj., 875 ; 1892, L. maj., 1,049 ; 1886, L. maj., 1,309.

Mr. WILLIAM YOUNG, the son of an Aberdeenshire farmer, was born at Brackley Farm, Glenmuick, in 1863, and educated at Ballater Public School ; appointed in 1891 to represent the interests of Messrs. Mathison and Co., bankers and merchants, of London, in Mexico City, where he established himself as a merchant ; resides in this country, paying occasional visits to Mexico.

WEST (8,547).—UNIONIST GAIN.

Tullibardine, The Marquis of (U.)	3,864
Morrison, T. B., K.C. (L.) ..	3,566
Unionist majority ..	298

1906.—L., 3,890 ; U., 3,087—L. maj., 803.
1900.—U., 3,598 ; L., 2,913—U. maj., 685.
1895.—U., 3,379 ; L., 3,087—U. maj., 292.
1892.—U., 3,422 ; L., 3,053—U. maj., 369.
1886.—U., 3,269 ; L., 2,329—U. maj., 940.

The MARQUIS OF TULLIBARDINE, born in 1871, is the eldest surviving son of the Duke of Atholl. After education at Eton he held a lieutenant in the 3rd Battalion Royal Highlanders (Black Watch), and afterwards transferred to the Royal Horse Guards. He served with the Egyptian Cavalry as Staff officer to Colonel Broadwood during the Nile Expedition, 1898, being present at the battles of Atbara and Khartum, and twice mentioned in despatches ; and in South Africa, where he was first attached to the Royal Dragoons, and afterwards commanded the 1st and 2nd Scottish Horse ; he was three times mentioned in despatches, and holds the Queen's medal with six clasps and the King's with two. He is M.V.O. and D.S.O.

RENFREWSHIRE (2).

EAST (20,947).—UNIONIST GAIN.

Gilmour, Capt. J. (U.) ..	9,645
*Laidlaw, Sir R. (L.) ..	8,771
Unionist majority ..	874

1906.—L., 6,896 ; U., 6,801—L. maj., 95.
1900 and 1895.—U. unop.
1892.—U. maj., 1,087 ; 1886, U. maj., 1,368.

CAPTAIN JOHN GILMOUR, the eldest son of Sir John Gilmour, of Montrave, was born in 1876, and educated at Edinburgh and Cambridge Universities ; served in the Imperial Yeomanry in South Africa ; major in the Fife and Forfar Yeomanry and a member of the Bodyguard of the Royal Company of Archers ; is largely interested in agriculture, and a member of several Scottish agricultural societies and organizations ; was for four years Master of the Fife Hounds ; opposed Mr. Asquith in East Fife in 1906.

WEST (13,900).—No change.

Greig, Col. (L.)	6,480
Cuninghame, J. C. (U.) ..	5,631
Liberal majority ..	849

1906.—L., 5,858 ; U., 4,490—L. maj., 1,368.
1900.—U., 4,323 ; L., 4,053—U. maj., 270.
1895.—U. maj., 603 ; 1892, U. maj., 451 ; 1886, U. maj., 553.

COLONEL JAMES WILLIAM GREIG, B.A., LL.B., who commands the London Scottish, is a barrister by profession, and was born in London in 1859 of Scottish parents. He is a son of the late Mr. John Borthwick Greig, W.S., and Parliamentary agent, of 18, Abingdon-street, Westminster, and grandson of the late Mr. James Greig, W.S., Edinburgh.

ROSS AND CROMARTY (8,211).—No change.

*Weir, J. Galloway (L.) ..	4,430
Maclean, N. (U.) ..	1,418
Liberal majority ..	3,012

1906.—L., 3,883 ; U., 1,771—L. maj., 2,112.
1900.—L., 3,554 ; U., 1,651—L. maj., 1,903.
1895.—L. maj., 863 ; 1892 L. maj., 758 ; 1886, L. maj., 3,066.

Mr. JAMES GALLOWAY WEIR was born in 1839, and is a retired manufacturer. He has been returned to the London County Council and is a member of the committee of the Scottish Corporation. In 1885 he unsuccessfully contested Falkirk Burghs, and went in 1892 to Ross and Cromarty, which has never wavered in its allegiance since. His inquiring mind has often made him a thorn in the flesh of the Scottish Office.

ROXBURGHSHIRE (6,025).—No change.

*Jardine, Sir J. (L.)	2,943
Scott, Lord Henry (U.) ..	2,626
Liberal majority ..	317

1906.—L., 2,829 ; U., 2,514—L. maj., 315.
1900.—U., 2,682 ; L., 2,323—U. maj., 359.
1895.—U. maj., 561 ; 1892, L. maj., 158 ; 1886, U. maj., 428.

SIR JOHN JARDINE was born in 1844 and educated at Christ's College, Cambridge, where he took the Chancellor's Gold Medal for English verse in 1864. In that year he entered the Bombay Civil Service, and in the later stages of a distinguished career became successively Judicial Commissioner of Burma, Chief Secretary to the Bombay Government, holding the Political, Secret, Educational, Persian, and Judicial portfolios, and a Judge of the High Court of Bombay. He acted as Chief Justice in 1895, and retired with a K.C.I.E. in 1897. Various writings on Burmese and Buddhist law and history have come from his pen.

STIRLINGSHIRE (20,144).—No change.

Chapple, A. (L.)	10,122
Horne, R. S. (U.)	6,417
Liberal majority ..	3,705

1906.—L., 9,475 ; U., 5,806—L. maj., 3,669.
1900.—U., 6,325 ; L., 6,023—U. maj., 302.
1895.—U. maj., 427 ; 1892, L. maj. over U., 746 ; 1886, L. maj., 707.

Dr. CHAPPLE is a native of New Zealand, but of Scottish descent, his mother having been born in Glasgow. He studied at Glasgow University, and at a later period took the diploma for public health at Dublin University. For 20 years afterwards he carried on a medical practice in New Zealand. In 1906 he retired from his profession, and he has since spent his time travelling and writing. He has had political experience as representative of the Tuapeka constituency in the Colonial Parliament.

SUTHERLAND (3,055).—No change.

*Morton, A. C. (L.)	1,607
Cameron of Lochiel (U.) ..	951
Liberal majority ..	656

1906.—L., 1,383 ; U., 933.—L. maj., 450.
1900.—U., 1,224 ; L., 752—U. maj., 472.
1895.—L. maj., 495 ; 1892, L. maj., 846 ; 1886, L. maj., 880.

Mr. ALPHEUS CLEOPHAS MORTON was born in Canada in 1840 and educated privately. He is an architect and surveyor, and has been a member of the Corporation of the City of London since 1882 ; a City Guardian, a member of the City and Guilds Institute, governor of St. Thomas's Hospital, and member of the Thames Conservancy Board. He contested Hythe in 1885, Christchurch in 1886, and represented Peterborough, 1889-95. He was returned for Sutherland in 1906.

WIGTOWNSHIRE (5,683).—No change.

*Dalrymple, Viscount (U.) ..	2,777
Macpherson, J. A. (L.) ..	2,142
Unionist majority ..	635

1906.—U., 2,866 ; L., 2,127—U. maj., 739.
1900 and 1895.—U. unop.
1892.—U. maj., 1,225 ; 1886, U. maj., 1,201.

VISCOUNT DALRYMPLE is the only son of the Earl of Stair. He was born in 1879, educated at Harrow and Sandhurst, and entered the Scots Guards. in 1898. He served in the South African War from 1900 to 1902.

IRELAND (CITIES AND BOROUGHS).

BELFAST (4).

EAST (16,330).—No change.
*Wolff, G. W. (U.)

1906.—U. unop.
1900.—U. unop.
1895.—U. unop. ; 1892, U. unop.; 1886, U. maj., 3,816.

Mr. GUSTAV WILHELM WOLFF was formerly a member of the great Belfast shipbuilding firm of Harland and Wolff, and is now chairman of the Belfast Ropeworks Company and a director of the Union-Castle Steamship Company ; born at Hamburg in 1834, and educated first in that city and afterwards in Liverpool ; has sat for East Belfast since March, 1892.

NORTH (11,829).—No change.

Thompson, R. (U.)	6,275
Gageby, R. (Lab.)	3,951
Unionist majority	2,324

By-election, April, 1907—U., 6,021 ; Lab., 4,194—U. maj., 1,827.
1906.—U., 4,907 ; Lab., 4,616—U. maj., 291.
1900.—U., 4,172 ; Ind. U., 1,855—U. maj., 2,317.
1895.—U. unop. ; 1892, U. unop.
1886.—U., 4,522 ; Nat., 732—U. maj., 3,790.

Mr. ROBERT THOMPSON is engaged in the spinning trade in Belfast, where he has taken some part in local politics.

SOUTH (10,622).—No change.

Chambers, J., K.C. (U.)	5,772
*Sloan, T. H. (Ind. U.)	3,552
Unionist majority	2,220

1906.—Ind. U., 4,450 ; U., 3,634—Ind. U. maj., 816.
1900, 1895, 1892.—U. unop.
1886.—U., 4,542 ; Nat., 657—U. maj., 3,885.

Mr. JAMES CHAMBERS, K.C., is a leading member of the Irish Bar and resides in Dublin ; was educated at Dublin University and called to the Bar in 1886, and has been a prominent figure in local politics ; a member of the North-Eastern Circuit.

WEST (9,230).—No change.

*Devlin, J. (Nat.)	4,651
Carpenter, J. Boyd (U.)	4,064
Magee, P. J. (Ind. Nat.)	75
Nationalist majority	587

1906.—Nat., 4,138 ; U., 4,122 ; L., 153—Nat. maj. over U., 16.
1900 and 1895.—U. unop.
1892.—U., 4,266 ; Nat., 3,427—U. maj., 839.
1886.—Nat., 3,832 ; U., 3,729—Nat. maj., 103.

Mr. JOSEPH DEVLIN, who was born in 1872, made his entry at Westminster as the unopposed representative of North Kilkenny in 1902, being given the seat during his absence on a political mission in the United States. He was returned both by Kilkenny and by West Belfast in 1906, and decided to sit for his present constituency. For a long time he has been the recognized leader of the Belfast Nationalists and in the forefront of Nationalist politics. He is general secretary of the United Irish League of Great Britain and president of the executive council of the United Irish League in Belfast.

CORK CITY (2) (13,797).—No change.

O'Brien, W. (Ind. Nat.)	4,535
*Roche, A. (Nat.)	4,438
*Healy, M. (Ind. Nat.)	4,229
Murphy, Dr. W. (Nat.)	3,776
FitzGerald, Sir E. (Ind.)	2,061
Successful Ind. N. maj. over defeated N.	759
Successful N. maj. over defeated Ind. N.	202

By-election, 1909, Ind. Nat., 4,706 ; Nat., 3,547—Ind. Nat maj., 1,159.
1906.—Two Nats. unop.
1900.—Nat., 5,812 ; Nat., 5,513 ; Nat., 2,235 ; Nat., 1,985—Nat. maj., 3,278.
1895.—Nat., 5,327 ; Nat., 5,169 ; P., 4,994 ; P., 4,966—Nat. maj., 175.
1892.—Nat., 5,273 ; Nat., 4,759 ; P., 3,186 ; P., 3,077—Nat. maj., 1,573.
1886.—Two Nats. unop.

Mr. WILLIAM O'BRIEN, who has played a large part in Irish Nationalist politics and who founded the United Irish League, has had a chequered Parliamentary career ; has sat at different times for Mallow, South Tyrone, North-East Cork, and Cork City (twice) ; resigned his seat for the last-named constituency during the Session of 1909 ; born in 1852, and is a journalist and author.

Mr. AUGUSTINE ROCHE was born at Cork and educated privately ; was High Sheriff in 1902 and Lord Mayor of the city two years later ; unsuccessfully contested the constituency in 1895 and was elected in 1905 ; a wholesale wine merchant.

DUBLIN (4).

COLLEGE GREEN (8,739).—No change.

*Nannetti, J. P. (Nat.)	4,559
O'Connor, Major G. B. (U.)	1,239
Nationalist majority	3,320

1906.—N. unop.
1900.—N., 2,467 ; U., 2,173—N. maj., 294.
1895.—P. unop. ; 1892, P. maj. over U., 1,127 ; 1886, N. unop.

Mr. JOSEPH PATRICK NANNETTI, who is foreman printer on the *Freeman's Journal*, was born in Dublin in 1851, and educated at Baggot-street Convent and Christian Brothers' Schools, Dublin ; has been twice Lord Mayor of the city; has represented the College Green Division since 1900.

HARBOUR (9,038).—No change.
*Harrington, T. (Nat.).
1906.—Nat. maj., 2,766.
1900.—Nat. unop.
1895.—Nat. unop.; 1892, Parnellite maj. over Nat., 3,106; 1886, Nat. unop.

Mr. TIMOTHY HARRINGTON was born in 1851, educated at the Catholic University and Trinity College, Dublin, and is a barrister. He was at one time secretary of the Irish National League and a Parnellite, but in 1897 he took up an independent position as a Nationalist. He has been several times Lord Mayor of Dublin, and has represented the Harbour Division in Parliament since 1885. He was formerly proprietor of *United Ireland* and the *Kerry Sentinel*.

ST. PATRICK'S (8,882).—No change.
*Field, W. (Nat.).
1906.—Nat. unop.
1900.—Nat. unop.
1895.—Nat. unop.; 1892, Parnellite maj. over Nat., 2,584; 1886, Nat. unop.

Mr. WILLIAM FIELD, born at Blackrock in 1848, was educated at the Catholic University, St. Stephen's Green. He is a victualler, and president of the Irish Cattle Traders' and Stock Owners' Association, hon. secretary of the Dublin Victuallers' Association, vice-president of the National Federation of Meat Trades of the United Kingdom and of the Dublin Bimetallic League, a member of the Dublin Port Docks Board, and a governor of the Royal Irish Veterinary College. He has represented the division in Parliament since 1892.

ST. STEPHEN'S GREEN (7,099).—No change.
Brady, P. J. (Nat.) 3,683
Conner, H. D., K.C. (U.).. 3,021

Nationalist majority .. 662
1906.—N., 4,055; U., 2,581—N. maj., 1,474.
1900.—N., 3,429; U., 2,873—N. maj., 556.
1895.—U. maj., 456; 1892, U. maj. over P., 15; 1886, N. maj., 2,443.

Mr. PATRICK J. BRADY is a solicitor residing in Kingstown, where he has a considerable practice, and a member of the Blackrock Urban Council.

GALWAY (2,306).—No change.
*Gwynn, S. L. (Nat.).
By-election, 1906.—Nat., 983; Devolutionist, 559—Nat. maj., 424.
1906.—Nat. unop.
1900.—U. maj., 119.
1895.—Nat. maj. over Parnellite, 131; 1892.—Nat. maj. over P., 51; 1886—Nat. unop.

Mr. STEPHEN LUCIUS GWYNN, the son of Dr. J. Gwynn, for several years Professor of Divinity in Trinity College, Dublin, was born in 1864, and educated at St. Columba's College, Rathfarnham, and Brasenose College, Oxford; was a teacher of classics and literature, and is a journalist and author; has represented the city since November, 1906.

KILKENNY (1,742).—No change.
*O'Brien, P. (Nat.).
1906.—Nat. unop.
1900.—Nat. unop.
1895.—Parnellite maj. over Nat., 14; 1892.—Nat. maj. over P., 140; 1886—Nat. unop.

Mr. PATRICK O'BRIEN, one of the Whips of the Nationalist Party in the House of Commons, has,

except for an interval of three years, been in Parliament since 1886; was born at Tullamore, and is an engineer; was imprisoned under the Crimes Act.

LIMERICK (4,686).—No change.
*Joyce, M. (N.) 2,137
Rice, J. H. (Ind. Nat.) .. 973

Nationalist majority .. 1,164
1906.—Nat. unop.
1900.—Nat., 2,521; U., 474—Nat. maj., 2,047.
1895.—P. unop; 1892, Nat. maj., 388; 1886, Nat. unop.

Mr. M. JOYCE, a pilot by occupation, has taken an active part in the affairs of the City of Limerick, of which he is an alderman; has represented Limerick since the year 1900.

LONDONDERRY (5,068).—No change.
*Hamilton, the Marquis of (U.) 2,435
Leslie, Shane (Nat.) .. 2,378

Unionist majority .. 57
1906.—U. unop.
1900.—U., 2,361; Nat., 2,294—U. maj., 67.
1895.—Nat., 2,033; U., 1,994—Nat. maj., 39.
1892.—U., 1,986; Nat., 1,960—U. maj., 26.
1886.—U., 1,781; Nat., 1,778—U. maj., 3.

The MARQUIS of HAMILTON is the eldest son of the Duke of Abercorn. Educated at Eton, he entered the 1st Life Guards in 1892, resigning as captain in 1903. Londonderry elected him in 1900, and he acted as Treasurer to the Household, 1903-1905, and as one of the Junior Opposition Whips during the late Parliament.

NEWRY (2,021).—No change.
*Mooney, J. J. (N.) 1,079
Cusack, J. (U.) 542

Nationalist majority .. 537
1906.—Nat. maj. over Nat., 66.
1900.—Nat., unop.
1895.—Nat. maj., 359; 1892, N. maj., 163; 1886, N. maj., 467.

Mr. JOHN J. MOONEY, who has had a seat in Parliament since 1900, first for Dublin County South and then for Newry, was born in 1874, and educated at Ushaw College, Durham, and Trinity College, Dublin; a member of both the Irish and the English Bars; takes a great interest in private Bill legislation; director of Mooney and Co., wine and spirit merchants, London.

WATERFORD (3,104).—No change.
*Redmond, J. (Nat.)
1906.—Nat. unop.
1900.—Nat. unop.
1895.—Parnellite maj. over Nat., 559; 1892, P. maj. over Nat., 383; 1886, Nat. unop.

Mr. JOHN EDWARD REDMOND is chairman of the Irish Party. He was born in 1856—eldest son of William Archer Redmond, who sat in Parliament for Wexford borough from 1872 till his death in 1880—and for a time was a clerk in the House of Commons. This position he resigned in 1881 on his election as a Nationalist for New Ross. When the Irish Party was split on the question of Mr. Parnell's leadership in December, 1890, he took sides with the Parnellites and succeeded to the leadership of this section of the Nationalists on the death of Mr. Parnell in October, 1891. In 1900 the Parnellites and Anti-Parnellites were re-united, and Mr. Redmond since then has been leader of the Nationalists. He was called to the Bar by Gray's Inn in 1886 and to the Irish Bar in 1887.

IRELAND (COUNTIES).

ANTRIM (4).
EAST (8,959).—No change.
*McCalmont, Col. J. M. (U.).
1906.—U., 4,496; L., 2,145—U. maj., 2,351.
1900.—U., 3,852; Ind. U., 2,653—U. maj., 929.
1895, 1892, 1886, U. unop.

COLONEL JAMES MARTIN MCCALMONT was born in 1847, and educated at Eton. He joined the 8th Hussars as cornet in 1886, retired as captain in 1874, and is now Hon. Colonel of the Royal Antrim Artillery. He has served as aide-de-camp to two Viceroys of Ireland—the late Duke of Marlborough and Earl Cowper. He is Deputy Grand Master of the Orangemen of Ireland. In 1885 he was first returned for East Antrim.

MID (7,219).—No change.
O'Neill, the Hon. A. (U.).
1906.—U., 3,367; Ind. U., 2,577—U. maj., 790.
1900.—U. unop.
1895.—U. unop.; 1892, U. unop.; 1886, U. maj. over Nat., 3,698.

The HON. ARTHUR EDWARD BRUCE O'NEILL is a new member. The eldest son and heir of Lord O'Neill, of Shane's Castle, Antrim, he was born in 1876, and married in 1902 Lady Annabel Crewe-Milnes, eldest daughter of the Earl of Crewe. He was educated at Eton and is captain and adjutant in the 2nd Life Guards. He served in the South African War, when he received a medal with three clasps.

NORTH (7,516).—UNIONIST GAIN.
Kerr-Smiley, P. (U.)	..	3,519
Baxter, Sir W. (L.)	..	3,135
Unionist majority	..	384

1906.—U., 3,757; U., 2,969—U. maj. over U., 788.
1900 and 1895.—U. unop.
1892.—U. maj., 2,639; 1886, U. maj., 2,519.

LIEUTENANT PETER KERR-SMILEY is the second son of the late Sir Hugh H. Smiley and brother of the present baronet, Sir John Smiley, who contested West Belfast at the last General Election. Lieutenant Kerr-Smiley was born in 1879, and is a lieutenant in the 21st Lancers (Reserve of Officers).

Mr. R. Glendinning was returned in 1906 as an Independent Liberal Unionist, but he crossed the floor of the House before the close of the Parliament.

SOUTH (9,900).—No change.
*Craig, C. C. (U.)	..	5,310
Clow, W. M. (L.)	..	2,340
Unionist majority	..	2,970

1906.—U. unop.
1900.—U., 3,674; Ind. U., 3,081—U. maj., 593.
1895, 1892, and 1886.—U. unop.

Mr. CHARLES CURTIS CRAIG, a brother of Captain Craig, M.P. for East Down, was born in 1869 and educated at Clifton College; has represented the division since 1903.

ARMAGH (3).
MID (7,072).—No change.
*Lonsdale, J. B. (U.).
1906.—U. unop.
1900.—U. unop.
1895.—U. unop.; 1892, U. unop.; 1886, U. maj. over Nat., 1,638.

Mr. JOHN BROWNLEE LONSDALE, who is hon. secretary to the Irish Unionist Party, was born in 1849, and has sat for Mid Armagh since 1900.

NORTH (7,581).—No change.
*Moore, W. (U.).
By-election, 1906.—U., 4,229; Ind. U., 1,443—U. maj., 2,796.
1906.—U. unop.
1900.—U. maj. over Ind. U., 1,111.
1895.—U. unop.; 1892, U. unop.; 1886, U. maj. over Nat., 2,893.

Mr. WILLIAM MOORE is a K.C. (Ireland). He was born in 1864. From 1899 to 1905 he represented North Antrim, and for a time was private secretary (unpaid) to the Chief Secretary for Ireland. He was defeated in North Antrim, for which he was returned in 1899, in 1906, and in November of the same year was elected for North Armagh.

SOUTH (6,810).—No change.
*O'Neill, Dr. C. (Nat.).
By-election, 1909.—Nat. unop.
1906.—Nat. unop.
1900, Nat. maj. over Nat., 385.
1895.—Nat. maj. over U., 1,383; 1892, Nat. maj. over U., 1,197; 1886, Nat. unop.

DR. CHARLES O'NEILL, who was born in 1844, was first returned for the division at the 1909 by-election. He is a doctor in practice at Coatbridge, near Glasgow.

CARLOW (5,905).—No change.
Molloy, M. (Nat.)
By-election, 1908, Nat. unop.
1906, 1900, Nat. unop.
1895, Nat. maj. over U., 2,406; 1892, Nat. maj. over U., 2,925; 1886, Nat. unop.

Mr. MICHAEL MOLLOY is a trader in Carlow town. He succeeds in the representation of the county Mr. MacMorrough Kavanagh—returned at the by-election of 1908—who retired on account of his disagreement with the Irish Party on the question of the Budget.

CAVAN (2).
EAST (8,981).—No change.
*Young, S. (Nat.).
1906.—Nat. unop.
1900.—Nat. unop.
1895.—Nat. unop.; 1892, Nat. maj. over U., 4,664; 1886, Nat. unop.

Mr. SAMUEL YOUNG was born in 1822 and educated at the Old Presbyterian College, Belfast. He is a whisky distiller in Belfast and chairman of a firm of millers and bakers. He was first returned for East Cavan in 1892. He was the oldest member of the House of Commons in the late Parliament.

WEST (8,605).—No change.
*Kennedy, V. P. (Nat.).

1906.—Nat. unop.
1900.—Nat. unop.
1895.—Nat. unop.; 1892, Nat. maj. over U., 4,508; 1886, Nat. unop.

Mr. VINCENT PAUL KENNEDY was born in 1876, and is a solicitor in Cavan. He has sat for West Cavan since 1904.

CLARE (2).
EAST (8,709).—No change.
*Redmond, W. (Nat.).

1906.—Nat. unop.
1900.—Nat. unop.
1895.—Parnellite maj. over Nat., 57; 1892, P. maj. over Nat., 444; 1886, Nat. unop.

Mr. WILLIAM REDMOND, who is the younger brother of Mr. J. Redmond, the leader of the Irish Party, was born in 1861. He was first returned to Parliament in 1883, and has sat uninterruptedly since then for different Irish constituencies.

WEST (8,834).—No change.
*Lynch, A. (Nat.).

By-election, 1909.—Nat. unop.
1906.—Nat. unop.
1900.—Nat unop.
1895.—Nat. maj. over Parnellite, 403; 1892, P. maj. over Nat., 1,007; 1886, Nat. unop.

Mr. ARTHUR LYNCH, journalist and author, was first returned for West Clare at the by-election of 1909. He was born at Ballarat, Victoria, in 1861, and is an M.A. and C.E. of Melbourne University. After practising for a short time as an engineer in Melbourne he came to Europe, and lived in London and Paris as a journalist. During the South African war he was "Colonel of the Irish Brigade No. II." on the Boer side. In November, 1901, he was elected M.P. for Galway City, defeating Sir (then Mr.) Horace Plunkett, who stood as a Unionist. On coming to London he was arrested, convicted of high treason on January 23, 1903, and condemned to death. The sentence was commuted to penal servitude for life. On January 23, 1904, Mr. Lynch was released on licence, and received a free pardon from the Crown on June 10, 1907. Among the books he has written are "Our Poets!" (1895) and "Human Documents" (1896).

CORK (7).
EAST (6,316).—No change.
*Donelan, Captain A. J. C. (Nat.).

1906.—Nat. unop.
1900.—Nat. unop.
1895, 1892, 1886, Nat. unop.

CAPTAIN ANTHONY JOHN CHARLES DONELAN is the only son of the late Colonel Anthony Donelan, 48th Regiment, and was born in 1846. He was educated privately and at Sandhurst, and has served in the Army. Since 1892 he has represented East Cork. He is Chief Whip of the Irish Party.

MID (6,599).—No change.

*Sheehan, D. D. (Ind. Nat.) ..	2,824
Fallon, W. (Nat.)	1,999
Ind. Nationalist majority ..	825

1906, 1900, 1895, 1892, and 1886.—Nat. unop.

Mr. DANIEL D. SHEEHAN, who was born in 1874, is a journalist and law student; president of Irish Land and Labour Association, and connected officially with the United Irish League; has sat for Mid Cork since 1901; resigned his seat in January, 1907, as a protest against his exclusion from the Nationalist Party, and was re-elected unopposed.

NORTH (6,655).—IND. NATIONALIST GAIN.

Guiney, P. (Ind. Nat.) ..	2,888
Barry, Michael (Nat.) ..	1,798
Ind. Nationalist majority ..	1,090

1906, 1900, 1895, 1892, and 1886.—Nat. unop.

Mr. P. GUINEY belongs to the farming class, has held various offices on local councils, and is a member of the United Irish League.

NORTH-EAST (6,634).—INDEPENDENT NATIONALIST GAIN.

O'Brien, W., M.P. (Ind. Nat.)	2,984
*Abraham, W. (Nat.) ..	1,510
Ind. Nationalist majority	1,474

1906, 1900, 1895, 1892, and 1886.—Nat. unop.

Mr. WILLIAM O'BRIEN was also returned as an Independent Nationalist at the head of the poll for Cork City. He must inform the Speaker for which constituency he will sit when Parliament meets. Brief details of his Parliamentary career appear on page 104 under "Cork City."

SOUTH (6,199).—No change.
*Barry, E. (Nat.).

1906.—Nat. unop.
1900.—Nat. unop.
1895, 1892, 1886, Nat. unop.

Mr. EDWARD BARRY was born in 1852, and is a farmer. He has sat for South Cork since 1906.

SOUTH-EAST (6,734).—No change.

*Crean, E. (Ind. Nat.).. ..	2,300
Burke, J. M. (Nat.) ..	1,757
Ind. Nationalist majority..	543

1906.—Nat. unop.
1900.—Nat. maj. over Nat., 528.
1895 and 1886.—Nat. unop; 1892, Nat. maj., 3,417.

Mr. EUGENE CREAN, who has had a seat in Parliament since 1892, first for the Ossory Division of Queen's County and then for South-East Cork, was born in 1856, and is closely associated with the municipal and industrial life of Cork, of which he was Mayor in 1899.

WEST (5,727).—IND. NATIONALIST GAIN.

*Gilhooly, J. (Ind. Nat.) ..	2,155
O'Leary, D. (Nat.) ..	1,382
Ind. Nationalist majority ..	773

1906, 1900, 1895, and 1886.—Nat. unop.
1892.—Nat. maj., 2,826.

Mr. JAMES GILHOOLY, in business at Bantry as a draper, is the son of an officer in the Coastguard Service, and was born in 1845; has sat for the West Division of the county since 1885, and was imprisoned three years after his first election under the Crimes Act.

DONEGAL (4).
EAST (6,454).—No change.

Kelly, E. (Nat.)	3,415
Harrison, T. (U.)	2,202
Nationalist majority ..	1,213

1906.—Nat. unop.
1900.—Nat., 3,113; U., 2,660—Nat. maj., 453.
1895.—Nat. maj., 663; 1892, Nat. maj., 763; 1886, Nat. maj., 1,421.

Mr. EDWARD KELLY is a young man who has just completed a successful career at the Royal University of Ireland.

NORTH (6,650).—No change.
*O'Doherty, P. (Nat.).

1906.—Nat. unop.
1900.—Nat. maj. over Nat., 950.
1895.—Nat. unop.; 1892, Nat. maj. over Parnellite, 2,711; 1886, Nat. maj. over U., 3,349.

Mr. PHILIP O'DOHERTY is a solicitor practising in Londonderry, and is 39 years old.

SOUTH (6,091).—No change.
*MacNeill, J. G. Swift (Nat.).

1906.—Nat. unop.
1900.—Nat. unop.
1895.—Nat. maj. over U., 2,301; 1892, Nat. maj., 2,530; 1886, Nat. maj., 3,349.

Mr. JOHN GORDON SWIFT MACNEILL, K.C., is the only son of the late Rev. J. G. Swift MacNeill, chaplain of the Richmond Bridewell, Dublin, and was born in 1849. He was educated at Christ Church, Oxford (B.A., 1873; M.A., 1875), and was called to the Irish Bar in 1876. He has sat for South Donegal since 1887. Among the books he has written are "The Irish Parliament" and "How the Union was Carried." He has been appointed Professor of Constitutional Law in the new National University of Ireland, which was established last year.

WEST (6,642).—No change.
*Law, H. A. (Nat.).

1906, 1900, 1895, 1892, 1886, Nat. unop.

Mr. HUGH ALEXANDER LAW is the son of the late Right Hon. H. Law, Lord Chancellor of Ireland. He was born in 1872, and was educated at Rugby, and University College, Oxford. He is a J.P. for county Donegal, and has sat in Parliament for the West Division since 1902.

DOWN (4).
EAST (7,895).—No change.

*Craig, Capt. J. (U.).. ..	4,028
Wood, J. (L.)	3,054
Unionist majority ..	974

1906.—U., 4,011; U., 3,341—U. maj over U., 670.
1900, 1895, and 1892.—U. unop.; 1886, U. maj., 2,532.

CAPTAIN JAMES CRAIG was elected for East Down in 1906; was born in 1871 and educated at Merchiston Castle School, Edinburgh; is an hon. captain in the Army and served in the South African War, 1900-2; a J.P. for Belfast.

NORTH (9,912).—No change.
*Corbett, T. L. (U.).

1906.—U., 4878; Ind. U., 2,603—U. maj., 2,275.
1900.—U., 4,493; Ind. U., 3,230—U. maj., 1,263.
1895, 1892, U. unop.; 1886, U. maj. over Nat., 3,995.

Mr. THOMAS LORIMER CORBETT was born at Glasgow in 1854. He was a member of the London County Council for many years, and was deputy chairman as well as discharging the duties of Whip of the Moderate Party. He has sat for North Down since 1898. Mr. Cameron Corbett, who has been elected as an Independent Liberal for the Tradeston Division of Glasgow, is his brother.

SOUTH (7,753).—No change.

*MacVeagh, J. (Nat.).. ..	3,815
Macassey, L. (U.).. ..	3,180
Nationalist majority ..	635

1906.—Nat., 3,190; U., 3,262—Nat. maj., 648.
1900.—Nat. unop.
1895.—Nat. maj., 679; 1892, Nat. maj. over U., 571; 1886, Nat. maj., 970.

Mr. JEREMIAH MACVEAGH, who is a journalist, and was for some years in the Press Gallery of the House of Commons, has represented South Down since February, 1902; born at Belfast in 1872, and educated at St. Malachy's College, Belfast.

WEST (8,253).—No change.
*MacCaw, W. J. (U.).

By-election, 1908.—U., 4,051; L., 2,760—U. maj., 1,291.
By-election, 1907.—U., 3,702; L., 2,918—U. maj., 784.
1903, 1900, 1895, 1892.—U. unop.; 1886, U. maj. over Nat., 5,390.

Mr. WILLIAM JOHN MACGEAGH MACCAW was born in 1850 at Cheetham, near Manchester. He is a solicitor, and has large business interests in India and the Far East. He was first returned for the division at a by-election in 1908.

DUBLIN (2).
NORTH (13,044).—No change.
*Clancy, J. J. (Nat.)

1906.—Nat. unop.
1900.—Nat. unop.
1895.—Nat maj., 2,240; 1892, Parnellite maj. over Nat., 1,295; 1886, Nat. unop.

Mr. JOHN JOSEPH CLANCY, born in Galway in 1847, received his education at Summer Hill, Athlone, and Queen's College, Galway. He took the degree of M.A. at the Royal University of Ireland with honours in Ancient Classics, and was classical master at Holy Cross School, Tralee, from 1867 to 1870. From 1870 to 1885 he was on the editorial staff of the *Nation* ; from 1886 to 1890 he was editor of the Irish Press Agency in England ; and from 1891 to 1902 he was on the editorial staff of the *Irish Daily Independent.* Called to the Irish Bar in 1887, he became K.C. in 1906. He has written various political pamphlets, has contributed to many reviews, and has represented the division since 1885.

SOUTH (12,009).—No change.

Cooper, Capt. Bryan (U.) ..	5,072
Cotton, W. F. (Nat.) ..	5,006
Unionist majority ..	66

1906.—U., 5,269 ; Nat., 3,926—U. maj., 1,343.
1900.—Nat., 3,410 ; U., 2,906 ; U., 1,539—Nat. maj., 504.
1895.—U. maj., 1,939 ; 1892, U. maj., 2,110 ; 1886, Nat. maj., 1,768.

CAPTAIN BRYAN COOPER, of Markree Castle, County Sligo, comes of a family which was represented in the Irish Parliament for 30 years before the Union, and afterwards in the Imperial Parliament for 41 years ; educated at Eton and at the Royal Military Academy, Woolwich, and served in the Royal Field Artillery ; left the service three years ago and has since then been an officer in the Special Reserve ; a member of the executive committee of the Irish Unionist Alliance ; his large property in County Sligo has recently been sold to the tenants under the Land Purchase Acts.

FERMANAGH (2).
NORTH (4,895).—No change.

*Fetherstonhaugh, G., K.C. (U.)	2,474
Kerr, J. G. (L.)	2,124
Unionist majority ..	350

1906.—U., 2,419 ; U., 2,331—U. maj. over U., 88.
1900.—U. unop.
1895.—U. maj., 376 ; 1892, U. maj., 317 ; 1886, Nat. maj., 206.

Mr. GODFREY FETHERSTONHAUGH, K.C., was born in 1859. He is M.A. Dublin University, and a member of both the English and Irish Bars. He was first returned for North Fermanagh in 1906.

SOUTH (5,317).—No change.

*Jordan, J. (Nat.)	2,693
Battersby, T. S. F., K.C. (U.)	2,098
Nationalist majority ..	595

1906.—Nat. unop.
1900.—Nat., 2,753 ; U. 1,982—Nat. maj., 771.
1895.—Nat.maj., 696 ; 1892, Nat. maj., 621 ; 1886, Nat. maj., 1,233.

Mr. JEREMIAH JORDAN, who was born in 1830 and educated at the National School and the Royal School, Enniskillen, is a provision merchant and tenant farmer ; a member of the county council and of local bodies ; was first returned to Parliament in 1885, and has represented South Fermanagh since 1895.

GALWAY (4).
CONNEMARA (6,248).—No change.
*O'Malley, W. (Nat.).
1906, 1900, 1895.—Nat. unop.
1892.—Nat. maj. over Parnellite, 2,039 ; 1886, Nat. unop.

Mr. WILLIAM O'MALLEY was born in Connemara in 1857, and has represented the division since 1895. He was at one time a schoolmaster in Liverpool, and is now a journalist in London.

EAST (7,242).—No change.
*Roche, J. (N.).
1906, 1900, 1895, Nat. unop.
1892.—Nat. maj. over Parnellite, 2,039 ; 1886, Nat. unop.

Mr. JOHN ROCHE, who is a miller in Woodford, county Galway, was born in 1848. He was imprisoned for opposing the eviction proceedings on the estate of the Marquis of Clanricarde ; and when the occasion presented itself in 1890 the people of the district sent him to Parliament.

NORTH (7,713).—No change.
*Hazleton, R. (Nat.).
By-election, 1906.—Nat. unop.
1906.—Nat. maj. over Nat., 1,521 ; 1900, Nat. unop. ; 1895, Nat. maj. over Parnellite, 565 ; 1892, Parnellite maj. over N., 389 : 1886, Nat. unop.

Mr. RICHARD HAZLETON, who was defeated by Mr. T. M. Healy in the contest for North Louth, was returned unopposed for the constituency which he has represented since 1906. He was born in 1880, the son of the senior partner of a big drapery firm in Dublin, and is interested in the promotion of temperance and the revival of Gaelic as a spoken language in Ireland.

SOUTH (6,292).—No change.
*Duffy, W. J. (Nat.).
1906, 1900, 1895.—Nat. unop.
1892.—Nat. maj. over Parnellite, 1,212 ; 1886, Nat. unop.

Mr. WILLIAM JOHN DUFFY was born in 1865. He is a shopkeeper in Loughrea, the principal town of the division, for which he was first returned in 1900.

KERRY (4).
EAST (5,766).—No change.

O'Sullivan, E. (Ind. Nat.)	2,643
*Murphy, J. (Nat.) ..	2,154
Ind. Nationalist majority ..	489

1906.—Nat., 2,185 ; Nat., 2,131—Nat. maj. over Nat., 54.
1900 and 1895.—Nat. unop.
1892.—Nat. maj., 2,347 ; 1886, Nat. unop.

Mr. EUGENE O'SULLIVAN is a farmer and a member of various local bodies.

NORTH (5,536).—No change.

*Flavin, M. J. (Nat.)	2,637
Stack, T. N. (Ind. Nat.) ..	885
Nationalist majority..	1,752

1906, 1900, and 1895.—Nat. unop.
1892.—Nat. maj. over P., 2,082 ; 1886, Nat. unop.

Mr. MICHAEL JOSEPH FLAVIN, a merchant in Listowel and Tralee, was born in 1866 and educated at the national schools, St. Michael's College, Listowel, and privately; a member of the Kerry County Council, and M.P. for the North Division since 1896.

SOUTH (5,858).—No change.
*Boland, J. P. (Nat.).
1906, 1900, 1895, Nat. unop.
1892.—Nat. maj. over Parnellite, 1,871; 1886, Nat. unop.

Mr. JOHN PIUS BOLAND was born in 1870 and educated at the Oratory School, Edgbaston. He is B.A. London University and M.A. Oxford. In 1897 he was called to the English Bar by Inner Temple. He has been in Parliament since 1900, and interests himself in education and commercial questions affecting Ireland.

WEST (5,848).—No change.
*O'Donnell, T. (Nat.).
1906.—Nat. unop.
1900.—Nat., 2,464; Ind. Nat., 1,065—Nat. maj., 1,399.
1895.—Nat. unop.; 1892, Nat. maj. over Parnellite, 1,347; 1886, Nat. unop.

Mr. THOMAS O'DONNELL is a farmer's son, and was born in 1872. He was a national school teacher before his return for West Kerry in 1900, and was called to the Irish Bar in 1905.

KILDARE (2).
NORTH (4,711).—No change.
*O'Connor, John (Nat.).
1906.—Nat. unop.
1900.—Nat. maj. over Nat., 232.
1895.—Nat. maj. over Parnellite, 232; 1892, Nat. maj. over P., 446; 1886, Nat. unop.

Mr. JOHN O'CONNOR was called to the English Bar in 1893. He sat for South Tipperary from 1885 to 1892, and was elected for North Kildare in 1905. He was born in 1850.

SOUTH (4,958).—No change.
*Kilbride, D. (Nat.).
1906.—Nat. unop.
1900.—Nat. unop.
1895.—Nat. unop; 1892, Nat. maj. over Parnellite, 1,667; 1886, Nat. unop.

Mr. DENIS KILBRIDE was born in 1848. He is a farmer, and was the first tenant evicted under the Plan of Campaign on the Marquis of Lansdowne's estate in Queen's County. He was returned to Parliament in 1887; he did not stand in 1900, but got back in 1903 for South Kildare.

KILKENNY (2).
NORTH (4,847).—No change.
*Meagher, M. (Nat.).
1906.—Nat. unop.
1900.—Nat. unop.
1895.—Nat. unop.; 1892, Nat. maj. over Parnellite, 140; 1886, Nat. unop.

Mr. MICHAEL MEAGHER was born in 1846. He is a farmer, and was returned for North Kilkenny in 1906.

SOUTH (4,985).—No change.
*Keating, M. (Nat.).
By-elections, 1909 and 1907, Nat. unop.
1906, 1900, 1895, Nat. unop.
1892.—Nat. maj. over U., 3,093; 1886, Nat. unop.

Mr. MATTHEW KEATING, who was born in Wales, the son of a miner, was first returned at the by-election of 1909. He is a manufacturer's agent in London.

KING'S COUNTY (2).
BIRR (4,410).—No change.
*Reddy, M. (Nat.).
1906.—Nat. unop.
1900.—Nat. maj. over Nat., 270.
1895.—Nat. unop.; 1892, Nat. maj. over U., 2,609; 1886, Nat. maj. over U., 2,555.

Mr. MICHAEL REDDY is a farmer, and has represented the Birr Division since 1900.

TULLAMORE (4,472).—No change.
*Haviland-Burke, E. (Nat.).
1906.—Nat. unop.
1900.—Nat. unop.
1895.—Nat. unop.; 1892, Nat. unop.; 1886, Nat. unop.

Mr. EDMUND HAVILAND-BURKE was born in 1864, the son of E. Haviland-Burke, at one time M.P. for Christchurch, Hants. He is a Whip to the Irish Party.

LEITRIM (2).
NORTH (6,282).—No change.
*Meehan, F. E. (Nat.).
By-election, 1908.—Nat., 3,103; Sinn Feiner, 1,157—Nat. maj, 1,946.
1906.—Nat. unop.
1900.—Nat. maj. over U., 3,642.
1895.—Nat. unop.; 1892, Nat. maj. over U., 3,857; 1886, Nat. unop.

Mr. FRANCIS EDWARD MEEHAN was born in 1870, and is a shopkeeper in Manorhamilton. The by-election of 1908, when he was returned, was the first contest between a Sinn Feiner and a Nationalist.

SOUTH (5,727).—No change.
*Smyth, T. F. (Nat.).
1906.—Nat. unop.
1900.—Nat. unop.
1895.—Nat. unop.; 1892, Nat. maj. over U 3,725; 1886, Nat. unop.

Mr. THOMAS F. SMYTH, the son of a farmer, was born in 1875. He is in business as an auctioneer and insurance agent in county Leitrim. He was returned for South Leitrim in 1906.

LIMERICK (2)
EAST (7,455).—No change.
*Lundon, T. (Nat.)	3,077
Bennett, T. W. (Ind. Nat.)	2,918
Nationalist majority ..	159

By-election, June, 1909.—Nat., 2,664; Nat., 1,686—Nat. maj. over Nat., 978.
1906, 1900, and 1895.—Nat. unop.
1892.—Nat., 2,903; P., 1,174—Nat. maj., 1,729.
1886.—Nat. unop.

Mr. THOMAS LUNDON is the son of Mr. William Lundon, who sat for the division from 1900 to his death in 1909, and whom he succeeded in the representation.

WEST (7,550).—No change.
*O'Shaughnessy, P. J. (Nat.).
1906.—Nat. unop.
1900.—Nat. unop.
1895.—Nat. unop.; 1892, Nat. maj. over Parnellite, 2,741; 1886, Nat. unop.

Mr. PATRICK JOSEPH O'SHAUGHNESSY was born

in 1872, the son of a farmer, and has represented West Limerick since 1900.

LONDONDERRY (2).
NORTH (9,349).—No change.
*Barrie, H. T. (U.).
1906.—U., 4,806; Ind. U., 2,699—U. maj., 2,107.
1900.—U. unop.
1895.—U. maj. over L., 2,225; 1892, U. maj., 3,190; 1886, U. unop.

Mr. HUGH T. BARRIE was born at Glasgow in 1860, and is in business there as a grain and produce merchant. He was elected for North Londonderry in 1906.

SOUTH (8,052).—No change.
*Gordon, J., K.C. (U.)	..	3,985
Keightley, Dr. S. R. (L.)..		3,678
Unionist majority	..	307

1906.—U., 3,847; Ind. U., 3,776—U. maj. over Ind. U., 71.
1900.—U. unop.
1895.—U. maj., 417; 1892, U. maj., 501; 1886, U. maj., 108.

Mr. JOHN GORDON, K.C., was born in 1849, and educated at the Royal Academical Institute, Belfast, and Queen's College, Belfast; is B.A. and LL.D. of the Royal University, Ireland; one of the leaders of the Irish Bar, to which he was called in 1877; unsuccessfully contested Mid Armagh in February, 1895, and was returned unopposed for his present seat in 1900.

LONGFORD (2).
NORTH (3,632).—No change.
*Farrell, J. P. (Nat.).
1906.—Nat unop.
1900.—Nat. unop.
1895.—Nat. unop.; 1892, Nat. maj. over U., 2,538; 1886, Nat unop.

Mr. JAMES PATRICK FARRELL, who is a local journalist and newspaper owner, was born in 1865. He was returned for the division in 1900 on the resignation of Mr. Justin McCarthy.

SOUTH (3,691).—No change.
*Phillips, J. (N.).
By-election, 1907, 1906, 1900, 1895, Nat. unop.
1892, Nat. maj. over U., 2,538; 1886, Nat. unop.

Mr. JOHN PHILLIPS was returned for the division at the 1907 by-election, and is a magistrate of the county.

LOUTH (2).
NORTH (5,868).—No change.
*Healy, T. M. (Ind. Nat.)	..	2,432
†Hazleton, R. (Nat.)	..	2,333
Ind. Nationalist majority	..	99

1906.—Nat. unop.
1900.—Nat., 1,604; Nat., 1,285—Nat. maj., 319.
1895.—Nat., 2,294; P., 1,433—Nat. maj., 861.
1892.—Nat., 2,268; Ind., 1,569—Nat. maj., 699.
1886.—Nat. unop.

Mr. TIMOTHY HEALY is the Ishmael of Nationalist politics, for in recent years he has been in disagreement on one point or another with nearly all his colleagues. From 1885 onwards he has been a member of the Parliamentary Party, but since the downfall of Mr. Parnell, to which he actively contributed, has followed an independent course. He is a member of the Bar both in England and Ireland, and enjoys a large practice. In Parliament he is an authority on Irish land legislation and consistently opposed the Budget last Session in a series of witty and incisive speeches.

SOUTH (4,802).—No change.
*Nolan, J. (Nat.).
1906.—Nat. unop.
1900.—Nat. maj. over Nat., 299.
1895.—Nat. maj. over Parnellite, 962; 1892, Nat. maj. over P., 1,325; 1886, Nat. unop.

Mr. JOSEPH NOLAN is a commission agent in London. He has represented South Louth since 1900.

MAYO (4).
EAST (7,816).—No change.
*Dillon, J. (Nat.).
1906.—Nat. unop.
1900.—Nat. unop.
1895.—Nat. unop.; 1892, Nat. maj. over Parnellite, 2,207; 1886, Nat. unop.

Mr. JOHN DILLON, one of the best-known members of the Irish Party, was born in 1851, the son of the late John Blake Dillon, M.P. for Tipperary. He is a licentiate of the Irish College of Surgeons. He was leader of the Anti-Parnellite section of the Nationalists in succession to Mr. Justin McCarthy from 1896 to 1900, when, on the reunion of the Nationalists, he gave way to Mr. J. Redmond. In 1895 he married a daughter of the late Sir J. Mathew, Judge of the High Court (she died in 1907). Except for an interval of about two years, has had a seat in Parliament since 1880.

NORTH (6,977).—No change.
Boyle, Daniel (Nat.) ..	..	1,861
Egan, Bernard (Ind. Nat.)		1,821
Nationalist majority	..	40

1906.—Nat unop.
1900.—Nat., 2,504; Nat., 1,116—Nat. maj., 1,388.
1895.—Nat. maj., 621; 1892, Nat. maj., 804; 1886, Nat. unop.

ALDERMAN DANIEL BOYLE was born in Ireland about 50 years ago, and, coming to England at an early age, settled at Manchester. For many years he was organizer in Lancashire for the United Irish League, but is now engaged in commercial pursuits in Manchester, and is an alderman of the city council.

SOUTH (7,883).—No change.
*O'Donnell, J. (Ind. Nat.)	..	2,667
†O'Kelly, Conor (Nat.)	..	2,226
Ind. Nationalist majority	..	441

1906, 1900, 1895, 1892, and 1886.—Nat. unop.

Mr. JOHN O'DONNELL, who has sat for South Mayo since 1900, is a journalist, and founded the *Connaught Champion* newspaper; first organizer, and for five years general secretary, of the United Irish League; born at Westport and educated at the national school.

WEST (8,261).—No change.
Doris, W. (Nat.).
1906.—Nat. unop.
1900.—Nat. unop.
1895.—Nat. unop.; 1892, Nat. maj. over Ind. Nat., 2,845; 1886, Nat. unop.

Mr. WILLIAM DORIS is a new member. He succeeds

Dr. R. Ambrose, London, who represented the division from 1893, but failed to be selected at the Nationalist Convention. Mr. Doris is a journalist at Westport.

MEATH (2).

North (5,662).—No change.
*White, P. (Nat.).

1906.—N. unop.
1900.—Nat., 1,453 ; Ind. Nat., 1,316—Nat. maj., 137.
1895.—Nat. maj. over Parnellite, 32 ; 1892, Nat. maj. over P., 403 ; 1886, Nat. unop.

Mr. Patrick White has represented the division since 1900. He was born in 1860, and is in business as a tailor in Dublin.

South (5,584).—No change.
*Sheehy, D. (Nat.).

1906.—Nat. unop.
1900.—Nat. unop.
1895.—Parnellite maj. over Nat., 43 ; 1892, Nat. maj. over P., 13 ; 1886, Nat. unop.

Mr. David Sheehy is one of the staff officials of the United Irish League. He was born in 1844, sat for South Galway from 1885 to 1900, and was returned for South Meath in 1903.

MONAGHAN (2).

North (6,435).—No change.

*Lardner, J. C. R. (Nat.)	..	3,477
Knight, M. E. (U.)	.. ..	2,005
Nationalist majority	..	1,472

1906 and 1900.—Nat. unop.
1895.—Nat. maj., 1,283 ; 1892, Nat. maj., 1,437 ; 1886, Nat. maj., 1,471.

Mr. James Carrige Rush Lardner, who was born in 1879, and educated at Christian Brothers' School and St. McCarten's College, Monaghan, and Clongowes Wood College, Co. Kildare, is a solicitor, and has represented this division since June, 1907.

South (6,449).—No change.

*McKean, J. (Ind. Nat.)	..	2 611
Laverty, C. (Nat.)	..	1,903
Ind. Nationalist majority	..	708

1906 and 1900.—Nat. unop.
1895.—Nat. maj., 2,870 ; 1892, Nat. maj., 3,236 ; 1886, Nat. maj., 3,706.

Mr. John McKean, who was born at Castleblayney and educated at the local seminary, is a barrister and occasional contributor to the Press ; defended the late King Leopold's government of the Congo in the course of the debates on that question in the House of Commons.

QUEEN'S COUNTY (2).

Leix (4,872).—No change.
*Meehan, P. A. (Nat.).

1906, 1900, 1895.—Nat. unop.
1892.—Nat. maj. over U., 2,748 ; 1886, Nat. maj. over U., 3,122.

Mr. Patrick Aloysius Meehan was born in 1852, and is a grocer and spirit merchant at Maryborough.

Ossory (4,786).—No change.
*Delany, W. (N.).

1906, 1900, Nat. unop.
1895, Nat. maj. over U., 2,356 ; 1892, Nat. maj. over U., 3,143 · 1886, Nat. unop.

Mr. William Delany was born in 1855 and is a farmer. He has been in Parliament since 1900.

ROSCOMMON (2).

North (8,528).—No change.
*O'Kelly, J. (Nat.).

1906, 1900.—Nat. unop.
1895.—Parnellite maj. over Nat., 476 ; 1892, Nat. maj. over P., 52 ; 1886, Nat. unop.

Mr. James O'Kelly was born in Dublin in 1845. He was educated at the Sorbonne, Paris, whence he passed into the French Army, and served in the Franco-German War. After the fall of Paris he went to New York and turned journalist. In the war with Cuba he represented the *New York Herald*, and has published a book recounting his experiences, entitled " The Mambi Land, a history of personal adventures with President Cespides in the Cuban Insurrection." In 1884 he went to the Sudan for the *Daily News* with the intention of joining the Mahdi, but was stopped at Dongola by order of the Egyptian Government. He first entered Parliament in 1880, and on the suppression of the Land League was imprisoned in Kilmainhan with Mr. Parnell. At the split of the Irish Party in 1890 Mr. O'Kelly took sides with Mr. Parnell, and at the General Election of 1892 lost his seat by the narrow majority of 52, but recovered it in 1895.

South (8,362).—No change.
*Hayden, J. P. (Nat.).

1906.—Nat. unop.
1900.—Nat. unop.
1895.—Parnellite maj. over Nat., 954 ; 1892, P. maj. over Nat., 1,571 ; 1886, Nat. unop.

Mr. John P. Hayden was born in 1863, and is a journalist and newspaper proprietor. He has represented South Roscommon since 1897.

SLIGO (2).

North (7,993).—No change.
*Scanlan, T. (Nat.).

By-election, 1909.—Nat. unop.
1906.—Nat. unop.
1900.—Nat. unop.
1895.—Nat. maj. over U., 3,195 ; 1892, Nat. maj. over U., 3,752 ; 1886, Nat. unop.

Mr. Thomas Scanlan, who was returned for the division at the by-election of 1909, is a solicitor in Glasgow.

South (7,096).—No change.
*O'Dowd, J. (Nat.).

1906.—Nat. unop.
1900.—Nat. unop.
1895.—Nat. maj. over U., 3,195 ; 1892, Nat. maj. over U., 3,752 ; 1886, Nat. unop.

Mr. John O'Dowd was born in 1856. He is a

IRELAND (COUNTIES).

farmer and shopkeeper, and has written a book of Nationalist poems called "Lays of South Sligo."

TIPPERARY (4).
East (5,610).—No change.
*Condon, T. J. (Nat.).
1906.—Nat. unop.
1900.—Nat. unop.
1895.—Nat. unop.; 1892, Nat. maj. over Parnellite, 2,107; 1886, Nat. unop.

Mr. Thomas Joseph Condon was born in 1850, and has been Mayor of Clonmel, his native town, for several years. He has sat for East Tipperary since 1885.

Mid (6,105).—No change.
Hackett, J. (Nat.).
1906.—Nat. unop.
1900.—Nat. over Nat., 1,729; 1895, Nat., unop.; 1892, Nat. maj. over Parnellite, 2,397; 1886, Nat. unop.

Mr. John Hackett is a new member. He is a shopkeeper in Thurles, the chief town of the division.

North (5,421).—No change.
*Hogan, M. (Nat.).
1906.—Nat. unop.
1900.—Nat. unop.
1895.—Nat. unop.; 1892, Nat. maj. over U., 3,602; 1886, Nat. unop.

Mr. Michael Hogan was born in 1851. He is a farmer in county Tipperary, and was returned for the North Division in 1906.

South (4,917).—No change.
*Cullinan, J. (Nat.)
1906.—Nat. unop.
1900.—Nat. unop.
1895.—Nat. maj. over Nat., 501; 1892, Nat. maj. over Parnellite, 1,798; 1886, Nat. unop.

Mr. John Cullinan was born in 1858. He was several times imprisoned for his action in the Nationalist movement, and has sat for South Tipperary since 1900.

TYRONE (4).
East (6,526).—No change.
*Kettle, T. M. (Nat.)	..	3,208
Saunderson, A. D. (U.)	..	3,096
Nationalist majority	..	112

By-election, July, 1906.—Nat., 3,019; U., 3,000—Nat., maj. 19.
1906.—Nat., 3,053; U., 3,022—Nat. maj., 31.
1900.—Nat., 3,126; U., 3,050—Nat. maj., 76.
1895.—Nat. maj., 152; 1892, Nat. maj., 208; 1886, Nat. maj., 468.

Mr. Thomas Michael Kettle, who was returned for the division at a by-election in July, 1906, by 19 votes, was born in 1880 and educated at the Christian Brothers' School, Clongowes, and University College, Dublin; a journalist and barrister (called in 1906); received a professorial appointment at University College, Dublin, in October, 1909.

Mid (6,512).—Unionist Gain.
Brunskill, G. F. (U.)	..	2,475
Valentine, J. (Nat.)	..	2,070
*Murnaghan, G. (Ind. Nat.)		1,244
Unionist majority	..	405

1906 and 1900.—Nat. unop.
1895.—Nat. maj., 1,507; 1892, Nat. maj., 1,069; 1886, Nat. maj., 1,670.

Mr. Gerald Fitzgibbon Brunskill, the son of an official in the Bank of Ireland, is a member of the Irish Bar and practises in Dublin and on the North-East Circuit; educated at Christ's Hospital, London, and at Trinity College, Dublin; elected in 1889 to the much-coveted office of auditor of the College Historical Society; called to the Bar at the beginning of 1901, but a little later, having married a daughter of Mr. Robinson, head of a well-known firm of solicitors in Dublin, he relinquished the Bar and became a member of the solicitors' profession; two or three years afterwards he returned to the Bar, where he now enjoys a considerable practice.

North (6,572).—No change.
*Barry, Redmond, K.C. (L.)	..	3,238
Herdman, E. C. (U.)	..	3,136
Liberal majority	..	102

By-election, 1907.—L., 3,013; U., 3,006—L. maj., 7.
1906.—L., 2,966; U., 2,957—L. maj., 9.
1900.—L., 2,869; U., 2,814—L. maj., 55.
1895, L. maj., 91; 1892, U. maj., 49; 1886, U. maj., 352.

Mr. Redmond John Barry, who was first Solicitor-General and afterwards became Attorney-General for Ireland in the late Government on the elevation of Mr. Cherry to the Irish Bench, first obtained a seat in the House in March, 1907, when he defeated his Unionist opponent, Mr. Denis Henry, K.C., by seven votes; born in 1866, and educated in Cork and at the Royal University of Ireland; called to the Irish Bar in 1888, took silk 11 years later, and is a Bencher of King's Inn, Dublin.

South (6,059).—Unionist Gain.
Horner, A. L., K.C. (U.)	..	3,054
*Russell, Rt. Hon. T. W. (L.)		2,770
Unionist majority	..	284

1906.—L., 2,954; L.U., 2,671—L. maj., 283.
1900.—U., 2,499; N., 2,409; I.U., 303—U. maj. over N., 303.
1895.—U. maj., 193; 1892, U. maj., 372; 1886, U. maj., 99.

Mr. Andrew L. Horner, K.C., is a member of the Irish Bar, and practises in Dublin. He was called to the Bar in 1887. At the last General Election he was defeated by Mr. T. W. Russell.

WATERFORD (2).
East (4,216).—No change.
*Power, P. J. (Nat.).
1906.—Nat. unop.
1900.—Nat. unop.
1895.—Nat. unop.; 1892, Nat. maj. over Parnellite, 1,519; 1886, Nat. unop.

Mr. Patrick Joseph Power was born in 1850 and educated at Stonyhurst College. He is a magistrate for Waterford county. He has been in the House of Commons since 1884, and was a temporary Chairman of Committees in the late Parliament.

West (4,139).—No change.
*O'Shee, J. J. (Nat.)	..	1,753
Ryan, E. A. (Ind. Nat.)	..	1,309
Nationalist majority	..	444

1906, 1900, 1895, 1892, and 1886, Nat. unop.

Mr. James John O'Shee, a solicitor, and hon. secretary of the Irish Land and Labour Association, was born at Newtown, Carrick-on-Suir, in 1866, and educated at Rockwell College, Cashel, and University College, Dublin; has sat for the division since 1895.

WESTMEATH (2).

NORTH (5,245).—IND. NAT. GAIN FROM NAT.

*Ginnell, L. (Ind. Nat.) .. 1,996
McKenna, Patrick (Nat.) .. 1,379

Ind. Nationalist majority .. 617

1906.—Nat. unop.
1900.—Nat., 1,763; Nat., 1,418—Nat. maj., 345.
1895.—Nat. unop.; 1892, Nat. maj. over P., 2,499; 1886, Nat. unop.

Mr. LAURENCE GINNELL, who " invented " cattle-driving as a political instrument, and who has suffered imprisonment for contempt of Court in connexion with this practice, was born in 1854, and, according to " Dod's Parliamentary Companion," is self-educated; a member of both the English and the Irish Bars; one of the founders of the Irish Literary Society; unsuccessfully contested the division in 1900, but was elected in 1906.

SOUTH (6,755).—No change.

*Nugent, Sir W. (Nat.).

By-election, 1907, Nat. unop.
1906.—Nat. unop.
1900.—Nat. unop.
1895.—Nat. unop.; 1892, Nat. maj. over Parnellite, 1,455; 1886, Nat. unop.

SIR WALTER RICHARD NUGENT was returned for the division in the by-election of 1907. He was born in 1865.

WEXFORD (2).

NORTH (8,835).—No change.

*Esmonde, Sir T. (Nat.)

1906.—Nat. unop.
1900.—Nat. maj. over Nat., 1,670.
1895.—Nat. maj. over U., 3,903; 1892, Nat. maj. over U., 4,834; 1886, Nat. unop.

SIR THOMAS GRATTAN ESMONDE, born in 1862, is a great-grandson of Henry Grattan. He has sat in Parliament as a Nationalist since 1885.

SOUTH (8,557).—No change.

*Ffrench, P. (Nat.)

1906.—Nat. unop.
1900.—Nat. unop.
1895.—Nat. unop.; 1892, Nat. maj. over U., 4,550; 1886, Nat. unop.

Mr. PETER FFRENCH, who was born in 1844, is a farmer in Wexford and a coroner of the county. He was first returned in 1893.

WICKLOW (2).

EAST (4,710).—No change.

*Muldoon, J. (Nat.)

By-election, 1907.—Nat. unop.
1906.—Nat. unop.
1900.—Nat. unop.
1895.—Nat. maj. over U., 87; 1892, Nat. maj., 208; 1886, Nat. maj., 2,117.

Mr. JOHN MULDOON was born in 1865, and is a barrister-at-law. He was elected for East Wicklow in 1907.

WEST (4,417).—No change.

*O'Connor, James (Nat.).

1906.—Nat. unop.
1900.—Nat. unop.
1895.—Nat. unop.; 1892, Nat. maj. over U., 1,798; 1886, Nat. maj. over U., 2,675.

Mr. JAMES O'CONNOR was born in 1836. He was on the staff of the *Irish People*, the organ of the Fenian movement, published in Dublin, and on the suppression of the paper in 1865 was arrested, found guilty of treason felony, and sentenced to seven years' penal servitude. He was liberated before the term had expired, and has since been connected with the editorial staffs of different Nationalist newspapers.

THE UNIVERSITIES.

OXFORD (2) (6,895).—No change.

*Anson, Sir W. R. (U.)
Cecil, Lord Hugh (U.)

1906.—U. unop.
1900.—U. unop.
1895.—U. unop.; 1892, U. unop.; 1886, U. unop.

SIR W. R. ANSON, who held the office of Parliamentary Secretary to the Board of Education, 1902-5, was born in 1843, educated at Eton and Balliol College; elected to a fellowship of All Souls' College, 1867, and became Warden 1881. He was called to the Bar in 1869; contested West Staffordshire as a Liberal in 1880; has been chairman of the Oxfordshire Quarter Sessions since 1894, and Chancellor of the Diocese of Oxford from 1899. He became Vice-Chancellor of the University in 1898, and resigned the office in the following year to become one of its representatives in Parliament as a Liberal Unionist. He is the author of works on " The Law of Contract " and " The Law and Custom of the Constitution."

LORD HUGH CECIL, the fifth son of the late Marquis of Salisbury, was born in 1869, and educated at Eton and University College, Oxford; Fellow of Hertford College, Oxford, since 1891; was private secretary to his father while the latter was Secretary of State for Foreign Affairs; was Unionist member for Greenwich from 1895 to 1906; is opposed to the policy of Tariff Reform.

CAMBRIDGE (2) (7,145).—No change.

*Butcher, S. H. (U.)
*Rawlinson, J. F. P., K.C. (U.)

1906.—U. maj. over U. (Sir J. Gorst), 1,323.
1900.—U. unop.
1895.—U. unop.. 1892, U. unop.; 1886, U. unop.

Mr. SAMUEL HENRY BUTCHER, a distinguished man of letters, and a recognised authority on such diverse subjects as Greek literature and the Irish agrarian problem ; born in 1850, the son of a former Bishop of Meath, and educated at Marlborough and at Trinity College, Cambridge ; was Lecturer at Trinity College, Cambridge, and University College, Oxford, Professor of Greek, University of Edinburgh (1882-1903) ; is joint author with Mr. Andrew Lang of a prose translation of the *Odyssey*, and has written other works ; is one of the most cultured speakers in the House of Commons, which he entered in 1906.

Mr. JOHN FREDERICK PEEL RAWLINSON, youngest son of the late Sir C. Rawlinson, Chief Justice of Madras, was born in 1860, and educated at Eton and Trinity College, Cambridge ; was called to the Bar (Inner Temple) in 1884, took silk in 1897, and has been a member of the Bar Council since its formation ; represented the Treasury at the South Africa Committee inquiry into the Jameson Raid (1896) ; is Recorder of Cambridge and Commissary of Cambridge University ; unsuccessfully contested Ipswich in 1900.

LONDON (6,070).—No change.

*Magnus, Sir P. (U.)	2,625
Ridgeway, Sir J. West (L.)	1,928
Unionist majority	697

1906.—U., 1,840 ; L., 1,816—U. maj., 24.
1900, 1895, and 1892, U. unop.
1886.—U. maj., 798.

SIR PHILIP MAGNUS, first elected for the University of London at the General Election of 1906, was born in 1842 and educated at University College School, University College, London, and at the Berlin University ; has had a distinguished educational career, particularly on the technical side ; is a member of several learned societies, and Fellow and member of the Senate of the London University. In Parliament he has specialized on educational questions, and has given close attention to all matters affecting the University and education in its broadest sense. He was knighted in 1886.

GLASGOW AND ABERDEEN (11,705).—No change.

*Craik, Sir H. (U.)	4,879
Pollock, Sir F. (U.F.T.)	3,411
Unionist majority	1,468

The details of the polling are as follows :—

	Glasgow.	Aberdeen.
Sir H. Craik	3,030	1,849
Sir F. Pollock	2,275	1,133

1906.—U., 3,543 ; L., 2,450 ; U., 1,240—U. maj. over L., 1,093.
1900, 1895, 1892, and 1886, U. unop.

SIR HENRY CRAIK is a son of the late Dr. James Craik, a former Moderator of the General Assembly of the Church of Scotland. He was educated at the High School, Glasgow, Glasgow University, and Balliol College, Oxford. In 1870 he was appointed an examiner in the Education Department and senior examiner in 1878, and from 1885 to 1904 he was Secretary to the Scottish Education Department at Whitehall. Among other literary works he is the author of a " Life of Swift " and of "A Century of Scottish History."

EDINBURGH AND ST. ANDREWS (11,319).—No change.

Finlay, Right Hon. Sir R. B., K.C. (U.)	5,205
Simpson, Sir Alexander (L.)	2,693
Unionist majority	2,512

1906.—U., 4,893 ; U.F.T., 2,310—U. maj., 2,583.
1900, 1895, 1892, 1886, U. unop.

SIR ROBERT BANNATYNE FINLAY, K.C., was born in 1842, and was educated at Edinburgh Academy and Edinburgh University, where he graduated in medicine. He was called to the Bar in 1867, and has been a Bencher of the Middle Temple. The office of Solicitor-General was held by him from 1895 to 1900, and in that year he became Attorney-General, holding the office until the dissolution of that Parliament.

DUBLIN (2) (5,020).—No change.

*Carson, Rt. Hon. Sir E., K.C. (U.)
*Campbell, Rt. Hon. J. H., K.C. (U.)

1906.—U. unop.
1900.—U. unop.
1895.—U. unop. ; by-election, 1895, U. maj. over U., 746 ;
1892, U. maj. over U., 712 ; 1886, U. maj. over Nat., 1,810.

SIR EDWARD HENRY CARSON was born in 1854 and educated at Dublin University. He was called to the Irish Bar in 1877 and to the Middle Temple in 1893, took silk in Ireland in 1889 and in England in 1894, and is a Bencher of the King's Inns and the Middle Temple. He was Solicitor-General for Ireland for a few months in 1892, and Solicitor-General from 1900 to 1905. He has represented the University in Parliament since 1892. He was made a Privy Councillor of Ireland in 1896 and of Great Britain in 1905.

Mr. JAMES HENRY M. CAMPBELL was born in 1851, and educated at Stackpoole's School, Kingstown, and Trinity College, Dublin. He was called to the Irish Bar in 1878 and to the English Bar 20 years later, taking silk in 1890, and is a Bencher of King's Inns and of Gray's Inn. He was Solicitor-General for Ireland from 1901 to 1905, and afterwards for a brief period Attorney-General. He is a member of the Irish Privy Council. He has sat for the University since 1903.

CONSTITUENCIES.

	PAGE
Abercromby—see Liverpool	
Aberdeen, N.	93
,, S.	93
Aberdeenshire, E.	98
,, W.	98
Aberdeen and Glasgow Universities—see Glasgow	
Abingdon—see Berks	
Accrington—see Lancs	
Altrincham—see Cheshire	
Andover—see Hants	
Anglesey	90
Antrim, E.	103
,, Mid	103
,, N.	103
,, S.	106
Appleby—see Westmorland	
Arfon—see Carnarvonshire	
Argyllshire	98
Armagh, Mid	106
,, N.	106
,, S.	106
Ashburton—see Devon	
Ashford—see Kent	
Ashton-under-Lyne	30
Aston Manor	30
Attercliffe—see Sheffield	
Aylesbury—see Bucks	
Ayr District	93
Ayrshire, N.	98
,, S.	98
Banbury—see Oxford	
Banffshire	98
Barkston Ash—see Yorks	
Barnard Castle — see Durham	
Barnsley—see Yorks	
Barnstaple—see Devon	
Barrow-in-Furness	31
Basingstoke—see Hants	
Bassetlaw—see Notts	
Bath	31
Battersea	21
Bedford	31
Bedfordshire, Biggleswade	54
,, Luton	54
Belfast, E.	104
,, N.	104
,, S.	104
,, W.	104
Berkshire, Abingdon	55
,, Newbury	55
,, Wokingham	55

	PAGE
Bermondsey—see Southwark	
Berwick-on-Tweed — see Northumberland	
Berwickshire	98
Bethnal-green, N.E.	22
,, S.W.	22
Bewdley — see Worcestershire	
Biggleswade — see Beds	
Birkenhead	31
Birmingham, Bordesley	31
,, Central	31
,, E.	32
,, Edgbaston	32
,, N.	32
,, S.	32
,, W.	32
Birr—see King's County	
Bishop Auckland — see Durham	
Blackburn	32
Blackfriars — see Glasgow	
Blackpool — see Lancs	
Bodmin — see Cornwall	
Bolton	33
Bootle — see Lancs	
Bordesley — see Birmingham	
Boston	33
Bosworth — see Leicester	
Bow and Bromley — see Tower Hamlets	
Bradford, Central	33
,, E.	33
,, W.	33
Brecknockshire	90
Brentford — see Middlesex	
Bridgeton—see Glasgow	
Bridgwater—see Somerset	
Brigg—see Lincs	
Brighton	34
Brightside—see Sheffield	
Bristol, E.	34
,, N.	34
,, S.	34
,, W.	34
Brixton—see Lambeth	
Bromley—see Tower Hamlets	
Buckingham, Aylesbury	55
,, Buckingham	55
,, Wycombe	55
Buckrose—see Yorks	

	PAGE
Burnley	35
Burton—see Staffs	
Bury (Lancs)	35
Bury St. Edmunds	35
Buteshire	99
Caithness	99
Camberwell, Dulwich	22
,, N.	22
,, Peckham	22
Camborne—see Cornwall	
Cambridge	35
Cambridge University	115
Cambs, Chesterton	55
,, Newmarket	56
,, Wisbech	56
Camlachie—see Glasgow	
Canterbury	35
Cardiff	88
Cardiganshire	90
Carlisle	35
Carlow	106
Carmarthen District	88
Carmarthenshire, E.	91
,, W.	91
Carnarvon District	89
Carnarvonshire, Arfon	91
,, Eifion	91
Cavan, E.	106
,, W.	107
Chatham	35
Chelmsford—see Essex	
Chelsea	22
Cheltenham	36
Chertsey—see Surrey	
Cheshire, Altrincham	56
,, Crewe	56
,, Eddisbury	56
,, Hyde	56
,, Knutsford	56
,, Macclesfield	57
,, Northwich	57
,, Wirral	57
Chester	36
Chesterfield—see Derby	
Chester-le-Street—see Durham	
Chesterton—see Cambs	
Chichester—see Sussex	
Chippenham—see Wilts	
Chorley—see Lancs	
Christchurch	36
Cirencester—see Gloucester	
City of London—see London	

CONSTITUENCIES.

	PAGE
Clackmannan and Kinross	99
Clapham	21
Clare, E.	107
,, W.	107
Cleveland—see Yorks	
Clitheroe—see Lancs	
Cockermouth—see Cumberland	
Colchester	36
College Green—see Dublin	
Colne Valley—see Yorks	
Connemara—see Galway	
Cork, City	104
Cork, E.	107
,, Mid	107
,, N.	107
,, N.E.	107
,, S.	107
,, S.E.	107
,, W.	108
Cornwall, Bodmin	57
,, Camborne	57
,, Launceston	57
,, St. Austell	57
,, St. Ives	58
,, Truro	58
Coventry	36
Crewe—see Cheshire	
Cricklade—see Wilts	
Cromarty—see Ross	
Croydon	23
Cumberland, Cockermouth	58
,, Egremont	58
,, Eskdale	58
,, Penrith	58
Darlington	36
Dartford—see Kent	
Darwen—see Lancs	
Denbigh Dist.	89
Denbighshire, E.	91
,, W.	91
Deptford	23
Derby	36
Derbyshire,, Chesterfield	59
,, High Peak	59
,, Ilkeston	59
,, Mid	59
,, N.E.	59
,, S.	59
,, W.	59
Devizes—see Wilts	
Devonport	37
Devonshire, Ashburton	60
,, Barnstaple	60
,, Honiton	60
,, South Molton	60
,, Tavistock	60
,, Tiverton	60
,, Torquay	60
,, Totnes	61
Dewsbury	37
Doncaster—see Yorks	
Donegal, E.	108
,, N.	108
,, S.	108
,, W.	108
Dorset, E.	61
,, N.	61
,, S.	61
,, W.	61

	PAGE
Dover	37
Down, E.	108
,, N.	108
,, S.	108
,, W.	108
Droitwich—see Worcester	
Dublin, College Green	104
,, Harbour	105
,, St. Patrick's	105
,, St. Stephens Green	105
Dublin Co.—N.	108
,, S.	109
Dublin University	115
Dudley	37
Dulwich—see Camberwell	
Dumbartonshire	99
Dumfries District	93
Dumfriesshire	93
Dundee	94
Durham	37
Durham, Barnard Castle	61
,, Bishop Auckland	61
,, Chester-le-Street	62
,, Houghton-le-Spring	62
,, Jarrow	62
,, Mid	62
,, N.W.	62
,, S.E.	62
Ealing—see Middlesex	
Eastbourne—see Sussex	
East Grinstead—see Sussex	
East Lothian—see Haddington	
East Toxteth—see Liverpool	
Eccles—see Lancs	
Ecclesall—see Sheffield	
Eddisbury—see Cheshire	
Edgbaston—see Birmingham	
Edinburgh, Central	94
,, E.	94
,, S.	94
,, W.	94
Edinburgh and St. Andrews University	115
Edinburghshire (Mid Lothian)	99
Egremont—see Cumberland	
Eifion—see Carnarvonshire	
Elgin District	94
Elgin and Nairn	100
Elland—see Yorks	
Enfield—see Middlesex	
Epping—see Essex	
Epsom—see Surrey	
Eskdale—see Cumberland	
Essex, Chelmsford	62
,, Epping	63
,, Harwich	63
,, Maldon	63
,, Romford	63
,, S.E.	63
,, Saffron Walden	63
,, Walthamstow	63
Everton—see Liverpool	
Evesham—see Worcester	
Exchange—see Liverpool	
Exeter	37
Eye—see Suffolk	
Falkirk District	95
Falmouth—see Penryn	

	PAGE
Fareham—see Hants	
Faversham—see Kent	
Fermanagh, N.	109
,, S.	109
Fife, E.	100
,, W.	100
Finsbury, Central	23
,, E.	23
,, Holborn	23
Flint District	89
Flintshire	91
Forest of Dean—see Glo'ster	
Forfarshire	100
Frome—see Somerset	
Fulham	23
Gainsborough—see Lincs	
Galway	105
Galway, Connemara	109
,, E.	109
,, N.	109
,, S.	109
Gateshead	38
Glamorganshire, E.	92
,, Gower	92
,, Mid	92
,, Rhondda	92
,, S.	92
Glasgow, Blackfriars	95
,, Bridgeton	95
,, Camlachie	95
,, Central	95
,, College	95
,, St. Rollox	96
,, Tradeston	96
Glasgow and Aberdeen Universities	115
Gloucester	38
Gloucester, Cirencester	64
,, Forest of Dean	64
,, Stroud	64
,, Tewkesbury	64
,, Thornbury	64
Gorton—see Lancs	
Govan—see Lanark	
Gower—see Glamorgan	
Grantham	38
Gravesend	38
Great Grimsby	38
Great Yarmouth	38
Greenock	96
Greenwich	23
Guildford—see Surrey	
Hackney, Central	24
,, N.	24
,, S.	24
Haddington	100
Haggerston—see Shoreditch	
Halifax	38
Hallam—see Sheffield	
Hallamshire—see Yorks	
Hammersmith	24
Hampshire, Andover	64
,, Basingstoke	64
,, Fareham	65
,, Isle of Wight	65
,, New Forest	65
,, Petersfield	65
Hampstead	24
Handsworth—see Staffs.	
Hanley	39

	PAGE
Harborough—see Leicester	
Harbour—see Dublin	
Harrow—see Middlesex	
Hartlepool	39
Harwich—see Essex	
Hastings	39
Haverfordwest—see Pembroke	
Hawick District	96
Henley—see Oxon	
Hereford	39
Hereford, Leominster	65
,, Ross	65
Hertford, Hertford	65
,, Hitchin	66
,, St. Albans	66
,, Watford	66
Hexham—see Northumberland	
Heywood—see Lancs	
High Peak—see Derby	
Hitchin—see Hertford	
Holborn—see Finsbury	
Holderness—see Yorks	
Holmfirth—see Yorks	
Honiton—see Devon	
Horncastle—see Lincs	
Hornsey—see Middlesex	
Horsham—see Sussex	
Houghton-le-Spring — see Durham	
Howdenshire—see Yorks	
Hoxton—see Shoreditch	
Huddersfield	39
Hull, Central	39
,, E.	39
,, W.	40
Hunts, Huntingdon	66
,, Ramsey	66
Hyde—see Cheshire	
Hythe	40
Ilkeston—see Derbyshire	
Ince—see Lancs	
Inverness District	96
Inverness-shire	100
Ipswich	40
Isle of Thanet—see Kent	
Isle of Wight—see Hants	
Islington, E.	24
,, N.	24
,, S.	25
,, W.	25
Jarrow—see Durham	
Keighley—see Yorks	
Kendal—see Westmorland	
Kennington—see Lambeth	
Kensington, N.	25
,, S.	25
Kent, Ashford	66
,, Dartford	66
,, Faversham	66
,, Isle of Thanet	67
,, Medway	67
,, St. Augustine's	67
,, Sevenoaks	67
,, Tunbridge	67
Kerry, E.	109
,, N.	109
,, S.	110
,, W.	110

	PAGE
Kidderminster	40
Kildare, N.	110
,, S.	110
Kilkenny	105
Kilkenny, N.	110
,, S.	110
Kilmarnock District	96
Kincardineshire	100
King's Co., Birr	110
,, Tullamore	110
King's Lynn	40
Kingston—see Surrey	
Kingswinford—see Staffs	
Kirkcaldy District	96
Kirkcudbrightshire	101
Kirkdale—see Liverpool	
Knutsford—see Cheshire	
Lambeth, Brixton	25
,, Kennington	25
,, N.	25
,, Norwood	25
Lanark, Govan	101
,, Mid	101
,, N.E.	101
,, N.W.	101
,, Partick	101
,, S.	102
Lancashire, Accrington	68
,, Blackpool	67
,, Bootle	70
,, Chorley	68
,, Clitheroe	68
,, Darwen	68
,, Eccles	68
,, Gorton	69
,, Heywood	69
,, Ince	70
,, Lancaster	68
,, Leigh	70
,, Middleton	69
,, Newton	70
,, North Lonsdale	68
,, Ormskirk	70
,, Prestwich	69
,, Radcliffe-cum-Farnworth	69
,, Rossendale	68
,, Southport	70
,, Stretford	69
,, Westhoughton	69
,, Widnes	70
Lancaster—see Lancs	
Launceston—see Cornwall	
Leamington—see Warwick	
Leeds, Central	40
,, E.	41
,, N.	41
,, S.	41
,, W.	41
Leek—see Staffs	
Leicester	41
Leicestershire, Bosworth	71
,, Harborough	71
,, Loughborough	71
,, Melton	71
Leigh—see Lancs	
Leith District	97
Leitrim, N.	110
,, S.	110
Leix—see Queen's Co.	

	PAGE
Leominster—see Hereford	
Lewes—see Sussex	
Lewisham	26
Lichfield—see Staffs	
Limehouse — see Tower Hamlets	
Limerick	105
Limerick, E.	110
,, W.	110
Lincoln	41
Lincolnshire, Brigg	71
,, Gainsborough	71
,, Horncastle	72
,, Louth	72
,, Sleaford	72
,, Spalding	72
,, Stamford	72
Linlithgowshire	102
Liverpool, Abercromby	42
,, East Toxteth	42
,, Everton	42
,, Exchange	42
,, Kirkdale	42
,, Scotland	42
,, Walton	43
,, West Derby	43
,, West Toxteth	43
London, City of	21
London University	115
Londonderry	105
Londonderry, N.	111
,, S.	111
Longford, N.	111
,, S.	111
Lonsdale, N.—see Lancs	
Loughborough—see Leicester	
Louth, N.	111
,, S.	111
Louth—see Lincs	
Lowestoft—see Suffolk	
Ludlow—see Shropshire	
Luton—see Beds	
Lynn Regis—see King's Lynn	
Macclesfield—see Cheshire	
Maidstone	43
Maldon—see Essex	
Malton—see Yorks	
Manchester, E.	43
,, N.	43
,, N.E.	43
,, N.W.	44
,, S.	44
,, S.W.	44
Mansfield—see Notts	
Marylebone, E.	26
,, W.	26
Mayo, E.	111
,, N.	111
,, S.	111
,, W.	111
Meath, N.	112
,, S.	112
Medway—see Kent	
Melton—see Leicester	
Merionethshire	92
Merthyr Tydvil	89
Middlesbrough	44
Middlesex, Brentford	72
,, Ealing	72

CONSTITUENCIES.

	PAGE
Middlesex, Enfield	73
,, Harrow	73
,, Hornsey	73
,, Tottenham	73
,, Uxbridge	73
Middleton—see Lancs	
Mid Lothian—see Edinburgh	
Mile End—see Tower Hamlets	
Monaghan, N.	112
,, S.	112
Monmouth District	44
Monmouthshire, N.	73
,, S.	73
,, W.	73
Montgomery District	89
Montgomeryshire	92
Montrose District	97
Morley, Yorks	
Morpeth	44
Nairn—see Elgin and Nairn	
Newark—see Notts	
Newbury—see Berks	
Newcastle-on-Tyne	44
Newcastle-under-Lyme	45
New Forest—see Hants	
Newington, Walworth	26
,, West	26
Newmarket—see Cambs	
Newport—see Shropshire	
Newry	115
Newton—see Lancs	
Norfolk, E.	74
,, Mid	74
,, N.	74
,, N.W.	74
,, S.	74
,, S.W.	74
Normanton—see Yorks	
Northampton	45
Northants, E.	75
,, Mid	75
,, N.	75
,, S.	75
North Lonsdale—see Lancs	
North Shields—see Tynemouth	
Northumberland, Berwick	75
,, Hexham	75
,, Tyneside	75
,, Wansbeck	76
Northwich—see Cheshire	
Norwich	45
Norwood—see Lambeth	
Nottingham, E.	45
,, S.	46
,, W.	46
Notts, Bassetlaw	76
,, Mansfield	76
,, Newark	76
,, Rushcliffe	76
Nuneaton—see Warwickshire	
Oldham	46
Orkney and Shetland	102
Ormskirk—see Lancs	
Osgoldcross—see Yorks	
Ossory—see Queen's Co.	
Oswestry—see Shropshire	
Otley—see Yorks	

	PAGE
Oxford	46
Oxford, Banbury	76
,, Henley	76
,, Woodstock	76
Oxford University	114
Paddington, N.	26
,, S.	27
Paisley	97
Partick—see Lanark	
Peckham—see Camberwell	
Peebles and Selkirk	102
Pembroke and Haverfordwest	90
Pembrokeshire	93
Penrith—see Cumberland	
Penryn and Falmouth	46
Perth	97
Perthshire, E.	102
,, W.	102
Peterborough	47
Petersfield—see Hants	
Plymouth	47
Pontefract	47
Poplar—see Tower Hamlets	
Portsmouth	47
Preston	48
Prestwich—see Lancs	
Pudsey—see Yorks	
Queen's Co., Leix	112
,, Ossory	112
Radcliffe-cum-Farnworth—see Lancs	
Radnorshire	93
Ramsey—see Hunts	
Reading	48
Reigate—see Surrey	
Renfrewshire, E.	103
,, W.	103
Rhondda—see Glamorgan	
Richmond—see Yorks	
Ripon—see Yorks	
Rochdale	48
Rochester	48
Romford—see Essex	
Roscommon, N.	112
,, S.	112
Ross—see Hereford	
Ross and Cromarty	103
Rossendale—see Lancs	
Rotherham—see Yorks	
Rotherhithe—see Southwark	
Roxburghshire	103
Rugby—see Warwick	
Rushcliffe—see Notts	
Rutland	77
Rye—see Sussex	
Saffron Walden—see Essex	
St. Albans—see Hertford	
St. Andrews District	97
St. Andrews Univ.—see Edinburgh	
St. Augustine's—see Kent	
St. Austell—see Cornwall	
St. George's, Hanover-sq.	27
St. George's-in-the-East—see Tower Hamlets	
St. Helens	48
St. Ives—see Cornwall	
St. Pancras, E.	27
,, N.	27

	PAGE
St. Pancras, S.	27
,, W.	27
St. Patrick's—see Dublin	
St. Rollox—see Glasgow	
St. Stephen's Green—see Dublin	
Salford, N.	48
,, S.	48
,, W.	49
Salisbury	49
Scarborough	49
Scotland Division—see Liverpool	
Selkirk—see Peebles and Selkirk	
Sevenoaks—see Kent	
Sheffield, Attercliffe	49
,, Brightside	49
,, Central	49
,, Ecclesall	49
,, Hallam	50
Shipley—see Yorks	
Shoreditch, Haggerston	28
,, Hoxton	28
Shrewsbury	50
Shropshire, Ludlow	77
,, Newport	77
,, Oswestry	77
,, Wellington	77
Skipton—see Yorks	
Sleaford—see Lincs	
Sligo, N.	112
,, S.	112
Somerset, Bridgewater	77
,, E.	78
,, Frome	78
,, N.	78
,, S.	78
,, Wellington	78
,, Wells	78
Southampton	50
South Molton—see Devon	
Southport—see Lancs	
South Shields	50
Southwark, Bermondsey	28
,, Rotherhithe	28
,, West	28
Sowerby—see Yorks	
Spalding—see Lincs	
Spen Valley—see Yorks	
Stafford	50
Staffs, Burton	78
,, Handsworth	78
,, Kingswinford	79
,, Leek	79
,, Lichfield	79
,, N.W.	79
,, W.	79
Stalybridge	51
Stamford—see Lincs	
Stepney—see Tower Hamlets	
Stirling District	97
Stirlingshire	103
Stockport	51
Stockton	51
Stoke-on-Trent	51
Stowmarket—see Suffolk	
Strand	28
Stratford-on-Avon—see Warwick	

		PAGE			PAGE			PAGE
Stretford—see Lancs			Tyneside—see Northumberland			Wigtownshire	..	103
Stroud—see Gloucester						Wilton—see Wilts		
Sudbury—see Suffolk			Tyrone, E.	..	113	Wilts, Chippenham	..	83
Suffolk, Eye	..	79	,, Mid	..	113	,, Cricklade	..	83
,, Lowestoft	..	79	,, N.	..	113	,, Devizes	..	83
,, Stowmarket	..	80	,, S.	..	113	,, Westbury	..	83
,, Sudbury	..	80	Uxbridge—see Middlesex			,, Wilton	..	83
,, Woodbridge	..	80	Wakefield	..	52	Wimbledon—see Surrey		
Sunderland	..	51	Walsall	..	52	Winchester	..	53
Surrey, Chertsey	..	80	Walthamstow—see Essex			Windsor	..	53
,, Epsom	..	80	Walton—see Liverpool			Wirral—see Cheshire		
,, Guildford	..	80	Walworth—see Newington			Wisbech—see Cambs		
,, Kingston	..	81	Wandsworth..	..	29	Wokingham—see Berks		
,, Reigate	..	81	Wansbeck—see Northumberland			Wolverhampton, E...	..	53
,, Wimbledon..	..	81				,, S...	..	53
Sussex, Chichester	..	81	Warrington	..	52	,, W.	..	53
,, Eastbourne..	..	81	Warwick and Leamington	..	52	Woodbridge—see Suffolk		
,, East Grinstead	..	81	Warwick, Nuneaton	..	82	Woodstock—see Oxford		
,, Horsham	..	81	,, Rugby	..	82	Woolwich	..	30
,, Lewes	..	81	,, Stratford-on-Avon	..	82	Worcester	..	54
,, Rye	..	82	,, Tamworth	..	82	Worcester, Bewdley	..	83
Sutherland	..	103	Waterford	..	105	,, Droitwich	..	84
Swansea	..	90	Waterford, E.	..	113	,, E.	..	84
Swansea District	..	90	,, W.	..	113	,, Evesham	..	84
			Watford—see Herts			,, N.	..	84
Tamworth—see Warwick			Wednesbury	..	52	Wycombe—see Bucks		
Taunton	..	51	Wellington—see Shropshire			Yarmouth—see Great Yarmouth		
Tavistock—see Devon			Wellington—see Somerset					
Tewkesbury—see Glo'ster			Wells—see Somerset			York	..	54
Thanet, Isle of—see Kent			West Bromwich	..	52	Yorks, Barkston Ash	..	85
Thirsk and Malton—see Yorks			Westbury—see Wilts			,, Barnsley	..	85
			West Derby—see Liverpool			,, Buckrose	..	84
Thornbury—see Glo'ster			West Ham, N.	..	29	,, Cleveland	..	85
Tipperary, E.	..	113	,, S.	..	30	,, Colne Valley	..	85
,, Mid	..	113	Westhoughton—see Lancs			,, Doncaster	..	86
,, N.	..	113	Westmeath, N.	..	114	,, Elland	..	86
,, S.	..	113	,, S.	..	114	,, Hallamshire	..	86
Tiverton—see Devon			Westminster..	..	30	,, Holderness	..	84
Torquay—see Devon			Westmorland, Appleby	..	82	,, Holmfirth	..	86
Totnes—see Devon			,, Kendal	..	83	,, Howdenshire	..	84
Tottenham—see Middlesex			West Toxteth — see Liverpool			,, Keighley	..	86
Tower Hamlets, Bow and Bromley		28				,, Morley	..	86
			Wexford, N.	..	114	,, Normanton..	..	87
,, Limehouse		28	,, S.	..	114	,, Osgoldcross.	..	87
,, Mile End..		29	Whitby—see Yorks			,, Otley	..	87
,, Poplar		29	Whitechapel — see Tower Hamlets			,, Pudsey	..	87
,, St. George's		29				,, Richmond	..	85
,, Stepney		29	Whitehaven	..	53	,, Ripon	..	87
,, Whitechapel		29	Wick District	..	97	,, Rotherham..	..	87
Toxteth—see Liverpool			Wicklow, E...	..	114	,, Shipley	..	87
Tradeston—see Glasgow			,, W.	..	114	,, Skipton	..	88
Truro—see Cornwall			Widnes—see Lancs			,, Sowerby	..	88
Tullamore—see King's Co.			Wigan	..	53	,, Spen Valley	..	88
Tunbridge—see Kent			Wight, Isle of—see Hants			,, Thirsk and Malton..	..	85
Tynemouth and North Shields		52				,, Whitby	..	85

THE NEW PARLIAMENT.

The following is a list of members returned to the new Parliament. An asterisk denotes that the member elected sat in the last Parliament at the time of the Dissolution :—

MEMBERS.	CONSTITUENCIES.	L.	LAB.	N.	U.
*Abraham, Rt. Hon. W.	Glamorganshire, Rhondda	..	1	..	..
*Acland-Hood, Rt. Hon. Sir A. F.	Somerset, Wellington	..	..	..	1
Adam, Maj. W. A.	Woolwich	..	..	..	1
Addison, C.	Hoxton	1	..	..	..
*Adkins, W. R.	Middleton	1	..	..	..
*Agar-Robartes, Hon. T.	Cornwall, Mid	1	..	..	..
*Agnew, G. W.	Salford, W.	1	..	..	..
*Ainsworth, J. S.	Argyllshire	1	..	..	..
*Akers-Douglas, Rt. Hon. A.	St. Augustine's	..	..	..	1
*Alden, P.	Tottenham	1	..	..	..
*Allen, C. P.	Stroud	1	..	..	..
Anderson, A.	Ayrshire	1	..	..	..
*Anson, Sir W.	Oxford Univ.	..	..	..	1
Arbuthnot, G. A.	Burnley	..	..	..	1
Archer-Shee, Maj. M.	Finsbury, C.	..	..	..	1
*Arkwright, J. S.	Hereford	..	..	..	1
*Armitage, R.	Leeds, C.	1	..	..	..
*Ashley, W. W.	Blackpool	..	..	..	1
*Ashton, T. G.	Luton	1	..	..	..
*Asquith, Rt. Hon. H. H.	Fife, E.	1	..	..	..
*Atherley-Jones, L., K.C.	Durham, N.W.	1	..	..	..
Attenborough, W. A.	Bedford	..	..	..	1
*Aubrey-Fletcher, Rt. Hon. Sir H.	Lewes	..	..	..	1
Bagot, Lieut.-Col. J. F.	Kendal	..	..	..	1
Baird, J. L.	Rugby	..	..	..	1
Baker, H.	Accrington	1	..	..	..
*Baker, J. A.	Finsbury, E.	1	..	..	..
Baker, Sir R.	Dorset, N.	..	..	..	1
*Balcarres, Lord	Chorley	..	..	..	1
*Baldwin, S.	Bewdley	..	..	..	1
*Balfour, Rt. Hon. A. J.	City of London	..	..	..	1
Balfour, R.	Partick	1	..	..	..
*Banbury, Sir F.	City of London	..	..	..	1
Barclay, Sir T.	Blackburn	1	..	..	..
*Baring, Capt. G. V.	Winchester	..	..	..	1
*Barlow, Sir J. E.	Frome	1	..	..	..
*Barnes, G. N.	Glasgow, Blackfriars	..	1	..	..
Barnston, H.	Cheshire, Eddisbury	..	..	..	1
*Barran, R. H.	Leeds, N.	1	..	..	..
*Barran, Sir J.	Hawick Burghs	1	..	..	..
*Barrie, H. T.	Londonderry, N.	..	..	..	1
*Barry, E.	Cork, S.	..	..	1	..
*Barry, Redmond, K.C.	Tyrone, N.	1	..	..	..
Barton, A. W.	Oldham	1	..	..	..
Bathurst, Charles	Wilton	..	..	..	1
Bathurst, Col. the Hon. A. B.	Cirencester	..	..	..	1
*Beach, Hon. M. Hicks	Tewkesbury	..	..	..	1
*Beale, W. P., K.C.	Ayrshire, S.	1	..	..	..
*Beckett, the Hon. Gervase	Whitby	..	..	..	1
*Belloc, H.	Salford, S.	1	..	..	..
Benn, J. H.	Greenwich	..	..	..	1
*Benn, W. Wedgwood	St. George's-in-the-East	1	..	..	..
Bentham, G. J.	Gainsborough	1	..	..	..
Beresford, Lord C.	Portsmouth	..	..	..	1
*Bethell, Sir J. H.	Romford	1	..	..	..
Bird, A. F.	Wolverhmptn, W.	..	..	..	1
*Birrell, Rt. Hon. A.	Bristol, N.	1	..	..	..
*Black, A. W.	Biggleswade	1	..	..	..
*Boland, J. P.	Kerry, S.	..	..	1	..
*Bottomley, H.	Hackney, S.	1	..	..	..
*Bowerman, C. W.	Deptford	..	1	..	..
Bowles, T. G.	King's Lynn	1	..	..	..
Boyle, D.	Mayo, N.	..	..	1	..
Boyle, W. L.	Norfolk, Mid	..	..	..	1
Boyton, J.	Marylebone, E.	..	..	..	1
*Brace, W.	Glamorganshire, S.	..	1	..	..
Brackenbury, Capt. H. L.	Lincolnsh., Louth	..	..	..	1
Brady, P. J.	Dublin, St. Stephen's Green	..	..	1	..
Brassey, Capt. R. B.	Banbury	..	..	..	1
Brassey, H. L. C.	Northamp'shire, N.	..	..	..	1
*Bridgeman, W. C.	Oswestry	..	..	..	1

Members.	Constituencies.	L.	Lab.	N.	U.
*Brigg, Sir J.	Keighley	1			
*Brocklehurst, Col. W. B.	Macclesfield	1			
*Brotherton, E. A.	Wakefield				1
*Brunner, J. F. L.	Northwich	1			
Brunskill, G. F.	Tyrone, Mid				1
*Bryce, J. A.	Inverness Burghs	1			
*Bull, Sir W. J.	Hammersmith				1
*Burdett-Coutts, W. L. A. B.	Westminster				1
Burgoyne, A.	Kensington, N.				1
*Burns, Rt. Hon. J.	Battersea	1			
*Burt, Rt. Hon. T.	Morpeth	1			
Butcher, J. G., K.C.	York				1
*Butcher, S. H.	Cambridge Univ.				1
Buxton, C. R.	Ashburton	1			
Buxton, Noel	Norfolk, N.	1			
*Buxton, Rt. Hon. S.	Poplar	1			
*Byles, W. P.	Salford, N.	1			
Calley, Col. T.C.P.	Cricklade				1
*Cameron, R.	Houghton-le-Spring	1			
*Campbell, Rt. Hon. J. H. M., K.C.	Dublin University				1
*Carlile, E. H.	St. Albans				1
*Carr-Gomm, H.	Rotherhithe	1			
*Carson, Rt. Hon. Sir E. H., K.C.	Dublin University				1
*Castlereagh, Viscount	Maidstone				1
Cator, J.	Huntingdon				1
Cautley, H. S.	East Grinstead				1
*Cave, G., K.C.	Kingston				1
Cavendish - Bentinck, Lord H.	Nottingham, S.				1
Cawley, H. T.	Heywood	1			
*Cawley, Sir F.	Prestwich	1			
*Cecil, E.	Aston Manor				1
Cecil, Lord Hugh	Oxford Univ.				1
Chaloner, Col. R. G. W.	Liverpool, Abercromby				1
*Chamberlain, Rt. Hon. Austen	Worcestershire, E.				1
*Chamberlain, Rt. Hon. J.	Birmingham, W.				1
Chambers, J., K.C.	Belfast, S.				1
Chancellor, H. G.	Haggerston	1			
*Channing, Sir F. A.	Northamptonshire, E.	1			
*Chaplin, Rt. Hon. H.	Wimbledon				1
Chapple, A.	Stirlingshire	1			
*Churchill, Rt. Hon. Winston S.	Dundee	1			
*Clancy, J. J.	Dublin Co., N.			1	
Clay, Capt. H. Spender	Tunbridge				1
*Cleland, J. W.	Glasgow, Bridgeton	1			
*Clive, Capt. P. A.	Herefordshire, Ross				1
*Clough, W.	Skipton	1			
*Clyde, J. A., K.C.	Edinburgh, W.				1
*Clynes, J. R.	Manchester, N.E.		1		
*Coates, Major E.F.	Lewisham				1
Colefax, H. A.	Manchester, S.W.				1
*Collings, Rt.Hon. J.	Birmingham, Bordesley				1
Collins, G. P.	Greenock	1			
*Collins, S.	Kennington	1			
*Collins, Sir W.	St. Pancras, W.	1			

Members.	Constituencies.	L.	Lab.	N.	U.
Compton, Lord A. F.	Brentford				1
*Compton-Rickett, Sir J.	Osgoldcross	1			
*Condon, T. J.	Tipperary, E.			1	
Cooper, Capt. Bryan	Dublin County, S.				1
Cooper, R. A.	Walsall				1
*Corbett, A. Cameron	Glasgow, Tradeston	1			
*Corbett, T. L.	Down, N.				1
*Cornwall, Sir E. A.	Bethnal-green, N.E.	1			
*Cory, Sir C. J.	St. Ives	1			
*Courthope, G. L.	Rye				1
*Cowan, W. H.	Aberdeenshire, E.	1			
*Craig, C. C.	Antrim, S.				1
*Craig, Capt. J.	Down, E.				1
*Craig, H. J.	Tynemouth	1			
Craig, Norman C., K.C.	Thanet				1
*Craik, Sir H.	Glasgow & Aberdeen Univs.				1
Crawshay-Williams, E.	Leicester	1			
*Crean, E.	Cork, S.E.			1	
Cripps, Sir C. A., K.C.	Wycombe				1
Croft, H. Page	Christchurch				1
*Crosfield, A. H.	Warrington	1			
*Crossley, Sir W. J.	Altrincham	1			
*Cullinan, J.	Tipperary, S.			1	
*Dalrymple, Viscount	Wigtownshire				1
Dalziel, D.	Brixton				1
*Dalziel, Sir J. H.	Kirkcaldy Burghs	1			
*Davies, D.	Montgomeryshire	1			
*Davies, Ellis W.	Eifion	1			
*Davies, Sir W. H.	Bristol, S.	1			
Dawes, J. A.	Walworth	1			
*Delany, W.	Queen's Co., Ossory			1	
Denman, Hon. R. D.	Carlisle	1			
*Devlin, J.	Belfast, W.			1	
*Dewar, A, K.C.	Edinburgh. S.	1			
*Dewar, Sir J. A.	Inverness-shire	1			
*Dickinson, W. H.	St. Pancras, N.	1			
*Dilke, Rt. Hon. Sir C. W.	Forest of Dean	1			
*Dillon, J.	Mayo, E.			1	
Dixon, C. H.	Boston				1
*Donelan, Capt. A. J. C.	Cork, E.			1	
Doris, W.	Mayo, W.			1	
Du Cros, Alfred	Bow and Bromley				1
*Du Cros, Arthur	Hastings				1
*Duffy, W. J.	Galway, S.			1	
Duke, H. E., K.C.	Exeter				1
*Duncan, C.	Barrow-in-Furness		1		
*Duncan, J. H.	Otley	1			
Duncannon, Viscount	Cheltenham				1
*Dunn, A. E.	Camborne	1			
Dunn, Sir W. H.	Southwark, W.				1
*Edwards, E.	Hanley		1		
*Elibank, Master of	Mid Lothian	1			
*Ellis, Rt. Hon. J. E.	Rushcliffe	1			
Elverston, H.	Gateshead	1			
*Emmott, Rt. Hon. A.	Oldham	1			
*Esmonde, Sir T.	Wexford, N.			1	

THE NEW PARLIAMENT.

MEMBERS.	CONSTITUENCIES.	L.	LAB.	N.	U.
*Esslemont, G. B.	Aberdeen, S.	1	.	.	.
Evans, L. Worthington ..	Colchester	.	.	.	1
*Evans, Sir S. T., K.C. ..	Glamorgansh. Mid	1	.	.	.
Eyres-Monsell, B.	Evesham..	.	.	.	1
*Faber, Capt. W.V.	Hampshire, W.	.	.	.	1
*Faber, G. D.	Clapham	.	.	.	1
*Falconer, J.	Forfarshire	1	.	.	.
Falle, B. G.	Portsmouth	.	.	.	1
*Farrell, J. P.	Longford, N.	.	.	1	.
*Fell, A.	Great Yarmouth	.	.	.	1
*Fenwick, C.	Wansbeck	1	.	.	.
*Ferens, T. R.	Hull, E. ..	1	.	.	.
*Fetherstonhaugh, G., K.C.	Fermanagh, N. ..	.	.	.	1
*Ffrench, P.	Wexford, S.	.	.	1	.
*Field, W...	Dublin, St. Pat'k's	.	.	1	.
Finlay, Rt. Hon. Sir R. B., K.C.	Edinburgh and St. Andrews Univs.	.	.	.	1
Fisher, W. Hayes	Fulham	.	.	.	1
Fitzroy, E. A.	Northamp'shire, S.	.	.	.	1
Flannery, Sir F.	Essex, Maldon	.	.	.	1
*Flavin, M. J.	Kerry, N.	.	.	1	.
Fleming, V.	Henley	.	.	.	1
*Fletcher, J. S.	Hampstead	.	.	.	1
*Forster, H. W.	Sevenoaks	.	.	.	1
Foster, H. S.	Lowestoft	.	.	.	1
Foster, J. K.	Coventry..	.	.	.	1
*Foster, P. S.	Stratford-on-Avon	.	.	.	1
*Foster, Rt. Hon. Sir W. ..	Ilkeston ..	1	.	.	.
France, G.	Morley	1	.	.	.
*Fuller, J. M. F.	Westbury	1	.	.	.
*Furness, Sir C.	Hartlepool	1	.	.	.
Gardner, E.	Wokingham	.	.	.	1
Gastrell, Maj. H.	Lambeth, N.	.	.	.	1
Gelder, Sir W. A.	Brigg	1	.	.	.
Gibbs, Lt.-Col.G.A.	Bristol, W.	.	.	.	1
*Gibson, Sir J.	Edinburgh, E.	1	.	.	.
*Gilhooly, J.,	Cork Co., W.	.	.	1	.
*Gill, A. H.	Bolton	.	1	.	.
Gilmour, Capt. J.	Renfrewshire, E.	.	.	.	1
*Ginnell, L.	Westmeath, N. ..	.	.	1	.
Glanville, H. J.	Bermondsey	1	.	.	.
*Glover, T.	St. Helens	.	1	.	.
*Goddard, Sir D.	Ipswich ..	1	.	.	.
Goldman, C. S.	Penryn & Falm'th	.	.	.	1
Goldsmith, F.	Stowmarket.	.	.	.	1
*Gooch, H. C.	Peckham..	.	.	.	1
Gordon, J., K.C.	Londonderry, S.	.	.	.	1
*Goulding, E. A.	Worcester	.	.	.	1
Grant, J. A.	Cumberland, Egremont ..	.	.	.	1
Greene, Raymond	Hackney, N.	.	.	.	1
*Greenwood, G. C.	Peterborough	1	.	.	.
Greig, Colonel	Renfrewshire, W.	1	.	.	.
Grenfell C. A.	Bodmin ..	1	.	.	.
*Gretton, J.	Rutlandshire	.	.	.	1
*Grey, Rt.Hon.SirE.	Berwick-on-Tweed	1	.	.	.
*Griffith, J. Ellis	Anglesey	1	.	.	.
Griffiths, J. N.	Wednesbury	.	.	.	1
Guest, Capt. the Hon. F.	Dorset, E...	1	.	.	.
Guiney, P.	Cork Co., N.	.	.	1	.
*Guinness, Hon.W.	Bury St. Edmunds	.	.	.	1
*Gulland, J. W.	Dumfries Burghs	1	.	.	.
*Gwynn, S. L.	Galway ..	.	.	1	.
Gwynne, R. S.	Eastbourne	.	.	.	1
Hackett, J.	Tipperary, Mid	.	.	1	.
*Haddock, G. B.	North Lonsdale	.	.	.	1
*Haldane, Rt. Hon. R. B., K.C.	Haddingtonshire	1	.	.	.
Hall, Douglas B.	Isle of Wight	.	.	.	1
Hall, E. Marshall, K.C.	Liverpool, E. Toxteth	.	.	.	1
*Hall, F.	Normanton	.	1	.	.
Hambro, Angus V.	Dorset, S.	.	.	.	1
Hamersley, A. St. G., K.C.	Woodstock	.	.	.	1
*Hamilton, Marquis of	Londonderry	.	.	.	1
Hamilton, Ld. C.	Kensington, S.	.	.	.	1
*Hancock, J. G.	Derbyshire, Mid	.	1	.	.
*Harcourt, Rt. Hon. Lewis	Rossendale	1	.	.	.
*Harcourt, R. V.	Montrose Burghs	1	.	.	.
*Hardie, J. Keir	Merthyr Tydvil ..	.	1	.	.
*Hardy, L.	Kent, Ashford	.	.	.	1
*Harmood-Banner, J. S.	Liverpool, Everton	.	.	.	1
*Harmsworth, R. Leicester	Caithness-shire	1	.	.	.
*Harrington, T.	Dublin, Harbour..	.	.	1	.
*Harris, F. Leverton	Stepney ..	.	.	.	1
Harris, H. P.	Paddington, S. ..	.	.	.	1
Harrison-Broadley, Col. H. E.	Howdenshire	.	.	.	1
*Harvey, A. G.	Rochdale	1	.	.	.
Harvey, T. E.	Leeds, W.	1	.	.	.
*Harvey, W. E.	Derbyshire, N.E.	.	1	.	.
*Harwood, G.	Bolton	1	.	.	.
*Haslam, J.	Chesterfield	.	1	.	.
*Haslam, L.	Monmouth Dist.	1	.	.	.
Havelock-Allan, Sir H.	Bishop Auckland	1	.	.	.
*Havieland-Burke, E.	Tullamore	.	.	1	.
*Haworth, A. A.	Manchester, S.	1	.	.	.
*Hayden, J. P.	Roscommon, S.	.	.	1	.
Hayward, E.	Durham, S.E.	1	.	.	.
*Hazleton, R.	Galway, N.	.	.	1	.
*Healy, T. M, K.C.	Louth, N.	.	.	1	.
Heath, Col. A. H.	Staffordshire, Leek	.	.	.	1
*Heaton, J. Henniker	Canterbury	.	.	.	1
*Helme, N. W.	Lancaster	1	.	.	.
*Helmsley, Viscount	Thirsk and Malton	.	.	.	1
*Hemmerde, E. G., K.C.	Denbighshire, E.	1	.	.	.
*Henderson, A.	Barnard Castle	.	1	.	.
*Henderson, J. M.	Aberdeenshire, W.	1	.	.	.
Henderson, Maj. H. G.	Abingdon	.	.	.	1
*Henry, C. S.	Shropshire, Mid..	1	.	.	.
*Herbert, Colonel Sir I.	Monmouthshire, S.	1	.	.	.
*Hermon-Hodge, Sir R.	Croydon ..	.	.	.	1
Hickman, Col. T.	Wolverham'ton, S.	.	.	.	1
*Higham, J. S.	Sowerby ..	1	.	.	.
*Hill, Sir C. L.	Shrewsbury	.	.	.	1
Hillier, Dr. A.	Hitchin ..	.	.	.	1
*Hills, J. W.	Durham	.	.	.	1
Hindle, F. G.	Darwen ..	1	.	.	.
Hoare, S. J. G.	Chelsea ..	.	.	.	1
*Hobhouse, Rt. Hon. C.	Bristol, E.	1	.	.	.
*Hodge, J.	Gorton	.	1	.	.

16—2

Members.	Constituencies.	L.	Lab.	N.	U.
*Hogan, M.	Tipperary, N.	.	.	1	.
Hohler, G. F., K.C.	Chatham	.	.	.	1
*Holland, Sir W.	Rotherham	1	.	.	.
*Holt, R. D.	Hexham	1	.	.	.
*Hooper, A. G.	Dudley	1	.	.	.
Hope, H.	Buteshire	.	.	.	1
*Hope, J. D.	Fife, W.	1	.	.	.
*Hope, J. F.	Sheffield, C.	.	.	.	.
Horne, Rev. C. Silvester	Ipswich	1	.	.	.
Horne, W. E.	Guildford	.	.	.	1
Horner, A. L., K.C.	Tyrone, S.	.	.	1	.
Houston, R. P.	Liverpool, W. Toxteth	.	.	.	1
Howard, Hon. Geoffrey	Eskdale	1	.	.	.
Hudson, W.	Newcastle-on-Tyne	.	1	.	.
Hughes, S. L.	Stockport	1	.	.	.
Hume-Williams, W.E., K.C.	Bassetlaw	.	.	.	1
'Hunt, R.	Ludlow	.	.	.	1
Hunter, Sir C.	Bath	.	.	.	1
Hunter, W., K.C.	Govan	1	.	.	.
*Illingworth, P.	Shipley	1	.	.	.
*Isaacs, Rufus, K.C.	Reading	1	.	.	.
Jackson, Lt.-Col. J. A.	Whitehaven	.	.	.	1
Jackson, Sir J.	Devonport	.	.	.	1
Jardine, E.	Somerset, E.	.	.	.	1
*Jardine, Sir J.	Roxburghshire	1	.	.	.
Jessel, Capt. H. M.	St. Pancras, S.	.	.	.	1
*Johnson, W.	Warwickshire Nuneaton	.	1	.	.
Jones, E.	Merthyr Tydvil	1	.	.	.
Jones, Haydn	Merionethshire	1	.	.	.
*Jones, Sir D. Brynmor, K.C.	Swansea Dist.	1	.	.	.
*Jones, W.	Arfon	1	.	.	.
*Jordan, J.	Fermanagh, S.	.	.	1	.
*Jowett, F. W.	Bradford, W.	.	1	.	.
*Joyce, M.	Limerick	.	.	1	.
*Keating, M.	Kilkenny, S.	.	.	1	.
Kelly, E.	Donegal, E.	.	.	1	.
Kemp, Sir G.	Manchester, N.W.	1	.	.	.
*Kennedy, V. P.	Cavan, W.	.	.	1	.
Kerr-Smiley, P.	Antrim, N.	.	.	.	1
*Kerry, Earl of	Derbyshire, W.	.	.	.	1
*Keswick, W.	Epsom	.	.	.	1
*Kettle, T. M.	Tyrone, E.	.	.	1	.
*Kilbride, D.	Kildare, S.	.	.	1	.
*Kimber, Sir H.	Wandsworth	.	.	.	1
King, J.	Somerset, N.	1	.	.	.
*King, Sir H. S.	Hull, C.	.	.	.	1
Kinloch-Cooke, Sir C.	Devonport	.	.	.	.
Kirkwood, J. E. Morrison	Essex, S.E.	.	.	.	1
Knight, Capt. E.A.	Kidderminster	.	.	.	1
Knott, J.	Sunderland	.	.	.	1
'Lambert G.	South Molton	1	.	.	.
'Lane-Fox, G. R.	Barkston Ash	.	.	.	1
*Lardner, J. C.	Monaghan, N.	.	.	1	.
*Law, A. Bonar	Dulwich	.	.	.	1
*Law, H. A.	Donegal, W.	.	.	1	.
Lawson, Hon. H. L. W.	Mile-end	.	.	.	1
*Layland-Barratt, Sir F.	Torquay	1	.	.	.
Leach, C.	Colne Valley	1	.	.	.
*Lee, A. H.	Fareham	.	.	.	1
*Lehmann, R. C.	Leicestershire, Harborough	1	.	.	.
*Levy, Sir M.	Loughborough	1	.	.	.
*Lewis, J. H.	Flintshire	1	.	.	.
Lewisham, Viscount	West Bromwich	.	.	.	1
Lincoln, J. T.	Darlington	1	.	.	.
Lloyd, G. A.	Staffordshire, W.	.	.	.	1
*Lloyd George, Rt. Hon. D.	Carnarvon Dist.	1	.	.	.
Locker-Lampson G.	Salisbury	.	.	.	1
Locker-Lampson, O.	Hunts, Ramsey	.	.	.	1
*Lockwood, Rt. Hon. Col. A.R.M.	Epping	.	.	.	1
*Long, Rt. Hon. W.	Strand	.	.	.	1
*Lonsdale, J. B.	Armagh, Mid	.	.	.	1
*Lough, Rt. Hon. T.	Islington, W.	1	.	.	.
Low, Sir F., K.C.	Norwich	1	.	.	.
*Lowe, Sir F. W.	Birmingham, Edg.	.	.	.	1
*Lowther, Rt. Hon. J. W.	Cumberld., Penrith	.	.	.	1
*Lundon, T.	Limerick, E.	.	.	1	.
*Luttrell, H. C. F.	Tavistock	1	.	.	.
*Lynch, A.	Clare, W.	.	.	1	.
*Lyttelton, Rt. Hon. A.	St. George's, Hanover-square	.	.	.	1
Lyttelton, Hon. J. C.	Droitwich	.	.	.	1
*McArthur, C.	Liverpool, Kirkdale	.	.	.	.
McCallum, J.	Paisley	1	.	.	.
*McCalmont, Col. J. M.	Antrim, E.	.	.	.	1
*MacCaw, W. J. MacG.	Down, W.	.	.	.	.
McCurdy, C. A.	Northampton	1	.	.	.
*Macdonald, J.A.M.	Falkirk Burghs	1	.	.	.
*MacDonald, J. R.	Leicester	.	1	.	.
*McKean, J.	Monaghan, S.	.	.	1	.
*McKenna, Rt. Hon. R.	Monmouthshire, N.	1	.	.	.
Mackinder, H. J.	Glasgow, Camlachie	.	.	.	1
McLaren, F.	Lincolnshire, Spalding	1	.	.	.
*McLaren, Rt. Hon. Sir C., K.C.	Bosworth	1	.	.	.
Macmaster, D., K.C.	Chertsey	.	.	.	1
*Macnamara, Dr.	Camberwell, N.	1	.	.	.
*MacNeill, J. G. Swift	Donegal, S.	.	.	1	.
'MacVeagh, J.	Down, S.	.	.	1	.
*Magnus, Sir P.	London Univ.	.	.	.	1
Mallaby-Deeley, H. C.	Harrow	.	.	.	1
*Mallet, C. E.	Plymouth	1	.	.	.
*Manfield, H.	Northamptonshire Mid	1	.	.	.
*Markham, A. B.	Mansfield	1	.	.	.
*Marks, G. C.	Launceston	1	.	.	.
Martin, Hon. J., K.C.	St. Pancras, E.	1	.	.	.
*Mason, J. F.	Windsor	.	.	.	1
*Masterman, C.F.G.	West Ham, N.	1	.	.	.
*Meagher, M.	Kilkenny, N.	.	.	1	.
*Meehan, F. E.	Leitrim, N.	.	.	1	.
*Meehan, P. A.	Queen's Co., Leix	.	.	1	.

THE NEW PARLIAMENT.

Members	Constituencies	L.Lab.	N.	U.
*Menzies, Sir W.	Lanarkshire, S.	1	.	.
*Meysey-Thompson, E. C.	Handsworth	.	.	1
*Middlebrook, W.	Leeds, S.	1	.	.
*Middlemore, J. T.	Birmingham, N.	.	.	1
*Mildmay, F. B.	Devon, Totnes	.	.	1
Millar, J. D.	St. Andrews Burghs	1	.	.
Mills, Hon. C. T.	Uxbridge	.	.	1
Mitchell, W. Foot	Dartford	.	.	1
Molloy, M.	Carlow	.	1	.
*Moiteno, P. A.	Dumfriesshire	1	.	.
*Mond, A.	Swansea Town	1	.	.
*Montagu, Hon. E.S.	Chesterton	1	.	.
*Mooney, J. J.	Newry	.	1	.
*Moore, W.	Armagh, N.	.	.	1
*Morgan, G. Hay	Truro	1	.	.
*Morgan, J. Lloyd, K.C.	Carmarthenshire, W.	1	.	.
*Morpeth, Viscount	Birmingham, S.	.	.	1
Morrison-Bell, Maj. A. C.	Honiton	.	.	1
Morrison, Captain J. A.	Nottingham, E.	.	.	1
*Morton, A. C.	Sutherland	1	.	.
Mount, W. A.	Newbury	.	.	1
*Muldoon, J.	Wicklow, E.	.	1	.
Munro, R.	Wick Burghs	1	.	.
*Munro-Ferguson, R. C.	Leith Burghs	1	.	.
*Murray, Capt. the Hon. A. C.	Kincardineshire	1	.	.
Muspratt, M.	Liverpool, Exchange	1	.	.
*Nannetti, J. P.	Dublin, Coll. Green	.	1	.
*Neilson, F.	Cheshire, Hyde	1	.	.
*Newdegate-Newdegate, F. A.	Tamworth	.	.	1
Newman, J. R. Pretyman	Enfield	.	.	1
Newton, H. K.	Harwich	.	.	1
*Nicholson, C. N.	Doncaster	1	.	.
*Nicholson, W. G.	Petersfield	.	.	1
*Nield, H.	Ealing	.	.	1
*Nolan, J.	Louth, S.	.	1	.
*Norton, Capt. C.	Newington, W.	1	.	.
*Nugent, Sir W.	Westmeath, S.	.	1	.
*Nussey, Sir W.	Pontefract	1	.	.
*Nuttall, H.	Lancs, Stretford	1	.	.
*O'Brien, Patrick	Kilkenny	.	1	.
O'Brien, W.	Cork City	.	1	.
O'Brien, W.	Cork, N.E.	.	1	.
*O'Connor, James	Wicklow, W.	.	1	.
*O'Connor, John	Kildare, N.	.	1	.
*O'Connor, T. P.	Liverpool, Scotland	.	1	.
*O'Doherty, P.	Donegal, N.	.	1	.
*O'Donnell, J.	Mayo, S.	.	1	.
*O'Donnell, T.	Kerry, W.	.	1	.
*O'Dowd, J.	Sligo, S.	.	1	.
Ogden, F.	Pudsey	1	.	.
*O'Grady, J.	Leeds, E.	1	.	.
*O'Kelly, J.	Roscommon, N.	.	1	.
*O'Malley, W.	Connemara	.	1	.
O'Neill, Hon. A.	Antrim, Mid	.	.	1
*O'Neill, Dr. C.	Armagh, S.	.	1	.
Orde-Powlett, Hon. W. G. A.	Yorks, Richmond	.	.	1
Ormsby-Gore, Hon. W.	Denbigh District	.	.	1

Members	Constituencies	L.Lab.	N.	U.
O'Shaughnessy, P. J.	Limerick, W.	.	1	.
*O'Shee, J. J.	Waterford	.	1	.
O'Sullivan, E.	Kerry, E.	.	1	.
Paget, A. H.	Cambridge	.	.	1
Palmer, G.	Jarrow	1	.	.
*Parker, Sir G.	Gravesend	.	.	1
*Parker, J.	Halifax	.	1	.
*Parkes, E.	Birmghm., Central	.	.	1
*Partington, O.	High Peak	1	.	.
*Pearce, W.	Limehouse	1	.	.
*Pearson, H.	Suffolk, Eye	1	.	.
Peel, Capt. R. F.	Woodbridge	.	.	1
*Peel, Hon. W.	Taunton	.	.	1
Perkins, W. F.	New Forest	.	.	1
Peto, B. E.	Devizes	.	.	1
*Philipps, Sir O. C.	Pembroke and Haverfordwest	1	.	.
*Philipps, Lt.-Col. Ivor	Southampton	1	.	.
*Phillips, J.	Longford, S.	.	1	.
*Pickersgill, E. H.	Bethnal-green, S.W.	1	.	.
*Pirie, D. V.	Aberdeen, N.	1	.	.
*Pointer, J.	Sheffield, Attercliffe	1	.	.
*Pollard, Sir G. H.,	Eccles	1	.	.
Pollock, E. M., K.C.	Warwick and Leamington	.	.	1
*Ponsonby, A.	Stirling Burghs	1	.	.
*Power, P. J.	Waterford, E.	.	1	.
*Pretyman, E. G.	Chelmsford	.	.	1
*Price, C. E.	Edinburgh, C.	1	.	.
*Price, Sir R. J.	Norfolk, E.	1	.	.
*Priestley, A.	Grantham	1	.	.
*Priestley, Sir W. E.	Bradford, E.	1	.	.
Primrose, Hon. Neil	Wisbech	1	.	.
Pringle, W. M. R.	Lanarkshire, N.W.	1	.	.
Proby, Col. D. J.	Saffron Walden	.	.	1
Quilter, W. E. C.	Suffolk, Sudbury	.	.	1
*Radford, G. H.	Islington, E.	1	.	.
Raffan, R. W.	Leigh	1	.	.
*Rainy, A. R.	Kilmarnock B'rghs	1	.	.
*Randles, Sir J. S.	Cockermouth	.	.	1
Rankin, Sir J.	Leominster	.	.	1
*Raphael, H. H.	Derbyshire, S.	1	.	.
*Ratcliff, R. F.	Burton	.	.	1
*Rawlinson, J. F. P., K.C.	Camb. University	.	.	1
Rawson, Col. R.H.	Reigate	.	.	1
*Rea, W. Russell	Scarborough	1	.	.
*Reddy, M.	King's Co., Birr	.	1	.
*Redmond, J.	Waterford	.	1	.
*Redmond, W.	Clare, E.	.	1	.
*Rees, J. D.	Montgomery Dist.	1	.	.
*Remnant, J. F.	Holborn	.	.	1
*Rendall, A.	Gloucestershire, Thornbury	1	.	.
Rice, Hon. W. F.	Brighton	.	.	1
*Richards, T.	Monmouthshire, W.	1	.	.
Ridley, S. F.	Rochester	.	.	1
*Roberts, C. H.	Lincoln	1	.	.
*Roberts, G. H.	Norwich	1	.	.
*Roberts, S.	Sheffield, Ecclesall	.	.	1
*Roberts, Sir J. H.	Denbighshire, W.	1	.	.
*Robertson, J. M.	Tyneside	1	.	.
*Robertson, Sir G.	Bradford, C.	1	.	.
*Robinson, S.	Brecknockshire	1	.	.
*Robson, Sir W.	South Shields	1	.	.

Members.	Constituencies.	L.	Lab.	N.	U.
*Roch, W. F.	Pembrokeshire	1	.	.	.
*Roche, A.	Cork City	.	.	1	.
*Roche, J.	Galway, E.	.	.	1	.
*Roe, Sir T.	Derby	1	.	.	.
Rolleston, Sir J.	Hertford	.	.	.	1
*Ronaldshay, Earl of	Hornsey	.	.	.	1
Rothschild, Lionel	Aylesbury	.	.	.	1
Rowntree, A.	York	1	.	.	.
Royds, E.	Sleaford	.	.	.	1
*Runciman, Rt. Hon. W.	Dewsbury	1	.	.	.
*Rutherford, W.W.	Liverpool, W. Derby	.	.	.	1
*Salter, A. C., K.C.	Basingstoke	.	.	.	1
Samuel, J.	Stockton-on-Tees	1	.	.	.
*Samuel, Rt. Hn. H.	Cleveland	1	.	.	.
Samuel, Sir H.	Norwood	.	.	.	1
*Samuel, Stuart	Whitechapel	1	.	.	.
Sanders, R. A.	Bridgwater	.	.	.	1
Sanderson, L., K.C.	Westmorland, Appleby	.	.	.	1
*Sandys, Col. T. M.	Bootle	.	.	.	1
Sandys, G. J.	Wells	.	.	.	1
*Sassoon, Sir E.	Hythe	.	.	.	1
*Scanlan, T.	Sligo, N.	.	.	1	.
*Schwann, Sir C.	Manchester, N.	1	.	.	.
*Scott, A. H.	Ashton-under-Lyne	1	.	.	.
*Scott, Sir S.	Marylebone, W.	.	.	.	1
*Scott Dickson, Rt. Hon. C., K.C.	Glasgow, C.	.	.	.	1
*Seddon, J. A.	Lancashire, Newton	.	1	.	.
*Shackleton, D. J.	Clitheroe	.	1	.	.
*Shaw, Sir C. E.	Stafford	1	.	.	.
*Sheehan, D. D.	Cork, Mid	.	.	1	.
*Sheehy, D.	Meath, S.	.	.	1	.
*Sherwell, A. J.	Huddersfield	1	.	.	.
Shortt, E.	Newcastle-on-Tyne	1	.	.	.
*Simon, J. A., K.C.	Walthamstow	1	.	.	.
*Smith, F. E., K.C.	Liverpool, Walton	.	.	.	1
Smith, H. B. Lees	Northampton	.	.	.	.
*Smyth, T. F.	Leitrim, S.	.	.	1	.
*Snowden, P.	Blackburn	.	1	.	.
*Soames, A. W.	Norfolk, S.	1	.	.	.
*Soares, E. J.	Barnstaple	1	.	.	.
*Spicer, Sir A.	Hackney, C.	1	.	.	.
*Stanier, B.	Shropshire, Newport	.	.	.	1
*Stanley, Albert	Staffordshire, N.W.	.	1	.	.
Stanley, Capt. G. F.	Preston	.	.	.	1
*Stanley, Hon. A.	Ormskirk	.	.	.	1
*Starkey, J. R.	Newark	.	.	.	1
*Staveley-Hill, H.	Staffs, Kingswinford	.	.	.	1
Steel-Maitland, A. D.	Birmingham, E.	.	.	.	1
Stewart, G.	Wirral	.	.	.	1
Stewart, Sir M. J. McT.	Kirkcudbrightshire	.	.	.	1
Storey, S.	Sunderland	.	.	.	1
*Strachey, Sir E.	Somerset, S.	1	.	.	.
Strauss, A.	Paddington, N.	.	.	.	1
Summers, J. W.	Flint District	1	.	.	.
*Sutherland, J. E.	Elgin Burghs	1	.	.	.
Sutton, J. E.	Manchester, E.	.	1	.	.
Sykes, A. J.	Knutsford	.	.	.	1
*Talbot, Lord E.	Chichester	.	.	.	1
*Taylor, J. W.	Chester-le-Street	.	1	.	.
*Taylor, T. C.	Radcliffe-cum-Farnworth	1	.	.	.
*Tennant, H. J.	Berwickshire	1	.	.	.
Terrell, G.	Chippenham	.	.	.	1
Terrell, H., K.C.	Gloucester	.	.	.	1
*Thomas, A., K.C.	Carmarthensh., E.	1	.	.	.
*Thomas, D. A.	Cardiff	1	.	.	.
Thomas, J. H.	Derby	.	.	1	.
*Thomas, Sir A.	Glamorganshire, E.	1	.	.	.
Thompson, R.	Belfast, N.	.	.	.	1
*Thorne, G. R.	Wolverhampton, E.	1	.	.	.
*Thorne, W.	West Ham, S.	.	1	.	.
Thynne, Ld. A.	Bath	.	.	.	1
Tobin, Alfred A., K.C.	Preston	.	.	.	1
*Tomkinson, Rt. Hon. J.	Crewe	1	.	.	.
*Toulmin, G.	Bury	1	.	.	.
*Trevelyan, C. P.	Elland	1	.	.	.
Tryon, Capt. G. C.	Brighton	.	.	.	1
Tullibardine, Marquis of	Perthshire, W.	.	.	.	1
Twist, H.	Wigan	.	1	.	.
*Ure, Rt. Hon. A., K.C.	Linlithgowshire	1	.	.	.
*Valentia, Viscount	Oxford	.	.	.	1
*Vaughan-Davies, M. L.	Cardiganshire	1	.	.	.
Venables-Llewellyn, C. T.	Radnorshire	.	.	.	1
*Verney, F. W.	Buckingham	1	.	.	.
Verrall, G. H.	Newmarket	.	.	.	1
*Vivian, H.	Birkenhead	1	.	.	.
*Wadsworth, J.	Hallamshire	.	1	.	.
*Walker, Col. W.H.	Widnes	.	.	.	1
*Walker, H. de R.	Leicestershire, Melton	.	.	.	1
*Walrond, Hon. W. L. C.	Tiverton	.	.	.	1
*Walsh, S.	Ince	.	1	.	.
*Walters, J. T.	Sheffield, Brightside	1	.	.	.
*Walton, J.	Barnsley	1	.	.	.
Ward, A. S.	Watford	.	.	.	1
Ward, D.	Southampton	1	.	.	.
Ward, J.	Stoke-on-Trent	1	.	.	.
*Warde, Col. C. E.	Medway	.	.	.	1
*Wardle, G. J.	Stockport	.	1	.	.
Waring, Capt. W.	Banffshire	1	.	.	.
*Warner, T. C.	Lichfield	1	.	.	.
*Wason, Rt. Hon. E.	Clackmannan and Kinross	1	.	.	.
*Wason, J. C.	Orkney and Shetland	1	.	.	.
*Waterlow, D. S.	Islington, N.	1	.	.	.
*Watt, H. A.	Glasgow, College	1	.	.	.
*Wedgwood, J. C.	Newcastle-under-Lyme	1	.	.	.
*Weir, J. Galloway	Ross & Cromarty	1	.	.	.
Wheler, G. C. H.	Faversham	.	.	.	1
*White, J. D.	Dumbartonshire	1	.	.	.
White, Maj. Dalrymple	Southport	.	.	.	1
*White, P.	Meath, N.	.	.	1	.
*White, Sir G.	Norfolk, N.W.	1	.	.	.
*White, Sir L.	Buckrose	1	.	.	.
Whitehouse, J. H.	Lanark, Mid	1	.	.	.
*Whitley, J. H.	Halifax	1	.	.	.
*Whittaker, Rt. Hon. Sir T. P.	Spen Valley	1	.	.	.

Members.	Constituencies.	L.	Lab.	N.	U.
Whyte, A. F.	Perth	1	.	.	.
*Wiles, T.	Islington, S.	1	.	.	.
*Wilkie, A.	Dundee	.	1	.	.
Williams, A.	Plymouth	1	.	.	.
*Williams, Col. R.	Dorset. W.	.	.	.	1
*Williams, J.	Glamorganshire, Gower	.	1	.	.
Williams, P.	Middlesbrough	1	.	.	.
*Williams, W. Llewellyn	Carmarthen Dist.	1	.	.	.
*Williamson, Sir A.	Elgin and Nairn	1	.	.	.
*Willoughby de Eresby, Lord	Horncastle	.	.	.	1
Willoughby, Maj. the Hon. C.	Lincs, Stamford	.	.	.	1
*Wilson, Hon. Guy	Hull, W.	1	.	.	.
*Wilson, H. J.	Holmfirth	1	.	.	.
*Wilson, John	Durham, Mid	1	.	.	.
*Wilson, J. W.	Worcestershire, N.	1	.	.	.
*Wilson, Maj. Stanley	Yorks, Holderness	.	.	.	1
Wilson, T. F.	Lanarkshire, N.E.	1	.	.	.
*Wilson, W. T.	Westhoughton	.	1	.	.
*Winfrey, L.	Norfolk, S.W.	1	.	.	.

Members.	Constituencies.	L.	Lab.	N.	U.
Wing, T.	Grimsby	1	.	.	.
*Winterton, Earl	Horsham	.	.	.	1
*Wolff, G. W.	Belfast, E.	.	.	.	1
Wood, Hon. E.	Ripon	.	.	.	1
Wood, J.	Stalybridge	.	.	.	1
*Wood, T. McKinnon	Glasgow, St. Rollox	1	.	.	.
*Wortley, Rt. Hon. C. B. Stuart	Sheffield, Hallam	.	.	.	1
*Wyndham, Rt. Hon. G.	Dover	.	.	.	1
Yerburgh, R.	Chester	.	.	.	1
*Young, S.	Cavan, E.	.	.	1	.
Young, W.	Perthshire, E.	1	.	.	.
*Younger, G.	Ayr Burghs	.	.	.	1
Younger, W.	Peebles and Selkirk	1	.	.	.
*Yoxall, Sir J. H.	Nottingham, W.	1	.	.	.

	275	40	82	273
	397			273

Total 670

The Times
WEEKLY EDITION.

Price 2d.   To be obtained from any Newsagent, or from the Publisher.

Published every Friday Morning, containing, in an abbreviated form, the news from **The Times** for the preceding six days, together with some of the most important **Speeches, Leading Articles, Headed Articles,** and Correspondence in full, and a specially prepared report for the week of the **Money Market.** Also a **Chess Column weekly,** and a **Serial Story by a well-known and popular Author.** With the **Literary Supplement,** price 3d.

Special Editions are issued for Australasia and India, for Canada and the United States, and for South Africa, containing matter particularly interesting to dwellers in those countries.

SUBSCRIPTIONS.

	3 Months.	6 Months.	12 Months.
Inland	2s. 9d.	5s. 6d.	11s. 0d.
,, With Literary Supplement	3s. 10d.	7s. 8d.	15s. 4d.
Abroad	3s. 3d.	6s. 6d.	13s. 0d.
,, With **one** of The Times Special Supplements*	4s. 10½d.	9s. 9d.	19s. 6d.

*Engineering, Literary, or Financial, identical with those issued with The Times without extra charge on Wednesdays, Thursdays, and Fridays respectively.

APPLY TO ANY NEWSAGENT, OR TO

The Publisher, The Times Office, Printing House Square, London
from whom Bound Volumes can also be obtained.

REPORTS of COMMERCIAL CASES

Reported by J. S. HENDERSON, *Barrister-at-Law.*

¶ This work produces in very clear type and in convenient form the reports of such cases as are of peculiar interest to the mercantile community.

THESE REPORTS MAY BE CITED AS "COM. CAS."

¶ Published at intervals during Term.   Yearly subscription, 15s. ; separate parts, 2s. 6d. each. Part I., Vol. XV., is now ready.   Bound volumes are also issued ; Vol. XIII. is now ready.

¶ Of any newsagent ; of Messrs. BUTTERWORTH & CO., 12, Bell-yard, Temple-bar ; or of THE PUBLISHER, The Times Office, London.

The Mail.

A reproduction of the substance of The Times, with the Latest Intelligence,

APPEARS ON

MONDAY, WEDNESDAY, and *FRIDAY* in each week.

— PRICE 2d. —

Published Half-Yearly in quarto size, half bound in morocco, 10s. 6d.
The Volume for the Second Half of 1908 is the 36th.

ISSUES.

Financiers, Bankers, Insurance Managers, Actuaries, Accountants, and Company Promoters, and Solicitors having business relations therewith, frequently find "ISSUES" of great value as a work of reference, containing as it does

Prospectuses Reprinted from The Times of

Public Companies,
Government Loans,
Increases and Decreases of Capital,

Changes in Articles of Association,
Amalgamations, and
Schemes of Arrangement.

Results of Tenders and Auctions and a Statistical Table of Issues by Subscription are appended.

An important Feature in Vols. 30, 32, 34, and 36 is

the full text of the Notices, as published in *The Times*, of

all Bills promoted by Local Authorities, Public Companies, &c.,

for Introduction to Parliament in the ensuing Session.

The additions from time to time made to the Stock Exchange Official List will be found for the first time in Vol. 31.

The Times Office, Printing House Square, Blackfriars, E.C.
Also at the City Office of The Times, 15, Copthall-avenue, E.C.

SCHOOLS In ENGLAND or ABROAD For BOYS and GIRLS.

Messrs. J. & J. PATON, having an intimate knowledge of the BEST SCHOOLS and TUTORS in this Country and on the Continent, will be pleased to aid parents in their selection by sending (free of charge) prospectuses and full particulars of reliable and highly recommended establishments. When writing, please state the age of pupil, the district preferred, and give some idea of the fees to be paid.

J. & J. PATON,
Educational Agents,
143 CANNON STREET, LONDON, E.C.
Tel. 5053 Central.

PATON'S LIST OF SCHOOLS AND TUTORS.
Twelfth Edition, 1,176 pages. Red cloth. Post free, 2s. 6d. Contains abridged Prospectuses, Fees, &c., of over 750 good Schools. Also a Map of England, and Articles on How to Enter the Army, Navy, Civil Service, Medical and Engineering Professions.

PATON'S GUIDE TO CONTINENTAL SCHOOLS.
240 pages. Blue cloth. Post free, 1s. 4d.

The Times
OFFICIAL INDEX.

Price 3s. 6d., post free.

Published at the end of the month, each part of this invaluable work is a complete mirror of the past month's human history, and furnishes the key to any event or information that has been dealt with in *The Times* during the month. The headings are diverse, and are amplified by numerous cross-references that lead the inquirer to what he seeks without delay and with the minimum of trouble.

Annual Subscription £2.

Orders should be addressed to THE PUBLISHER, *The Times*, PRINTING HOUSE SQUARE, E.C.

The Times Guide
to the
House of Commons
1911

The Times

HOUSE OF COMMONS
1911

(GENERAL ELECTION, DECEMBER, 1910.)

With Brief Biographies of Members and Full Details of the Polls: also an ANALYSIS OF THE RESULTS AND COMPARISONS WITH PREVIOUS ELECTIONS, A Survey of Changes in Counties and Boroughs, Statistical Tables, &c.

LONDON:
PRINTED AND PUBLISHED BY JOHN PARKINSON BLAND AT THE TIMES OFFICE
PRINTING HOUSE-SQUARE, E.C.

1910.

CONTENTS.

	PAGE
INDEX TO CANDIDATES	1
RESULT OF THE GENERAL ELECTION	8
PARTY GAINS AND LOSSES	11
COMPOSITION OF THE HOUSE OF COMMONS: DECEMBER, 1910, AND AFTER THE GENERAL ELECTION IN JANUARY, 1910	11
THE LABOUR PARTY	11
AN ANALYSIS OF THE VOTING	12
OLD MEMBERS DEFEATED: FORMER MEMBERS RE-ELECTED	15
THE CONSTITUENCIES: A COMPARATIVE RECORD IN 1906 AND 1910	16
POLLS AND BIOGRAPHIES :—	
ENGLAND—LONDON	21
,, —BOROUGHS	32
,, —COUNTIES	59
WALES —BOROUGHS	97
,, —COUNTIES	99
SCOTLAND —BURGHS	102
,, —COUNTIES	108
IRELAND —BOROUGHS	114
,, —COUNTIES	117
UNIVERSITIES	127
INDEX TO CONSTITUENCIES	129
THE NEW PARLIAMENT	134

The first pollings took place on December 3; *and the last on December* 19.

ALLIANCE
ASSURANCE COMPANY, Ltd.

Head Office: **BARTHOLOMEW LANE, LONDON, E.C.**

Established 1824.

Accumulated Funds exceed £17,000,000.

Directors.
The Right Hon. LORD ROTHSCHILD, G.C.V.O., Chairman.

IAN H. AMORY, Esq.	FRANCIS WILLIAM BUXTON, Esq.	Hon. HENRY BERKELEY PORTMAN.
CHARLES EDWARD BARNETT, Esq.	JOHN CATOR, Esq., M.P.	Hon. N. CHARLES ROTHSCHILD.
F. CAVENDISH BENTINCK, Esq.	His Grace The DUKE OF DEVONSHIRE.	Sir MARCUS SAMUEL, Bart.
A. V. DUNLOP BEST, Esq.	Col. the Hon. EVERARD C. DIGBY.	H. MELVILL SIMONS, Esq.
FRANCIS AUGUSTUS BEVAN, Esq.	Captain GERALD M. A. ELLIS.	Right Hon. LORD STALBRIDGE.
PERCIVAL BOSANQUET, Esq.	JOHN HAMPTON HALE, Esq.	HENRY ALEXANDER TROTTER, Esq.
HON. KENELM P. BOUVERIE.	C. SHIRREFF HILTON, Esq.	The RIGHT HON. THE EARL OF VERULAM
THOMAS HENRY BURROUGHES, Esq.	W. DOURO HOARE, Esq.	SIR CHARLES RIVERS WILSON, G.C.M.G., C.B.
	FRANCIS ALFRED LUCAS, Esq.	

THE OPERATIONS OF THE COMPANY EMBRACE ALL BRANCHES OF INSURANCE.

DEATH DUTIES.—Special forms of Policies have been prepared by the Company providing for the payment of Death Duties, thus avoiding the necessity of disturbing investments at a time when it may be difficult to realise without loss.

INCOME TAX.—Under the provisions of the Act, Income Tax is not payable on that portion of the Assured's income which is devoted to the payment of annual premiums on an assurance on his life, or on the life of his wife. Having regard to the amount of the tax, this abatement (which is limited to one-sixth of the Assured's income) is an important advantage to Life Policyholders.

Full particulars of all classes of Insurance, together with Proposal Forms and Statement of Accounts, may be had on application to any of the Company's Offices or Agents.

Applications for Agencies invited.

ROBERT LEWIS, General Manager.

INDEX TO CANDIDATES.

In the following list of candidates those who were unsuccessful are distinguished by italics. Members of the last Parliament are indicated by asterisks.

A

	PAGE
*Abraham, Rt. Hon. W.	101
*Abraham, W.	115
Acland, F. D.	62
*Acland-Hood, Rt. Hon. Sir A.	86
Adam, Major W. A.	31
Adamson, W.	110
Addinsell, W. A.	24
*Addison, Dr. C.	29
Adkins, W. R., K.C.	75
*Agar-Robartes, Hon. T.	62
*Agnew, Sir G. W.	52
Ahearn, J.	119
*Ainsworth, J. S.	108
Aitken, W. Max	32
*Akers-Douglas, Rt. Hon. A.	73
*Alden, Percy	80
Allen, A. A.	109
*Allen, C. P.	69
Amery, L. S.	29
*Anderson, A. M., K.C.	108
Anson, Sir W. R.	127
Anstruther-Gray, Major W.	107
Arbuthnot, G. A.	36
*Archer-Shee, Major M.	23
*Arkwright, J. S.	42
*Armitage, R.	43
Armstrong, Sir G.	54
Arnold, S.	93
*Ashley, W. W.	73
Ashmead-Bartlett, E.	30
Ashton, A. J., K.C.	62
*Ashton, T. G.	59
Aske, Dr. R. W.	42
*Asquith, Rt. Hon. H. H.	110
Astor, Waldorf	50
*Atherley-Jones, L., K.C.	67
Attenborough, W. A.	32

B

	PAGE
Badlay, J.	44
Bagley, E. A.	75
*Bagot, Lt.-Col. J. F.	91
Bailey, A. J.	53
*Baird, J. L.	90
Baker, H. A.	56
*Baker, Harold T.	74
*Baker, J. Allen	23
*Baker, Sir R.	66
*Balcarres, Lord	73
Baldwin, J. H. L.	41
*Baldwin, S.	92
*Balfour, Rt. Hon. A. J.	21
Balfour, G.	111
Balfour, Major K.	54
Balfour, R.	112
*Banbury, Sir F. G.	21
Barbour, G. F.	113
Barclay, R. L.	87
Baring, G.	39
*Baring, Capt. the Hon. G. V.	57
Barlow, C. Montague	52
*Barlow, Sir J. E.	85
Barnard, E. B.	43
*Barnes, G. N.	104
*Barnston, H.	61
*Barran, Sir J.	106
*Barran, R. H.	44
*Barrie, H. T.	123
Barry, E.	119
*Barry, Redmond, K.C.	126
*Barton, A. W.	49
*Bathurst, Lieut.-Col. Hon. A. B.	69
*Bathurst, C.	92
Baxter, Sir G. W.	103
*Beach, Hon. M. Hicks	70
*Beale, W. P., K.C.	108
Beauchamp, E.	87
Beauchamp, F. B.	85
Beck, A. C. T.	69
Beck, A. E.	38
*Beckett, Hon. Gervase	94
Belilios, R. E.	27
Bell, McKenzie	28
Bellairs, C. W.	69
Benn, A. Shirley	50
*Benn, Ian H.	24
Benn, Sir J.	22
*Benn, W. W.	30
Bennett, E. N.	84
Bennett, T. J.	78
*Bentham, G. J.	78
*Beresford, Lord C.	51
Bernacchi, L. C.	37
Bernard, F. T. H.	60
Berridge, T. H.	56
*Bethell, Sir J. H.	68
Beyfus, G. H.	69
Bigham, Capt. C.	45
Bigland, A.	33
Bignold Sir A.	107
Birchall, J. D.	44
Bird, A. F.	58
*Birrell, Rt. Hon. A.	36
Black, A. W.	59
Black, J. B.	106
Black, W. G.	25
Blaiklock, G.	24
Blayney, J. J.	74
Bliss, J.	74
Blyth, B. H.	110
*Boland, J. P.	121
Booth, F. H.	50
Boulton, A. C. F.	72
Borwick, G.	87
*Bottomley, Horatio W.	24
*Bowerman, C. W.	23
*Bowles, T. G.	43
Bowring, F. C.	45
Boyd, R. N.	126
*Boyle, Daniel	124
*Boyle, W. L.	81
Boyton, J.	27
*Brace, W.	101
Brackenbury, Capt. H. L.	78
Brady, J.	115
*Brady, P. J.	115
Branch, J.	79
*Brassey, H. L. C.	82
Brassey, Capt. R. B.	83
Brett, Hon. O.	72
*Bridgeman, W. C	84
*Brigg, Sir J.	95
Bright, Allan	54

2—2

Name	PAGE
Brocklehurst, F.	75
*Brocklehurst, Col. W. B.	61
Bromley - Davenport, Lt.-Col. W.	86
Brooke, Sir A. De Capell-	81
Brooke, Stopford W.	83
Brookes, Dr. Clifford	92
Brookes, Warwick	27
*Brotherton, E. A.	56
Brown, C. Clifton	30
Brown, W. H.	123
Browne, Capt. E. M.	30
*Brunner, J. F. L.	61
*Brunskill, G. F., K.C.	126
*Bryce, J. A.	106
Buckmaster, S. O., K.C.	37
*Bull, Sir W. J.	24
*Burdett-Coutts, W. L. A. B.	31
Burdon, Col. R.	68
*Burgoyne, A.	25
Burn, Col. C. R.	66
*Burns, Rt. Hon. J.	21
Burrows, J. H.	69
*Burt, Rt. Hon. T.	48
Burt, W.	50
Burton, B. H.	43
*Butcher, J. G., K.C.	58
*Butcher, S. H.	127
Butler, A. E.	34
*Buxton, C. R.	65
*Buxton, Noel	81
*Buxton, Rt. Hon. S.	30
*Byles, W. P.	52

C

Name	PAGE
*Calley, Col. T. C. P.	91
Cameron, A. G.	67
*Cameron, R.	67
Cameron, R. M.	103
Campbell, Capt. D.	108
Campbell, Capt. the Hon. J. B.	109
Campbell, J. G. D.	74
Campbell-Johnston, M.	95
*Campbell, Rt. Hon. J. H. M., K.C.	128
Campbell, R.	54
*Campion, W. R.	90
*Carlile, E. H.	71
Carpenter, Capt. A. Boyd	94
Carpenter, J. Boyd	111
Carpenter, W. B. Boyd	34
Carr, W. H.	51
*Carr-Gomm, H.	29
*Carson, Rt. Hon. Sir E. H., K.C.	128
Carson, F. M.	25
Carthew, Capt. T.	31
Cassel, Felix, K.C.	28
*Castlereagh, Viscount	46
*Cator, J.	72
*Cautley, H. S.	89
*Cave, G., K.C.	88
*Cavendish-Bentinck, Lord H.	49
*Cawley, Sir F.	75
Cawley, H. T.	75
*Cecil, E.	32
*Cecil, Lord Hugh	127
Cecil, Lord R.	60
*Chaloner, Col. R. G. W.	45
*Chamberlain, Rt. Hon. Austen	92
*Chamberlain, Rt. Hon. J.	34
Chamberlayne, A. R.	105
*Chambers, J., K.C.	114
*Chancellor, H. G.	28
*Chaplin, Rt. Hon. H.	89
Chapman, S.	105
*Chapple, A.	113
Chaytor, A. H.	82
Chetwynd, A.	87
*Churchill, Rt. Hon. Winston S.	103
Churchman, A. C.	43
*Clancy, J. J.	120
Clark, E.	48
Clarke, Capt. A. E. S.	81
Clarke, G. F.	76
Clarke, W. H.	43
*Clay, Capt. H. Spender	73
*Clive, Capt. P. A.	71
*Clough, W.	96
*Clyde, J. A., K.C.	104
Clynes, J. R.	47
*Coates, Major E. F.	26
Coates, G.	62
Coats, S. A.	23
Cochrane, C. A.	39
Cochran-Patrick, N. K.	113
Cockerill, Major	70
Cockerill, Pepys	83
Cockshutt, N.	51
*Colefax, H. A.	47
Collier, J. V.	48
*Collings, Rt. Hon. J.	33
*Collins, G. P.	105
*Collins, S.	26
*Collins, Sir W.	28
Collum, Capt. A.	120
*Compton, Lord A. F.	79
Compton-Rickett, Sir J.	95
*Condon, T. J.	125
Constable, A. H. B., K.C.	104
Cooke-Taylor, C. R.	23
*Cooper, Capt. Bryan	120
*Cooper, R. A.	56
*Corbett, A. Cameron	105
Corcoran, Timothy	118
*Cornwall, Sir E. A.	22
*Cory, Sir C. J.	62
Cotton, W. F.	120
Court, Dr. J.	64
*Courthope, G. L.	90
*Cowan, W. H.	108
*Craig, C. C.	117
Craig, E. F.	61
*Craig, H. J.	56
*Craig, Capt. J.	119
*Craig, Norman, C., K.C.	72
Craighead, W.	108
*Craik, Sir H.	128
Craven-Hoyle, Lt.-Col. J.	74
*Crawshay-Williams, E.	44
*Crean, E.	119
Cremlyn, J. W. J.	100
Crichton-Stuart, Ld. N.	97
*Cripps, Sir C. A., K.C.	60
*Croft, H. Page	38
Cronin, T. B.	121
Crooks, W.	31
*Crosfield, A. H.	56
*Crossley, Sir W. J.	60
Crumley, P.	120
*Cullinan, J.	125
Cummins, J.	127

D

Name	PAGE
*Dalrymple, Viscount	114
*Dalziel, D.	26
*Dalziel, Sir J. H.	106
Davey, Hon. A. J.	88
*Davies, D.	101
*Davies, Ellis W.	100
Davies, J.	42
Davies, T.	78
*Davies, Sir W. H.	36
*Dawes, J. A.	27
de Eresby, Lord Willoughby	78
de Gruyther, L., K.C.	87
de Knoop, J.	61
*Delany, W.	124
*Denman, Hon. R. D.	37
Dennis, E. R. B.	49
Dent, B.	61
de Pass, H.	31
Derry, J.	53
*Devlin, J.	114
*Dewar, Sir J. A.	111
*Dickinson, W. H.	28
*Dickson, Rt. Hon. C. Scott, K.C.	105
*Dilke, Rt. Hon. Sir C. W.	69
*Dillon, J.	123
Disraeli, Coningsby	83
*Dixon, C. H.	35
*Donelan, Capt. A. J. C.	118
Dore, S. L.	25
*Doris, W.	124
Doughty, Sir G.	40
Douglas, Dr. C. M.	112
Dransfield, J. H.	96
*Du Cros, Arthur	41
Duffy, W. J.	121
*Duke, H. E., K.C.	40
Dummett, R. E.	79
Dumphreys, J.	29
*Duncan, C.	32
Duncan, J. B.	110
*Duncan, J. H.	96
*Duncannon, Viscount	37
*Dunn, Sir W. H.	29
Dunne, Major E. M.	77
Dunstan, R.	66
Dyson, W.	48

E

Name	PAGE
Earle, S. R.	29
Edwards, A. C.	101
*Edwards, E.	41
Edwards, Sir F.	102
Edwards, J. H.	101
*Elibank, Master of	110
Elliston, W. R.	88
*Elverston, H.	40
Emery, J. N.	84

INDEX TO CANDIDATES.

Name	Page
*Emmott, Rt. Hon. A.	49
Esmonde, Dr. J.	125
*Esmonde, Sir T.	127
Essex, R. W.	54
*Esslemont, G. B.	102
*Evans, L. Worthington	38
*Eyres-Monsell, B.	92

F

Name	Page
*Faber, G. D.	22
*Faber, Capt. W. V.	70
Fairbairn, J.	31
Fairbairn, R. R.	58
*Falconer, J.	110
*Falle, B. G.	51
*Farrell, J. P.	123
*Fell, A.	41
*Fenwick, C.	83
*Ferens, T. R.	42
*Ferguson, R. C. Munro	106
*Fetherstonhaugh, G., K.C.	120
*Ffrench, P.	127
*Field, W.	115
Fiennes, Hon. Eustace	83
Fiennes, Hon. G. R. C.	57
Filmer, Sir R.	44
*Finlay, Rt. Hon. Sir R. B., K.C.	128
*Fisher, W. Hayes	24
Fisher, W. J.	37
Fitch, Cecil	69
Fitzgibbon, John	124
*Fitzroy, Hon. E. A.	82
*Flannery, Sir F.	68
*Flavin, M. J.	121
*Fleming, V.	84
*Fletcher, J. S.	25
Flower, Sir E.	35
Foot, I.	62
Ford, P. J.	106
Forester, Capt. G. C. B. W.	85
Forestier-Walker, L.	80
*Forster, H. W.	73
*Foster, H. S.	87
*Foster, J. Kenneth	38
*Foster, P. S.	90
Foxcroft, C. T.	85
*France, G.	95
Francis, J.	29
Francombe, J. T.	36
Franklin, L. B.	27
Freeman, B.	91
Freeman, M.	64
Frewen, Moreton	118
*Fuller, Sir J. M. F.	91
*Furness, S.	41

G

Name	Page
Galbraith, J. F. W.	41
*Gardner, E.	59
Garowski, Count D. B.	77
Gaskell, F. H.	101
*Gastrell, Maj. H.	26
Geen, H.	65
*Gelder, Sir W. A.	78
*George, Rt. Hon. D. Lloyd	97
*Gibbs, Lt.-Col. G. A.	36
*Gibson, Sir J.	103
*Gilhooly, J.	119

Name	Page
*Gill, A. H.	34
*Gilmour, Capt. J.	113
*Ginnell, L.	126
*Glanville, H. J.	29
*Glover, T.	52
Glyn, Major G. C.	59
Glyn, Maurice	66
Glyn, R. G. C.	105
*Goddard, Sir D.	43
Goldberg, H. W.	89
*Goldman, C. S.	50
Goldney, F. B.	37
Goldsmid, S. H.	22
*Goldsmith, F.	87
Goldstone, F. W.	55
Gooch, G. P.	32
*Gooch, H. C.	22
Gordon, J.	43
*Gordon, J., K.C.	123
Gosling, H.	26
*Goulding, E. A.	58
*Grant, J. A.	63
Gray, E.	74
Grayson, A. Victor	26
*Greene, Raymond	24
*Greenwood, G. G.	50
Greenwood, Hamar	55
Greg, T. T.	71
*Greig, Colonel	113
*Gretton, J.	84
*Grey, Rt. Hon. Sir E.	82
*Griffith, J. Ellis	99
Griffith-Boscawen, Col.	39
*Griffiths, J. N.	56
Griggs, W. P.	68
Gritten, W. G. H.	41
Grogan, Capt. E. S.	48
Guedella, F. M.	28
Guest, Capt. the Hon. F.	66
*Guest, Maj. the Hon. H.	98
*Guiney, P.	118 & 121
*Guinness, Hon. R.	28
*Guinness, Hon. W.	37
*Gulland, J. W.	103
*Gwynn, S. L.	116
*Gwynne, R. S.	89

H

Name	Page
*Hackett, J.	125
*Haddock, G. B.	74
*Haldane, Rt. Hon. R. B., K.C.	110
*Hall, Douglas B.	70
*Hall, E. Marshall, K.C.	45
Hall, F.	22
*Hall, F.	95
*Hambro, Angus V.	66
*Hamersley, A. St. G., K.C.	84
*Hamilton, Lord C.	26
Hamilton Lord John	126
*Hamilton, Marquis of	116
*Hancock, J. G.	64
Hannon, P. J.	36
Harben, H. D.	51
*Harcourt, Rt. Hon. Lewis	74
*Harcourt, R. V.	106
Hardicker, J. O.	67
*Hardie, J. Keir	98
Hardy, G. A.	32

Name	Page
*Hardy, L.	72
Hargreaves, G. de la P.	47
*Harmood-Banner, J. S.	45
*Harmsworth, R. Leicester	109
Harrington, Col. Sir J.	21
*Harris, H. P.	27
Harris, Hon. J. W.	24
Harris, L. W.	25
*Harrison-Broadley, Col. H. B.	93
Hartley, E. L.	36
Hartshorn, V.	101
*Harvey, A. G.	51
*Harvey, T. E.	44
*Harvey, W. E.	64
*Harwood, G.	34
*Haslam, J.	63
*Haslam, L.	47
*Havelock-Allan, Sir H.	67
*Haviland-Burke, E.	122
*Haworth, A. A.	47
*Hayden, J. P.	125
*Hayward, E.	68
Hazel, Dr. A. E. W.	57
*Hazleton, R.	121 & 123
*Healy, M.	115
Healy, M. F., jun	126
*Healy, T. M., K.C.	123
Hedges, A. P.	73
*Helme, N. W.	73
*Helmsley, Viscount	93
*Hemmerde, E. G., K.C.	51
Hemphill, Captain F.	35
*Henderson, A.	66
*Henderson, Maj. H. G.	59
*Henderson, J. M.	108
Henlé, F. H.	27
*Henry, C. S.	85
Herbert, Hon. Aubrey	85
*Herbert, Col. Sir I.	80
Herbert, Capt. Lord	115
Hesketh, Col. G.	34
Hewins, Prof. W. A. S.	75
*Hickman, Col. T.	58
Hickman, J. O.	59
Hicks, Harold	85
*Higham, J. S.	97
Hiley, F. S.	68
*Hill, Sir C.	53
Hillier, Dr. A.	71
*Hills, J. W.	39
*Hindle, F. G.	74
Hinds, J.	100
Hoare, C. H.	82
Hoare, Hugh	23
*Hoare, S. J. G.	23
*Hobhouse, Rt. Hon C.	36
*Hodge, J.	75
Hoffgaard, E.	22
Hogge, J. M.	104
*Hohler, G. F., K.C.	37
Holt, R. D.	82
Hood, A.	100
*Hooper, A. G.	39
*Hope, H.	109
Hope, Major J. A.	110
*Hope, J. D.	110
*Hope, J. F.	53
Hopkins, J. W. W.	28

2—3

		PAGE
*Horne, C. Silvester	..	43
Horne, F. ..	..	94
Horne, R. S.	..	113
*Horne, W. E.	..	88
*Horner, A. L., K.C.	..	126
Horsley, Sir V.	..	128
House, W. ..	..	67
*Houston, R. P.	..	46
Howard, Col.	..	98
*Howard, Hon. Geoffrey	..	63
Howard, Hon. H. M.	..	127
Howard, J. ..	..	37
Howell, H. E.	..	46
*Hudson, W.	..	48
*Hughes, S. L.	..	54
*Hume-Williams, W. E., K.C.	..	83
*Hunt, Rowland	..	84
*Hunter, Sir C. R.	..	32
*Hunter, W., K.C.	..	111
Hutchinson, R. A. L.	..	75
Hutchinson, St. J.	..	90
Hutchison, W.	..	104
Hutchison, G. A. C.	..	108
Hyde, Sir Clarendon	..	97
Hyndman, H. M.	..	36

I

*Illingworth, P. H.	..	96
Ingleby, H.	..	43
Irving, D. D.	..	51
*Isaacs, Sir Rufus, K.C.	..	51

J

*Jackson, Sir J.	..	39
*Jackson, Lt.-Col. J. A.	..	57
Jackson, J. P. T.	..	73
Jacobs, H.	..	28
*Jardine, E.	..	85
*Jardine, Sir J.	..	113
Jardine, Willoughby	..	68
Jenkins, S. R.	..	40
Jephcott, A. R.	..	107
Jessel, A. H., K.C.	..	24
*Jessel, Capt. H. M.	..	28
Jodrell, N. P.	..	81
John, E. T.	..	100
Johnson, A. W. F.	..	41
*Johnson, W.	..	90
Johnston, J. Weir	..	120
Johnston, W. J.	..	123
Jones, A. L.	..	97
*Jones, Sir D. Brynmor	..	99
*Jones, Edgar	..	98
Jones, G. W. H.	..	44
*Jones, Haydn	..	101
Jones, Leif	..	83
*Jones, W.	..	100
Jones, W. S. Glyn	..	30
*Jowett, F. W.	..	35
*Joyce, M.	..	116
Joynson-Hicks, W.	..	55

K

Kaye, J. H.	..	42
*Keating, M.	..	122
Kebty-Fletcher, J. R.	..	60
Keith, H. S.	..	111
Kellaway, F.	..	32
Kelley, F.	..	97

		PAGE
*Kelly, E.	..	119
*Kemp, Sir G.	..	47
*Kennedy, V. P.	..	118
*Kerr-Smiley, P.	..	117
*Kerry, Earl of	..	64
Kessack, J. O'C.	..	104
*Keswick, William	..	88
Kidd, J.	..	112
*Kilbride, D.	..	122
*Kimber, Sir H.	..	31
King, H. D.	..	81
*King, Sir H. Seymour	..	42
*King, J.	..	85
King, W.	..	90
King-Farlow, S. E.	..	24
*Kinloch-Cooke, Sir C.	..	39
Kirkley, J.	..	67
*Kirkwood, J. H. Morrison	..	69
*Knight, Capt. E.	..	43
Knight, M. E.	..	124
Kyd, D. H.	..	69
*Kyffin-Taylor, Col.	..	45

L

Lamb, E. H.	..	51
*Lambert, G.	..	65
Lambert, R. C.	..	91
*Lane-Fox, G. R.	..	94
Lansbury, G.	..	29
*Lardner, J. C. R.	..	124
*Law, A. Bonar	..	47
*Law, H. A.	..	119
*Lawson, Hon. H.	..	30
Lawson, Sir W.	..	63
*Layland-Barratt, Sir F.	..	66
*Leach, C.	..	94
*Lee, A. H.	..	70
Leon, A. L.	..	23
Leslie, Shane	..	116
Lester, W. R.	..	81
Lever, A. Levy	..	58
*Levy, Sir M.	..	77
*Lewis, J. H.	..	100
Lewis, J. Windsor	..	93
Lewis, Price	..	58
*Lewisham, Viscount	..	57
Lias, W. J.	..	46
Linfield, F. C.	..	78
Lister, R. A.	..	70
Lithgow, S.	..	39
Lloyd, C.	..	99
*Lloyd, G. A.	..	87
Lloyd, Harold	..	101
Lloyd, J. S.	..	103
Lobjoit, W. G.	..	79
*Locker-Lampson, G.	..	52
*Locker-Lampson, O.	..	72
*Lockwood, Col. Sir A. R. M.	..	68
Logan, J. W.	..	77
*Long, Rt. Hon. W.	..	29
*Lonsdale, J. B.	..	117
Lord, W. G.	..	76
Lort-Williams, J. R.	..	54
*Lough, Rt. Hon. T.	..	25
Low, W.	..	106
*Low, Sir F., K.C.	..	48
*Lowe, Sir F.	..	33
Lowther, Claude	..	63
*Lowther, Rt. Hon. J. W.	..	63

		PAGE
Lucas, Col. F. A.	..	26
*Lundon, T.	..	122
*Luttrell, A. C. F.	..	65
*Lyell, C. H.	..	103
Lygon, Hon. H.	..	50
*Lynch, A.	..	118
Lynch, H. F. B.	..	40
*Lyttelton, Rt. Hon. A.	..	28
*Lyttelton, Hon. J. C.	..	92

M

Macafee, W.	..	117
*McCalmont, Col. J. M.	..	117
McCall, Major Pollok	..	103
*McCallum, J.	..	107
*MacCaw, W. J. M.	..	120
*McCurdy, C. A.	..	48
*Macdonald, J. A. M.	..	104
*MacDonald, J. Ramsay	..	44
McGhee, R.	..	126
McIntyre, T. W.	..	108
*McKean, J.	..	124
*McKenna, Rt. Hon. R.	..	80
McKerrell, T.	..	45
*Mackinder, H. J.	..	104
*McLaren, F.	..	78
McLaren, H. D.	..	77
*McLaren, W. S. B.	..	61
Maclean, D.	..	112
McLeod, A.	..	109
*Macmaster, D., K.C.	..	88
McMicking, Major G.	..	111
McMordie, R. J.	..	114
*Macnamara, Dr. T. J.	..	22
McNeill, R.	..	111
*MacNeill, Swift, K.C.	..	119
Maconochie, A. W.	..	112
Macpherson, J. I.	..	113
MacQuisten, F. A.	..	106
*MacVeagh, J.	..	120
Maddison, F.	..	38
Maddocks, H.	..	90
Magnus, L.	..	36
*Magnus, Sir P.	..	128
Main, A. P.	..	105
Malcolm, Ian	..	23
*Mallaby-Deeley, H. C.	..	79
*Mallet, C. E.	..	50
Mallik, M. C.	..	80
*Manfield, H.	..	82
Manton, Henry J.	..	33
March-Phillipps, Capt. L.	..	59
*Markham, A. B.	..	83
Markham, G. E.	..	67
*Marks, G. C.	..	62
Marsden-Smedley, J. B.	..	64
Marshall, A. H.	..	56
Marshall, Sir H.	..	77
*Martin, Hon. J.	..	28
Mason, D. M.	..	38
*Mason, J. F.	..	57
Mason, W. J. P.	..	23
*Masterman, C. F. G.	..	31
Mathias, R.	..	37
Mayer, S.	..	24
Meager, D. V.	..	99
*Meagher, M.	..	122
Meakin, W.	..	87
Mechan, H.	..	113

INDEX TO CANDIDATES.

	PAGE
*Meehan, F. E.	122
*Meehan, P. A.	124
*Menzies, Sir W.	112
Meyer, F. C.	80
Meynell, F.	32
*Meysey-Thompson, E. C.	86
Micklem, N., K.C.	71
*Middlebrook, W.	44
*Middlemore, J. T.	33
*Mildmay, F. B.	66
*Millar, J. D.	107
*Mills, Hon. C. T.	80
Mirrlees, W. J.	104
Mitchell, Rosslyn	109
*Mitchell, W. Foot	72
*Mitchell-Thomson, W.	120
*Molloy, M.	118
Molony, T. F.	46
Molson, Dr. J. E.	22
*Molteno, P. A.	109
Monckton-Arundell, Hon. G. V. A.	52
*Mond, Sir A.	99
Money, L. G. Chiozza	81
*Montagu, Hon. E. S.	60
Montefiore, R. M. Sebag	42
Moon, A.	28
Moon, Dr. R. O.	27
*Mooney, J. J.	116
*Moore, W., K.C.	117
*Morgan, G. Hay	63
Morgan, J.	56
Morgan, Prof. J. H.	104
Morgan, L.	101
Morison, H.	89
*Morpeth, Visct.	34
Morrell, P.	36
Morris, A.	35
*Morrison, Capt. J. A.	49
*Morrison-Bell, Maj. Clive	65
Morrison-Bell, Capt. E. F.	65
Mortimer, R.	35
*Morton, A. C.	114
Moulsdale, W. E.	63
*Mount, W. A.	59
Moynagh, S. H.	117
*Muldoon, J.	127
*Munro-Ferguson, Rt. Hon. R. C.	106
*Munro, R.	107
Murison, Prof.	105
Murphy, N. J.	122
*Murray, Capt. Hon. A. C.	111
Murray, C. D., K.C.	103
Murray, W.	109
*Muspratt, Max	45

N
	PAGE
*Nannetti, J. P.	115
Neal, A.	53
Needham, C. T.	47
*Neilson, F.	61
Neville, R. J.	57
*Newdigate-Newdegate, F. A.	90
*Newman, J. R. P.	79
Newton, G. D. C.	60
*Newton, H. K.	68
Nicholls, G.	72
*Nicholson, C. N.	94

	PAGE
Nicholson, G. C. N.	84
Nicholson, Col. J. S.	54
Nicholson, W.	44
*Nicholson, W. G.	70
Nickalls, M.	35
*Nield, H.	79
*Nolan, Joseph	123
Norman, Sir H.	34
Norris, F.	93
*Norton, Capt. C.	27
*Nugent, Sir W.	126
*Nuttall, H.	75

O
	PAGE
*O'Brien, P.	116
*O'Brien, W.	115, 118, & 124
Ocklestone, T. O.	45
O'Connor, H.	122
*O'Connor, John	122
*O'Connor, T. P.	45
Oddy, J. J.	96
*O'Doherty, P.	119
*O'Donnell, T.	122
*O'Dowd, J.	125
O'Dwyer, M.	125
*Ogden, F.	96
*O'Grady, J.	43
*O'Kelly, E. P.	127
*O'Kelly, J.	125
O'Leary, D.	119
O'Malley, Sir E.	26
*O'Malley, W.	121
*O'Neill, Hon. A.	117
*O'Neill, Dr. C.	117
*Orde-Powlett, Hon. W.G.A.	93
*Ormsby-Gore, Hon. W.	98
*O'Shaughnessy, P. J.	123
*O'Shee, J. J.	126
O'Sullivan, T.	121
Oversby, W. T.	76
Owen, A. Humphreys	98

P
	PAGE
Pace, T.	53
*Paget, A. H.	37
Paget, T. F. G.	82
Paine, W.	71
*Palmer, G.	67
Palmer, G. L.	91
Parker, C. S.	65
Parker, F. C.	48
*Parker, Sir G.	40
*Parker, J.	41
*Parkes, E.	33
Parkin, G. H.	79
*Partington, O.	64
Paul, E.	38
Pauling, G.	35
Pawle, G. S.	71
Pearce, R.	86
*Pearce, W.	30
*Pearson, Hon. W. H. M.	87
Pease, H. Pike	38
*Pease, Rt. Hon. J. A.	96
Peel, Mervyn	99
*Peel, Capt. R. F.	88
*Peel, Hon. W.	55
Percy, C.	56

	PAGE
*Perkins, W. F.	70
Permewan, Dr. W.	46
Perowne, Lieut.-Col.	65
*Peto, B. E.	91
*Philipps, Col. Ivor	54
Phillimore, R. C.	71
*Phillips, J.	123
Phillips, J. F. L.	98
Phillips, V.	46
Phillips, W. F.	101
*Pickersgill, E. H.	22
Pilditch, P. E.	25
*Pirie, D. V.	102
Platt, Major E.	41
Pocock, S. J.	91
*Pointer, J.	53
Pole-Carew, Lt.-Gen. Sir R.	62
*Pollard, Sir G. H.	74
*Pollock, E. M., K.C.	56
*Ponsonby, A.	107
Poole, Lt.-Col. T. G.	47
Potter, C. H.	52
Powell, E.	84
*Power, P. J.	126
Pownall, Assheton	29
Preston, W. R.	30
*Pretyman, E. G.	68
*Price, C. E.	103
*Price, Sir R. J.	80
*Priestley, A.	40
*Priestley, Sir W. E.	35
*Primrose, Hon. Neil	60
Pringle, A. S.	112
*Pringle, W. M. R.	112
*Proby, Col. D. J.	69
Proby, R. G.	46
Pryce-Jones, Col. E.	98
Pyman, W. H. S.	94

Q
	PAGE
*Quilter, W. E. C.	88

R
	PAGE
Radcliffe, G. R. Y.	103
*Radford, G. H.	25
Radford, G. W.	63
Rae, H. N.	96
*Raffan, P. W.	76
Raine, G. E.	52
*Rainy, A. R.	106
Ramsbotham, H.	73
Ramsden, G. T.	94
*Randles, Sir J. S.	63
Rankin, Sir J.	71
*Raphael, H. H.	64
*Ratcliff, R. F.	86
*Rawlinson, J. F. P., K.C.	127
*Rawson, Col. R. H.	89
Raymond, Irvine	37
*Rea, Rt. Hon. Russell	54
*Rea, Walter R.	52
Reddy, M.	122
*Redmond, J.	116
*Redmond, W.	115 & 118
Redmond, W. A.	125
Rees, G. C.	98
Reid, D. D.	125
Reid, G. R.	26

	PAGE		PAGE		PAGE
Reiss, R.	89	*Schwann, Sir C.	46	Sturdy, E. V.	80
*Remnant, J. F.	23	*Scott, A. H.	32	*Summers, J. W.	98
*Rendall, A.	70	Scott, A. MacCallum	104	Surtees, Col.	40
Rhys, Sir D.	64	Scott, Leslie, K.C.	45	*Sutherland, J. E.	104
Rice, J. H.	116	*Scott, Sir S.	27	*Sutton, J. E.	46
*Rice, Hon. W. F.	35	Scott-Brown, R.	102	Swift, Rigby	52
*Richards, T.	80	*Scott Dickson, Rt. Hon. C.,		*Sykes, A. J.	61
Richards, T. F.	81	K.C.	105	Sykes, Major Mark	93
Richardson, A.	22	Scrymgeour, E.	103	Symmons, I. A.	68
Richardson, A.	49	Seaverns, J. H.	26		
Richardson, H. Ashton	55	*Seddon, J. A.	76	**T**	
Richardson, T.	57	*Seely, Rt. Hon. J. E. B.	64		
Ricketts, G. W.	57	Shaw, C. N. L.	21	*Talbot, Lord E.	89
Ridley, Hon. Jasper	48	Shaw, Col. J. R.	50	Taylor, A.	47
*Ridley, S. F.	51	Shaw, W. T.	109	*Taylor, J. W.	67
Riley, H. L.	34	*Sheehan, D. D.	118 & 123	*Taylor, T. C.	75
Rittner, G. H.	41	*Sheehy, D.	124	Telfer - Smollett, Lt.-Col.	
*Roberts, C.	44	*Sherwell, A. J.	42	C. E. D.	107
*Roberts, G.	48	*Shortt, E., K.C.	48	*Tennant, H. J.	109
*Roberts, Sir J. H.	100	Shrubsall, G.	26	*Terrell, G.	91
Roberts, R. H.	24	*Simon, Sir J. A., K.C.	69	*Terrell, H., K.C.	40
*Roberts, S.	53	Simpson, E. O.	39	Thomas, A. A.	82
*Robertson, Sir G.	35	Skelton, A. N.	112	*Thomas, A., K.C.	99
Robertson, H. M.	82	Sloan, T. H.	114	*Thomas, J. H.	38
*Robertson, J. M.	82	Smiley, Sir J.	114	Thomas, S. J.	55
Robertson, W.	102	Smillie, R.	111	Thompson, J. W. H.	85
*Robinson, S.	99	Smith, Albert	74	*Thompson, R.	114
*Roch, W. F.	102	Smith, D. T.	95	Thompson, W. W.	96
*Roche, A.	115	Smith, F.	37	*Thorne, G. R.	57
*Roche, J.	121	*Smith, F. E., K.C.	46	*Thorne, W.	31
*Roe, Sir T.	38	Smith, G.	108	*Thynne, Lord A.	32
Rogers, F. E. N.	92	Smith, Harold	56	Timins, D.	92
*Rolleston, Sir J.	71	*Smith, H. B. Lees	48	Timmis, T. S.	81
Ronaldshay, Earl of	79	Smith, T.	61	*Tobin, Alfred A., K.C.	51
Rose, Sir C. D.	60	Smith, W. C., K.C.	102	Touche, G. A.	25
Rose-Innes, P.	30	Smith-Carington, N. W.	77	*Toulmin, G.	36
Rosenheim, F.	23	*Smyth, T. F.	122	Treffry, E.	62
*Rothschild, Lionel N. de	59	Snell, H.	42	Trestrail, A. E. Y.	65
Roundell, R. F.	96	Snowden, H. G.	40	*Trevelyan, C. P.	94
Rowlands, J.	72	*Snowden, P.	34	*Tryon, Capt. G. C.	35
*Rowntree, A.	58	*Soames, A. W.	81	*Tullibardine, Marquis of	113
Royce, W. S.	78	*Soares, E. J.	65	*Twist, H.	57
*Royds, E.	78	Somervell, W. H.	91		
*Runciman, Rt. Hon. W.	39	Spalding, H. N.	89	**U**	
Russell, C.	52	Spear, J. W.	65		
Rutherford, Col. J.	74	*Spicer, Sir A.	24	*Ure, Rt. Hon. A., K.C.	112
*Rutherford, W. W.	46	Spicer, Evan	22	**V**	
Ryan, F. W.	122	Spokes, A. H.	27		
*Rylett, Harold	86	Sprot, Col. A.	110	*Valentia, Viscount	50
		Stafford, Marquis of	114	*Vaughan-Davies, M. L.	99
S		*Stanier, B.	84	*Venables-Llewelyn, C.	102
		*Stanley, Hon. A.	76	*Verney, F. W.	38
St. Maur, H.	40	*Stanley, Albert	87	Verney, Sir Harry	60
*Salter, A. C., K.C.	70	Stanley, Hon. A. L.	61	*Verrall, G. H.	60
Samson, E. M.	102	*Stanley, Major Hon. G. F.	51	Vickers, D.	53
Samuel, A. M.	75	Stanton, C. B.	101	Vincent, Sir E.	38
*Samuel, Rt. Hon. H.	93	*Starkey, J. R.	83	*Vivian, H.	33
*Samuel, Sir H.	26	*Staveley-Hill, H.	86		
*Samuel, J.	55	Steel, S. Strang	112	**W**	
Samuel, S.	55	*Steel-Maitland, A. D.	33		
*Samuel, Stuart	30	Stevens, J. V.	33	*Wadsworth, J.	95
*Sanders, R. A.	85	Stevens, J. W.	36	Walker, S.	53
*Sanderson, L., K.C.	91	*Stewart, G.	62	*Walker, Col. W. H.	77
Sands, M. H.	59	Stewart-Smith, D., K.C.	49	Wallis, R. B.	83
*Sandys, G. J.	86	Stobart, H. G.	66	*Walrond, Hon. W. L. C.	65
*Sandys, Col. T. M.	76	*Strachey, Sir E.	85	Walsh, J.	119
*Sassoon, Sir E.	42	Straus, B. S.	30	*Walsh, S.	76
*Scanlan, T.	125	*Strauss, A.	27	*Walters, J. T.	53
Scaramanga-Ralli, C.	70	Strauss, E. A.	29	*Walton, Sir J.	94
Schunck, J. E.	55			Wanklyn, J. L.	116

INDEX TO CANDIDATES.

	PAGE
Ward, A. L.	42
*Ward, A. S.	71
*Ward, D.	54
*Ward, J.	55
*Warde, Col. C. E.	73
*Wardle, G. J.	54
*Waring, Capt. W.	108
Warner, C. J.	52
*Warner, Sir T. C.	87
*Wason, Rt. Hon. E.	109
*Wason, J. C.	112
*Waterlow, D. S.	25
*Watt, H. A.	105
Watts, J. H.	98
Webb, H.	71
*Wedgwood, J. C.	48
Weigall, Capt. A.	78
*Weir, J. Galloway	113
*Wheler, G. C. H.	72
White, C. F.	64
*White, Major Dalrymple	77
*White, Sir G.	81
White, H.	75
*White, Sir L.	93
*White, P.	124
*Whitehouse, J. H.	111
Whiteside, R. B.	57
*Whitley, J. H.	41
*Whittaker, Rt. Hon. Sir T. P.	97
Whitworth, C. W.	94
Whitworth, J. H.	61
*Whyte, A. F.	107
Wild, E. E.	31
*Wiles, T.	25
*Wilkie, A.	103
Wilkinson, J. R.	82
*Williams, Aneurin	50
Williams, A. F. B.	90
Williams, C.	63
Williams, Lt.-Col. D. E.	80
*Williams, J.	101
Williams, J. F.	50
Williams, J. H.	99
*Williams, P.	47
*Williams, Col. R.	66
Williams, R. Vaughan	62
*Williams, W. Llewellyn	97
*Williamson, Sir A.	110
Williamson, J.	119
*Willoughby, Maj. the Hon. C.	79
*Willoughby de Eresby, Lord	78
Wills, A. O.	86
Wills, A. W.	66
Wilshere, A. M.	44
*Wilson, Hon. Guy	42
*Wilson, H. J.	95
*Wilson, John	67
*Wilson, J. W.	92
Wilson, Capt. Leslie	51
Wilson, P. W.	91
*Wilson, Stanley	93
*Wilson, T. F.	111
*Wilson, W. T.	76
*Winfrey, R.	81
*Wing, T.	40
*Winterton, Earl	89
Wolmer, Viscount	76
*Wood, Hon. E.	96
*Wood, J.	54
Wood, S. Hill	64
*Wood, T. McKinnon	105
Woodcock, H. D.	77
*Wortley, Rt. Hon. C. B. Stuart	53
Wright, B. S.	49
Wrigley, J.	49
*Wyndham, Rt. Hon. G.	39

Y

Yate, Col. C.	77
*Yerburgh, R.	38
Young, D. H. L.	104
Young, Hilton	51
*Young, S.	118
*Young, W.	112
*Younger, G.	102
*Yoxall, Sir J. H.	49